Netflix Nostalgia

Remakes, Reboots, and Adaptations

Series Editors: Carlen Lavigne, Red Deer College
Paul Booth, DePaul University

Broad-ranging and multidisciplinary, this series invites analysis of remakes, reboots, and adaptations in contemporary media from video games to television to the internet. How are we reusing and remixing our stories? What does that tell us about ourselves, our cultures, and our times? Scholars use multidisciplinary approaches from areas such as gender studies, race, sexuality, disability, cultural studies, fan studies, sociology, or aesthetic and technical research. Titles in the series set out to say something about who we are, where we've come from, and where we're going, as read in our popular culture and the stories we tell ourselves over and over again.

Titles in the Series

Screening Gender in Shakespeare's Comedies: Film and Television Adaptations in the Twenty-First Century, by Magdalena Cieślak
Netflix Nostalgia: Streaming the Past on Demand, edited by Kathryn Pallister

Netflix Nostalgia

Streaming the Past on Demand

Edited by Kathryn Pallister

LEXINGTON BOOKS
Lanham • Boulder • New York • London

Published by Lexington Books
An imprint of The Rowman & Littlefield Publishing Group, Inc.
4501 Forbes Boulevard, Suite 200, Lanham, Maryland 20706
www.rowman.com

6 Tinworth Street, London SE11 5AL

British Library Cataloguing in Publication Information Available

Library of Congress Cataloging-in-Publication Data

Names: Pallister, Kathryn, editor.
Title: Netflix nostalgia : streaming the past on demand / edited by Kathryn Pallister ; afterword by
    Ann M. Ciasullo.
Description: Lanham : Lexington Books, 2019. | Series: Remakes, reboots, and adaptations | Includes
    bibliographical references and index.
Identifiers: LCCN 2019014096 (print) | LCCN 2019014423 (ebook) | ISBN 9781498583060 (elec-
    tronic) | ISBN 9781498583053 (cloth : alk. paper) | ISBN 9781498583077 (pbk. : alk. paper)
Subjects: LCSH: Nostalgia on television. | Netflix (Film) | Streaming video—Social aspects.
Classification: LCC PN1992.8.N67 (ebook) | LCC PN1992.8.N67 N48 2019 (print) | DDC 791.45/
    653—dc23
LC record available at https://lccn.loc.gov/2019014096

Printed in the United States of America

Contents

Acknowledgments

I would like to extend my sincere appreciation to the Red Deer College Professional Development Program, Torben Anderson, Jane MacNeil, and Krista Robson for providing their support for this project from its very beginnings. I owe a debt of gratitude to all of the contributors to this collection for allowing me to include their interesting and insightful work. Thanks to my many colleagues at Red Deer College, including Carlen Lavigne, coeditor of this book series (along with Paul Booth); Trish Campbell, who was game to cowrite a chapter with me for this book; and Cindy Brooks, for the regular stream of cat memes to keep me motivated. And, finally, big thanks to my parents (even though they limited the amount of *The Brady Bunch* reruns I was allowed to watch in my childhood) and of course, the two guys who share my Netflix account—Greg and Myles.

Introduction

Kathryn Pallister

Whether it's "Throwback Thursday" or "Flashback Friday," the streaming juggernaut Netflix fuels and is fueled by audience desire for nostalgic content, as both a platform for audiences to rewatch beloved content from the past and a creator of original content with nostalgic impulses. My path to *Netflix Nostalgia* began in the summer of 1975, though at age five, I was blissfully unaware of the "nostalgia boom" going on in American popular culture at the time.[1] Having traveled from our family's home on an army base in Germany to my mother's hometown in Illinois, I sat on the beach and cried because I was missing reruns of *The Brady Bunch* while everyone else enjoyed a sunny afternoon at the lake. At the time, I had very little access to American television, so my grandparents' cable subscription, with its seemingly endless catalog of programs, opened up a whole new world of access to me, including series that no longer regularly aired like *The Brady Bunch* and current (at the time) nostalgic series like *Happy Days*. I didn't know it then, but one day, Netflix would expand that access exponentially, opening up a whole new universe of nostalgia for me and over 130 million other subscribers around the world.[2]

In part a response to my childhood obsession with television, and nostalgic programs in particular, this edited volume aims to interrogate the complex and contradictory notions of nostalgia through the contemporary lens of Netflix. Contributors examine angles such as the Netflix business model, the role of streaming platforms such as Netflix in audiences' consumption of nostalgia, and the ideological nature of nostalgic representation in Netflix series. The chapters in this volume analyze a range of Netflix content, providing timely and original analysis by established and emerging scholars in a variety of disciplines. As a part of the series "Reboots, Remakes and Adaptations" originated by series editors Dr. Carlen Lavigne and Dr. Paul Booth, this work asks the question: What can we learn about ourselves, our times, our cultures, in response to an examination of "Netflix Nostalgia"?

Most people think of nostalgia with a sort of benign indulgence, like my students who give courtesy laughs to my references to 1980s popular culture in class, though the word was first used as a medical term in the late seventeenth century by Johannes Hofer, in response to displaced soldiers, domestic workers and students who developed symptoms in response to their profound homesickness.[3] Etymologically, as Fred Davis notes, "*Nostalgia* is from the Greek *nostos*, to return home, and *algai*, a painful condition; thus, a painful yearning to return home,"[4] emphasizing the melancholy undertone of the term. The identification and proliferation of this notion of medical nostalgia came at a time when notions of time and space were evolving as society became more secular, global and industrial, while it also became a by-product of the questioning of progress, what Svetlana Boym calls "a disease of the modern age."[5] With the rise of modernity, the original definition of nostalgia slipped away, eroding the focus on the psychiatric connotations of the word as well as its overt reference to "home."[6] While "postmodern" expressions of nostalgia are often characterized by a "kind of ironic double vision,"[7] nostalgic content has become a multifaceted and significant component of our mass media of late, including but not limited to the Netflix catalog. And, while nostalgia can seduce audiences into sitting down on their couches for a one-night stand of a viewing session, the Netflix platform invites them to sit and stay for a while, turning the seduction into a long-term relationship.

The connections between nostalgia and mass media have been addressed by many scholars seeking to understand why the past retains such a strong siren's song. Stefanie Armbruster, for example, categorizes television nostalgia in two ways: first, by texts that have content producers create as intentionally nostalgic (such as Netflix original *Stranger Things*, set in the 1980s and borrowing generously from popular culture of the time, including Steven Spielberg's films) and series revivals/reboots (like the four-episode Netflix revival *Gilmore Girls: A Year in the Life)*. Second, Armbruster notes that nostalgia can also be categorized by audiences, based on their feelings of nostalgia while watching programming that producers would not have created as intentionally nostalgic (such as would be the case when watching a show like *Friends* on Netflix; the content itself isn't nostalgic, but viewing it twenty years later, the audience typically responds with feelings of nostalgia).[8] Similarly, Paul Grainge identifies the mood (experience or response) and mode (style) of nostalgia.[9] While Grainge privileges the mode or style of nostalgia, Hutcheon and Valdes emphasize the importance of the mood or response, explaining that "nostalgia is not something you 'perceive' *in* an object; it is what you 'feel' when two different temporal moments, past and present, come together for you and, often, carry considerable emotional weight."[10] Taking both of these perspectives into consideration, Netflix, then, becomes both a producer of nostalgia and an access point for nostalgic responses to previously circulated content. It provides that seemingly infinite catalog I only dreamed of as a five-year-old looking for a television fix.

Furthermore, an audience's nostalgic responses to texts can function both individually and collectively, expanding the types of audiences who view content from a nostalgic perspective. As Boym writes, "nostalgia is about the relationship between individual biography and the biography of groups or nations, between personal and collective memory."[11] Thus, viewers who consume content they previously enjoyed or that otherwise links them to their past connect to the text with a primarily individual nostalgic response, while viewers first encountering this same content would understand the text with a sort of residual or collective nostalgic response, often due to a mediated knowledge of that earlier time period and its popular culture. Davis locates nostalgia as a key factor in how we construct and reconstruct our identities, both individually and collectively (or generationally), as well as how we maintain continuity in our identities, particularly in the fact of instability or threats (such as the 1970s, when Davis was writing, or in the late part of the 2010s).[12] Mass media play a key role in the formation of this collective memory, according to Davis, generating what Boym calls secondhand memories.[13]

As both a creator and distributor of media texts, Netflix takes great advantage of a wide variety of audience nostalgic responses, banking on attracting audiences who seek out nostalgic content that takes them back in time, as well as new audiences who discover "old" and reimagined content. As Schwindt points out, "Netflix didn't invent nostalgia, but it's certainly leaning into it," at least in part as an attempt to gain subscribers, especially those in the Generation X or Baby Boomer demographic.[14] Netflix's brand strategy relies heavily on nostalgia-related content, and as Bojalad notes, the streaming service has "complex algorithms and tech folks analyzing our viewing habits to determine what we want to see and apparently the answer was 'everything I saw when I was a kid.'"[15] Quality is also important, however, as nostalgia "can get a viewer to the table but by its very definition nostalgia is fleeting. We love to feel the pain of an old wound sometimes but dragging that melancholy out for hours on end is just not sustainable,"[16] emphasizing the contradictory pleasure/pain aspect of the nostalgic impulse inherent in its earliest definitions. The author of the Afterword in this collection, Ann Ciasullo, in her article, "Not a Spaceship but a Time Machine: Mad Men and the Narratives of Nostalgia," argues more specifically that the emotional realism we see in nostalgic content is what draws us in, as she sees the show as "keeping us grounded in the wounds that we have felt and will continue to feel not because we live in a troubled time, not because we long for a past that was so much easier than things are now, but because we, like the characters of *Mad Men*, are human."[17]

These broad emotional responses underpin the function of nostalgia, particularly in the impetus to reevaluate the past and its juxtapositioning with the present. Armbruster argues that "scholars agree that nostalgia is a reaction on modern times,"[18] though the exact nature of this reaction is debatable. Is it a regressive desire to return "home" to an earlier time period in the past, away from a present that seems undesirable or overwhelming? Or is it a more optimistic reaction, whereby a trip back in time reminds us of progress, where we see that past with all its shortcomings? Ryan Lizardi argues that contemporary media typically deploy what he calls *narcissistic nostalgia,* when audiences connect emotionally to nostalgic content without really acknowledging the historical conditions of the past.[19] Pickering and Keightley, on the other hand, represent scholars who see the possibility of the nostalgic return to the past as correlated with "dissatisfaction" with the present, as the past is constructed as something we would like to emulate in our flawed present.[20] Thus, nostalgia can work progressively, rather than regressively engendering audiences' wallowing in the past. The nostalgic discourse, according to Lyne, can be seen as "offering a portal to a cherished realm that's not quite how you remember it."[21] This perspective invites audiences to consider nostalgia critically; as Lyne goes on to say:

> If re-examining the movies and music we grew up with can sometimes feel like looking back at embarrassing photos of our teenage selves, then the process at least forces us to reckon with our own fallibility, and that of others. If you once considered Duckie from *Pretty in Pink* a viable love interest, as opposed to a psychopathic timebomb, then who knows what you're wrong about now.[22]

One component of the progressive/regressive function of nostalgia of particular interest to many, including several of the contributors to this volume, is the way nostalgic content represents and connects us to issues of diversity. Mathur takes the current status of nostalgia in popular culture to task, writing that, "Right now, Hollywood is stuck in a cycle of bringing back old properties. The white male childhood still reigns supreme. The industry will need to experience a seismic change to get out of this routine."[23] For Lizardi, nostalgic mass media is often "myopic, individual, and uncritical,"[24] as platforms such as Netflix, Hulu, and iTunes enable audiences to curate individualized "playlists" devoid of any real critical stance. When nostalgic content remedies the lack of diverse characters in mass media of previous time periods, a failure to interrogate the real challenges faced by marginalized people results, what Lizardi identifies as "a misrecognized and idealized form of past reality that refuses to question and discuss the past as an adaptive tool for the present."[25] Ciasullo attempts to respond to this sort of criticism with her identification of the "two contradictory narratives" in *Mad Men*, focusing on how nostalgia can be deployed both in a positive or sentimental way through the narratives *about* the show (such as the style and fashion featured so prominently) and a negative or realistic way through the narratives *of* the show (such as the oppression and discontent experienced by the characters).[26] Ciasullo says positive nostalgia "depends upon an erasure of those aspects of the past that are negative or even painful"[27] and that audiences often "want the style, but they don't want the substance."[28] While the contributing authors in this collection approach nostalgia from diverse theoretical and personal perspectives, a common theme that runs through many of the subsequent chapters is the navigation of the positive, pleasurable aspects of nostalgia that Ciasullo acknowledges with the sort of critical perspective Lizardi emphasizes.

The chapters in this volume address the issues and tensions discussed above from a variety of standpoints and methods, looking at a number of genres of texts in their analysis of the intersection of Netflix and nostalgia. Following this introduction, the first set of chapters addresses broad issues that impact how and why nostalgic content has become such a prevalent part of the Netflix model and its success. Taurino and Stephan look at issues such as industry and branding in Netflix's use of nostalgic content, while Chinen Biesen's and Murray's chapters focus on the interplay between nostalgic content and viewership. Gauthier's chapter examines the progressive potential of nostalgic content in Netflix series, which provides a transition into a focus on diversity and nostalgic media texts. The next set of chapters begins with Freeman's and Mcclantoc's discussions of queer representation in Netflix programming such as *Stranger Things, GLOW,* and *Black Mirror*'s "San Junipero" episode. Next, Davis's and Yanders's chapters discuss race and ethnicity, using the series *The Get Down, Luke Cage* and *One Day at a Time.* Maganzani's chapter on the Spanish-language series *Cable Girls,* as well as Castellano and Meimaridis's chapter on Brazilian viewers' responses to *Gilmore Girls,* expand the discussion to include globalized perspectives on Netflix nostalgia. In the last set of chapters, authors look at temporal elements of Netflix programming. Sirianni analyzes nostalgic content in *Stranger Things* from a generational perspective, and Campbell and Pallister's chapter addresses the use of "old" and "new" communication technology in the series *13 Reasons Why.* In the final chapter, Tembo addresses the interplay of nostalgic content with futurism in *Cowboy Bebop.*

Finally, Ann M. Ciasullo provides an Afterword that quite appropriately bookends this collection. Ann and I met as undergraduate students at Gonzaga University, where Ann now teaches, bonding over our shared love of nostalgic popular culture. Alert readers will notice how closely Ann's opening anecdote in the Afterword mimics the start of this Introduction, hearkening back to the central role that television—especially nostalgic television—played in both of our childhoods. This inadvertent "happy accident" serves as a reminder that nostalgia, while deeply personal, also provides a powerful social connection that helps us understand ourselves, our times, and our cultures.

NOTES

1. Fred Davis, "Nostalgia, Identity, and the Current Nostalgia Wave," *The Journal of Popular Culture* 11, no. 2 (1977): 421, /doi.org/10.1111/j.0022-3840.1977.00414.x.

2. Netflix, *Letter to Shareholders* (Third Quarter Earnings, October 18, 2018). https://ir.netflix.com/financials/quarterly-earnings/default.aspx.

3. Svetlana Boym, *The Future of Nostalgia* (New York: Basic Books, 2001).

4. Davis, "Nostalgia Wave," 414.

5. Boym, *The Future of Nostalgia,* 7.

6. Davis, "Nostalgia Wave," 415.

7. Linda Hutcheon and Mario J. Valdes, "Irony, Nostalgia, and Postmodern: A Dialogue." Online PDF, *Poligraphias* 3 (1998-2000): 23, revistas.unam.mx/index.php/poligrafias/article/download/31312/28976 .

8. Stefanie Armbruster, *Watching Nostalgia: An Analysis of Nostalgic Television Fiction and Its Reception* (Bielefeld: Transcript, 2016), 12.

9. Paul Grainge, "Nostalgia and Style in Retro America: Moods, Modes, and Media Recycling," *American Culture* 23, no. 1 (2000): 38, https://doi.org/10.1111/j.1537-4726.2000.2301_27.x.

10. Hutcheon and Valdes, "Irony, Nostalgia and the Postmodern," 22.

11. Boym, *The Future of Nostalgia,* xvi.

12. Davis, "Nostalgia Wave."

13. Boym, *The Future of Nostalgia,* 54.

14. Oriana Schwindt, *"Stranger Things* Tests Limits of Netflix's Nostalgia Strategy," *Variety,* July 25, 2016, https://variety.com/2016/tv/news/stranger-things-netflix-fuller-house-nostalgia-strategy-1201822075/.

15. Alex Bojalad, *"Stranger Things*: In Defense of Nostalgia," *Den of Geek,* November 2, 2017, http://www.denofgeek.com/us/tv/stranger-things/268649/stranger-things-in-defense-of-nostalgia.

16. Bojalad, "In Defense of Nostalgia."

17. Ann M. Ciasullo, "Not a Spaceship but a Time Machine: Mad Men and the Narratives of Nostalgia," in *Lucky Strikes and a Three Martini Lunch: Thinking about Television's Mad Men* (Second Edition), ed. Jennifer C. Dunn, Danielle M. Stern, and Jimmie Manning (Newcastle Upon Tyne: Cambridge Scholars Publishing, 2015), 50.

18. Armbruster, *Watching Nostalgia,* 34.

19. Ryan Lizardi, *Mediated Nostalgia: Individual Memory and Contemporary Mass Media* (Lanham, MD: Lexington Books, 2014), 7.

20. Michael Pickering and Emily Keightly, "The Modalities of Nostalgia," *Current Sociology* 54, no. 6 (2006): 937, https://doi.org/10.1177/0011392106068458.

21. Charlie Lyne, "How Nostalgia Took over the World (and Why That's No Bad Thing)," *The Guardian,* July 9, 2016, https://www.theguardian.com/film/2016/jul/09/the-ghostbusters-reboot-and-nostalgia-in-pop-culture.

22. Lyne, "How Nostalgia Took over the World."

23. Manish Mather, "How Pop Culture Nostalgia Privileges Some (and Excludes Others)," *Bitch Flicks,* August 25, 2016, http://www.btchflcks.com/2016/08/how-pop-culture-nostalgia-privileges-some-and-excludes-others.html#.XCcCgVVKh0w.

24. Lizardi, *Mediated Nostalgia,* 19.

25. Lizardi, *Mediated Nostalgia,* 38.

26. Ciasullo, "Not a Spaceship," 39-40.

27. Ciasullo, "Not a Spaceship," 41.

28. Ciasullo, "Not a Spaceship," 46.

BIBLIOGRAPHY

Armbruster, Stefanie. *Watching Nostalgia: An Analysis of Nostalgic Television Fiction and Its Reception.* Bielefeld: Transcript, 2016.

Bojalad, Alex. "*Stranger Things*: In Defense of Nostalgia." *Den of Geek.* November 2, 2017. http://www.denofgeek.com/us/tv/stranger-things/268649/stranger-things-in-defense-of-nostalgia.

Boym, Svetlana. *The Future of Nostalgia.* New York: Basic Books, 2001.

Ciasullo, Ann M. "Not a Spaceship but a Time Machine: Mad Men and the Narratives of Nostalgia." In *Lucky Strikes and a Three Martini Lunch: Thinking about Television's Mad Men* (Second Edition), edited by Jennifer C. Dunn, Danielle M. Stern, and Jimmie Manning. Newcastle Upon Tyne: Cambridge Scholars Publishing, 2015.

Davis, Fred. "Nostalgia, Identity, and the Current Nostalgia Wave." *The Journal of Popular Culture* 11, no. 2 (1977): 414-424. /doi.org/10.1111/j.0022-3840.1977.00414.x.

Grainge, Paul. "Nostalgia and Style in Retro America: Moods, Modes, and Media Recycling." *American Culture* 23, no. 1 (2000): 28-33. https://doi.org/10.1111/j.1537-4726.2000.2301_27.x.

Hutcheon, Linda, and Mario J. Valdes, "Irony, Nostalgia, and the Postmodern: A Dialogue." Online PDF. *Poligraphias* 3 (1998-2000): 18-41. revistas.unam.mx/index.php/poligrafias/article/download/31312/28976.

Lizardi, Ryan. *Mediated Nostalgia: Individual Memory and Contemporary Mass Media.* Lanham, MD: Lexington Books, 2014.

Lyne, Charlie. "How Nostalgia Took over the World (and Why That's No Bad Thing)." *The Guardian.* July 9, 2016. https://www.theguardian.com/film/2016/jul/09/the-ghostbusters-reboot-and-nostalgia-in-pop-culture.

Mather, Manish. "How Pop Culture Nostalgia Privileges Some (and Excludes Others)." *Bitch Flicks.* August 25, 2016. http://www.btchflcks.com/2016/08/how-pop-culture-nostalgia-privileges-some-and-excludes-others.html#.XCcCgVVKh0w.

Netflix. *Letter to Shareholders* (Third Quarter Earnings), October 18, 2018. https://ir.netflix.com/financials/quarterly-earnings/default.aspx.

Pickering, Michael, and Emily Keightly. "The Modalities of Nostalgia." *Current Sociology* 54, no. 6 (2006): 919-941. https://doi.org/10.1177/0011392106068458.

Schwindt, Oriana. "*Stranger Things* Tests Limits of Netflix's Nostalgia Strategy." *Variety.* July 25, 2016. https://variety.com/2016/tv/news/stranger-things-netflix-fuller-house-nostalgia-strategy-1201822075/.

ONE

Crossing Eras

Exploring Nostalgic Reconfigurations in Media Franchises

Giulia Taurino

A SYNTAX OF NETFLIX NOSTALGIA

Over the past few years, as television began to build a more solid history, televisual products have been affected by a nostalgic wave that led to the revival of several old-time favorite franchises. Such a trend is one of the consequences of a wider technological environment, where television content is more and more interconnected and somehow serialized, not only through space, whether fictional, virtual or real, but also through time, in a continuous dialogue between media of the past and media of the present. This reticular mechanism, which involves processes of recycling and remediation among others, contributed to consolidate a preexisting association between the domain of media and forms of nostalgia. As Dominik Schrey explains, "media can serve as a means of virtually accessing the past, and are thus an important resource for cultural memory. Consequently, they often establish the precondition for a nostalgic perspective on things past (and present)."[1] Elsewhere, Ryan Lizardi talks about this phenomenon as a form of "mediated nostalgia," to describe how "media consistently make available a media-defined past."[2]

While nostalgia doesn't appear as a new paradigm in contemporary history, since it has been affecting human societies starting from their ancient years, the emergence of digital media indeed created alternative premises for triggering nostalgic practices in cultural industries worldwide. Being easily accessible in libraries online, always available, mediated nostalgia turns a self-generated state of longing into an externally prompted condition, which responds to technological changes, socio-cultural dynamics and commercial parameters. As a multifaceted concept, it carries several meanings and implications, ranging from an economical to a cultural understanding of the production of storytelling practices. This chapter will investigate the concept of mediated nostalgia in the digital age, by analyzing its role in contemporary television seriality, as well as its effects on textual forms and narrative structures, and on the industry that surrounds them.

An underlying assumption in every discussion about nostalgia is that it implies memory: there is no nostalgia without some form of memory. In the wake of Richard Terdiman's memory studies, memory is to be intended here as a transformative and transhistorical individual and social condition.[3] In this respect, memory is also a multidirectional force, meaning "subject to ongoing negotiation, cross-referencing, and borrowing,"[4] which ultimately contributes to the constitution of multiple identities in a constant laboring process that happens in the present and reference to the past. When inserted in mass media environments, memory can acquire a higher resonance as a widespread nostalgic cultural phenomenon. What does cultural memory mean in the context of a mediated environment?

Perhaps one of the most central notions to investigate, in relation to both mediated nostalgia and cultural memory, is that of repository. Beyond a subjective, individual memory, and probably even stronger when it comes to triggering large-scale phenomena of cultural revival, a broader, collective memory is, to a certain extent, guaranteed by archives and related practices of preservation. Technological advances and an increasing movement toward digitization nourished the archival process, and while several "physical" archives still remain trapped in issues of inaccessibility and auto-referentiality, digital archives, here comprised online databases and virtual platforms, represent new resources for assuring the persistence of memory and the access to it. As "new media" were able to generate a sedimentation of content not only in physical archives, but also in virtual repositories, they freed nostalgia from the constraints and frailties of human memory. Today nostalgia is not so much about memory as it is about the media industry itself.

Starting from these general considerations, mediated nostalgia on Netflix will be explored in the specific context of streaming television, a nonlinear environment independent from the restrictions of a rigid programming schedule typical of linear television. As a streaming platform, Netflix gives shape and organization to a library of content, very much similar to an interactive archive. The metaphor of the library, or of a catalog, containing a collection of audiovisual texts, results particularly effective to describe Netflix's inner dynamics. When the memory of a movie or a television show is not only stored in an inventory, but also indexed and made available to search, mediated nostalgia can become an intrinsic property for the sustainability of the Netflix archive and its business model, in multiple ways. Observing a syntax of Netflix nostalgia leads to a general classification of different typologies of nostalgia, as they occur and take shape in the current "mediascape."[5] If we consider nostalgia as a spectrum, nostalgic iterations can be found mainly on three levels: genre, setting and/or content/plot.

For instance, the most recent revivals of old media products are often prompted by an algorithmic-driven nostalgia, or nostalgia-by-indexing, which ultimately turns out to be a genre-based form of nostalgia. Such a category, particularly in the case of television series, can be seen on a macroscopic level in the structure of the platform itself. As Netflix largely relies on statistics and data collected from users' behavior, a form of algorithmic-driven recommendation allows the platform to organize the content into clusters. In this environment, nostalgia becomes a genre itself and contributes to arrange content into subgenres. For example, digging through the Netflix library, as of April 2018 we found content browsed by genres like "Nostalgic '90s"[6] or "Totally Awesome '80s."[7] Users can go as far back as 1960s or 1970s television,[8] or climb the catalog up until the more rich category "TV from 2000 on."[9] Although it may vary depending on the country, nostalgia-by-indexing looks more like a modern-day form of rerun for nonlinear television: old content is made available for contemporary audiences and algorithmic clustering dictates a principle of organization, in which content is separated by decade and yet interconnected through meta-tags.

On the opposite end, nostalgia can be found through close-reading and textual analysis, most often attached to the setting. Beyond the genre itself, a series like *Stranger Things* (Netflix, 2016-), for example, offers many textual clues for the audience to relate to a nostalgic view of the 1980s, not least the historical setting, as well as a certain visual aesthetic typical of US made, Spielbergian coming-of-age movies, such as *The Goonies* (1985) or *Stand by Me* (1986). What has been defined by the press, with respect to this specific case, as a "Goonies-Inflected Nostalgia"[10] is a nostalgia built upon narrative and visual citations of Stephen King's stories and Steven Spielberg's movies, as well as on popular culture references to the 1980s and 1990s decades. Far from being a purely aesthetic choice, this longing-for-the-past comes with simulacra and objects fitting in the plot, in order to take the audience back to another era, similarly to what Baz Luhrmann and Stephen Adly Guirgis did, while reimagining New York's 1970s in another, lesser known Netflix series, *The Get Down* (2016-2017).

In this respect, nostalgia programming is not at all a new model in North-American television seriality. Already in 2007, *Mad Men*, with its vintage vibe, was bringing a feeling of nostalgia to the cable channel

AMC. Such nostalgic practices related to the setting could be said to correspond to Robert Buerkle's definition of "nostalgia-by-proxy." As he explains, "the target audience for nostalgic media frequently does not have a direct relationship with the time being evoked, but rather a tangential relationship via the generation that came before them. This is nostalgia-by-proxy. In truth, *Charlie's Angels* is not so much designed for the show's original fan base as it is for Millennials who are aware of the cultural capital of *Charlie's Angels*."[11] Reasoning about nostalgia in terms of cultural capital is particularly interesting for a comparative analysis that crosses different eras. As an article in *The Guardian* points out when presenting one of the latest television hybrid experiments, *Stranger Things*, "television's latest hit show combines a distribution model that represents the future of screen entertainment with content that harks back to its past."[12]

Even more effective to this aim is a third type of nostalgia, which will be examined more closely in the following analysis: a nostalgia-by-serialization, that of revivals—or else, remakes, reboots, sequels, prequels, spin-offs. Netflix, as well as other platforms and networks, adopted this solution as a response to the uncertainties brought by the introduction of new business models in television, which now tend to skip the traditional pilot release in favor of a straight-to-series commitment. The proliferation of revivals, as forms of storytelling based on the rehabilitation of a pre-existing "narrative ecosystem,"[13] is indicative of a landscape where old media dynamics are changing toward a more flexible model, in which the audience gains more power and freedom. In the precarious context of digital television, revivals are a good solution to assure, within a certain limit, profitable revenues based on the previous reputation among the viewers of a show already tested. Adopting the definition given by Constantine Verevis when he examines the characteristics of remakes, revivals can be described as "commercial products that repeat successful formulas in order to minimize risk and secure profits in the marketplace."[14] However, revivals don't account exclusively for commercial exploitation and financial security; on the contrary, these more strictly economical mechanisms have additional impacts on cultural production, distribution and reception.

NETFLIX REVIVALS AND INTERGENERATIONAL NOSTALGIA

The renewed interest for old television products, triggered among other factors by nonlinear television's platforms and their complex algorithmic apparatuses, opens up several possibilities of analysis, which were briefly summed up in the previous paragraph by distinguishing between different types of nostalgia. In the wake of much older revival practices, dating back to the early days of audiovisual media and even before, Netflix revivals enhance processes of reappropriation of a former audience, which in some cases has remained silent and inactive, but it is nonetheless already existing as a consolidated fan base. As mentioned before, acknowledging the presence of a fandom and unmuting its voice can have a strong influence on the economic factor, providing a relatively reliable prediction of future revenues and thus decreasing the financial risks of producing a high-budget, quality content. Before turning into a nostalgic practice, a revival seems to be first and foremost a financial operation.

It is therefore worth asking, more specifically, what makes a revival a truly nostalgic product from a cultural standpoint. In other terms, what is the difference between a 2017 television adaptation of a 2015 movie, such as the Italian series *Suburra: Blood on Rome* (Netflix, 2017-), and a product like *Lost in Space* (Netflix, 2018-), from the homonymous series by CBS (1965-1968), itself based on Johann David Wyss' novel *The Swiss Family Robinson* (1812)? To answer this question, we should consider nostalgia not only as a "formatting practice,"[15] but more importantly as a sociocultural dynamic, made of processes of historicization, instead of pure serialization. While all forms of revival—remakes/reboots or sequels, prequels and so on—are made of both repetition and variation, as the main properties of serial narratives,[16] the nostalgia effect is created when there is a sense of return perceived by the audience, rather than a simple pattern of reiteration.

In this sense, in order to create nostalgia a revival should come after a time gap and involve a historical rupture, a fracture, an interval that allows the presence of an "intergenerational nostalgia,"[17] ultimately made possible through a remediated experience. In order to trigger nostalgia in the revival formula, a cross-historical displacement is required, giving the viewer a perception of distance. In *Media of Serial Narratives*,[18] Frank Kelleter and Kathleen Loock address the specific case of remakes as a "second-order serialization" that entails a process of self-reflexive historicization. Revivals can be therefore studied as places for cultural negotiation, where "a cultural reflective form of nostalgia" happens, "one that might provide information or comparative answers about the past in relation to the present."[19] By giving a sense of longing and return, this sort of nostalgia "goes beyond the simple idea of intertextuality, and begins to become an interconnected web of the past aimed at the heart of a viewer's and player's constructed dependency on nostalgia."[20]

Taking into account their audience-oriented nature, Netflix nostalgic revivals can be studied as experimental narrative spaces to reinvent preexisting narrative forms and to adapt them to the contemporary nonlinear television environment, which consistently diverges from the linear environment of traditional broadcasting that originally created and distributed such television products. Moreover, by stimulating a fandom previously formed, revivals and other ways of recycling stories serve as processes of serialization. By doing this, they add further value to the narrative repository, not only by impacting the final commercial result, but also by broadening and reinventing the story for a new audience and televisual scape, as it will be shown in detail in the following paragraph. Besides serving as financial triggers, television revivals can function as additional narrative places for updating and expanding the fictional universe, giving it a renewed format shape able to fit the structure and composition of streaming platforms.

"YOU CAN'T DO A SLASHER MOVIE AS A TV SERIES"[21]: THE CASE OF *SCREAM*

An interesting operation of "cultural reflective nostalgia" is the series *Scream: The TV Series* (MTV/Netflix, 2015-). As in other cases, like the teen drama *Riverdale* (The CW, 2017-), this series is not strictly a Netflix's original production, even though it received the label of "Netflix Original" on non-US Netflix platforms. First released on MTV in the United States, the exclusive international distribution rights were soon acquired by Netflix, which inserted it on the platform and distributed it in countries all over the world. The aspect of acquisition and distribution is an important point in the analysis, as it shows how nostalgia on Netflix does not respond exclusively to a branding or creative factor (such as in the case of Netflix originals), but also to other and more complex platform dynamics, which deal with the necessity to think about the cultural capital of the series on a global scale, and insert in local libraries a content that can be considered transnational.

Going back to the initial film tetralogy, based on the numbers reported on the website Box Office Mojo, "not only did *Scream* gross $173 million worldwide on a slim $15 million production budget, but it spawned a series of copycats, from the *I Know What You Did Last Summer* franchise to the *Scary Movie* franchise, which mimicked both its basic comedy-horror paradigm and its popular success."[22] This mimetic wave of slasher-like movies and parodies officially initiated the long-term and influential success of *Scream* in popular culture, and not only in the United States, but also in foreign film markets. *Scream*-like sleeper hits invaded English-speaking countries like Great Britain and Australia, as well as other countries in Europe and Asia. Such a cultural resonance helped to set the premises for a relatively safe economic bet on the televisual revival, not only envisaged to be released within the United States, but also to be exported abroad. This means that, while recurring to the nostalgia element, Netflix is asked to account for its function of distributing non-original content internationally. A shared sentiment of nostalgia for a single product and its cultural capital can help Netflix to overcome the barriers of local markets and their specificities.

As a cross-cultural phenomenon, financially speaking, inserting *Scream* in Netflix's libraries represents a long-term investment, both for its narrative capital and its ability to relate to other products in different countries. Its status of formulaic serial product inscribed in a predefined genre, which "operates across the cultural realms of media industries, audiences, policy, critics, and historical contexts,"[23] together with television's tendency toward a certain hybridization of forms, makes *Scream* a televisual product that "exists as a nexus of often conflicting influences and factors."[24] While inheriting a transnational dimension as a worldwide acclaimed franchise, *Scream: The TV Series* has to conform its narrative space to at least three contextual factors: the cultural scape, as already partially discussed, industrial transformations and new audiences.

From a cultural standpoint, what makes this case study interesting is the possibility of analyzing the television series within the franchise, as part of a dense web of intertextual references and nostalgic relations that became typical, over the years, of the slasher genre and postmodern horror. The nostalgic content of the series finds its roots in the origins of the slasher genre itself and its rise to popularity in the 1980s, which immediately led to the 1990s impulse to rethink the genre in a satirical way. To quote Frances Pheasant-Kelly, when she discusses the success of *Scream*, "its uniqueness arises from the fact that even as it is composed of fragments of previous 'texts,' these are reframed to generate a set of revised aesthetic and narrative characteristics for the genre, which, in turn, provide a template for subsequent slasher films."[25] This alternate movement of both employing and subverting horror clichés at the same time is present all along the *Scream* franchise, which was originally conceived as a trilogy, starting with Wes Craven's movies in 1996, 1997 and 2000, and then went through a first cinematic revival in 2011. As Valerie Wee notes,

> Just as the first three films' heightened postmodern and self-referential characteristics were tied to macro-industrial forces—the rise of a new youth demographic, Dimension's leveraging then-parent company Disney's multiple content platforms, and trends in media marketing— *Scre4m* was also a response to key social, industrial, and technological developments that unfolded prior to its production and release.[26]

While another sequel, *Scream 5*, was announced but never shot, television turned out to be the perfect place for a revival experiment, since seriality is a preferential activator of nostalgia. Looking at the industrial circumstances around the series, as the *Scream* franchise thrives to survive in the contemporary television industry, and so does the media conglomerate Viacom, owner of the teen-oriented channel, the deal between MTV and Netflix offers a viable option to insert *Scream* in the race of nonlinear platforms. While nurturing Netflix's libraries and their nostalgic component, it also helped to bridge the gap between the cable-satellite television channel and the video-on-demand service. The series was released on

MTV on June 30, 2015, and the agreement with Netflix was reached soon after, with the first season of *Scream* becoming available to stream on Netflix worldwide in October of the same year, and on Netflix U.S. in May 2016, before the start of the second season. The second season streamed on Netflix following a weekly schedule and a one-day delayed release after the first broadcast on MTV, an unusual choice for the streaming service that most often opts for a full-season release strategy, probably motivated by the need to align to the original weekly release. With regard to its form and content, the series maintains the revival structure that seeks variation in repetition, with the classic slasher main plot and the everybody's-a-suspect formula stretched over a longer narrative arc.

Interestingly, the series is set to be rebooted for a third season, with a new story and new characters, adopting a form that is establishing a new tradition in television seriality, that of the seasonal anthology, which fulfills Netflix's audience spread habit to binge-watch entire seasons at once as autonomous narrative units. *Scream: The TV Series* is not the only series to follow this emerging trend and bring the anthology format to Netflix. Recently, Netflix announced a collaboration with the director Guillermo del Toro for the production of its first original horror anthology, which will go by the name *Guillermo del Toro Presents 10 After Midnight* (upcoming). Another horror anthology TV show, *Slasher* (Super Channel/Netflix, 2017-), originally a Canadian production, has secured itself a place on the platform, with Netflix acquiring the rights for the second season. As much as in *Scream: The TV Series*, *Slasher* conforms its main themes to the cultural context of the digital age and to a new generation of targeted teen audience. Under these circumstances, the acquisition of a slasher TV series for international distribution therefore perfectly makes sense within Netflix's strategy of targeting and localizing the viewers into differentiated streams of products that are indexed in the library—such as, perhaps, horror anthology shows.

Additionally, as a cult TV product, it "draws a niche audience, [. . .] has a nostalgic appeal, [. . .] is considered emblematic of a particular subculture."[27] Nostalgia can be found in *Scream: The TV Series* on many levels, not only in cultural production and distribution, but also on the level of reception. Being part of a cult franchise with a "nostalgic appeal" means also being able to sustain a dialogue with the audience and provide material for their interpretative practices, including the creation of communities or the production of fan-fiction and tertiary texts. The series *Scream* responds to this need by inserting multiple metafictional references to a conversation with the viewers and by celebrating relative fan practices, such as Noah Foster's podcast *The Morgue*, in the second season, which replaces Piper Shaw's podcast *Autopsy of a Crime*, appeared in the first season as a major plot element. Overall, the series is updated for a modern-day audience that takes a center-stage in the plot, attesting that nostalgia is not only in the creative process of televisual production, but first and foremost in the active role of the viewers, as they nostalgically immerse themselves in the story. As Xavier Mendik and Graeme Harper reminds us, a cult—and nostalgic, as it is argued here—product "draws on a (hard) core of audience interest and involvement which is not just the result of random, directionless entertainment seeking, but rather a combination of intense physical and emotional involvement."[28]

SLASHER NOSTALGIA ON NETFLIX:
BUILDING A COMPLEX NETWORK

In May 2016 the chief executive of Showtime, David Nevins, declared to the *New York Times*: "we now live in a world where TV shows never die."[29] This is a scenario where a large amount of televisual content is produced every year, with close to five hundred original scripted TV series released only in the United States in the decade from 2009 to 2017[30] and put on online libraries containing seemingly unlimited content. Most of them were commissioned by over-the-top services like Netflix, Amazon Prime, and Hulu.[31] As reported on Variety, the FX Networks' CEO John Landgraf pointed at this seemingly unsustainable model already in 2015, when, during the Television Critics Association Summer Press Tour, he coined the term "peak television" and commented with the phrase: "there's simply too much television."[32]

Over-the-top players are essential factors in this exponential growth of televisual production. Very much like the arrival of cable television did in the 1980s, they opened a new space for content. To officially enter the race, a platform like Netflix started to set its own standards for supplying the demand of content and become a competitive player. The production and distribution of exclusive content was the most direct solution to differentiate the catalog and make it unique, and nostalgic revivals represent one of the best options for generating a resilient form of adaptation, which is there to stay and potentially encourage a further production of content. Without necessarily being nostalgic, even the first Netflix original was referencing to a previous product: *House of Cards* (Netflix, 2013-2018), the American political thriller created by Beau Willimon and produced by David Fincher, comes from a same genre 1990s miniseries by the BBC, which was based itself on a novel by Michael Dobbs published in 1989.

Whether Netflix's choice of acquiring a nostalgic revival of *Scream* was profitable or not for MTV is not clear yet. Furthermore, if we think about reviving a former audience, who comes back to the show with a feeling of belonging, there is probably more nostalgia in the revival *Gilmore Girls: A Year in the Life* (Netflix, 2016-). However, *Scream: The TV Series*, as well as other slasher-like television series, still looks relevant in the context of

Netflix nostalgia for the reasons outlined. By itself, it puts together all three kinds of nostalgia—nostalgia-by-indexing, nostalgia-by-proxy, nostalgia-by-serialization—thus facilitating the process of classification, as well as an intergenerational exchange and a self-reflexivity typical of the serial form. Netflix's bet on nostalgic content seems to have many advantages if we consider the platform logic.

Beyond the debate on quality and the actual success, *Scream: The TV Series* responds to the necessity of managing the amount of television series on Netflix by generating a flow of interconnected content, via a recommendation system. For instance, the form of the anthology allows by itself to create a basin for collecting different serialized spin-off seasons related to the franchise. A point of entrance is now opened, and the viewer is encouraged to explore and navigate the library by subgroups: movies linked to the same franchise, content related to the slasher super-category, or other products listed in the horror macro-genre. "These include the creation of a [. . .] playlist past through the increased availability of a digital-archive apparatus, the behavioral repetition of nostalgia [. . .], the epistemology of the film remake in the age of the re-imagined 'classic,' and the commodity flow of nostalgia through all areas of televisual content."[33]

Calling this TV series a simple revival might be limiting, if we refer uniquely to a recurring branded nostalgia often seen in slasher movies, with their temporary closures and resolutions in the story, which ends up reopening in a constant hunt. Even a broader definition of "horror nostalgia" doesn't really account for the complexity of the current television scenario. To quote Stefanie Armbruster, "across the boundaries of genres, nostalgia is a decisive characteristic of contemporary television fiction and its reception, 'not only,' as Feyerabend highlights in a more general context of contemporary nostalgia, 'on a national level but indeed on a more global or transnational scope'"[34] It is probably more appropriate to talk about a cultural nostalgia that feeds into the Netflix's library through a series of intertextual links.

In the Netflix universe, where data dictate cultural preferences and tendencies, form and content in nostalgia-making practices should be analyzed for their potentialities of generating adjacent fictional universes and dynamics of "intertextual dialogism,"[35] that in some cases can go transnational. It is widely known in the media industry that nostalgia stimulates the audience through an archive of historical and cultural memories, by referencing a shared heritage or a collective imagery. Repurposing old content through commercial deals is not exclusively a Netflix business model, but a widely diffused bet of the contemporary television industry. However, Netflix made nostalgia one of the pillars of its brand. The idea of an archive, with a dynamic catalog, where practices of storage and retrieval are strictly interconnected, shows that, in a less abstract point of view and in more practical ways, nostalgia can be thought of as the formation of a network of intertextual references that eventually fosters dynamics of algorithmic indexing and "preferential attachment."[36]

With the purpose of verifying dynamics of preferential attachment involved in recommendation systems, an interesting study has been conducted by Mariano Beguerisse Díaz, Mason A. Porter and Jukka-Pekka Onnela who analyzed Netflix as a "catalog network." As they explain, "the Netflix network can be studied using such a catalog network framework; it starts completely disconnected, nobody has rated any videos, and the users start choosing and rating videos from the catalog."[37] Through this model they observed that "the number of ratings for a given video is driven almost completely by its popularity (preferential attachment) and only in very small measure by the intrinsic preferences of users."[38] Of course, as it is also underlined in their paper, in order to infer a general rule from this initial observation, one would also need to look at other factors that can influence the popularity of a product, both internally (actual scores, age of the video, demographic of the users and so on) and externally (launch and promotional campaigns, for example). Nevertheless, this study still serves as a starting point for investigating the popularity of a TV show on a VOD platform, using at the same time quantitative and qualitative analysis. A similar interdisciplinary approach to television studies could help us understand whether nostalgic products do actually function as gatherings of popularity, like a solely qualitative analysis would suggest.

Either way, it is clear that by acting in this nostalgic perimeter, Netflix revivals can be ways of facing and challenging old televisual standardized formats, through a practice of constant reboot and update that conforms to current television industry dynamics. As cultural products, such revivals find themselves at the intersection between the past and the future, both inheriting an audiovisual tradition and aiming to create new processes and inputs for storytelling. Additionally, they show the adaptability of nostalgic practices and their capacity to reinvent themselves, throughout different narrative, cultural and technological forms. Nostalgic reconfigurations in the *Scream* media franchise helped us in providing a specific case study for such a phenomenon. However, what we aim to bring to the academic attention is the existence of a spreading tendency in nonlinear television toward the creation of algorithmic networks for indexing content, a phenomenon which is worth investigating as part of the way digital technologies and streaming platforms are impacting the production of nostalgic narrative forms.

NOTES

1. Dominik Schrey, "Analogue Nostalgia and the Aesthetics of Digital Remediation." In *Media and Nostalgia: Yearning for the Past, Present and Future*, edited by Katharina Niemeyer (London: Palgrave Macmillan, 2014), 29.

2. Ryan Lizardi, *Mediated Nostalgia: Individual Memory and Contemporary Mass Media* (Lanham: Lexington Books, 2015), 137.

3. Richard Terdiman, *Present Past: Modernity and the Memory Crisis* (Ithaca, NY: Cornell University Press, 1993).

4. Michael Rothberg, *Multidirectional Memory: Remembering the Holocaust in the Age of Decolonization* (Stanford: Stanford University Press, 2009), 3.

5. For a definition of mediascape see Arjun Appadurai, "Disjuncture and Difference in the Global Cultural Economy," *Theory Culture & Society*, 7 (1990).

6. "Nostalgic '90s," Netflix, accessed April 7, 2018, https://www.netflix.com/browse/genre/2691941 .

7. "Totally awesome 80s," Netflix, accessed April 7, 2018, https://www.netflix.com/browse/genre/2314106 .

8. "TV shows from the 1960s," Netflix, accessed April 7, 2018, https://www.netflix.com/browse/genre/7316 ; "TV shows from the 1970s," Netflix, accessed April 7, 2018, https://www.netflix.com/browse/genre/7341 .

9. "TV from 2000 on," Netflix, accessed April 7, 2018, https://www.netflix.com/browse/genre/1716137 .

10. Michelle Dean, "Stranger Things: A Dose of Goonies-Inflected Nostalgia," *The New Republic*, last modified July 20, 2016, https://newrepublic.com/article/135320/stranger-things-dose-goonies-inflected-nostalgia .

11. Robert Buerkle. "Playset Nostalgia: LEGO Star Wars: The Video Game and the Transgenerational Appeal of the LEGO Video Game Franchise." In *LEGO Studies: Examining the Building Blocks of a Transmedial Phenomenon*, edited by Mark J. P. Wolf (New York: Routledge, 2014), 128.

12. Mark Lawson, "Nostalgic Nightmares: How Netflix Made *Stranger Things* a Watercooler Smash," *The Guardian*, last modified August 5, 2016, https://www.theguardian.com/tv-and-radio/2016/aug/05/netflix-hit-stranger-things-highlights-tvs-trend-for-nostalgia .

13. For a definition of the concept of "narrative ecosystem" in television seriality, see Guglielmo Pescatore and Veronica Innocenti, "Information Architecture in Contemporary Television Series," *Journal of Information Architecture*, 4 (2012): 57-72.

14. Constantine Verevis, *Film Remakes* (New York: Palgrave Macmillan, 2005), 37.

15. Frank Kelleter, *Media of Serial Narrative* (Columbus: The Ohio State University Press, 2017).

16. See Umberto Eco, "Tipologia della ripetizione," in *L'immagine al plurale. Serialità eripetizione nel cinema e nella televisione*, edited by Francesco Casetti (Venezia: Marsilio, 1984).

17. Fred Davis, *Yearning for Yesterday: A Sociology of Nostalgia* (New York: The Free Press, 1979).

18. Frank Kelleter, *Media of Serial Narrative* (Columbus: The Ohio State University Press, 2017).

19. Ryan Lizardi, *Mediated Nostalgia: Individual Memory and Contemporary Mass Media* (Lanham: Lexington Books, 2015), 50.

20. Ryan Lizardi, *Mediated Nostalgia: Individual Memory and Contemporary Mass Media* (Lanham: Lexington Books, 2015), 31.

21. *Scream*'s show-running executive producer Jill Blotevogel declared in an interview that a common reaction to his televisual project was: "You can't do a slasher movie as a TV series. It doesn't make sense. It doesn't fit into the format, the time frame," a statement that ended up being embedded in a catchy line of the first episode of the first season, openly declaring from the very beginning the will of the series to "go meta."

22. Pansy Duncan, *The Emotional Life of Postmodern Film: Affect Theory's Other* (London: Routledge, 2015), 88-89.

23. Jason Mittell, *Genre and Television: From Cop Shows to Cartoons in American Culture* (New York: Routledge, 2004), xii.

24. Lorna Jowett and Stacey Abbott, *TV Horror: Investigating the Dark Side of the Small Screen* (London and New York: I.B. Tauris, 2013).

25. Frances Pheasant-Kelly, "Reframing Parody and Intertextuality in Scream: Formal and Theoretical Approaches to the 'Postmodern' Slasher," in *Style and Form in the Hollywood Slasher Film,* edited by Wickham Clayton (London: Palgrave Macmillan, 2015), 149.

26. Valerie Wee, "'New Decade, New Rules': Rebooting the Scream Franchise in the" Digital Age." In *Merchants of Menace: The Business of Horror Cinema,* edited by Richard Nowell (New York: Bloomsbury, 2014), 147-148.

27. Sara Gwenllian-Jones and Roberta Pearson (eds.), *Cult Television* (Minneapolis: The University of Minnesota Press, 2004), ix.

28. Xavier Mendik and Graeme Harper (eds.), *Unruly Pleasures: The Cult Film and Its Critics* (Guildford: FAB Press, 2000), 7.

29. Michael M. Grynbaum, "TV's Big Bet on Nostalgia," *The New York Times,* last modified May 16, 2016, https://www.nytimes.com/2016/05/17/business/media/looking-to-its-future-television-revisits-its-past.html.

30. "Number of original scripted TV series in the United States from 2009 to 2017," *Statista,* accessed April 23, 2018, https://www.statista.com/statistics/444870/scripted-primetime-tv-series-number-usa .

31. Ashley Rodriguez, "The End of 'Peak TV' Must Finally, Mercifully Be Nigh," *Quartz,* January 13, 2018, accessed April 23, 2018, https://qz.com/999827/the-end-of-peak-tv-must-finally-mercifully-be-nigh/ .

32. Cynthia Littleton, "FX Networks Chief John Landgraf: 'There Is Simply Too Much Television,'" *Variety,* August 7, 2015, accessed April 23, 2018, http://variety.com/2015/tv/news/tca-fx-networks-john-landgraf-wall-street-1201559191.

33. Ryan Lizardi, *Playlist Pasts: New Media, Constructed Nostalgic Subjectivity and the Disappearance of Shared History* (State College: The Pennsylvania State University, 2012), iii.

34. Stefanie Armbruster, *Watching Nostalgia: An Analysis of Nostalgic Television Fiction and Its Reception* (Bielefeld: Transcript, 2016), 12.

35. Umberto Eco, "Tipologia della ripetizione," in *L'immagine al plurale. Serialità e ripetizione nel cinema e nella televisione,* edited by Francesco Casetti (Venezia: Marsilio, 1984).

36. In relation to dynamics of preferential attachment in online network, we refer more specifically to the distinction made by Kunegis, Blattner and Moser who investigate preferential attachment in rating networks: "In other words, preferential attachment in rating networks refers to the fact that items with many items will receive more ratings in the future. Note that this statement is independent of the actual ratings given, but only refers to the information of whether a rating was or will be given." J. Kunegis, M. Blattner, and C. Moser, "Preferential Attachment in Online Networks: Measurement and Explanations," *Proc. Web Sci. Conf.* (2013): 208

37. Mariano Beguerisse Díaz, Mason A. Porter and Jukka-Pekka Onnela, "Competition for Popularity in Bipartite Networks," *Chaos,* 20, no. 4 (2010), https://www.math.ucla.edu/~mason/papers/mariano_final.pdf.

38. Díaz, Porter, and Onnela, "Competition for Popularity in Bipartite Networks."

BIBLIOGRAPHY

Appadurai, Arjun. "Disjuncture and Difference in the Global Cultural Economy." *Theory Culture & Society* 7, no. 2 (1990): 295-310.

Armbruster, Stefanie. *Watching Nostalgia: An Analysis of Nostalgic Television Fiction and its Reception.* Bielefeld: Transcript, 2016.

Buerkle, Robert. "Playset Nostalgia: LEGO Star Wars: The Video Game and the Transgenerational Appeal of the LEGO Video Game Franchise." In *LEGO Studies: Examining the Building Blocks of a Transmedial Phenomenon,* edited by Mark J. P. Wolf, 118–152, New York: Routledge, 2014.

Davis, Fred. *Yearning for Yesterday: A Sociology of Nostalgia.* New York: Free Press, 1979.

Dean, Michelle. "*Stranger Things*: A Dose of Goonies-Inflected Nostalgia." The New Republic, last modified July 20, 2016, https://newrepublic.com/article/135320/stranger-things-dose-goonies-inflected-nostalgia .

Díaz, Mariano Beguerisse, Mason A. Porter and Jukka-Pekka Onnela. "Competition for popularity in bipartite networks." *Chaos,* 20, no. 4 (October 2010)-https://www.math.ucla.edu/~mason/papers/mariano_final.pdf .

Duncan, Pansy. *The Emotional Life of Postmodern Film: Affect Theory's Other.* London: Routledge, 2015.

Eco, Umberto. "Tipologia della ripetizione." In *L'immagine al plurale. Serialità e ripetizione nel cinema e nella televisione,* edited by Francesco Casetti, 19-36, Venezia: Marsilio, 1984.

Grynbaum, Michael M. "TV's Big Bet on Nostalgia," *The New York Times,* last modified May 16, 2016, https://www.nytimes.com/2016/05/17/business/media/looking-to-its-future-television-revisits-its-past.html.

Gwenllian-Jones, Sara and Roberta Pearson (Eds.). *Cult Television.* Minneapolis: The University of Minnesota Press, 2004.

Jowett, Lorna, and Stacey Abbott (Eds.). *TV Horror: Investigating the Dark Side of the Small Screen.* London and New York: I.B. Tauris, 2013.

Kelleter, Frank. *Media of Serial Narrative.* Columbus: The Ohio State University Press, 2017.

Kunegis, Jérôme, Marcel Blattner and Christine Moser. "Preferential Attachment in Online Networks: Measurement and Explanations." In *Proceedings of the 5th Annual ACM Web Science Conference, WebSci '13,* (2013): 205-214, https://arxiv.org/pdf/1303.6271.pdf

Lawson, Mark. "Nostalgic Nightmares: How Netflix Made *Stranger Things* a Watercooler Smash." *The Guardian,* last modified August 5, 2016, https://www.theguardian.com/tv-and-radio/2016/aug/05/netflix-hit-stranger-things-highlights-tvs-trend-for-nostalgia.

Littleton, Cynthia. "FX Networks Chief John Landgraf: 'There Is Simply Too Much Television,'" *Variety,* last modified August 7, 2015, http://variety.com/2015/tv/news/tca-fx-networks-john-landgraf-wall-street-1201559191.

Lizardi, Ryan. *Playlist Pasts: New Media, Constructed Nostalgic Subjectivity and the Disappearance of Shared History.* State College: The Pennsylvania State University, 2012.

———. *Mediated Nostalgia: Individual Memory and Contemporary Mass Media.* Lanham: Lexington Books, 2015.

Mendik, Xavier, and Graeme Harper (Eds.). *Unruly Pleasures: The Cult Film and Its Critics.* Guildford: FAB Press, 2000.

Mittell, Jason. *Genre and Television: From Cop Shows to Cartoons in American Culture.* New York: Routledge, 2004.

Netflix, "Nostalgic 90s," *Netflix,* accessed April 7, 2018, https://www.netflix.com/browse/genre/2691941.

———. "Totally awesome 80s," *Netflix,* accessed April 7, 2018, https://www.netflix.com/browse/genre/2314106.

———. "TV shows from the 1960s," *Netflix,* accessed April 7, 2018, https://www.netflix.com/browse/genre/7316 .

———. "TV shows from the 1970s," *Netflix,* accessed April 7, 2018, https://www.netflix.com/browse/genre/7341 .

———. "TV from 2000 on," *Netflix,* accessed April 7, 2018, https://www.netflix.com/browse/genre/1716137.

Niemeyer, Katharina. *Media and Nostalgia: Yearning for the Past, Present and Future.* London: Palgrave Macmillan, 2014

Pescatore, Guglielmo, and Innocenti, Veronica. "Information Architecture in Contemporary Television Series." *Journal of Information Architecture* 4 (2012): 57-72.

Pheasant-Kelly, Frances. "Reframing Parody and Intertextuality in Scream: Formal and Theoretical Approaches to the 'Postmodern' Slasher." In *Style and Form in the Hollywood Slasher Film,* edited by Wickham Clayton, 149-160, London: Palgrave Macmillan, 2015.

Rodriguez, Ashley. "The End of 'Peak TV' Must Finally, Mercifully Be Nigh," *Quartz,* last modified January 13, 2018, https://qz.com/999827/the-end-of-peak-tv-must-finally-mercifully-be-nigh/.

Rothberg, Michael. *Multidirectional Memory: Remembering the Holocaust in the Age of Decolonization.* Stanford: Stanford University Press, 2009.

Statista. "Number of original scripted TV series in the United States from 2009 to 2017," *Statista,* accessed April 23, 2018, https://www.statista.com/statistics/444870/scripted-primetime-tv-series-number-usa.

Terdiman, Richard. *Present Past: Modernity and the Memory Crisis.* Ithaca, NY: Cornell University Press, 1993.

Verevis, Constantine. *Film Remakes.* New York: Palgrave Macmillan, 2005.

Wee, Valerie. "'New Decade, New Rules': Rebooting the Scream Franchise in the Digital Age." In *Merchants of Menace: The Business of Horror Cinema,* edited by Richard Nowell. New York: Bloomsbury, 2014, 147-160.

TWO

Branding Netflix with Nostalgia

*Totemic Nostalgia, Adaptation,
and the Postmodern Turn*

Matthias Stephan

NETFLIX, DISRUPTION, AND THE POSTMODERN TURN

The story of Netflix has been the story of disruption, which "describes a process whereby a smaller company with fewer resources is able to successfully challenge established incumbent businesses."[1] Netflix's business model has been just that, consisting of entering a market in its least profitable sectors before moving to more mainstream, and hence more profitable, sectors of the media landscape. This has proven highly successful and Netflix has become a worldwide company, now the leading provider of streaming media globally, accounting for 64.5 percent of digital video viewers in the United States, the world's biggest market, in 2018.[2] Yet, the period since 1997 did not just see disruption in one market (home-use digital video), but in virtually all of them, a wide scale digital revolution challenging traditional business practices in most cultural industries. The world is more global, more connected, than ever, which has brought us together, and brought the challenge of a mix of cultures, values, and perspectives. These challenges, as in the case of Netflix, have brought innovation, and technological advancements have moved forward rapidly. However, concurrently, faced with rapid change, not only technological, but also social, political, and cultural, there has been an expansion of underlying anxiety with the modern world, which the digital revolution has exacerbated.

Media disruption follows upon the larger change of the postmodern turn, which is increasingly pervasive. While the playful, metafictional elements associated with postmodernism have waned, what remains is the understanding of postmodern structure, leading to feelings of insecurity. Not only do we have the anxiety associated with modernism, including loss of identity and a fragmented nature, but with the postmodern turn, we have lost our faith that there are answers to be found. In the lack of underlying structure, we return to the organizing structures of the past, as the cultural default, even as the underpinnings of those norms have been challenged by postmodernism. Those residual cultural values are reinforced through the nostalgic trend of the past decade, partly because they reinforce what Matt Hills calls a self-narrative.[3]

This paper explores the underpinnings of the nostalgic narrative trend in contemporary society, especially as present in Netflix. Netflix Originals presents the streaming service an opportunity to root its programming in a highly affective and emotional frame, connecting viewers longing for the perceived stability of the past with the Netflix brand. Continuing programs with a dedicated audience reinforces this, and the creation of sequels like *Fuller House* and the successful *The Gilmore Girls: A Year in the Life* increasingly ties this affect to the brand. This paper will focus on *Stranger Things* and *GLOW*, both Netflix Original programming, and the CW series *Riverdale*, distributed globally by Netflix, and consider their use of setting, tone, and elements of adaptation theory to explain the construction of their nostalgic narratives. Each series builds on William Proctor's notion of *totemic nostalgia*, which ties fans' self-narrative to an object of fandom, and this paper demonstrates how each, through connections with 1980s gothic film traditions (*Stranger Things*), 1980s depictions of Hollywood (*GLOW*), and the adaptation of the Archie TV and movie franchises (themselves adaptations of the comics) from the 1970s (*Riverdale*), activate a sense of belonging through its appeal to nostalgia. Each, as the Netflix brand itself does through these series, roots its appeal in the nostalgic narrative, while also providing new takes in line with contemporary audiences.

NETFLIX AND THE NOSTALGIC NARRATIVE

According to Svetlana Boym, nostalgia "is a longing for a home that no longer exists or has never existed."[4] Nostalgia is a double bind, both a look back to an idealized past, but with a future trajectory, a hope that the romanticized past will become our future. Nostalgia can be a dangerous preoccupation, especially when used in what Boym calls the "restorative" variety, which seeks to reestablish the past, as described, directly into the future scenario, often eliding complications to the self-identity presented in this nostalgic narrative. This is particularly problematic, because, as Bauman notes, "what we as a rule 'return to' when dreaming our nostalgic dreams is not the past 'as such'—not that past 'as it genuinely was.'"[5]

Yet, recent sociological research suggests that nostalgia can have positive implications as well. As William Proctor[6] argues, "nostalgia presents an affirmative psychical bulwark, a 'meaning-making resource' and a 'resource for the self'[7] both of which counteract 'self-discontinuity and restores self-continuity.'"[8] Proctor ties this notion to *totemic nostalgia*, which centers on "an affective relationship with a fan-object" and builds upon the construction of a self-narrative that is also contingent on personal attachments to the past, often exemplified in cultural artifacts and media products. This positive track of nostalgia, Boym's alternative formulation of the nostalgic narrative, "reflective" nostalgia, suggests that "the past is not made in the image of the present, or seen as foreboding of some present disaster; rather the past opens up a multitude of potentialities, nonteleological possibilities of historical development."[9] In other words, the reflective formulation questions the construction of the idealized nature of the past, and opens up the past for revision, even as it is activated as a reference point in our construction of the future.

One benefit of the nostalgic narrative is the opportunity to provide ontological security, an anchoring in the fragmented world. Giddens argues that "to be ontologically secure is to possess, on the level of the unconscious and practical consciousness, 'answers' to fundamental existential questions which all human life in some way addresses."[10] After the postmodern turn, those answers are not only harder to come by, but we have had a loss of faith in our ability to answer these questions at all. In reaction, Jameson suggests "not the disappearance of the great masternarratives, but their passage underground as it were, their continuing but now *unconscious* effectivity as a way of 'thinking about' and acting in our current situation.'"[11] Jameson here postulates that faced with a loss of faith in the grand narratives of the past, and lacking an alternative anchor for the understanding of the modern (or postmodern) world, we continue to operate *as if* the previous patterns were still operable. This is done on both a social and personal level, and we engage this identity making in all forms of daily life, not least in our media consumption. Thus, the past becomes a central way to interpret the future.

Pickering and Keightley contend that "nostalgia is certainly a response to the experience of loss endemic in modernity and late modernity,"[12] but tend toward the reflective rather than restorative model. They argue that "nostalgia can then be seen as not only a search for ontological security in the past, but also as a means of taking one's bearings for the road ahead in the uncertainties of the present. . . . Nostalgia can be both melancholic and utopian."[13] This makes nostalgia not a means of constructing a past identity, but a progressive tool by which to construct a self-identity in the contemporary world. Our engagement with the past, however, is not limited to, or even exclusively derived from, our lived experiences, or even the direct stories told within families and communities. We have since the rise of mass media consumption and the advent of television been positioned as consumers of media narratives as direct and primary sources of meaningful self-narrative construction. Pickering and Keightley claim that "rather than remembering experiences, we are more likely to remember mediated experiences and as such, mediation of the past is a process by which the media can fix and limit social memory."[14] Thus, rather than constructing the past based on "real" events, we often create our self-narratives with a combination of real and media narratives, and increasingly, our personal experiences are also mediated narratives.

Michael Dwyer, in his study of the nostalgic turn in the construction of the 1950s, presents the notion of "pop nostalgia," the final feature of which is located not just in the texts, but in the "affective relationship between audiences and texts."[15] This presents nostalgia as a distinctly media product, constructed and interpreted by what look like Fishian "interpretative communities," but without the necessity of a historical accuracy. As he notes, the consumption of the 1950s in the Reagan-era of the 1980s uses a combination of traditional and pop nostalgia to sell a political message. Its effectiveness was not that it constructed Reagan as a nostalgic figure, but rather that it reconstituted its audience in the image, with this nostalgic narrative projected onto Reagan by the consumers of his political message. It reflects "not only to the shared cultural texts and practices but also—and crucially—the shared *identity* of a nation. In other words, the Fifties were not only important in American popular culture but central to American self-understanding in the Reagan Era."[16] However, this is not strictly about the construction of a political message, but rather the way in which we present our self-identity – which is increasingly constructed through mediated experience. The connections with the past, not the reality of it, but the iconic references, intertexts, and the "feel" of the age, allow us to construct the past as a strategic sounding board for how we construct our narrative moving forward. As Niemeyer notes, nostalgia is "more than only a cultural product we consume," but it is also "something we do actively, either superficially or profoundly, alone, with family or friends, or, on a larger scale, with media."[17] It is thus the mediated nostalgia that allows such broader connections to be made, through its collective experience and mapping of those experiences onto our identities.

Jonathan Simon, in his study of boot camps, argues that what is created is a notion of "willful nostalgia," which romanticizes parts of the past to allow it to fit into a version of the self-narrative. "The real past, even misrecognized, contains challenges as well as comforts. The ultimate retreat is escaping to a past that has been self-consciously and systematically revised to remove its jagged edges."[18] This narrative construction can be seen in Dwyer's study of 1950s pop nostalgia, and is arguably even more activated in our contemporary era, with less faith in accurate historical representation. Such nostalgia functions through Boym's restorative model as "willful nostalgia delivered in both films and politics seems to operate as a compensation for the anxieties generated by present uncertainties,"[19] yet Simon argues that "Rather than creating space from which the present can be subjected to evaluation, willful nostalgia cobbles together a past out of commodified (often popular culture) images that, because of their overtly consumable quality, deny the possibility of serious opposition to the present."[20] This plays into notions of postmodernity, specifically Jameson's invocation of the idea of blank parody, where parody is invoked without the characteristic motives, critique, and ridicule, and operates as reference or adaptation, without commentary or direction. This leaves the symbolism implicit in the reference to the totemic object open for interpretation and useful in the construction of new narratives moving forward. Activation of the nostalgic provides, as Bauman advocates, both (ontological) security as well as freedom to remake the images and even political message inherent in the totemic narrative. "In other words, Jameson's conceptualization of nostalgia/pastiche is that of a representational practice that *flattens, evacuates*, and eventually *elides* the authentic past."[21]

The construction of meaning through a mediated narrative happens at a number of levels. In the case studies, the nostalgic narrative is presented in setting and tone, the context of the stories, through totemic objects within the texts, including iconic technology, as well as through peripheral content such as music, intertextuality, and paratext. "Paratexts tell us what to expect, and in doing so, they shape the reading strategies that we will take with us 'into' the text, and they provide the all-important early frames through which we will examine, react to, and evaluate textual consumption."[22] Drawing on structuralist theorists, Gray presents framing material, like covers, commentary, ads, trailers, and spoilers (both official and unofficial), as meaningful in our interpretation and understanding of the text itself, to the extent that we are already framed in our interpretations of the text prior to ever consuming the text itself. This is not limited to peripheral material but also can include intertextual material and generic markers, which, while not formal parts of the texts, nonetheless shape our reading of the texts. He argues, for example, that "other, intangible entities can at times work in a paratextual fashion. Thus, for instance, while a genre is not a paratext, it can work paratextually to frame a text."[23] In essence, in order to understand what happens in a particular text, one also has to understand its nostalgic narrative context, as well as the interconnections of the paratext, the "void" between our contemporary understanding and all of the intertexts through which the narrative is constructed. We will now turn to the case studies, using the frames discussed above, nostalgia, totemic objects, as well as paratextual information and framing, and will first look at this through the upside-down world of *Stranger Things*, before proceeding to our other examples.

TOTEMIC NOSTALGIA AND PARATEXT IN *STRANGER THINGS*

Stranger Things is a critically acclaimed Netflix Original first produced in 2016. Set in Hawkins, Pennsylvania, in 1985, it revolves around strange, paranormal events in this small rural town. Much of the tale focuses on a small group of middle school children, who are directly affected through the vanishing of their friend Will Byers (Noah Schapp). In his stead, the town is introduced to the character of Eleven (Millie Bobby Brown), a young girl with telekinetic powers. The first season revolves around Will's disappearance, and the understanding of a parallel universe, the upside-down. The second season broadens the scope and makes the opposing entity less tangible.

The series evokes the totemic nostalgic effect, allowing Netflix to produce an affective attachment to the past through this series. The show is set in the 1980s, with its associated technology, allowing the presentation of certain social dynamics, such as the relative freedom the group of boys have in their environment because of the perceived safety of the small town atmosphere. This is further reinforced through 1980s technologies, including VHS tapes, the iconic wall telephone with an extended cord, and the main framing device of the first season, the role-playing game. This iconic game, which requires little in the way of electronic media, gives the show the metaphors it uses to fight the paranormal. The first season's main antagonist, from the upside-down, is the Demogorgon from Dungeons & Dragons, who represents the Prince of Demons and Lord of Darkness. This character, with classical and Christian references, also positions the opposition as one of clear lines between good (the inhabitants of Hawkins) and evil, reinforcing a clear hierarchy which helps to produce ontological security.

However, the character of Eleven is also presented as paranormal, and her character is pitched not only against the Demogorgon, but also against a group of scientists bent on using her abilities. This is clearly reminiscent of certain 1980s movies, not the least of which is *E.T.* and *Stranger Things* features iconic 1980s style bicycles as the group's primary mode of transportation. These are used, when Eleven joins the group, as a means of escape, with a scene which has direct parallels to the escaping E.T. The second season has further references to 1980s iconic scenarios, such as walking on train tracks (*Stand by Me*), a collection of five children facing off against a group of criminals of perhaps supernatural origin (*Goonies*), and iconically, the dressing up of the four main juvenile protagonists in *Ghostbusters* outfits. This foreshadows how they will fight Mind-Flayer (from season 2), and comments on the racial distribution of the

Ghostbusters, by using the assumption that Lucas (Caleb McLaughlin), as the only African-American member of the group should, by default, play Winston (the most recent member, and the only non-scientist), to comment on contemporary situations. Rather than whitewashing the past, the new Netflix original allows for a reconsideration of the past—invoking the iconic 1980s vibe but making the racial components, and gender dynamics, more up-to-date politically. This progressive use of nostalgia can be used to brand Netflix as both appealing to our sense of self-narrative while maintaining a connection to contemporary progressive attitudes in terms of race and gender, which are not reflective of either the historical realities of the 1980s or more conservative evocations of the same 1980s dynamic.

The series also uses a number of paratextual markers to provide the totemic attachment to the 1980s. One main reference is the casting of Winona Ryder as Joyce Byers. This is accomplished through intertextual parallels to the upside-down, which is visually represented as a more dystopic version of the rural town, flipped on its head (the otherside of the role-playing board provides the first visual). Winona Ryder, in an early role, plays a teenager in a haunted house in *Beetlejuice*, in which she is able to see the ghosts though her parents are not able to. In addition, if the ghosts in that film attempted to leave, they were confronted with a dystopic landscape beyond the safe confines of the house. Will Byers, especially as presented in paratextual material, is positioned as being able to see the upside-down even while being physically present in the "normal" universe, and that is reinforced through his mom having a totemic attachment to *Beetlejuice* through the common actress. This technique is further established in the second season with the addition of two characters, Dr. Sam Owens (Paul Reiser) and Bob Newby (Sean Astin). In the after-show *Beyond Stranger Things*, they provide short interview-style clips from both actors. Paul Reiser explicitly points to his casting as having a nostalgic resonance, to the character of a doctor he plays in *Aliens* (Carter J. Burke), who has similarly questionable allegiances within the universe of *Stranger Things*. Additionally, the casting of Sean Astin also provides clear references to *Goonies*, as well as to the quest narrative of the *Lord of the Rings* franchises. Sean Levy, in *Beyond Stranger Things*, mentions that they were hesitant to cast Astin, thinking the decision would seem too heavy-handed, but he occupied the character of Bob so well, that the decision seems to have proved worthwhile. Astin, once cast, improvises lines which parallel his character in *Goonies*, reinforcing the connection of that film's group of children with the cast of *Stranger Things*.

ADAPTATION, PROXIMATION, AND THE
GORGEOUS LADIES OF WRESTLING

GLOW (2017-) is an adaptation of a 1980s era women's wrestling program of the same name, which ran for four seasons from 1986 to 1990. The Netflix original differs from the original production in that it is a scripted production, which tells a fictionalized tale of the creation and presentation of the *Gorgeous Ladies of Wrestling*. The series is set in 1985 and uses period setting, tone, and other peripherals to create a nostalgic atmosphere. This challenges the conventions inherent in the original wrestling production, which had a distinctive comedic style, and produces an updated story focusing on the development of a primarily female cast in a time and setting which did not favor texts with female agency.

The feel of *GLOW* hearkens back to the 1980s, not only through costuming, props, and set design, but also through the cultural dynamics built into the show. The filming location, the iconic Valley from 1980s films as *The Karate Kid*, sets the tone and draws the viewer into a world of black and white, good versus evil dynamic. Alison Brie cites the authenticity of the 1980s dynamic as one of the reasons she embraced the TV role, stating: "I couldn't think of another thing that's on right now to compare it to. Even when I watch it, the feel and look of it is more like an '80s movie than like anything on TV right now."[24]

This is also highlighted in gender dynamics, with Ruth Wilder (Alison Brie) reading the "man's" role at an early audition, because men have all of the interesting lines. This highlights traditional gender roles, complimented by the character of Deborah Eagan (Betty Gilpin) who left her soap opera job to start a family, at the behest of her husband Mark (Rich Sommer). The family motif is furthered in the second season, with more emphasis placed on Eagan's role as a mother, both in the personal story, and through developments in the wrestling story, which *GLOW* increasingly parallels to the developments of key characters. The 1980s narrative is reinforced by the American vs. Russian dynamic, the main event in the diegetic wrestling program's first season, pitting Debbie "Liberty Belle" Eagan against Ruth "Zoya the Destroyer" Wilder, reenacting the contemporary Cold War, and returning us to the relatively clear world of the Reagan Era. This nostalgic narrative builds upon the affect and emotional connection to the 1980s to provide a stable launching point to allow the text to speak to the contemporary world. This brands Netflix with emotional appeal and provides the framework for it to challenge the conventions of the era.

The stability of the nostalgic narrative is reinforced, as in *Stranger Things*, through the use of totemic nostalgia. Here, the b-film aspects of Sam Sylvia (Marc Maron) present an opportunity to use both 1980s drug culture, with the availability of cocaine on the set, and technology. The use of the VHS tapes, as an archive of Sylvia's masterpieces, and featuring their rewritability refers us back to a time with more limited technology. This is also highlighted through the lack of communications, including the prank phone calls in the hotel rooms, and the possibility of Sam Sylvia and Sebastian "Bash" Howard (Chris Lowell) disappearing for longer periods.

While wrestling historically plays up binary oppositions and stereotypical characters, both in traditionally male and in the female *GLOW* versions, this Netflix version of *GLOW* allows us to see "behind the scenes" showing the level of doubt and hesitation in creating such an unnuanced presentation of cultural and historical dynamics. The diegetic male wrestling program, which Debbie Eagan and Carmen Wade (Brittany Murphy) attend, pits Mr. Monopoly (professional wrestler Joey Ryan) against working-class hero Steel Horse (professional wrestler Alex Riley), yet it is revealed that these personas are just an act. However, in that dynamic they represent relatively positive masculine values. *GLOW* questions how those roles are not available to women in the 1980s, which by proxy is a commentary on our current #metoo environment. Tammé Dawson (Kia Stevens, professional wrestler Awesome Kong) is one such example, through her "Welfare Queen" persona, which she argues, privately to Sam Sylvia, reinforces negative portrayals of African-American women, playing into the 1980s stereotype of African Americans being simultaneously less capable (welfare recipients) and devious and underhanded (the gaming of the system). Dawson's character highlights her children being upper middle class, attending Stanford University, and thus not conforming to this stereotyped representation, a motif picked up and emphasized in the second season when Dawson's son visits the filming.

Additionally, the character of Arthie "Beirut" Premkumar (Sunita Mari), both questions her role as an "Arab" (due to her own Indian ancestry, highlighting the othering of people of color both within the nostalgic frame), as well as the appropriateness of the character in light of the 1980s political landscape, in which the Beirut hostage crisis and its impact on the election also provides the backdrop to the narrative. This provides a parallel contemporary reference to the political turmoil in Syria and the Middle East, and points to President Trump's handling of that situation.

In an interview, Gilpin lays out how *GLOW*, and wrestling programs in general, simplifies the narrative to provide a relatively palatable and understandable timeline, one which can connect to the audience. In our current ever more fast-paced landscape, this is a sought-after comfort, and one in which the nostalgic narrative is particularly able to provide. By providing stereotypical characters, coupled by their wrestling motifs leading to the ultimate good versus evil battle between the Americans and the Russians (set in the Cold War), the original *GLOW* spoke to the anxieties of its era, and Netflix's nostalgic adaptation of that production allows that emotional appeal to speak to ours, simultaneously positioning Netflix as the provider of that ontological security within the audience's self-narrative, in the era of disruption. The structures in wrestling have parallels in other media, with the narrative element—found in television series, soap operas, and comic books—allowing for these women to connect to their totemic object and attach a totemic nostalgia to their watching and performing in these arenas. Now we will take a look at a comic book adaptation, and see how *Riverdale* also brands Netflix with its totemic nostalgic narrative.

THE UNCANNILY NOSTALGIC UNDERTONES OF THE *RIVERDALE* ADAPTATION

Riverdale is not a Netflix original, but is distributed worldwide by Netflix. The TV series (2017-) represents an adaptation based on the reboot of the Archie Comics iconic brand in 2014, and creator Aguirre-Sacasa's new direction for the comic book franchise after joining Archie in 2013. The series continues a long tradition of iconic characters, namesake Archie Andrews, girl next door Betty Cooper, social misfit Jughead Jones, and socialite Veronica Lodge. The framing of the new Riverdale also has a distinct nostalgic overtone, which connects it to the other case studies, both by using references to prior iterations of Archie key characters, and through paratextual material, iconic uses of technology, and parallels to other tropes and texts of the 1980s and 1990s. The success of the new *Riverdale* has already led to production of a spin-off series, based likewise on a darker version of one of Archie's other iconic brands, Sabrina the Teenage Witch, with *Chilling Adventures of Sabrina* appearing on Netflix. Of particular interest is how Netflix has brought the Archie Comics adaptations back in-house, learning from the success of *Riverdale* and its particular success with young online viewers, to both produce and distribute future Archie adaptations such as *Sabrina* and the rumored *Josie* series.

Riverdale was brought to fruition through the CW network, and this franchise was part of a collaboration between Netflix and CW to further distribute popular CW franchises through the internet streaming platform.[25] Announced in 2016, the agreement allows first-run original CW programming to stream on Netflix just eight days after it airs on CW, allowing it to acquire delayed viewers more rapidly, by which *Riverdale* built a strong audience through its streaming customers. *Riverdale*'s renewal for a second season was tied to the success of the Netflix partnership, which was also convenient for Netflix who distribute *Riverdale* worldwide.

The CW network, well-known for nostalgic narratives with *The Gilmore Girls*, first aired "new" *Riverdale* bringing forth the image of the original comic book series, which dates back to the 1940s, and presenting traditional characters. The use of iconic 1950s nostalgic devices, like the highlighting of Pop's Diner, serve both to construct the nostalgic narrative, as well as provide the appropriate setting for the Archie franchise. However, this new *Riverdale*, as we have discussed with other nostalgic narratives, both hearkens back and looks forward, modifying the franchise through modernization of themes, characters, and overall tone. In *Riverdale*, the iconic stereotypes, like in *GLOW*, are challenged and deconstructed. Archie, the preeminent jock, turns to an artistic streak, while all-American girl next door manifests a dark-side, Dark Betty. This is coupled with a distinct gothic overtone especially connected to the disappearance of Jason Blossom—which creates both a mystery and class dynamics between the largely middle-class Riverdale, the working (and suspect) class of Jughead and his family, and the elite represented by the Blossoms.

Riverdale's first season is dedicated to discovering the truth behind Blossom's disappearance and murder. The disruption to small-town America through death is reminiscent of classical crime dramas. As Bergin argues, this type of fiction allows us to reinforce stability, demonstrating that despite temporary breaches, order is always restored. "Golden Age crime fiction offers readers the cathartic release of knowing that evil has been expelled from the community, and that the community can now return to how it used to be."[26] However, *Riverdale* does not only map onto crime fiction, but also to the darker mystery elements, reminiscent of *Twin Peaks*. Aguirre-Sacasa is even noted as saying that *Twin Peaks*, and the overall gothic overtones, were part of the original pitch for *Riverdale*. He claims "When we finally kind of landed on the formula, we did kinda pitch it as John Hughes, via *Twin Peaks*, as a mashup."[27] Both of those references are clearly presented through paratextual features.

Riverdale's opening sequence is eerily reminiscent of the Washington found in Lynch's pioneering gothic tale. Additionally, the opening sequence used neon lettering (as do both *GLOW* and *Stranger Things*) producing a 1980s reminiscence, here without distinctly setting the story in the 1980s, as with the other cases. The homage to Lynch, a consistent refrain, continues with casting decisions. Madchen Amick's character in *Riverdale*, as Betty Cooper's mother Alice, evokes her role in Lynch's *Twin Peaks*. Additionally, the casting of the Andrews family also provides paratextual framing, attaching the show to the 1980s and 1990s. Luke Perry, most known for his role in *Beverly Hills 90210* takes the role of Fred Andrews, and provides the combination of the high school vibe from his prior role, as well as his unconventional overtones. As we learn later in the season, his estranged wife is played by John Hughes' muse, and iconic 1980s actress Molly Ringwald, reinforcing the nostalgic attachment through their presence, and totemically attaching her sense of innocence to both Betty and her sister Polly.

The show represents not just a pointing to the past, and a grounding of the franchise through its nostalgia, but also uses the created security in order to address contemporary issues and update its characters to reflect a post-millennial reality. The post-reboot introduction of an openly gay Kevin Keller continues in the franchise, and the storylines deal with contemporary issues such a sexual assault, and the agency of the female characters, even when faced with dark, gothic themes such as the disappearance of Jason Blossom, and the presence of the Black Hood in the second season (fought by the Red Circle, also a clear reference to Archie brands). Even the Southside gang, the Serpents, are interrogated in different ways, and not strictly postulated as the villains, a trajectory that is consistent with our postmodern reality, despite our longing for the more ontologically secure notion found in the nostalgic narrative.

BRANDING NETFLIX WITH NOSTALGIA

Each case finds a way to connect the nostalgic frame to our current era and to Netflix as a distributor or a producer. While *Stranger Things* and *GLOW* use explicit 1980s settings to create a distance between those social disruptions and the show, they also both represent Netflix original programming, tying our totemic attachment to these franchises with the platform. *GLOW*, as an adaptation, draws from its existing fanbase, as well as creating new connections for its audience with a larger mainstream collection of viewers, providing for the potential of cross-fan interests. *Stranger Things* activates a lot of intertextuality, from homage images to specific 1980s films, to the clever use of diegetic music in key scenes, but also as a meaning-making device with key lyrics and notes having resonances both for some characters, and members of the audience.

Riverdale has even a more complicated attachment. While the show has been distributed on CW in the United States (its primary market), which represents a collaborative effort between CBS and Warner Bros., the underlying Archie Comics frame is not co-owned. Thus, the current arrangement is a coproduction, with consequent sharing of trademark privileges with CBS, as it is a Warner Bros. franchise. This has two consequences. First, after the initial run on CW, the producers decided to license the show to Netflix in the off-season, which boosted viewership tremendously, and allowed the CW to push the current season to its own distribution in the United States. Netflix still retains the distribution rights abroad. Thus, while traditional practices suggest allowing the streaming or binging model might devalue the brand, it turns out that having it available on Netflix drove consumption of the franchise, and challenges the notion of original programming on traditional networks. Netflix becomes branded as both the provider of quality original content, but also associated with the ontological security which is created in providing audiences stories which will reinforce their self-narrative and the political agenda that the series' audience consists of. By looking back to the 1980s, we are looking back at what seems, from our vantage point, a simpler time. By associating Netflix with this positive emotional feeling, it rubs off, allowing us to conceive of Netflix branding itself as positive, through evocation of the past—creating a Nostalgic Netflix which continues to dominate economically.

NOTES

1. Clayton Christensen, Michael Raynor, and Rory McDonald, "What Is Disruptive Innovation?," *Harvard Business Review*, December 2015, 46.

2. "Leading Netflix Markets Worldwide in July 2018," *eMarketer*, accessed September 26, 2018, https://www.statista.com/statistics/499844/netflix-markets-penetration.

3. Matt Hills, "Psychoanalysis and Digital Fandom: Theorizing Spoilers and Fans' Self-Narratives," in *Producing Theory in a Digital World: The Intersection of Audiences and Production in Contemporary Theory*, ed. Rebecca Ann Lind, 105–122 (Frankfurt: Peter Lang, 2012): 144.

4. Svetlana Boym, *The Future of Nostalgia* (New York: Basic Books, 2001), xiv.

5. Zygmunt Bauman, *Retrotopia* (London: Polity, 2017), 10.

6. William Proctor, "'Bitches Ain't Gonna Hunt No Ghosts': Totemic Nostalgia, Toxic Fandom and the *Ghostbusters* Platonic," *Palabra Clave* 20, no. 4 (October 2017): 1115.

7. Matthew Vess, Jamie Arndt, Clay Routledge, Constantine Sedikides, and Tim Wildschut, "Nostalgia as a Resource for the Self." *Self and Identity* 11, no. 3: 280, Taylor & Francis Online.

8. Constantine Sedikides, Tim Wildischut, Clay Routledge, and Jamie Arndt, "Nostalgia Counteracts Self-Discontinuity and Restores Self-Continuity," *European Journal of Social Psychology* 45, no. 1 (October 2014): 52, Wiley-Blackwell Online.

9. Boym, *The Future of Nostalgia*, 54.

10. Anthony Giddens, *Modernity and Self-Identity: Self and Society in the Late Modern Age* (London: Polity, 1991), 47.

11. Frederic Jameson, "Preface," *The Postmodern Condition: A Report on Knowledge,*, trans. by Geoff Bennington and Brian Massumi (Minneapolis: University of Minnesota Press, 1984), xi-xii. Original emphasis.

12. Michael Pickering and Emily Keightley, "The Modalities of Nostalgia," *Current Sociology* 54, no. 6 (November 2006): 919.

13. Pickering and Keightley, "The Modalities of Nostalgia," 921.

14. Pickering and Keightley, "The Modalities of Nostalgia," 929.

15. Michael Dwyer, *Back to the Fifties: Nostalgia, Hollywood, and Popular Music of the Seventies and Eighties* (Oxford: Oxford University Press, 2015), 4.

16. Dwyer, *Back to the Fifties*, 6.

17. Katharina Niemeyer, "Introduction: Media and Nostalgia," *Media and Nostalgia: Yearning for the Past, Present and Future* (London: Palgrave Macmillan, 2014), 11.

18. Jonathan Simon, "They Died with Their Boots On: the Boot Camp and the Limits of Modern Penalty," *Social Justice* 22, no. 2 (Summer 1995): 32.

19. Simon, "They Died with Their Boots On," 32.

20. Simon, "They Died with Their Boots On," 32.

21. Dwyer, *Back to the Fifties*, 8.

22. Jonathan Gray, *Show Sold Separately: Promos, Spoilers, and Other Media Paratexts* (New York: New York University Press, 2010), 26.

23. Gray, *Show Sold Seperately*, 6.

24. Jackie Strause, "Alison Brie on Why 'GLOW' Is Part of Evolving TV Landscape for Women," *The Hollywood Reporter*, June 26, 2017, https://www.hollywoodreporter.com/live-feed/glow-alison-brie-season-1-spoilers-wrestling-potential-season-2-1016695.

25. "Netflix and the CW Announce New Agreement," *Netflix*. July 5, 2016. https://media.netflix.com/en/press-releases/netflix-and-the-cw-network-announce-new-agreement.

26. Tiffany Bergin, "Identity and Nostalgia in a Globalized World: Investigating the International Popularity of *Midsomer Murders*," *Crime Media Culture* 9, no. 1 (2012): 86.

27. Jenna Anderson, "*Riverdale* EP on the Show's John Hughes and *Twin Peaks* Influences," *Comicbook.com*, April 13, 2017. http://comicbook.com/tv-shows/2017/04/14/riverdale-molly-ringwald-john-hughes-twin-peaks/

BIBLIOGRAPHY

Aguirre-Sacasa, Roberto. *Riverdale*. Berlanti Productions, Archie Comics, Warner Bros. Television and CBS Television Studios, 2017.

Anderson, Jenna. "*Riverdale* EP on the Show's John Hughes and *Twin Peaks* Influences." *Comicbook.com*. April 13, 2017. http://comicbook.com/tv-shows/2017/04/14/riverdale-molly-ringwald-john-hughes-twin-peaks/.

Bauman, Zygmunt. *Retrotopia*. London: Polity, 2017.

Bergin, Tiffany. "Identity and Nostalgia in a Globalized World: Investigating the International Popularity of *Midsomer Murders*." *Crime Media Culture* 9, no. 1 (2012): 83-99.

Boym, Svetlana. *The Future of Nostalgia*. New York: Basic Books, 2001.

Christensen, Clayton, Michael Raynor, and Rory McDonald. "What is Disruptive Innovation?" *Harvard Business Review* 95, no. 12 (December 2015): 44-53.

Duffer, Matt, and Ross Duffer, creators. *Beyond Stranger Things*. Netflix, 2016.

Duffer, Matt, and Ross Duffer, creators. *Stranger Things*. 21 Laps Entertainment and Monkey Massacre, 2016.

Dwyer, Michael. *Back to the Fifties: Nostalgia, Hollywood, and Popular Music of the Seventies and Eighties*. Oxford: Oxford University Press, 2015.

eMarketer. *Leading Netflix Markets Worldwide in July 2018*. https://www.statista.com/statistics/499844/netflix-markets-penetration/. Accessed October 1, 2018.

Flahive, Liz and Carly Mensch, creators. *GLOW*. Tilted Productions, Perhapsatron and Fan Dancer, 2017.

Giddens, Anthony. *Modernity and Self-Identity: Self and Society in the Late Modern Age*. London: Polity, 1991.

Gray, Jonathan. *Show Sold Separately: Promos, Spoilers, and Other Media Paratexts*. New York: New York University Press, 2010.

Jameson, Frederic. "Preface." *The Postmodern Condition: A Report on Knowledge*. Trans. by Geoff Bennington and Brian Massumi. Minneapolis: University of Minnesota Press, 1984.

Hills, Matt. "Psychoanalysis and Digital Fandom: Theorizing Spoilers and Fans' Self-Narratives." *Producing Theory in a Digital World: The Intersection of Audiences and Production in Contemporary Theory*. Edited by Rebecca Ann Lind. Frankfurt: Peter Lang, 2012.

"Netflix and the CW Announce New Agreement," *Netflix*. July 5, 2016. https://media.netflix.com/en/press-releases/netflix-and-the-cw-network-announce-new-agreement.

Niemeyer, Katharina. "Introduction: Media and Nostalgia," *Media and Nostalgia: Yearning for the Past, Present and Future*. London: Palgrave MacMillan, 2014, 1-23.

Pickering, Michael and Emily Keightley. "The Modalities of Nostalgia." *Current Sociology* 54, no. 6 (November 2006): 919-941.

Proctor, William. "'Bitches Ain't Gonna Hunt No Ghosts': Totemic Nostalgia, Toxic Fandom and the *Ghostbusters* Platonic," *Palabra Clave* 20, no. 4 (October 2017): 1105-1141.

Sedikides, Constantine, Tim Wildischut, Clay Routledge and Jamie Arndt. "Nostalgia Counteracts Self-Discontinuity and Restores Self-Continuity." *European Journal of Social Psychology* 45: 52-61.

Simon, Jonathan, "They Died with Their Boots On: the Boot Camp and the Limits of Modern Penalty," *Social Justice* 22, no. 2 (Summer 1995): 32.

Strause, Jackie. "Alison Brie on Why 'GLOW' Is Part of Evolving TV Landscape for Women." *The Hollywood Reporter*, June 26, 2017. https://www.hollywoodreporter.com/live-feed/glow-alison-brie-season-1-spoilers-wrestling-potential-season-2-1016695.

Vess, Matthew, Jamie Arndt, Clay Routledge, Constantine Sedikides and Tim Wildschut. "Nostalgia as a Resource for the Self." *Self and Identity* 11 (July 2012): 272-284.

THREE

Binge Watching the Past

Netflix's Changing Cinematic Nostalgia from Classic Films to Long-Form Original Programs

Sheri Chinen Biesen

You're Norma Desmond. You used to be in silent pictures. You used to be big.

I am big. It's the pictures that got small.

— Sunset Boulevard

Netflix has always thrived on programming nostalgia. Back in the day, a decade ago, when Netflix became a popular way to rent movies, it was considered a great dream video store in the sky. Harkening back to an earlier age, Netflix featured an array of classic films to binge in a single sitting, or over a nostalgic cinema weekend, reliving the Golden Age of Hollywood by watching classic 1940s–1950s film noir movies *Double Indemnity* (1944), *Laura* (1944), *Sunset Boulevard* (1950), or *The Godfather* neo-noir trilogy. However, in recent years, the notion of video stores, movie rentals, and even Netflix sending films on DVD by mail or streaming an endless series of classic films seems like a nostalgic distant cinematic memory.

Netflix is continually reimagining and transforming itself. In transitioning to streaming, along with content creation of original programs, Netflix has expanded to become a distribution platform and content creator of nostalgic texts. Netflix has also transferred its nostalgia from older classic films to newer Netflix original long-form serial programs which

41

offer viewers the opportunity to relive and binge watch the past in innumerable ways. In this chapter, I will examine how Netflix has shifted and transformed to reimagine, re-create, and program nostalgia by taking viewers back in time via its long-form and "original series" period programs set in the past (e.g., *The Crown, GLOW, Marco Polo, Narcos, Babylon Berlin, The Same Sky, Five Came Back, D-Day, Generation War*), and weaves nostalgia into contemporary programming (e.g., *House of Cards* [screening and reciting dialogue from noir *Double Indemnity*], *Daredevil, Jessica Jones*), and binge watching series from other networks (e.g., CW's time-traveling *The Flash, Arrow*, AMC's 1950s–1960s *Mad Men*, or elaborate flashbacks in time in *Breaking Bad* and prequel *Better Call Saul*).

Netflix programming has evolved to infuse nostalgia into its changing array of films and long-form original series which evoke recollections of cinematic and televisual memories as it strategically repositions itself from a subscription-based "movie rental by mail" service to a streaming media company. Media scholar Rodrigo Muñoz-González suggests Netflix, the advent of digital streaming, and media companies such as Disney have spurred a burgeoning "production tendency whose main strategies are the continuation and expansion of successful narrative franchises, the adaptation of past media products to contemporary contexts in terms of plot, and the reworking of an original material in a different medium."[1] Thus, he argues that a "nostalgia economy" has emerged creating media "iterations" that "mirror" older or "previous" forms. "The nostalgic component is found, narratively, in all the connections with the original material," as he explains, and also "economically, in the purpose of engaging past viewers, or fans, with the return of a 'beloved' content and, at the same time, luring younger audiences to consume a product which appears to be new, but it is rooted in a sense of reminiscence."[2]

Moreover, this distinctive nostalgic "flow" of Netflix program content exemplifies scholar Henry Jenkins's notion of "convergence culture" and "transmedia storytelling" with a "whole new vision of synergy" in the "flow of content across multiple media platforms" to create an industrial, technological, social, and cultural context where "the art of story-telling has become the art of world-building, as artists create compelling environments that cannot be fully explored or exhausted within a single work or even a single medium."[3] In particular, Netflix reimagines traditional classic cinema and television series into media program content to recall the past and maximize long-form "binge watching" reception which creates a unique viewing experience that competing media companies strive to replicate.

Thus, in addition to such classic film noir movies of the 1940s–1950s as *Double Indemnity, Laura, Scarlet Street* (1945), and *Sunset Boulevard*, Netflix nostalgically reimagines these films in later contemporary "neo-noir" productions such as long-form original series *Babylon Berlin, Narcos, Jessica Jones, House of Cards, Daredevil*, and *The Same Sky*. In fact, Netflix's transformation as a changing media company and its shifting programming content is in itself a nostalgic harkening back to the past. As it spends a whopping $8 billion on content to produce seven hundred "original series" film/media programs in 2018,[4] while Netflix is considered the company that embodies the future of an evolving media production, distribution, exhibition, and reception climate, Netflix is also especially savvy at conveying nostalgia. Surpassing the competition, "An $8-billion annual content spend would put Netflix well ahead of rivals Amazon, Hulu and HBO," David Ng of the *Los Angeles Times* observes.[5] However, Netflix faces competition from fellow nostalgia merchant Disney and AT&T launching their own streaming services in 2019. Disney's acquisition of 21st Century Fox and creation of a new streaming service of extensive combined Disney/Fox film and TV libraries offers a formidable response to Netflix.[6] To take a nostalgic look back and put Netflix's production expenditure in context, a few years ago, Hollywood's entire output for 2015 was $7 billion to produce 109 films. In 2018, Netflix's goal of producing 80 films and 620 original series is remarkable.[7] And, nostalgia is definitely a strategy employed by Netflix in this prolific media production endeavor.

Significantly, nostalgia even infuses and informs the way in which Netflix is conceived and what media analysts think the nature of the company is. For instance, although Netflix began as a way to rent movies by mail, it is frequently considered in relation to nostalgia as a television channel. Netflix cofounder and CEO Reed Hastings describes it as a web-based internet TV "network."[8] Media scholars Thomas Schatz, Chuck Tryon, and industry analyst Tim Wu liken Netflix to cable television network HBO ("Netflix" suggests cinema-viewing, like "Home Box Office" [HBO] and Turner Classic Movies [TCM]) with a "premium" subscriber (rather than conventional commercial advertising) base. Reminiscent of premium cable television channels, Netflix produces and programs nostalgia and has shifted from exclusively screening films to also creating original high-quality long-form dramatic programming. And resembling the endless flow of 24-hour-a-day cinematic features, televisual long-form programs, and classic films on cable television, Netflix creates an ideal viewing reception climate to binge watch, reimagine, and experience its nostalgic media content. Schatz observes that Netflix "has taken binge-viewing practices to another level—and has pushed the term into the popular discourse—in its promotion of series like *Breaking Bad* and *Mad Men*, and in the strategic coordination of its full-season streaming releases with AMC's rollout of new seasons." He notes that "The veritable partnership with AMC in the marketing and dual launch (on cable and the Internet) of its hit series has been crucial to Netflix' climb in recent years."[9]

Yet, Netflix is more than a network. Netflix's tremendous success at streaming nostalgia has transformed media viewing. With the popularity of Netflix, other major media companies (e.g., TV networks,[10] film studios,[11] and other streaming companies[12]) have responded and tried to simulate Netflix in producing original content and streaming nostalgia in cinematic long-form dramas. Netflix has grown and proliferated to become a benchmark for other media companies. Even several years ago, Netflix was already a formidable company. The *Economist* reported that "If Netflix were a cable channel, its subscriber revenues in 2013 would put it third in America behind ESPN and HBO."[13] By May 25, 2018, *Variety*'s New York Digital Editor Todd Spangler reported that Netflix's total stock market value rose to become the world's most valuable media company, surpassing Disney and Comcast.[14] Responding to Netflix's success, Disney, HBO, CBS, Amazon (expanding from online retailer to emulate a film studio), and others are offering streaming services, competing with Netflix and heralding a "new era of à la carte television" and promising it will "look a lot like Netflix."[15]

Yet the "transformation" of these media companies would be "impossible," Wu insists, "without the path blazed by premium cable. HBO pioneered the subscription-fee model" and enabled the success of specialized premium network programming (e.g., AMC [originally "American Movie Classics"], TCM). He explains that "The DVD box set gave hardcore enthusiasts the first taste of the binge-viewing that is a Netflix trademark." Netflix's achievement, he contends, is to "bring it all together and target the entire TV-watching population—not just a few selected diehards, but every individual based on his or her own interests and obsessions."[16] Wu predicts "nearly all scripted shows" will "become streaming shows, whether they are produced or aggregated by Netflix or Amazon, CBS" or HBO.[17] Like Netflix nostalgia, other competing media conglomerates such as Comcast (NBCUniversal), Disney (Fox) and AT&T (Time-Warner/HBO) are adopting their own media streaming models which nostalgically simulate cable packages and channels. Yet, premium subscriber cable channels (HBO, AMC, and satellite television companies like DirectTV) are marketed not as conventional television, but rather harken back to suggest film-going nostalgia of a quality, high-caliber cinematic viewing experience.

In particular, Netflix's binge-worthy nostalgic long-form original programs are remarkably influential. Netflix's original Marvel series *Jessica Jones, Daredevil, Luke Cage, Iron Fist, The Punisher*, and *The Defenders* harken back to the brooding stylish shadows of classic 1940s "film noir" hardboiled crime movies, Marvel superhero film franchises and comics while referencing each other with characters moving between programs to create a nostalgic long-form "meta" narrative series (coproduced with Marvel/ABC). Such long-form production of nostalgia encourages binge watching on Netflix in a "meta" narrative of serialized long-form content as original 1980s period series *GLOW* includes recognizable stars (Alison Brie, Rich Sommer) from AMC's 1950s–1960s–1970s era *Mad Men*. Nostalgically reimagining the dark underworld of 1940s–1950s film noir and inspired by 1990s Marvel Comics and graphic novels, Netflix original *Jessica Jones* (Krysten Ritter) includes abundant noir shadows and venetian blind bars of entrapment, as well as a noir film within a series screening of Orson Welles's 1958 film noir *Touch of Evil* in the show. Additionally, *Jessica Jones* and *Better Call Saul* (recalling recent history in 2002) both feature actors/characters (Bob Odenkirk as Saul Goodman) from the 2007–2008 neo-noir black comedy drama *Breaking Bad*, with striking cinematography shot on location in the harsh deserts of New Mexico which is visually reminiscent of classic Hollywood John Ford Westerns such as *The Searchers* filmed in Monument Valley. Film noir-styled Marvel comic antihero *Daredevil* actor Charlie Cox is recognizable from his appearance as a bootlegging Irish gangster in HBO's 1920s Martin Scorsese nostalgic Jazz Age Prohibition-era neo-noir historical period series *Boardwalk Empire*.

Moreover, in an era of "cord cutting," other television series originally conceived and produced to be aired on a conventional broadcast or cable channel for an hour once a week at a certain time with commercial interruptions may never be viewed via conventional means. Instead, entire sequential seasons are later nostalgically "discovered" and "binge watched" on Netflix without commercial interruptions at home or traveling with a mobile device to produce fans of a series. Like 1980s Netflix original *GLOW* reimagining stars of AMC historical 1950s–1960s–1970s "period" drama *Mad Men,* even AMC's *Breaking Bad, Better Call Saul,* and the CW network's time traveling *The Flash* and *Arrow* series nostalgically reference and cross-promote each other between programs, and enjoyed greater popularity by being "binge watched" by viewers streaming the television shows on Netflix.

Netflix also creates nostalgia and reimagines the past through international partnerships, overseas productions and coproductions. Netflix's award-winning royal bio-pic period drama *The Crown* is set in the 1940s–1950s and stars Claire Foy as young Queen Elizabeth after nostalgically embodying Anne Boleyn married to and murdered by King Henry VIII in the 1530s BBC/PBS Thomas Cromwell era royal period drama *Wolf Hall*. Retro 1980s–1990s drug cartel drama *Narcos* star Pedro Pascal was in HBO's period fantasy *Game of Thrones*.

Stunning Netflix original series *Babylon Berlin*, touted as the most expensive German television series ever made, nostalgically re-creates the strife and free-wheeling hedonism of the 1929 Jazz Age city of Berlin in the tumultuous Weimar Germany era while invoking film noir, Weimar cinema, Bob Fosse *Cabaret*-styled noir musicals, hard-boiled detectives, showgirls, gritty crime, and political intrigue leading up to the rise of the Third Reich. In Netflix's nostalgic *Babylon Berlin*, Volker Bruch (recognizable star of *Generation War*) plays traumatized film noir-styled World War I veteran Gereon Rath, a hard-boiled, drug-addicted detective investigating murder, blackmail, and porn films with the aid of prostitute-turned-stenographer and aspiring female detective, Charlotte Ritter (Liv Lisa Fries). Rath and Ritter are fabulous dancers in Weimar nightclubs and surreal dream sequences that are reminiscent of Fosse's *Cabaret*, Dennis Potter's *Singing Detective* and *Pennies from Heaven*, and another Bruch Netflix period drama: ZDF German public broadcasting UFA/TeamWorx production *Generation War*, harkening back to World War II–Germany.

Nostalgia and its brilliant re-creation are the centerpieces of *Babylon Berlin*. In fact, Berlin is the "star of the show," Siobhán Dowling of the *New York Times* observes. "The lavish production lovingly re-creates the city's 1920s streets, cafes and nightclubs. Around 70 percent of the series was shot on location," she explains. Re-creating the Weimar era in the series' 1920s period nostalgia, other sequences in *Babylon Berlin* were "filmed on a massive set at the historic Babelsberg studios. Costing 38 million euros (about $44 million) to produce, the 180-day shoot involved three crews and three writer/directors" Tom Tykwer (who made *Run Lola Run*), Achim von Borries, and Henk Handloegten, who "sought to work together on a project based on this period" for a long time.[18] *Babylon Berlin* is also reminiscent of another Netflix offering: the Cold War espionage drama *The Same Sky*, set in 1970s East and West Berlin, produced by UFA Fiction/Beta Film/ZDF/Czech TV. *Babylon Berlin* conjures memories, films, and documentaries about World War I and Weimar Germany, reimaging the creative zeitgeist of UFA studio and Weimar cinema in experimental Modernist avant-garde opening credits paying homage to Walter Ruttmann's 1920s films *Opus I* and *Berlin: Symphony of a Great City*.

In addition to the popularity of nostalgic Netflix originals *The Crown*, *GLOW*, *Narcos*, *Jessica Jones*, *Babylon Berlin*, *Daredevil*, and *House of Cards*, AMC's *Mad Men*, *Breaking Bad*, and prequel *Better Call Saul* became highly viewed by being binge watched on Netflix. Moreover, nostalgically harkening back to watching cinema in a movie theater, Netflix promoted serial binge viewing of *Breaking Bad*, *House of Cards*, and *The Crown* in high definition 4K Ultra HD, for better quality cinematic images not always available on cable or satellite. Even series created for conventional viewing on regular TV with commercials once a week cross-promoting other shows, such as the CW network's *The Flash* and *Arrow*, are better when viewed in immersive commercial-free long-form nostalgic binge-watching sessions on Netflix rather than when aired on the conventional broadcast networks they were created and produced for with commercial interruptions that disrupt the flow of the meta narrative. These nostalgic long-form dramatic series are thus more ideally viewed on Netflix than on their original conventional television channels. Further, other competitor channels can actually impede the quality and viewing experience of nostalgia: When Hulu struck a deal with Criterion, pulling Criterion art cinema from Netflix, Hulu streamed Criterion's international art cinema classics, such as Akira Kurosawa masterwork *Ran*, interrupted by commercials. (Criterion and TCM later made deals to stream classic films and art cinema on FilmStruck commercial-free as on Netflix; Criterion is launching their own streaming service to supersede FilmStruck.)

The nostalgic nature of Netflix's long-form dramatic programs and programming platform for its media content has been encouraged by other media conglomerate competitors ending their deals with Netflix and pulling their media content (such as classic film titles) from its delivery platform for media streaming distribution. In response to Netflix's popularity, even media conglomerate companies and channels which previously had joint partnership deals with Netflix, such as Starz and Disney, increasingly view Netflix as a rival competitor and ended their agreements, opting instead to pull their film libraries and remove media content from Netflix and offer their own proprietary media streaming services to show films/programs to compete with Netflix. Other programs such as Jane Campion's 2013 neo-noir detective-crime-drama series *Top of the Lake*, starring *Mad Men*'s Elizabeth Moss, which enjoyed popularity on Netflix, later moved to competitor media streaming service Hulu.

In an ever-evolving streaming media production, distribution, and binge viewing climate, the very nature of Netflix and its cinematic televisual programs and media platform content has dramatically changed in intrinsic ways which foster nostalgia and greater long-form serialized binge watching. As Netflix became a successful conveyer of "aggregated" nostalgia and a film/television distribution outlet, global media conglomerates (e.g., film production studios, distributors, television cable companies) viewed Netflix as a competitor rather than a supplemental means of making movies/programs available to viewers. James Surowiecki of the *New Yorker* maintains that "Though Netflix still streams plenty of great films, no one really thinks of it as a dream video store in the sky anymore."[19]

Thus, Netflix offers fewer classic films to be viewed via "video on demand" media streaming. As video stores and art cinemas disappear, these classic films will be more difficult to find and see if they disappear from Netflix. Yet, media conglomerate competitors which terminate Netflix distribution deals and pull media content (such as classic films) from Netflix increasingly set up proprietary streaming services to compete with Netflix and ironically complain Netflix no longer offers classic cinema to binge on its media programming platform. As Tryon suggests, in an age of cord-cutting amid the growth of Netflix and media streaming options, "digital distribution raises new questions about how, when, and where we access movies and what this model means for entertainment culture." Yet, while digital media "seem to promise that media texts circulate faster, more cheaply, and more broadly than ever before," Tryon argues that despite the "promises of ubiquitous and immediate access to a wide range of media content, digital delivery has largely involved the

continued efforts of major media conglomerates to develop better mechanisms for controlling when, where, and how content is circulated."[20]

Nonetheless, Netflix US has featured an array of nostalgic offerings.
Recently, Netflix American screen releases have included classic Hollywood films such as Billy Wilder's *Sunset Boulevard* (1950), which yearns
for the 1920s with silent stars Gloria Swanson, Buster Keaton, H. B. Warner, and directors Erich von Stroheim and Cecil B. DeMille, as well as
Dragnet's Jack Webb and columnist Hedda Hopper. Netflix US viewers
can also binge Humphrey Bogart and Katharine Hepburn in John
Huston's *The African Queen* (1950), William Wyler's romantic reverie in
Roman Holiday (1953), Francis Ford Coppola's neo-noir *The Godfather* trilogy, Giuseppe Tornatore's remembrance of classic cinema in *Cinema Para-
diso* (1988), Kevin Costner's homage to 1920s baseball in *Field of Dreams*
(1989), Steven Spielberg's celebration of child-like innocence in *E.T.*
(1982) and memories of World War II Holocaust survivors in acclaimed
drama *Schindler's List* (1993), Peter Jackson's 2001–2003 *Lord of the Rings*
trilogy and 2005 reboot of 1933 *King Kong*, John Keats 1800s romance
Bright Star (2009), Woody Allen's Parisian Jazz Age *Midnight in Paris*
(2011), French historical dramas *A Promise* (2013) and *Come What May*
(2015), *Star Wars* prequel *Rogue One* (2016), and live-action *Beauty and the
Beast* (2017). Netflix US also offers classic TV series *M.A.S.H.*, *The Twilight
Zone*, *Star Trek*, and *The West Wing* to binge. Netflix originals reimagine
Homer's *Iliad* in *Troy* and stream history and nostalgia in *Versailles, Medi-
ci, Call My Agent,* and *Stranger Things*; reboot *Benji, Heidi, Full House,* and
Lost in Space; bring back talk show host David Letterman and former US
president Barack Obama then walk down memory lane to George Cloo-
ney's childhood home in *My Next Guest*.

Moreover, Netflix has aggressively moved into expanding their
streaming service globally and making international production deals for
original long-form dramatic programs while acquiring other series from
overseas for its diverse offering of Netflix originals.[21] Netflix advertises
nostalgic cinematic long-form quality dramatic original series (*The Crown,
Narcos, Jessica Jones, Daredevil, House of Cards,* and *Marco Polo*), during
televised cinema/awards broadcasts. Promotional metanarratives suggest
Netflix's original series media link to prestigious high quality art cinema
to stream in many ways on an array of devices, redefining and expanding
the "binge watching" viewing experience.

Netflix fosters nostalgia as it transforms traditional notions of cinema
and shifts conventional models of television to look more like cinema in a
home-viewing environment. In its deft invoking of nostalgia, Netflix has
harkened back to reveal that what we previously thought and conceived
of television itself is being reimagined entirely. Netflix has transformed
the television home media-viewing experience, the reception and distribution context of cinema-going (binge watching at home rather than in
the theater), and tapped into nostalgia to create its own personalized

cinematic experience for films and quality dramatic TV series nostalgically reformulated in the image of cinema. Netflix promotes its original productions (e.g., neo-noir *House of Cards* [based on the 1990 BBC series], *The Crown, Narcos, Jessica Jones,* and *Marco Polo*) in theaters, during televised movies and motion picture award shows (e.g., Oscars, Golden Globes) to simulate the communal cinematic experience in a new reception context. Netflix's move into producing original nostalgia programming has inspired other competitors, including new media technology companies Amazon Films and premium channel Starz, to replicate studios as entities producing and distributing original nostalgic films, television, and online media content, like Amazon's period originals reimaging post–World War II 1940s–1950s life: Parisian fashion drama *The Collection* and dystopian alternate world in *The Man in the High Castle.*

As it changes the media production/distribution climate, Netflix increasingly produces, distributes, and offers nostalgic programs that other major media companies would traditionally produce; moreover, they are viewed, binge watched and consumed in a way in which Netflix has made more popular and pervasive. For instance, Netflix streamed and made available Billy Wilder's classic 1944 film noir *Double Indemnity,* which then disappeared from Netflix programming content. However, invoking nostalgia, the neo-noir Netflix original series *House of Cards* showed a portion of the film in the fifth season and the actors recited the dialogue to each other as the film projected on the big screen in the background, thus recalling the film noir many viewers had already watched on Netflix.

Such nostalgic original Netflix series as *House of Cards, Narcos, The Crown, GLOW,* and *Five Came Back* are innovative quality long-form programming that would typically air on other conventional broadcast or premium cable channels such as HBO or the BBC. The BBC lamented it could not compete when Netflix produced *The Crown* (without BBC involvement), and Netflix's Steven Spielberg serial filmed adaptation of Mark Harris's *Five Came Back* is a quality long-form dramatic documentary that would typically be an HBO miniseries; however, it is shown in a way ideally suited for binge watching on Netflix, and is also accompanied by other related programs (the original World War II documentaries discussed in the Netflix original program) available to view on Netflix, shown in a way in which it would not have been seen on conventional television.

Netflix original series *The Crown,* a £50 million, fifty-part series set in the 1940s–1950s, starring Claire Foy as Great Britain's Queen Elizabeth and John Lithgow as Prime Minister Winston Churchill, written and produced by Peter Morgan, nostalgically recalls royal biopics on Netflix, such as *The Queen* (2006), starring Helen Mirren, based on Morgan's play *The Audience; The Royals; The Royal House of Windsor; Elizabeth at 90;* and *A Royal Night Out* (2015), where princesses Elizabeth and Margaret leave the palace for nightlife adventures without chaperones, like Audrey Hepburn in *Roman Holiday*. *The Crown* evokes other feature films, documentaries, BBC historical period drama biopics, royal history programs, and television mini-series on the royal family, Queen Elizabeth and Winston Churchill, including *The King's Speech* and *The Darkest Hour*.

In an increasingly international media-viewing environment with a changing distribution/reception context and greater demand for binge watching of long-form dramatic programs and streaming media, BBC admitted it "cannot compete" with Netflix to develop *The Crown*, a "quality" royal epic drama streaming production steeped in nostalgia about the "inside story of two of the most famous addresses in the world, Buckingham Palace and 10 Downing Street," although it was called a "classic BBC subject," similar to the quality "period" historical programming BBC had previously been known and acclaimed for.[22] In fact, *The Crown* powerfully employs nostalgia as it invokes viewers' memories of royal family scandals to engage them in the whole history and narrative drama based on real-life figures and historical events. *The Crown* spans six seasons of sixty episodes filmed extensively on location with sweeping views of palace interiors and grounds as it chronicles the lives of Queen Elizabeth and Prince Philip recalling romantic memories of sailing in Malta, a tranquil reverie on African safari, and reminiscing intrigue of palace affairs.

Netflix American reboot original series *House of Cards* is commended as a quality "prestige" production nostalgically invoking the original celebrated long-form British BBC series *House of Cards*, both written and coproduced by Andrew Davies, on par with "high-brow" British television, including Davies's 1995 BBC miniseries adapting Jane Austen's *Pride and Prejudice*, and international art cinema productions. As seen in *The Crown, Babylon Berlin,* and *House of Cards*, Netflix increasingly produces high-quality nostalgic cinematic long-form original dramatic programming that fosters nostalgia and creates an ideal viewing climate for reminiscing, binge-watching, and recalling memories of an earlier time.

While noir titles, classic films, and newer cinema releases come and go on Netflix, Netflix US recently included a series of *Bridget Jones's Diary* films. On Netflix US, Sharon Maguire's *Bridget Jones's Diary* (2001), written by Davies, reimagines Austen's *Pride and Prejudice* (adapting Helen Fielding's 1996 novel/column inspired by Davies's 1995 BBC adaptation of Austen's *Pride and Prejudice*), Beeban Kidron's sequel *Bridget Jones: The Edge of Reason* (2004, updating Fielding's 1999 sequel novel), and Maguire's *Bridget Jones' Baby* (2016). *Bridget Jones's Diary* nostalgically recalls romantic memories as it opens with a snowy winter scene in Snowshill, Gloucestershire reminiscent of a Christmas card as Bridget Jones (Renee Zellweger) remembers: "It all began on New Year's Day in my 32nd year . . ." The opening voice-over remembrance harkens back to Alfred Hitchcock's 1940 cinematic rendering of Daphne du Maurier's *Rebecca*.

The King's Speech star Colin Firth's incarnation of Darcy in Davies's BBC version of Austen's *Pride and Prejudice* inspired Fielding to nostalgically update and reboot the original in *Bridget Jones's Diary* films recasting Firth as arrogant Darcy opposite Hugh Grant (romantic male lead in 1995 *Sense and Sensibility*) as bad-boy Daniel Cleaver, in fierce jealous rivalry and sexual tension pursuing romantic affairs with Bridget. Invoking nostalgia, *Bridget Jones's Diary* reimagines Grace Kelly, Playboy bunnies, romantic landscapes, couples paddling boats, reciting Keats poetry, splashing into the lake like Darcy in *Pride and Prejudice*, Tower Bridge, and film noir.[23] Just as *Bridget Jones's Diary* conjures recognizable memories and characters/stars from BBC's incarnation of Austen's *Pride and Prejudice*, sequel *Bridget Jones: The Edge of Reason* recalls *Bridget Jones's Diary* and features striking atmospheric landscapes: stunning aerial shots of the heroine skydiving, which later shifts to spectacular travelogue images of the beaches, oceans and island cliffs of Thailand—which become a lost memory in real life because these images were shot right before the romantic vista was destroyed by the 2004 tsunami. Nostalgic cinematic spaces are juxtaposed with cramped, claustrophobic confines and imposing bars of entrapment recalling film noir as Bridget is thrown in prison until Darcy gets her released. Netflix also offers noir/neo-noir reimagining Charlotte Brontë's 1847 historical Gothic period romances *Jane Eyre* and Emily Brontë's 1847 *Wuthering Heights* in films and BBC/PBS/ITV productions.

However, Netflix original series such as *Babylon Berlin, The Crown, House of Cards, Narcos, Jessica Jones, Daredevil, GLOW*, and *Five Came Back* rival and are surprisingly better than several highly promoted but less impressive BBC, ITV, or PBS series such as *Poldark, Victoria*, or even some HBO programs, previously considered the gold standard of quality cinematic long-form television programming. Like HBO, Netflix has promoted itself as being better than ordinary television: specifically, a more cinematic quality long-form commercial free alternative to previous regular TV shows airing interrupted with ads for a specific duration at a certain time. Netflix executives have heralded, and media scholars and binge viewers acknowledge, that Netflix has transformed the very nature of television, its programs, what a TV show is, and changed the way we watch and experience media. As the nature of what constitutes television programs changes and evolves, Tryon suggests the "redefinition" of television which is rapidly occurring "takes place as TV itself becomes increasingly difficult to define."[24]

For a nostalgic dive into cinematic and televisual memories on screen, Netflix US viewers can binge watch and stream all three of Coppola's acclaimed epic neo-noir *The Godfather* trilogy (1972; 1974; 1990) postwar gangster-mafia movies, and an array of *Star Trek* shows, including the entire 1966–1969 original *Star Trek* television series, as well as various *Star Trek* motion pictures which come and go and are available periodically on Netflix, *Star Trek: The Next Generation* sequel television series, *Star*

Trek: The Animated Series, Star Trek: Deep Space Nine spin-off television series, *Star Trek: Voyager* another spin-off of the original television series, not to mention the *Enterprise* prequel television series. Jeremy Kay of *Screen Daily* reported a recent study from January 1–August 31, 2017, revealed that Netflix dramas dominate streaming originals demand in North America,[25] despite fierce competition by other major media conglomerates adding their own proprietary streaming services to the media viewing market. Moreover, popular Netflix original series are underestimated (since Netflix does not release ratings/viewing data) and are typically not tweeted on social media like live broadcasts. Yet, broadcast channel CBS, which includes commercial ads interrupting programs and is available to watch for free, nostalgically brought back and rebooted a new *Star Trek: Discovery* series, but only aired the first episode once, thus interrupting the flow of nostalgia, by then requiring viewers to pay (nearly as much as Netflix) every month to watch/stream the rest of the series episodes with commercial interruptions on CBS's "All Access" subscription service—a move widely panned on social media.

Netflix has re-created, reimagined, and transformed the way we consume nostalgia programming by taking viewers back in time via its long-form "original" serial "period" programs set in the past (e.g., *The Crown, GLOW, Marco Polo, Narcos, Babylon Berlin*), and weaving nostalgia into contemporary programming (e.g., *House of Cards* reimagining *Double Indemnity*, Marvel's *Daredevil* and *Jessica Jones*), and binge-watching series from other networks (e.g., AMC's *Mad Men, Breaking Bad, Better Call Saul,* CW's *The Flash,* and *Arrow*). In re-creating dramatic nostalgia, Netflix encourages binge watching by allowing spectators to automatically play/watch and skip the opening title credit sequences to create a more seamless, immersive "fluid" cinematic flow of sequential long-form media. Netflix original programs also re-create interactive narratives of memories, children's books, and animated films like *Puss in Book,* offering new ways for viewers to engage with media, determine story narratives and endings, and construct meaning as they binge and return to their childhood in a long-form metanarrative flow of nostalgia. Despite other media conglomerates increasingly endeavoring to compete with Netflix by offering their own streaming options,[26] Netflix offers the most ideal climate and media for nostalgic programming, the best streaming quality and experience for binging media programs, and dominates the nostalgia market. As evident in Disney ending its Netflix deal, pulling content from Netflix, and acquiring Fox, LucasFilm, *Star Wars* rights, and Major League Baseball Advanced Media (BamTech) streaming technology company to develop its own streaming service/channel[27] to rival Netflix and churn out nostalgia, the fact that all major media conglomerates (e.g., Comcast/NBCUniversal, AT&T/TimeWarner, Disney/Fox) are now trying to do what Netflix does (as a media streaming company producing and distributing long-form media nostalgia programs to "binge watch" on a streaming media platform) in order to compete with Netflix is extraordinary. These media industry developments are a remarkable testament to the tremendous influence of Netflix on the production, distribution, and televisual "binge watching" viewing reception of nostalgia to evoke recollections of cinematic and televisual memories on-screen.

NOTES

1. Rodrigo Muñoz-González, "The Nostalgia Economy: Netflix and New Audiences in the Digital Age," London School of Economics and Political Science, 2017, 3.

2. Muñoz-González, "The Nostalgia Economy," 3.

3. Henry Jenkins, *Convergence Culture: Where Old and New Media Collide* (New York: New York University Press, 2006), 104, 114.

4. Todd Spangler, "Netflix Eyeing Total of about 700 Original Series," *Variety*, 27 February 2018.

5. David Ng, "Netflix Saw Record Subscriber Growth in Fourth Quarter," *Los Angeles Times,* 22 January 2018.

6. Disney has been battling rival Comcast to acquire Fox in 2017-2018.

7. Meriah Doty, "US Film Production Spending Increased 11 Percent to $7 Billion in 2015," *The Wrap*, 15 June 2016.

8. Tim Wu, "Netflix's War on Mass Culture: Binge-Viewing Was Just the Beginning," *New Republic*, 4 December 2013.

9. Thomas Schatz, "HBO and Netflix—Getting Back to the Future," *Flow*, 19, 20 January 2014.

10. HBO, Showtime, CBS, TCM, Starz, ABC, et al.

11. Disney sparring with Comcast to acquire and merge with Fox.

12. Amazon Films, Hulu, Apple, Google/YouTube, FilmStruck/WarnerInstant, Dish/SlingTV, Roku, et. al.

13. "Thinking Outside the Set-Top Box," *The Economist*, 14 December 2013, 69.

14. Todd Spangler, "Netflix Stock Closes at All-Time High, Nudging Market Cap Ahead of Disney's Again," *Variety*, 25 May 2018.

15. Emily Steel, "Cord-Cutters Rejoice," "HBO Plans New Streaming Service," *New York Times*, 15-16 October 2014.

16. Wu, 2013.

17. Wu, 2013.

18. Siobhán Dowling, "Ahead of the Third Reich, a Dizzying Metropolis: Sex, Drugs and Crime in the Gritty Drama 'Babylon Berlin,'" *New York Times*, 7, 10 November 2017, C11.

19. James Surowiecki, "What's Next for Netflix?," *New Yorker*, 20 October 2014.

20. Chuck Tryon, *On-Demand Culture: Digital Delivery and the Future of Movies*, (New Brunswick, NJ: Rutgers University Press, 2013), 3-4.

21. Netflix expanded corporate partnerships with international telecom conglomerates: broadcast television channels even run T-Mobile cell phone ads that show Netflix original series *House of Cards* and *Narcos* to advertise free Netflix membership for new customers. Mark Scott, "In Global Expansion, Netflix Makes Friends With Carriers," *New York Times,* 26 February 2017.

22. Coproduced with Left Bank Pictures and Sony Pictures Television, released November 4, 2016, with a second season on December 4, 2017, *The Crown* was coproduced/directed by Stephen Daldry and Philip Martin, but BBC "couldn't compete with the amount of money that Netflix were prepared to pay for that production even though we would have loved to have been a co-producer with Netflix on it" and insisted they "tried to work with the US firm on the drama . . . but Netflix wanted to go it alone." John Plunkett, "BBC TV Chief Warns of US Threat after Big-Money Amazon Deals," *The Guardian*, 25 August 2015.

23. Darcy and Cleaver fight and crash through a shattering window onto glistening wet streets surrounded by broken glass among the shadows cast by the streetlights. In the sequel, Darcy and Cleaver engage in a wild brawl rife with "bromantic" sexual tension as they wrestle soaking wet while splashing in a water fountain.

24. Chuck Tryon, "TV Got Better: Netflix's Original Programming Strategies and Binge Viewing," *Media Industries Journal* 2, no. 2 (2015): 105.

25. Jeremy Kay, "Study: Netflix, dramas dominate streaming originals demand in North America," *Screen Daily*, 22 September 2017.

26. For example, Disney, CBS, HBO, Showtime, Starz, Amazon Films, Hulu, Apple, Google/YouTube, FilmStruck/TCM/WarnerInstant, Roku, etc.

27. Brooks Barnes and John Koblin, "Disney's Big Bet on Streaming Relies on Little-Known Tech Company," *New York Times*, October 8, 2017.

BIBLIOGRAPHY

Barnes, Brooks, and John Koblin. "Disney's Big Bet on Streaming Relies on Little-Known Tech Company," *New York Times*, October 8, 2017.

Biesen, Sheri Chinen. "Binge Watching 'Noir' at Home: Reimagining Cinematic Reception and Distribution via Netflix," in Kevin McDonald and Daniel Smith-Rowsey, eds. *The Netflix Effect: Technology and Entertainment in the 21st Century*. New York: Bloomsbury Academic Publishing, 2016.

———. *Blackout: World War II and the Origins of Film Noir*. Baltimore: Johns Hopkins University Press, 2005.

Doty, Meriah. "US Film Production Spending Increased 11 Percent to $7 Billion in 2015," *The Wrap*, 15 June 2016.

Dowling, Siobhán. "Ahead of the Third Reich, a Dizzying Metropolis: Sex, Drugs and Crime in the Gritty Drama 'Babylon Berlin,'" *New York Times*, 7, 10 November 2017, C11.

Jenkins, Henry. *Convergence Culture: Where Old and New Media Collide*. New York: New York University Press, 2006.

Kay, Jeremy. "Study: Netflix, dramas dominate streaming originals demand in North America," *Screen Daily*, 22 September 2017.

Muñoz-González, Rodrigo. "The Nostalgia Economy: Netflix and New Audiences in the Digital Age," London School of Economics and Political Science, 2017.

Ng, David. "Netflix Saw Record Subscriber Growth in Fourth Quarter," *Los Angeles Times*, 22 January 2018.

Plunkett, John. "BBC TV Chief Warns of US Threat after Big-Money Amazon Deals," *The Guardian*, 25 August 2015.

Schatz, Thomas. "HBO and Netflix—Getting Back to the Future," *Flow*, 19, 20 January 2014.

Scott, Mark. "In Global Expansion, Netflix Makes Friends with Carriers." *New York Times*, 26 February 2017.

Spangler, Todd. "Netflix Eyeing Total of about 700 Original Series," *Variety*, 27 February 2018.

———. "Netflix Stock Closes at All-Time High, Nudging Market Cap Ahead of Disney's Again," *Variety*, 25 May 2018.

Steel, Emily. "Cord-Cutters Rejoice," *New York Times*, 16 October 2014.

———. "HBO Plans New Streaming Service," *New York Times*, 14 October 2014.

Surowiecki, James. "What's Next for Netflix?," *New Yorker*, 20 October 2014.

Tryon, Chuck. "Digital Distribution, Participatory Culture, and the Transmedia Documentary," *Jump Cut* 53 (2011).

———. *On-Demand Culture: Digital Delivery and the Future of Movies*. New Brunswick, NJ: Rutgers University Press, 2013.

———. "TV Got Better: Netflix's Original Programming Strategies and Binge Viewing," *Media Industries*, 2, no. 2 (2015): 104-116.

"Thinking Outside the Set-Top Box," *The Economist*, 14 December 2013.
Wu, Tim. "Netflix's War on Mass Culture: Binge-Viewing Was Just the Beginning," *New Republic*, 4 December 2013.

FOUR

The Consumer Has Been Added to Your Video Queue

John C. Murray

Postmodern society has been paralyzed in a constant gaze of visual imagery. In *The Postmodern Condition: A Report on Knowledge*, Jean-Francois Lyotard famously "define[s] postmodern as incredulity toward metanarratives. . . . The narrative function [of which] is losing its functors, its great heroes, its great dangers, its great voyages, its great goal."[1] As the availability of new media technologies, such as streaming video, continues to grow, so too does the desire to produce and consume video artifacts of human experience within visual culture. When we view and value images, we do so to simplify the narrative complexities of human storytelling. Images are powerful and evocative tools that we use to represent the individual and constituent parts of human production and consumption. They can inspire speculation and debate by appearing to capture people and events within a visual totality. Unlike words, visual images are more literal. They may be used to decode conceptual and theoretical models for interpreting and valuing human experience. Postmodern technologies have been used to bridge the gap between still and video imagery and alter the language used to describe these representations. We use videos to replicate sounds and images and also to reconceptualize the boundaries of social space. From within this space, we assume a decentered subjectivity in response to the video event.

The evolution of visual culture and the growing demand for intuitive and multiplatform streaming services, such as Netflix, have nurtured a synthetic culture of passive voyeurs.[2] As agents of mass populism, which forms from rising consumer demand for streaming media and increasing pressures for innovation, viewers succumb to strategies of influence that connect them to the video event. As consumers transfer their viewing experiences across new streaming platforms, they misjudge the reflection of themselves in other consumers as well as the influence of their collective gaze. Currents of mass populism drive the home-video market by predicting consumers' preferences, and dissolving strategies of resistance that might resituate them as the highest commodity of visual culture. Instead, consumers are misdirected by affiliational thinking, and fall prey to a metanarrative of mass populism as the new form of anticritical intellectual banality.

In 1967, cultural critic Guy Debord redefined the term "spectacle" and deployed it in his broader comment on how modern life had been supplanted by visual representations. Debord defined the spectacle as "not [merely] a collection of images; rather, it is a social relationship between people that is mediated by images."[3] As a visionary thinker, Debord tested the limits of social criticism but could not anticipate how the accelerated growth of video smart technologies would stretch, distort, and inevitably dissolve the boundaries between public and private viewing. Visual imagery has been used to represent and supplement our understanding of social and cultural experiences. But the video form goes beyond supplementation and beyond representation by demonstrating its capacity for supplanting reality in its entirety. Video-based forms have been used to dilute viewers' subjectivity and critical responsiveness to the world around them.

Video stores provide a snapshot of the beginnings of this cultural transformation and the historical dispositions that encouraged it from the early 1980s to the present day. Video stores mapped the effects of affiliational thinking on video consumers' habits and desire for exclusivity. As neighborhood stores gave way to corporate rental chains, such as Blockbuster or West Coast Video, consumers were taught to value the privileges of membership within corporate rental chains. As these chains evolved into streaming video services, consumers' desire for comfort and convenience triggered changes in their viewing habits and preferences. Reboots of popular television shows, for example, allow viewers an online streaming glimpse into their nostalgic past. As Ryan Lizardi suggests, "media companies that seek to rehash pull off this feat by asking consumers to long for the past through techniques like rerelease and accessible digital archives like Netflix and use this encouraged nostalgia to spur consumptive desire for the remade versions that are made readily available to them."[4]

Consumers have been conditioned to await the video event, the temporal-image restoration of human experience, which is used to signify privileged status and affiliation to companies that evolved from physical stores, to DVDs by mail, to internet streaming services. As the companies changed, they also reimagined video consumers as component parts of a visual culture that reproduces its own patterns of serial assembly. Consumers erroneously believe that by viewing exclusive video products, they might contribute to a larger metanarrative of mass populism. Their presumed sense of control extends to market trends, which stimulated the parallel growth and expansion of the home video industry and the synthetic corporate structures designed to support and administer it.

Consumer involvement in the video market enabled the formation of physical and institutional structures of community that continue to drive populist sentiment. However, by rejecting mass populism and turning away from the collective gaze that empowers it, consumers might restore themselves as the true subject of the video event. Consumers supplement the limitations of physical communities with a collective audience that links viewers through axioms of brand identification. Ironically, the same axioms that foster affilitional thinking cannot be rejected by consumers until they challenge the "personalized taste-based algorithms"[5] that inform and reconstitute their individual choices within a collective audience. For example, Netflix has tailored its selection images in response to consumers' browsing habits. As Nick Nelson, Netflix's Global Manager of Creative Services suggests, "artwork was not only the biggest influencer to a member's decision to watch content, but it also constituted over 82% of their focus while browsing Netflix."[6] By showing consumers persuasive images, Netflix draws them into a pattern of habituated viewing in which individual preferences are reshaped by programmatic advertising and contexts.

As viewers connect to streaming services, they are greeted by a selection of choices that are grouped into categories and preferences used to profile them. Viewers enjoy being affirmed and allowed to create their own viewing experiences. As viewers gaze at the video event and their preferences are tabulated, and the gaze is turned back toward them in recognition. But in actuality, the "expectation" of the video event is "made of nonexpectation," and it merely provides the illusion of the viewer as subject, participant, and producer of culture.[7] As Paul Tassi explains, "[Y]ou would think that Netflix would have gotten enough clout to add a ton of movies at a reasonable pace, and yet the rate at which new movies were added is painfully slow . . . because of licensing deals . . . [and] what good movies they do have often depart after a few months."[8] In effect, viewers become conduits for strategies of corporate influence that cultivate their preferences and behavior within a range of predictable outcomes.

Viewers compensate for gaps in recent releases with "[o]lder shows that have exhausted all of their revenue streams and distribution windows, or those created before home video rights were a consideration, [now] find a welcoming home in streaming."[9] Netflix homogenizes viewing habits by allowing intergenerational viewers to consume nostalgic television content from distinct cultural nodal points. As one generation re-experiences episodic viewing of *Full House* (1987–1995), *Gilmore Girls* (2000–2007), or *Arrested Development* (2003–2006), another generation binge-watches these series in a single day. In so doing, different viewing habits of two generations are refashioned into a new preference-cluster that invariably "flattens generational distinctions and cultivates common taste . . . to get younger audiences attached to the same bankable properties as their older counterparts."[10] Thus, Netflix's subsequent revival of series, such as *Gilmore Girls: A Year in the Life* in 2014, *Fuller House* in 2016, and *Arrested Development* in 2018, might indicate its success in cultivating intergenerational sentiment for nostalgic viewing.

Video-based narratives provide viewers with realistic replications of human experience that might be as good or, in some instances, better than the real which can neither be replayed on demand, paused, stopped, fast-forwarded, nor rewound at our convenience. Replication is a process by which human experiences are recorded in order to enable the viewer to reengage a lost fragment of reality. The viewer's ability to choose from multiple realities provides a false sense of control over the video event. Video content is not left to the discretion of viewers. Licensing agreements regulate the ebb and flow of available movies and television shows to streaming media devices. As Lizardi suggests, "Streaming rights are a completely different story, as they must be continually negotiated across multiple competing companies,"[11] such as Netflix, Amazon Prime, Hulu, and YouTube.

In the past, video services delayed new releases to prevent the diminution of retail DVD and Blu-ray sales. Now, streaming video services give viewers the option to purchase new releases before renting them. To borrow from Jacek Tittenbrun's conceptions of ownership, internet video services accentuate "viewing exclusivity as the necessary feature of private ownership."[12] Binge-watching movies or television programs is misinterpreted by viewers to mean the same as watching whatever you wish and whenever you want. This misconception has caused consumers to multiply their subscriptions to unsatisfying streaming services in hopes that their viewing experience might be improved.

Corporate interest in the home video market has fostered a sophisticated model of distribution and consumption. Branding strategies have been used to create a unique consumer identity, particularly through original content that promotes differentiation and competition between rival corporate groups and their customer base. Within these competitive subsets, affiliational thinking has informed new fields of cultural production that treat the viewer-consumer as a commodity, rather than as a producer of visual culture. It is from within this ideological framework that we are taught the fears of scarcity and availability, rather than the correlative principles of production and consumption. Devoid of criticality, the viewer's identity is reconstituted within a commercial network that is "populated by self-validating hypotheses which, incessantly and monopolistically repeated, become hypnotic definitions or dictations"[13] of mass populism. As we trace social and economic movements through the nineteenth and twentieth centuries to the present, we might notice how cultural tendencies create an imbalance between production and consumption. In our assessment, we may dismiss our own failures to work with and within the visual culture that we helped reify, mediatize, and authenticate.

Popular culture is an expression of society's common values, interests, and experiences. It reminds us of our affiliations, relations, and obligations to one another. The use of video to replicate, archive, inform, and entertain us also spawned the birth of a synthetic culture that assumed the organizing properties of popular culture while separating consumers from their subjective narrative threads. The synthetic corporate culture employs algorithms to replicate behavior and reduces and modifies its identifiable properties to align with brand indicators that predict consumers' choices. In as much as the video event has been adapted to make it more accessible across various platforms of dissemination, synthetic corporate culture has been altered to align the production of brand identification with the restrictive labels imposed on video consumers.[14]

The home video industry provides iconography for a new visual cultural orientation. Visual images are material things that communicate privileges to the viewing audience by indulging individualistic concerns. The variety of images helps satisfy hedonistic impulses for immediate gratification. The commercial depiction of the domestic space, a living room with a couch and love seat, with friends and family gathered around an oversized flat screen television, portrays viewers' preoccupation with leisure, entertainment, and the flattery of tribal and hormonal instincts to "log onto Netflix and chill."[15] Home video advertisements work off of Victorian conceptions of home as a place of refuge, conceptions that became permanently embedded in the cultural psyché of the nineteenth century, a socially conditioned mindset that is still being realized in the present tense.

During the Victorian period, advertisements preyed on consumers' desire for physical and moral perfection. The visual expression of concerns about morality, spirituality, education, refinement, vitality, wealth, and status convinced consumers of the metaphysical powers of material commodities. "The advertisement became," as Lori Anne Loeb suggests in her seminal work *Consuming Angels*, "both a mirror and instrument of the social ideal."[16] Thus, even as Victorians were being inspired by the social idealism found in advertisements, they also were challenging its authenticity in novels. Victorian readers considered how the fictional realities of industrial novels reflected pervasive social issues of their time. By indulging in silent reading, Victorian readers secured themselves a modicum of privacy; they insulated themselves from political accountability; they disconnected themselves from the collective gaze of images;

and they decoded stories of human experience. From within these pockets of subjectivity, Victorian readers gradually developed a vocabulary for sharply critiquing the disjunctions within both their fictional and actual realities.

Contemporary video consumers are still working within the same constraints of social idealism to satisfy their own materialistic appetites. Video consumers, much like their Victorian counterparts, have come to recognize the symbolic power of imagery, and they employ video-based narratives within a new cultural model used for producing alternate reality. Through this process, video consumers allowed visual culture to supplement their dissatisfaction with the material world in actuality. Supplementation begins with the collection of aggregate data sets of personal information and viewing habits that inform marketing and advertising strategies of video streaming services. Images in advertisements foster a rhetoric used to support a materially defined, synthetic corporate culture of brand identification for video consumers. As consumers are increasingly absorbed within the video event, their social expectations and the language used to describe them are reconfigured.

The expansion of media technologies like text messaging delinguistified language by removing context cues from spoken discourse, and this change has profoundly altered the social spaces used for cultivating critical engagement. When we tweet to signal the "arrival" of an illusory moment, we make it virtual as well and blur the boundaries of our perceptual and conceptual frames of reference. In so doing, we remake our social expectations into "nonexpectations,"[17] accept our decentered subjectivity, and listen to the deafening sounds of mass populism.

In this context, "Language simply becomes a medium, an operator of visibility. It has lost its symbolic and ironic qualities, those which make language more important than what it conveys."[18] We create and consume images. The images become visual enticements that help us sustain the illusion of material possession and encourage a false sense of control over the creation of individual and collective narratives. When these images are assembled, sequenced, and given motion and sound, they become video events that replicate human experience. The video event is more than a visual record. It is, as Jacques Derrida suggests, the production of "artifactuality."[19] It necessitates a process of selection, revision, and performance, as well as a "fictional refashioning"[20] of reality. The video event has become "the acme of ideology because it fully exposes and manifests the essence of all ideological systems: the impoverishment, enslavement and negation of real life."[21]

For the video viewer, visual culture requires its practitioners to demonstrate visual competency: an intuitive ability to organize transmediated linkages between images and video and achieve narrative synthesis across various digital domains. By assembling these components within specular and discursive spaces, the viewer is able to experiment with cultural discourses, epistemologies, iconographies, and ideologies, and anticipate the social consequences of limitless permutations. As they recognize different contexts, so too do they realize the ways in which their identity is fragmented and dispersed across multiple platforms.

It is this sense of discontinuity that leads viewers to search for a coherent metanarrative, which might provide an organizing sense of closure through a unified field of reality. Metanarratives provide us "the hope to totalize . . . into a real unity"[22] but also allow for docility, irreversibility, and the negation of variety, which is repeated in the viewer's experience. The viewer becomes "both the outcome and goal"[23] of a synthetic corporate cultural hegemony that seeks to isolate him or her within the video event, itself.

In postmodern society, systems of surveillance are abundant and everywhere. There has never before been a period in history when human behavior has been so rigorously observed, recorded, replicated, and encoded through video time stamps. Video images and sounds become plausible representations of reality. Viewers abbreviate, edit, duplicate, disseminate, and value the images and sounds that comprise the video event. In so doing, they assume a false sense of empowerment. As Slavoj Žižek suggests, their gaze gives the illusion of control; instead, viewers are reduced to a state of impotence.[24] Their perceived authority over the video event is nothing more than "passive identification"[25] that ensures their placement within a discursive visual network. The viewer's desire to achieve placement within the visual network "supplants" human activity through distanciation and passive critique of the video event.[26] Contemporary viewers learn to observe and mimic one another while never fully acknowledging how their choices were influenced by conditioning.

In *Discipline and Punish: The Birth of the Prison*,[27] Michel Foucault discusses late-eighteenth-century philosopher Jeremy Bentham's theory of the panopticon and the effects of surveillance on human behavior. The panopticon was an inspection house designed to allow observers to see subjects while not being seen, in order to "help reform morals, preserve health, invigorate industry, diffuse instruction, and lighten public burdens."[28] Bentham's theory was later reworked into a psychoanalytic context by Jacques Lacan (self/other or mirror theory).[29] Lacan extended the process of surveillance to include shame in his formula of the gaze as a process in which "I see myself seeing myself." Lacan theorized the subject ("I") sees itself ("me") and begins to subconsciously monitor its own transgressions.

Foucault would suggest that our society has become so adept at monitoring us that we no longer need the intrusiveness of surveillance to influence human behavior. We monitor ourselves, are always aware of our transgressions, and experience a sense of shame that always inhibits us from acting radically by critiquing the status quo. Yet despite such knowledge, we continue to suffer the effects of producing and consuming visual imagery. We frame images and record videos to replicate ourselves for posterity and historicize our placement in visual culture. When we view visual forms, we begin to supplement and "deter every process by its operational double, a metastable, programmatic, perfect descriptive machine which provides all the signs of the real and short-circuits all its vicissitudes."[30]

Advertisements commonly persuade consumers to buy products that compensate for their own deficiencies. Consumers are told what they should eat, wear, watch, and think. Through the process of reinvention, they begin to subconsciously weigh their melancholy awareness of their imperfections. The visual images in advertisements become a constant reminder of the consumers' unsuitableness, and the persuasive rhetoric of advertisers becomes a clarion call for compulsive brand consumption. Consumers begin the process of self-examination and self-transformation by purchasing products and, in so doing, they take one step closer to embodying the persuasive messages of synthetic culture.

The arrangement between popular culture and synthetic culture is symbiotic: popular culture authenticates itself in terms of pluralism and inclusiveness. Synthetic culture projects a shadow image of popular culture; however, shadow images do not reproduce their subject fully. Instead, they invert their subject's properties. It is at this transmutative point that synthetic culture assumes the character of social exclusivism and displaces the viewer as original subject. Within both physical and virtual spaces, the symbiotic relationship between popular culture and synthetic culture has been documented. Unbeknownst to consumers, they have become the bridge between both cultures. Their predetermined choices affect their own hierarchical placement within antagonistic cultural forms that draw from the same value system.

Video stores were commonly arranged in an open floor plan, with wall-to-wall shelves that were stacked with videocassettes. Larger-than-life posters of popular movies adorned storefront windows to entice customers into paying for the privileges of membership. Unlike movie theaters, which served as a gathering place for community, video stores enabled a more singular, personal, and intimate viewing experience. Skillfully marketed advertisements promoted a doctrine of exclusivism and once segregated video consumers by their preference for either Netflix's mail-order or Blockbuster's brick-and-mortar rentals. Consumers delighted in their privilege of viewing exclusivity, but this privilege was nothing more than a commercial fallacy that obscured how easy it was to acquire a membership. Consumers struggled to scale an elitist hierarchy of membership that appeared to magnify their own contributions to a video event that continuously awaited signification.

Chart the histories of recently released videos and you might glean how mass populism affects the behavior of viewers of streaming video.

Rental videos were once shuffled onto new release shelves, then redistributed and arranged categorically by drama, comedy, action, and adventure, for children and so on. Did you ever consider how the reshuffling of videos might have affected the transitive value of not only the video event but the consumer as well?

It was the fall of 1983, and I went to a local store to rent *First Blood* for the *first* time, rather than go fishing with a childhood friend.[31] I will not debate the historical and political significance of Sylvester Stallone's character of John Rambo, nor will I analyze his influence on the mainstreaming of graphic violence for movie-going audiences. Let me simply say, I just wanted to watch "things get blown up." On my first attempt, I was told there were no copies available for rent. My persistent phone calls and repeated visits to the store finally convinced a beleaguered owner to yield to the demands of a petulant teenage boy. "I'll put it on hold for you, but you will need to pick it up within the hour," she said.

As I entered the store to retrieve the video, I heard other customers talking about *First Blood*, and they wondered aloud how they might convince an unenthusiastic store associate to procure them a copy of the movie. Renting the movie became a rite of passage for me, a movement toward being hip, cool, and in step with the times. Unfortunately, the movie left me uninspired, and hoping for a refund of my rental fee. Passively, I went back to the video store the next day and dropped the VHS tape ever so gingerly through the store's return slot. I never asked for a refund. Perhaps if I had spent a few more minutes perusing the shelves, I might have found a classic movie like *The Bridge on the River Kwai*, *The Godfather*, or *Jaws*.[32] Unfortunately my options were quite limited, but they were never influenced algorithmically. The choice was still mine to make.

As I walked home from the video store, I felt like I had been duped. I consoled myself in the thought that I was the first of my group of friends to view the video in the comforts of my home: a 12' x 8' childhood room, with a small and well-worn cherry wood dresser, 13" color TV, and a majestic black and silver VCR. My privileged access gave me a sense of entitlement and exclusivity but not a full awareness that I had in my possession the material representation of visual culture and all the fallacies it perpetuates. I was unable to comprehend how visual enticements might alter my viewing preferences and affect my desire to participate in mass populism as a young man.

How many times did you find yourself inconspicuously wandering the aisles of a rental store while listening in on conversations about release dates and video availability? How many times did you follow the returns-cart around a store before being told "We don't have it now, but a copy might come in later today"? Were you looking for a classic film or maybe a lesser-known movie? Were you searching for something historically informative or culturally relevant? More than likely, you were tripping over your own feet to locate a copy of *The Naked Gun* or *Lethal Weapon* (insert sequel number here!), because you saw other consumers doing the same thing, and you wanted to join in the collective gaze.[33] Because video selections were limited and unpredictable, many consumers opened accounts at different chain stores to satisfy their growing video habit. As small neighborhood stores closed and large video rental chains such as Blockbuster Video and West Coast Video replaced them, renting videos became less about finding the right movie and more about finding the right brand. Rental customers once flocked to the new release section of stores and moved with rapid speed to collect VHS copies of movies. How often did you see multiple shelves devoted to a new release, with twenty, thirty, or more copies in stock? How did that number come to signify your own value within the video event?

Viewers no longer need to wander store aisles and grapple over limited numbers of videos. Now, they may connect instantaneously to endless amounts of streaming video content and, in so doing, exaggerate their value. The market saturation of images has produced within consumers "waves of enthusiasm for particular products" and "moments of fervent exaltation similar to the ecstasies of the convulsions and miracles of the old religious fetishism."[34] Our fetish for commercial branding has not abated since the early nineteenth century. Instead, it has increased and expanded into all corners of our physical and virtual realities.

Do you remember entering a brick-and-mortar video store for the first time? You were directed down aisles and toward shelves only to be met by frustration in your search for entertainment. The available videos might have left you dissatisfied, but how frequently did you leave the store empty-handed? The same strategies of redirection have been integrated into streaming services, which now guide viewers through labyrinthine-like digital catalogs that repeat and recycle videos across various categories. In so doing, they prevent viewers from turning off their digital transmission before adding something new to their streaming queue. Netflix now uses auto-play trailers to entice viewers into selecting a video more quickly, rather than spending more time scrolling through movie synopses. Dan Jackson questions the value of the auto-play feature by asking, "If the video previews are actually decreasing the browsing time of the average user, does that mean you're getting a 'better' experience?"[35]

As retailers perceive it, customers value the availability and immediacy of video entertainment far greater than its artistic quality. Theorists such as Theodor Adorno and Max Horkheimer might caution us and ask us to question the intrinsic value of mass-produced entertainment that is stripped of vitality and nuanced by strategies of commercialism and populism.[36] Ultimately, what is being mass-produced is not only the movies and television shows we watch, but also us as video consumers. Small video stores and even the corporate chains that replaced them tried to predict our choices by turning our fascination with producing and consuming culture against us.

In more recent times, the ability of corporations to draw the consumer into the process of creating and consuming popular culture has promoted brand messaging and imaging. For example, Hollywood Video liquidated its inventory and closed its stores in February of 2010 as a direct result of its failure to compete with other video rental services, such as mail-order video rentals, video vending machines, and high-speed online video services. Consequently, the franchise was consumed within a competitive video-rental market. After defaulting on a loan from one of its major creditors, the franchise filed an agreement with the U.S. Bankruptcy Court for the Eastern District of Virginia in Richmond on May 3, 2010, which effectively ended its business operations and projected a tentative timeline for the closure of approximately 1,900 stores. In response, Redbox kiosks appeared at entry points to supermarkets and convenience stores across the nation, and they provided a steady supply of new releases at discounted fees. The comfort and convenience of home video viewing also necessitated the expansion of Netflix into internet streaming services in 2010.

Similarly, Blockbuster Video offered its members online video streaming and rentals via snail mail. It also signed deals with a number of major movie studios, including Warner Brothers, to secure exclusive rights to new releases for the first twenty-eight days at market. In its attempts to compete with Netflix, Blockbuster provided its customers a modicum of exclusivity that rivaled my own privileged viewing of *First Blood*. Blockbuster's advertising campaigns reminded members of their privileged access to new movies and asked them to "Rent It While It's Still a New Release." Nonmembers of Blockbuster were required to wait, with breathless anticipation, for the release of videos that were restricted by multiple distribution dates and only made accessible to members with particular brand affiliations.

At one time, customers increased their choices by maintaining accounts at various neighborhood rental stores. Video stores, much like the movies they stocked, were conceived as a way to produce and distribute popular culture for mass consumption. Rather than individuating consumers through personal preferences, video chains started to brand them according to choices that might be made under specific conditions, and from within such conditions might be found the logic of affiliational thinking. Video chains exhibited the properties of synthetic culture by promoting exclusivity and polarizing consumers into rival corporate camps, which grew beyond the limits of physical structures to include more interactive and mobile viewing experiences on the internet.

Rental cards once provided meager bits of information for tracking viewers' preferences. Now, our streaming queues are populated by videos that symbolize a shift in patterns of consumption. What we watch is now being surveilled by someone else, and the privileges of viewing exclusivity are no longer predicated by personal choice. Someone else is writing our viewing history, and they are deciding the future of what we should watch based on streaming rights that were determined long before we logged onto a video portal.

Recent innovations in internet technology and changes in corporate branding and subscription pricing affected consumer preferences for DVD by mail and/or online streaming services, particularly as rival companies focused on improving their business models to include more original content. In the present context, internet streaming services are increasing their memberships by exaggerating the benefits of consumer loyalty through the creation of original television shows and movies that are produced and distributed exclusively for their consumer base: for example, Netflix's *House of Cards* (2013), *Orange Is the New Black* (2013), and *Stranger Things* (2016). It is not uncommon for consumers to sign up for a streaming service just to view exclusive and original content, as television shows and movies jump periodically from Netflix to Amazon Prime, and so on. Streaming services promote affiliational thinking by producing original content that might never be seen anywhere else. These streaming services also unwittingly work together to cultivate an exclusivist value system for consumers, which is composed of layers of cultural influences and social groupings that are intertwined pluralistically.

The conceptual errors found common among video services are obvious and their operational missteps will continue until they have reached the limits of their corporate rhetoric. At which time, they will reflect on their diminished popularity, cultural irrelevance, and economic impotence, and regret they did not seize the opportunity to revalue the video viewer's contribution to a cultural metanarrative that encompasses the video event. They might also acknowledge their social and cultural connections to consumers that seek visual reminders of human experience, which are used for identifying patterns of production and expressing notions of consumption that alleviate the burden of possessive materialism.

When we visit a movie theater, we share a common social experience with other audience members by viewing imagery. As our enthusiasms and criticisms ebb and flow, we become aware of our participation in a larger cultural experience of mimicry. As we respond to the emotions of the crowd, its laughs and cries, its moans and groans, and its praises and curses, we perform a mimicry of the collective audience.

In contrast, videos provide us a more singular and personal experience. Separated from the collective audience, the viewer comes to regard himself or herself as master of the video event. In such moments, the viewer becomes isolated within the video event and reconstitutes himself or herself as the principal subject of inquiry. In creating and inhabiting such self-referential space, the viewer achieves a false sense of control over the video event. The viewer experiences auditory impulses and visual images as he or she gazes at the video event, and these stimuli allow the viewer to achieve a heightened singularity. Freed from the performative aspects of mimicry, the viewer struggles to recapture the feeling of inclusiveness from within his or her growing singularity. Binge-watching is not a social phenomenon but rather a predictable consequence of the isolated viewer trying to resume his or her mimicry of the collective audience. The viewer's desire to produce and consume culture draws him or her continuously to the video event, in which he or she experiences movement between popular and synthetic culture.

It is through these movements that viewers might recover intellectual intensities and symbolic meanings that dwarf and precede their own self-conceptions. It is through these movements that viewers conceptualize the merger of multilayers of culture and history, the archiving of memory, language, and meaning, and the pluralistic orchestration needed to sustain them. It is in these moments that viewers also try to rationalize the differences between popularism and pluralism.

Through video events, we are able to simulate, consume, repeat, or potentially resist models of representation "as a negation of life that has invented a visual form for itself." [37] Our movements toward or beyond models of representation happen within the ideological space between synthetic and popular cultures. From within these spaces, we begin a heterogeneous dialogue that antagonizes fears of anonymity, excites desires for popularity, and reveals distinct models of culture that we come to embody.

Media theorists have often debated how the images and sounds of video become pliable devices for constructing a comforting narrative for viewers. Synthetic corporate culture employs these devices to affect consumers' expectations of the video event. As consumers are conditioned to continuously anticipate the video event, their ability to access it signifies their perceived contribution to mass populism. Even by rejecting mass populism and differentiating themselves from algorithmically determined choices, consumers are not able to restore fully the connection between the video event and their subjective viewership.

Reclamation, alteration, selection, and so on, are words that have lost their evocativeness. The choices that allow for differentiation are not locatable within streaming networks of irreducible influence "in which subjects operate and which in turn conditions their freedom of action." [38] In order to free themselves, consumers must redirect their gaze away from the banalities of affiliational thinking and corporate branding and toward the fulfillment of individual subjectivity. Consumers must assist in the dissolution of narratives that do not present distinct and equally valued positions. They must assess the damage done by mass populism, reconstitute the language of criticality, and redress cultural narratives that might have been distorted, forgotten, misrepresented, or lost in total-ity. By fracturing, tearing, and destroying metanarrative configurations, "[we might] wean ourselves from the fiction of a 'true' [homogenous] vision and revel instead in the possibilities opened up by the scopic re-gimes we have already invented and the ones, now so hard to envision, that are doubtless to come."[39] In so doing, we allow new cultural models to form and welcome their contradictions and contradistinctions. We may restore subjective viewership and allow metanarratives to suffer a process of deconstruction from which they might yield endless possible significations. What is left in the wake of such change is an empowered viewer that attains self-knowledge by initiating endless permutations of becoming, which may far exceed the video catalogs of streaming services.

In their attempts to privilege viewing experiences, corporate video chains and the internet streaming services that followed them cultivated an audience that was desirous of their products. They continued to capi-talize on consumers like my younger self, who valued video-based enter-tainment as a new form of intellectual currency. VHS tapes, DVDs, Blu-rays, and streaming videos are historical and technological signposts that we might use for navigating the everchanging currents of visual culture. To that end, I recently found myself watching *First Blood*, again. I did not remember much about the video and found myself longing for my youth-ful past. I clicked the power button on my remote control, watched a giant plasma screen go dark, and saw my silhouette reflected back at me. I realized a synthetic version of me, a virtual iteration constructed from a complex arrangement of user profiles, cluster-preferences, and viewer metrics lingered somewhere deep inside the viewing experience. He was my replacement, a more adaptable version of me better suited for nostal-gic branding. Despite what the aggregate data might suggest, he simply was not me. He was merely an artificial reminder, a cue that some part of me had been either distorted, forgotten, misrepresented or lost, but not in full totality. He remained within his 60" cell and grew less noticeable as I reached for my phone to call a childhood friend and ask him if he would still like to go fishing with me.

NOTES

1. Jean-Francois Lyotard, *The Postmodern Condition: A Report on Knowledge*, trans. Geoff Bennington and Brian Massumi (Minneapolis: University of Minnesota Press, 1984), xxiv.

2. "'The Consumer' Has Been Added to Your Video Queue" was adapted for republication with the permission of Prafulla C. Kar and *The Journal of Contemporary Thought*. The article originally appeared in *The Journal of Contemporary Thought* 33 (Summer 2011): 153-70.

3. Guy Debord, *The Society of the Spectacle*, trans. Donald Nicholson-Smith (New York: Zone Books, 1994), 2.

4. Ryan Lizardi, *Nostalgic Generations and Media: Perception of Time and Available Meaning* (Lanham, MD: Lexington Books, 2017), 4.

5. John McMurria, *Republic on the Wire: Cable Television, Pluralism, and the Politics of New Technologies, 1948-1984* (New Brunswick: Rutgers University Press, 2017), 31.

6. Nick Nelson, "The Power of a Picture," *Netflix Media Center* (May 3, 2016), https://media.netflix.com/en/company-blog/the-power-of-a-picture.

7. Jacques Derrida and Bernard Stiegler, *Echographies of Television: Filmed Interviews*, trans. Jennifer Bajorek (Malden, MA: Polity Press, 2002), 13.

8. Paul Tassi, "What Is Wrong with Netflix?" *Forbes* (October 15, 2015), https://www.forbes.com/sites/insertcoin/2015/10/17/what-is-wrong-with-netflix/#645aede63a49.

9. Lizardi, 106.

10. Lizardi, 106.

11. Lizardi, 106.

12. Jacek Tittenbrun, *Economy in Society: Economic Sociology Revisited* (Newcastle Upon Tyne: Cambridge Scholars Publishing, 2011), 455.

13. Herbert Marcuse, *One-Dimensional Man* (Boston: Beacon Press, 1991), 24-25.

14. Though now commonly theorized, the term "corporate culture" was conceptualized by French-Canadian psychoanalyst Elliott Jaques. In *The Changing Culture of a Factory*, Jaques analyzed and evaluated how conscious organizational routines affect the unconscious patterns of production and consumption.

15. "Netflix and Chill," *Wikipedia*, last modified June 16, 2018, https://en.wikipedia.org/wiki/Netflix_and_chill.

16. Lori Ann Loeb, *Consuming Angels: Advertising and Victorian Women* (New York: Oxford University Press, 1996), 10.

17. Derrida and Steigler, 13.

18. Jean Baudrillard, "Dust Breeding," *CTheory.net* (October 8, 2001), trans. François Debrix, http://www.ctheory.net/articles.aspx?id=293.

19. Derrida and Steigler, 5.

20. Derrida and Steigler, 3.

21. Debord, 141.

22. Lyotard, 81.

23. Lyotard, 2.

24. Slavoj Žižek, "How the Non-Duped Err," *Qui Parle*, No. 1 (Fall 1990): 2.

25. Debord, 3.

26. Debord, 88.

27. Michel Foucault, *Discipline and Punish: The Birth of the Prison*, trans. Alan Sheridan (New York: Pantheon Books, 1977).

28. Tony Bennett, *Pasts Beyond Memory: Evolution, Museums, and Colonialism* (New York: Routledge, 2004), 81.

29. Jacques Lacan, "The Mirror Stage as Formative of the *I* Function, as Revealed in Psychoanalytic Experience," in *Ecrits: A Selection*, trans. Bruce Fink (New York: W.W. Norton & Company, 2004), 3-9.

30. Jean Baudrillard, *The Ecstasy of Communication*, trans. Paul Foss, Paul Patton, and Philip Beitchman (New York: Semiotext(e), 1988), 3.

31. *First Blood*, directed by Ted Kotcheff (1982; Burbank, CA, Thorn Emi; Warner Home Video, 1983), VHS.

32. *The Bridge on the River Kwai*, directed by David Lean (1957; Culver City, CA, RCA/Columbia Home Pictures Video, 1992), VHS; *The Godfather*, directed by Francis Ford Coppola (1972; Hollywood, CA, Paramount Home Video, 1992), VHS; *Jaws*, directed by Steven Spielberg (1975; Los Angeles, CA, MCA/Universal Home Video, 1980), VHS.

33. *The Naked Gun: From the Files of Police Squad!*, directed by David Zucker (1988; Hollywood, CA, Paramount Home Video, 1989), VHS; *Lethal Weapon*, directed by Richard Donner (1987; Burbank, CA, Warner Home Video, 1987), VHS.

34. Debord, 34.

35. Dan Jackson, "Netflix Does Not Care If You Hate the Auto-Play Trailer Feature," *Thrillist Entertainment* (April 30, 2018), https://www.thrillist.com/entertainment/nation/netflix-autoplay-previews-turn-off-hack.

36. Theodor Adorno and Max Horkheimer, "The Culture Industry: Enlightenment as Mass Deception," in *Dialectic of Enlightenment* (Stanford: Stanford University Press, 2002): 120-67.

37. Debord, 4.

38. Nicholas Mirzoeff, "The Subject of Visual Culture," in *The Visual Culture Reader*, ed. Nicholas Mirzoeff (London: Routledge, 2002), 6.

39. Martin Jay, "Scopic Regimes of Modernity," in *Vision and Visuality*, ed. Hal Foster (Bay Press: Seattle, 1988), 20.

BIBLIOGRAPHY

Adorno, Theodor, and Max Horkheimer. "The Culture Industry: Enlightenment as Mass Deception." In *Dialectic of Enlightenment*. Edited by Gunzelin Schmid Noerr. Translated by Edmund Jephcott, 120-67. Stanford: Stanford University Press, 2002.

Arrested Development. Performed by Jason Bateman, Michael Cera, and Portia de Rossi. Imagine Entertainment, 20th Century Fox Television, The Hurwitz Company, Imagine Television, 2003-. Television series.

Baudrillard, Jean. "Dust Breeding." *CTheory.net* (October 8, 2001). Edited by Arthur Kroker and Marilouise Kroker. Translated by François Debrix. http://www.ctheory.net/articles.aspx?id=293.

———. *The Ecstasy of Communication*. Translated by Paul Foss, Paul Patton, and Philip Beitchman. New York: Semiotext(e), 1988.

Bennett, Tony. *Pasts Beyond Memory: Evolution, Museums, and Colonialism*. New York: Routledge, 2004.

Bentham, Jeremy. *The Works of Jeremy Bentham Vol. 1*. Edinburgh: W. Tait, 1843.

Coppola, Francis F. dir. *The Godfather*. 1972; Hollywood, CA: Paramount Home Video, 1992. VHS.

Debord, Guy. *The Society of the Spectacle*. Translated by Donald Nicholson-Smith. New York: Zone Books, 1994.

Derrida, Jacques, and Bernard Stiegler. *Echographies of Television: Filmed Interviews*. Translated by Jennifer Bajorek. Malden, MA: Polity Press, 2002.

Donner, Richard. dir. *Lethal Weapon*. 1987; Burbank, CA: Warner Home Video, 1987. VHS.

Foucault, Michel Foucault. *Discipline and Punish: The Birth of the Prison*. Translated by Alan Sheridan. New York: Pantheon Books, 1977.

Full House. Performed by Bob Saget, John Stamos, and Dave Coulier. Jeff Franklin Productions, Lorimar Telepictures, and Lorimar Television, 1987–1995. Television series.

Fuller House. Performed by Candace Cameron Bure, Jodie Sweetin, and Andrea Barber. Jeff Franklin Productions, Miller/Boyett Productions, Warner Horizon Television, 2016–. Television series.

Gilmore Girls. Performed by Laura Graham, Alexis Beidel, and Keiko Agena. Dorothy Parker Drank Here Productions, Hofflund/Polone, Warner Bros. Television, 2000–2007. Television series.

Gilmore Girls: A Year in the Life. Performed by Laura Graham, Alexis Beidel, and Scott Patterson. Warner Bros. Television, 2016. Television series.

House of Cards. Performed by Kevin Spacey, Michel Gill, and Robin Wright. Media Rights Capital, Panic Pictures, Trigger Street Productions, 2013–. Television series.

Jackson, Dan. "Netflix Does Not Care If You Hate the Auto-Play Trailer Feature." *Thrillist Entertainment* (April 30, 2018). https://www.thrillist.com/entertainment/nation/netflix-autoplay-previews-turn-off-hack.

Jaques, Elliott. *The Changing Culture of a Factory*. London: Tavistock Publications, 1952.

Jay, Martin. "Scopic Regimes of Modernity." In *Vision and Visuality*. Edited by Hal Foster, 3-27. Bay Press: Seattle, 1988.

Kotcheff, Ted. dir. *First Blood*. 1982; Burbank, CA: Warner Home Video, 1983. VHS.

Lacan, Jacques. "The Mirror Stage as Formative of the *I* Function, as Revealed in Psychoanalytic Experience." In *Ecrits: A Selection*. Translated by Bruce Fink, 3-9. New York: W.W. Norton & Company, 2004.

Lean, David. dir. *The Bridge on the River Kwai*. 1957; Culver City, CA: RCA/Columbia Home Pictures Video, 1992. VHS.

Lizardi, Ryan. *Nostalgic Generations and Media: Perception of Time and Available Meaning*. Lanham, MD: Lexington Books, 2017.

Loeb, Lori Ann. *Consuming Angels: Advertising and Victorian Women*. New York: Oxford University Press, 1996.

Lyotard, Jean-Francois. *The Postmodern Condition: A Report on Knowledge*. Translated by Geoff Bennington and Brian Massumi. Minneapolis: University of Minnesota Press, 1984.

Marcuse, Herbert. *One-Dimensional Man*. Boston: Beacon Press, 1991.

McMurria, John. *Republic on the Wire: Cable Television, Pluralism, and the Politics of New Technologies, 1948-1984*. New Brunswick: Rutgers University Press, 2017.

Mirzoeff, Nicholas. "The Subject of Visual Culture." In *The Visual Culture Reader*. Edited by Nicholas Mirzoeff, 3-23. London: Routledge, 2002.

Murray, John C. "*The Consumer* Has Been Added to Your Video Queue." *The Journal of Contemporary Thought* 33 (Summer 2011): 153-70.

Nelson, Nick. "The Power of a Picture." *Netflix Media Center* (May 3, 2016). https://media.netflix.com/en/company-blog/the-power-of-a-picture. "Netflix and Chill." last modified June 16, 2018. https://en.wikipedia.org/ wiki/Netflix_and_chill.

Orange Is the New Black. Performed by Taylor Schilling, Danielle Brooks, and Taryn Manning. Tilted Productions, Lionsgate Television. 2013–. Television series.

Spielberg, Steven. dir. *Jaws*. 1975; Los Angeles, CA: MCA/Universal Home Video, 1980. VHS.

Stranger Things. Performed by Millie Bobby Brown, Finn Wolfhard, and Winona Ryder. 21 Laps Entertainment, Monkey Massacre 2016–. Television series.

Tassi, Paul. "What Is Wrong with Netflix?" *Forbes* (October 15, 2015). https://www.forbes.com/sites/insertcoin/2015/10/17/what-is-wrong-with-netflix/#645aede63a49.

Tittenbrun, Jacek. *Economy in Society: Economic Sociology Revisited*. Newcastle Upon Tyne: Cambridge Scholars Publishing, 2011.

Žižek, Slavoj. "How the Non-Duped Err." *Qui Parle*, No. 1 (Fall 1990): 1-20.

Zucker, David. dir. *The Naked Gun: From the Files of Police Squad!* 1988; Hollywood, CA: Paramount Home Video, 1989. VHS.

FIVE

Nostalgia as a Problematic Cultural Space

The Example of the Original Netflix Series GLOW (2017)

Philippe Gauthier

Most recent studies on the connection between nostalgia and the media—may they be a film, a television series or a song—focus on the way in which nostalgia is placed in the service of conservative or even regressive politics by means of the selective interpretation of the past (such as the appropriation of African-American culture by the white majority or the glamorizing of misogyny and homophobia). Whether it is a question of returning to the 1950s in the Reagan era through music or film[1] or of the circulating again today of iconic popular culture toys and texts from the 1980s,[2] scholars urge us to understand that the nostalgic recycling of culture not only deforms the past but also contributes actively to consumer society—quite simply through the consumption of goods literally taken from the past, or at least evoking that past, something Gary Cross calls consumed nostalgia.[3]

In the present article, I will extend these ideas about the complex relations between nostalgia and history. Thinking on this topic has recently intensified in the work of the scholars mentioned above, along with that of Svetlana Boym[4] and Christine Sprengler.[5] My goal is twofold. On the one hand, through study of a particular case, that of the original Netflix series GLOW (2017), I will demonstrate how different kinds of nostalgia function and clash within the same work, transforming it into a true site of tensions.[6] These tensions become *problems to be re-solved* in the public sphere for different social actors (filmmakers, critics, scholars, etc.). It is in this sense, on the other hand, and following Denis Simard, that I would describe nostalgia—or more precisely nostalgia films (or television series)[7] as defined by Le Sueur,[8] Jameson,[9] Sprengler[10] and Dwyer[11]—as a *problematic cultural space.*[12] I must clarify from the outset that my own analysis will focus on a specific Netflix series (*GLOW*) and that more research needs to be made in the near future in order to determine if different media (films, television series, etc.) employ nostalgia similarly/differently, and if so how.

I will not analyze here the form nostalgia takes in the series *GLOW*, for example through concepts such as "surface realism" or "deliberate archaism," each developed by Marc Le Sueur.[13] Rather, I will discuss how the different kinds of nostalgia present in *GLOW* make it possible not only to initiate new ways of interpreting and understanding history but also to invest the past and to place it in the service of the present. Series such as *GLOW* thus offer "new" visions of the 1980s which are a part of a redefinition of the United States to the benefit of the present. In the end, my conception of nostalgia as a problematic cultural space will enable me not only to call into question the position which holds that "'glossy' treatments of the past that idealize some aspects of history and erase others can *only* demonstrate an 'inability to create representations of our own present'"[14] but also, and more importantly, to render the connections between history and nostalgia more complex.

THE CONNECTIONS BETWEEN NOSTALGIA AND HISTORY

Fredric Jameson was one of the first intellectuals to decry the nostalgia in American popular culture for the way it deforms and falsifies history.[15] For Jameson, films depicting the past, or what he calls the "nostalgia film,"[16] do so only superficially, through suppositions and stereotypes, without engaging with the past in a critical and rigorous fashion. Nostalgia films thus replace the real past with mere aesthetic styles of the past. These films—and the nostalgic images they contain—encourage superficial relations with history. A film such as *American Graffiti* (George Lucas, 1973), set in 1962, is superficially steeped in the past through aesthetic references to the late 1950s and early 1960s, without really incorporating this decade's historical and social realities. Indeed, if "*American Graffiti* is stuffed to its customized tailpipes with little deuce coupes, rollerskating carhops, cherry cokes, copped feels, cooties, Clearasil—plus lots of vintage pop songs," as Michael Dempsey wrote in his review,[17] Lucas's film puts aside the "Fifties experience of women, African-Americans, homosexuals, and others, leaving huge swaths of the population out of its vision, and lionizes their invisibility."[18] The same is true, according to

Jameson, when Roman Polanski merely appropriated the film styles and cultural signs of the past when he re-created the United States of the 1930s in *Chinatown* (Roman Polanski, 1974).[19]

The result is a mere evoking or superficial impression of the past, a surface realism of the 1930s or 1950s through period fashion, architecture and objects. Jameson argues that the rise of nostalgia films in the 1970s and 1980s represents the inability of Western society to represent its own historical conditions and a desire to transform its "history" into a mere consumer product. These films are the sign of a crisis of historicity in which our true past is gradually erased from our collective memory and replaced by imagery confected from scratch. Nostalgia films thus contribute to a weakening of historicity and to society's inability to think about its history:

> As though, for some reason, we were unable today to focus our own present, as though we have become incapable of achieving aesthetic representations of our own current experience. But if that is so, then it is a terrible indictment of consumer capitalism itself or at the very least, an alarming and pathological symptom of a society that has become incapable of dealing with time and history.[20]

Jameson sees nostalgia films as images which, at best, reduce or simplify history and at worst evacuate or replace it entirely in favor of a process which ensures that capitalism will endure. For Jameson, the connection between nostalgia and history is thus that of a commodity, in that nostalgia films treat the past like one more piece of merchandise to be sold.

Following Jameson's work, other scholars, without denying the problematical connection between nostalgia and true access to history, have sought to depict this connection in a more complex light. Linda Hutcheon, in her book *The Politics of Postmodernism*, was one of the first to contest the fundamentally ahistorical nature of nostalgia in Jameson's account. For Hutcheon, nostalgia films have the potential to reveal that there exists a real past directly available to us today, in that these films highlight the distance between our present and the past they claim to depict.[21] In none of these films is there any evidence that contemporary society inhabits a "perpetual present,"[22] as Jameson suggested. According to Hutcheon, postmodern cinema (including the nostalgia film) is, on the contrary, obsessed not only with history but also with the way in which we today can know the past. How, Hutcheon wonders, can that be a weakening of historicity and society's inability to think about its history? A few years later, Vivian Sobchack aptly underscored the extent to which our era is marked by growing historical awareness: history is everywhere and exists in many forms, ready to be explored and consumed.[23]

Since then, several scholars have made the connection between nostalgia and history more complex. Christine Sprengler, in her book *Screening Nostalgia: Populuxe Props and Technicolor Aesthetics in Contemporary*

American Film, draws on the concepts "surface realism" and "deliberate archaism" developed by Marc Le Sueur[24]—to which I will return below—in order to better understand the role of props and the use of digital technology in the production of recent nostalgia films such as *The Aviator* (Martin Scorsese, 2004) and *The Good German* (Steven Soderbergh, 2006) in particular. For Sprengler, while an appearance of authenticity (surface realism) is communicated to viewers by the use of iconic objects from the historical period depicted, deliberate archaism reinterprets past visual styles. In the end, Sprengler succeeds in demonstrating that nostalgia films do more than simply cut our ties to the past. More precisely, she highlights the critical potential of the nostalgia film which can, for viewers invested in it, make them feel a greater connection with history. Finally, and most recently, Michael D. Dwyer explores the means and political ends of the recirculation of "the 1950s" in popular culture throughout the 1970s and 1980s. His book *Back to the Fifties: Nostalgia, Hollywood Film, and Popular Music of the Seventies and Eighties* shows how various invocations of the 1950s were used to a variety of and sometimes even concurrent ends: some of these were progressive, but several served the interests of conservative politics in order to redefine the United States past in the eyes of the voting public.[25]

Dwyer's argument is particularly relevant regarding our current fascination with nostalgia and how it connects to our recent historical conditions, especially in popular culture where the so-called postfeminist attitude—understood here as a regressive development—is still present.[26] Just to mention one evocative example, Kathleen Loock has astutely demonstrated how recent Netflix revivals of 1970s, 1980s and 2000s TV series such as *One Day at a Time*, *Fuller House* or *Gilmore Girls: A Year in the Life* entangle feminist and anti-feminist discourses, offering in the end "a more conservative, inherently nostalgic, and less challenging alternative to contemporary family sitcoms and complex TV, in particular new shows with female leads."[27]

INVESTING THE PAST FOR THE PRESENT

The idea of nostalgia serving the politics of the past is, however, not new. In a pioneering article entitled "Theory Number Five: Anatomy of Nostalgia Films: Heritage and Methods" and published in the *Journal of Popular Film*, Marc Le Sueur became one of the first to view nostalgia—and by extension nostalgia films—as a concept inseparable from history and whose operating principles few scholars had attempted to establish.[28] At this early date, Le Sueur was disputing critical ideas of the 1970s which saw nostalgia as an exclusively conservative phenomenon, arguing instead that it was sometimes joined with progressive social and political movements.[29] This is why, using concepts such as "deliberate archaism," he distinguished the "material" objects of nostalgia from our experience of them, thereby underscoring the potential presence of conservative and/or progressive uses of nostalgia, each having major social ramifications.

To account for such political divergences in the use of nostalgia, Le Sueur divided it into two types: restorative nostalgia and melancholic nostalgia. "Restorative nostalgia," somewhat like the nostalgia defined by Svetlana Boym,[30] represents an impulse motivated by attempts to capture the past anew and to revitalize it. Le Sueur suggests that restorative nostalgia fastens onto certain aspects of the past (either practices or desires) which continue to be relevant to the present. "Melancholic nostalgia," a little like Boym's "reflexive nostalgia,"[31] is by nature an escape mechanism and is characterized by a feeling of sadness tied to what has been lost over time. For Le Sueur, Hollywood is the principal producer of nostalgia, and its nostalgia is essentially melancholic. Nostalgic films of this kind are most often imprecise and evasive in their connection to the past. They often limit themselves to presenting highly romanticized images of a bygone era about which they supply little analysis and on which they provide little critical commentary. In Le Sueur's words, "the essentially uncritical methodology of especially melancholic nostalgia often creates a body of semi-truths which assume the proportions of legend in themselves."[32] Worse yet, for Le Sueur, these films contribute to what Jameson would decry in the 1980s, a deformation of the past: Stylistically, nostalgic artists promote these new myths by an attention to period detail, creating a surface realism which leads the viewer to confuse "the way it was" for, in the phrase of George Lucas, ". . . the way it should have been."[33]

Nevertheless, in its restorative form nostalgia makes it possible to initiate new ways of interpreting and understanding history. For Le Sueur, nostalgia films, those he identifies with restorative nostalgia, represent a way of investing the past and of placing it in the service of the present.[34] In this sense, these films are not very different from the discipline of history, in that history consists essentially in conceiving in time an object which the historian reconstructs in his or her present. More precisely, historians' methods vary depending on the society and era in which they work, as the historian and philosopher of history Michel de Certeau rightly points out: "If it is true that the organization of history is relative to a place and a time, this is first of all because of its techniques of production. Generally speaking, every society thinks of itself 'historically,' with the instruments that pertain to it."[35] Put differently, in the words this time of the historian Pierre Sorlin, "even completely lost in the midst of their archives, even isolated in the year 2000 BC, historians never respond to anything but the questions of their contemporaries."[36] It is thus on the basis of these methods, which enable it to construct and analyze its object of study, that history is rooted in the singular present of a given society. Like nostalgia, historical research begins in the present of a given social place (on the basis in particular of the historian's contemporary conceptual framework) and works its way back to the past. Historical writing, like nostalgia, thus reverses the order of the practices out of which it arises: "[chronology] applies the inverted image of time upon the text, an image that in research proceeds from the present to the past. Chronology follows this path in reverse."[37] Whether one is speaking of historical writing or of nostalgia, one moves from the present to the past in order to bring this past into our present.

In some cases, by means of this coming and going between present and past, a filmmaker or artist's nostalgic vision can lead viewers to become aware of a new version of the past by overcoming some of their preconceptions of quite precise periods.[38] In other words, some nostalgia films, once again employing a restorative nostalgia, can change people's opinions about past events or even entire periods. Through this function, which we could call "raising awareness," nostalgia makes it possible to expose individuals to new information about the world and its history. Marc Le Sueur even suggests that restorative nostalgia is sometimes associated with important social and political shifts such as revolutions; as a result, to categorize all nostalgia as escapism is to overlook the important social impact it can have.[39]

In the end, a nostalgia film's power of persuasion, like that of nostalgia itself, is not intrinsically dangerous or positive. Although (restorative) nostalgia can make it possible for previously suppressed histories to appear in the collective consciousness, melancholic nostalgia can substitute one set of myths with another, as in the film *American Graffiti*, which replaced the myth of the 1950s as "complacent" with the myth of those years as "optimistic."[40]

A PROBLEMATIC CULTURAL SPACE

Nostalgia films, as they have been defined by Jameson, Le Sueur, Dwyer or Sprengler, are rarely (or even never, I might add) entirely restorative or melancholy in nature. It may be that a particular kind of nostalgia will dominate in a nostalgia film, such as melancholic nostalgia in *American Graffiti*, but restorative nostalgia can also be present sporadically. This is why I would like to propose here that as a result we must conclude that nostalgia films are not simply imbued with a single kind of nostalgia. There is clearly little restorative nostalgia in *American Graffiti*, to refer once again to this widely commented upon film, but there is some just the same. According to this hypothesis, a nostalgia film will thus vacillate from beginning to end between restorative nostalgia and melancholic nostalgia, the two endpoints of the nostalgia spectrum. If it is possible to find both melancholic nostalgia and restorative nostalgia in a single nostalgia film, it is not surprising that they intersect and collide within it and as a result that the film would become a true site of tensions. As I mentioned above in my introduction, these tensions are *problems to be resolved* for the various social actors (filmmakers, critics, journalists, scholars, etc.). This is why I describe the nostalgia film and more generally nostalgia itself as a *problematic cultural space*.

To view the nostalgia film and nostalgia itself as *problematic cultural spaces* thus enables us to better understand the intersections and conflicting interpretations at work in certain works, which too often are viewed in a uniform manner. My approach, by recognizing the multiple connections between nostalgia and history, views the different visual forms nostalgia can take as spaces of negotiation. More than a concept, I propose the problematic cultural space as a *true theoretical paradigm*, enabling me to highlight cultural and media intersections which have been largely overlooked by scholars to date. This epistemological position has the principal advantage of making it possible to study the different cultural, social and institutional configurations of nostalgia films (or television series) in order to grasp the context in which they operate in all its complexity and the cultural and discursive practices associated with them. More precisely, this position makes it possible to cast new light on the diversity of historical interpretations found in different manifestations of nostalgia. In this way, by means of an analysis of the various discourses around the original Netflix series *GLOW*, it will be possible to grasp how the particularities of the various manifestations of nostalgia (restorative or melancholic) have been perceived in the different reception spaces in which they enter the present. Cultural confrontations, moreover, largely derive from a discursive construction: it is in discourses that they become manifest and take shape. I will thus seek to identify the principal features on which this confrontation is erected, but also to explain how these same discourses *invent* this confrontation out of "cultural knowledge" differences.

RESTORATIVE AND MELANCHOLIC NOSTALGIA IN *GLOW*

Distributed by INI (Independent Network Inc.) from 1986 to 1990, *Gorgeous Ladies of Wrestling* was a TV wrestling show in which women wrestled one other dressed in costumes of spangles and spandex. Its creator, David B. McLane, wanted to capitalize on the success of the World Wrestling Entertainment (known as the World Wrestling Federation at that time). Hoping to break into show business, the performers of *Gorgeous Ladies of Wrestling* were mostly actresses, stunt women, models or dancers. They embodied colorful and strong characters in over-the-top comedy sketches. Based loosely on this real television show, the Netflix series *GLOW*, created by Liz Flahive and Carly Mensch, tells the fictional story

of the creation of a similar TV wrestling show. Taking place in Los Angeles in 1985, *GLOW* features Ruth Wilder (played by Alison Brie), an
unemployed actress, who auditions alongside dozens of other women for
a televised female wrestling show. The Netflix series follows this group
of women who, without prior experience, get involved in the new program. *GLOW*'s first two seasons, made up of ten episodes each and
broadcast on Netflix starting June 23, 2017, for the first season and June
29, 2018, for the second one, covers the production process for the pilot
and the first season, from hiring the actresses to the shooting.

GLOW is part of what Oriana Schwindt has called Netflix's "nostalgia
strategy,"[41] which includes original shows (such as *Stranger Things* or
Everything Sucks!), new reboots/sequels (*Fuller House, Gilmore Girls: A
Year in the Life* or *Lost in Space*) or old movies and teleseries (such as *The
Princess Bride* or *Friends*). Using nostalgia as a "transgenerational magnet
programming,"[42] Netflix's goal is to attract (and keep!) both younger and
older nostalgic subscribers wanting to look (or to look back) on the 1980s,
1990s and early 2000s. Netflix's plans for creating original content leaning
toward nostalgia is so ambitious that it has been called by many commentators as the "nostalgia's reign."[43]

Beyond this marketing strategy, the two creators of *GLOW* saw in the
story behind the production of *Gorgeous Ladies of Wrestling* a great opportunity to explore the impact of the women's liberation movement of the
1970s in the United States. As Liz Flahive explained to the magazine
Rolling Stone, "we wanted to look back on the Seventies—coming out of
the women's movement—and into the Eighties, and ask the question: Did
it work? Did things get better?"[44] This question deserves to be asked
inasmuch as popular culture has often depicted the 1980s as a highly
conservative time.[45] And yet, despite the strict policies of the Ronald
Reagan presidency, numerous social movements emerged during this
period and thousands of American citizens were active in groups demanding greater social justice. The conservative politics of the Reagan era
were thus contested by several social groups, such as Greenpeace, the
Equal Rights Amendment (ERA), ACT UP and Food Not Bombs (without
this period being a golden age for the American left either). The 1980s in
the United States thus saw an increase in environmental awareness, mass
demonstrations against nuclear proliferation and against apartheid in
South Africa, protests against military intervention in Central America
and, what concerns us here, a consolidation of feminism.[46] It was precisely this final aspect of the 1980s that Liz Flahive and Carly Mensch wanted
to bring up-to-date with the series *GLOW*. They wanted to do "a sort of
double looking back"[47] as they were pitching the show during the 2016
US presidential campaign, a period where many Americans thought they
were about to elect their first female president. The consolidation of feminism is all the more relevant today in our current post–Trump era, as

many commentators view Trump's presidency as the worst ever seen for women.[48]

Through restorative nostalgia, *GLOW* is thus not only another important popular culture vehicle for decrying the pervasiveness of sexism in the United States in the 1980s and for confronting it with the present day—in order, in the end, to lead some viewers to become aware of a new version of the past by overcoming some of their preconceptions—but also, and perhaps more importantly, for keeping in the public sphere the important debate as to whether emancipation is possible through exploitation or even debasement. For many feminists, the logic according to which the women's empowerment can hinge to some extent on their sexualized bodies and their exploitation is directly linked to postfeminism.[49] However, as Abbott, Wallace and Tyler note, more libertarian feminists would argue that any form of social interdiction toward sexuality ultimately works against women's interests.[50]

GLOW's first season explored this topic unremittingly, without ever articulating a clear and unequivocal response, even when the character of Debbie "Liberty Belle" Eagan (played by Betty Gilpin) says at the end of episode 9 (first season): "I feel like I took back the control of my body. It does not belong to Mark [Debbie's husband] or Randy [her son] but to me. I feel like a fucking superhero." Several commentators, moreover, have commented on the way in which *GLOW* explores the process whereby women are emancipated through exploitation. For some observers, the women's wrestling league *Gorgeous Ladies of Wrestling* contributed to the emancipation of the women who took part in it. Hank Stuever writes:

> In *GLOW*'s case, the goal is to master the physically demanding stagecraft of pro wrestling, with some shred of dignity intact. The women who form *GLOW*—"Gorgeous Ladies of Wrestling," a real-life 1980s TV sensation on which this show is loosely based—must endure a series of humiliations and reckon with personal compromises. They must also learn to set aside their differences and cooperate to such a degree that, late in the series, they are borrowing tampons from one another because their menstrual cycles have synced. *From the wrestling ring, their sisterly empowerment arises.*[51]

For his part, Tom Phillips writes:

> *GLOW*'s feminism is made explicit from the outset. Despite the proposed show ostensibly being about "gorgeous ladies," the women are literally fighting the male gaze. The nuances of feminism within the show can be seen at first by the replacement of the white male trainer with Cherry Bang, a black woman. With Cherry in charge, the women find their way together, *relying only on themselves* to figure out how to wrestle. . . . As the series progresses, *the female wrestlers become more confident* in using their bodies as part of their performance, ultimately triumphing in the ring and winning over fans with their physical prow-

ess rather than their looks. As Cherry says to her fellow wrestlers: "*We're empowered, we're the heroes.*"[52]

For others, such as Jenna Scherer of the magazine *Rolling Stone*, both these things, exploitation and emancipation, are at work at the same time:

> The world of women's wrestling—particularly in the GLOW era—is portrayed in the series as being *simultaneously exploitative and empowering*. The women in the ring walk the line between being scantily clad objects to gawk at and performers given an arena to express themselves in a brash, physical way.[53]

Finally, for Rachel Aroesti of the British newspaper the *Guardian*, the women's wrestling league *Gorgeous Ladies of Wrestling* only exploits the women who took part in it, without contributing whatsoever to their emancipation:

> Then there are the things that are neither funny nor taboo-busting: the exasperating hashtag-empowerment vibe of the very concept of women's wrestling (the idea that women doing anything at all = feminism) that is never examined. The fact that the show-within-a-show is masterminded by two men (Sylvia and guileless WASPish producer Bash). That the titillating girl-on-girl action is predicated on catfights—and not just staged ones: the real scrap between Ruth and her ex-best friend is folded into the narrative.[54]

Although for some feminist scholars exploitation cannot lead to emancipation and in fact maintains the same system that has always profited from women's bodies,[55] the interest of *GLOW*'s restorative nostalgia lies in the way it invests the past—the history of the production of the women's wrestling series *Gorgeous Ladies of Wrestling* of the 1980s—in order to place it in the service of the present, meaning to add to the debate in the public sphere around the dual phenomenon of women's exploitation and emancipation.

The nostalgia present in *GLOW*, however, is not solely restorative. In some respects this Netflix series is one of a number of nostalgia films of the melancholic kind which, we should recall, are most often imprecise and evasive with respect to the past. As Caetlin Benson-Allott quite rightly notes, the women who acted in the real *Gorgeous Ladies of Wrestling* series were amazingly diverse for the 1980s,[56] even more so than the series *GLOW*, something which resonates with the various movements today decrying the lack of diversity in television and cinema. *GLOW*, however, does not succeed in taking advantage of the potential of this precedent. Benson-Allott accounts for this lack of diversity by the narrative structure chosen by Flahive and Mensch to tell the story of *Gorgeous Ladies of Wrestling*:

> The heterogeneity of *Gorgeous Ladies of Wrestling* could have facilitated a percipient critique of racism and sexism in television, but *GLOW*'s

structure precludes such innovation. Writer-producers Liz Flahive and Carly Mensch repeat a narrative formula made infamous by their executive producer, Jenji Kohan, whereby white protagonists dominate a story populated by more interesting characters of color in supporting roles.[57]

The lack of diversity in the cast of *GLOW*, compared to that of the real cast of *Gorgeous Ladies of Wrestling*, is an element of this same melancholic nostalgia which presents us with highly romanticized images of a bygone era about which they supply little analysis and on which they provide little critical commentary. Even if the ethnic diversity in *GLOW* can be seen as a comment in and of itself on the whiteness of 1980s television (or in other words can be seen as restorative nostalgia), it is mostly exploited for "laughs" (or melancholic nostalgia), like when, in episode 7 (first season), two black wrestlers—Cherry "Junk Chain" Bang (played by Sydelle Noel) and Tammé "Welfare Queen" Dawson (played by Kia Stevens)—fight against two "members of the KKK."

While *GLOW* brings the debate around to the emancipation of women through debasement back into the public sphere through restorative nostalgia, the series makes little contribution, because of its melancholic nostalgia, to the movement demanding more diversity in popular culture. In *GLOW*, it is the confrontation of these two kinds of nostalgia in image form which renders the series a problematic cultural space. Nostalgia, by virtue of its chaotic and multiple nature, cannot convey a single vision of the world. That is why we must see Netflix's "nostalgia strategy" as offering a multitude of interpretations of the past, which it asks viewers to confront, test, and affirm or condemn. In the end, it is up to individuals to give meaning to the resources offered up by nostalgia, and this is precisely what makes nostalgia so multifaceted.

NOTES

1. Michael D. Dwyer, *Back to the Fifties: Nostalgia, Hollywood Film, and Popular Music of the Seventies and Eighties* (Oxford: Oxford University Press, 2015).

2. Ryan Lizardi, *Mediated Nostalgia: Individual Memory and Contemporary Mass Media* (Lanham, MD: Lexington Books, 2014), and Ryan Lizardi, *Nostalgic Generations and Media: Perception of Time and Available Meaning* (Lanham, MD: Lexington Books, 2017).

3. Gary Cross, *Consumed Nostalgia: Memory in the Age of Fast Capitalism* (New York: Columbia University Press, 2015).

4. Svetlana Boym, *The Future of Nostalgia* (New York: Basic Books, 2001).

5. Christine Sprengler, *Screening Nostalgia: Populuxe Props and Technicolor Aesthetics in Contemporary American Film* (New York, NY: Berghahn Books, 2009).

6. My hypotheses are indebted to the ideas of Marc Le Sueur and in particular to his concepts restorative nostalgia and melancholic nostalgia. See Marc Le Sueur, "Theory Number Five: Anatomy of Nostalgia Films: Heritage and Methods," *Journal of Popular Film* 6, no. 2 (1977): 188-89.

7. Throughout this article I will use the standard expression "nostalgia film" even though, in the present case, I also use it to apply to television series.

8. Le Sueur, "Theory Number Five," 187-97.

9. Fredric Jameson, "Postmodernism or the Cultural Logic of Late Capitalism," *New Left Review* no. 146 (1984): 53-92.

10. Sprengler, *Screening Nostalgia*.

11. Dwyer, *Back to the Fifties*.

12. Denis Simard sees early cinema as a "problematic institutional space." See Denis Simard, "De la nouveauté du cinéma des premiers temps," in *Le cinéma en histoire. Institutions cinématographiques, réception filmique et reconstitution historique*, ed. André Gaudreault, Germain Lacasse and Isabelle Raynauld (Quebec/Paris: Nota Bene/Méridiens Klincsieck, 1995), 29-56.

13. Le Sueur, "Theory Number Five," 187-97. Christine Sprengler makes brilliant use of these two concepts in her analysis of the series *Mad Men*, when she demonstrates how an appearance of authenticity is communicated to viewers through the use of iconic 1950s objects and how the series reinterprets the visual styles of this period. See Christine Sprengler, "Complicating Camelot: Surface Realism and Deliberate Archaism," in *Analyzing Mad Men: Critical Essays on the Television Series*, ed. Scott F. Stoddart (Jefferson, North Carolina and London: McFarland & Company, 2011), 234-52.

14. Fredric Jameson, *Postmodernism, or, the Cultural Logic of Late Capitalism* (London: Verso, 1991), 21. My emphasis.

15. Jameson, "Postmodernism or the Cultural Logic of Late Capitalism"; Fredric Jameson, "Postmodernism and Consumer Society," in *The Anti-Aesthetic. Essays on Postmodernist Culture*, ed. Hal Foster (Port Townsend: Bay Press, 1985), 111-25; and Fredric Jameson, *Postmodernism, or, the Cultural Logic of Late Capitalism* (London: Verso, 1991).

16. Jameson, "Postmodernism or the Cultural Logic of Late Capitalism," 66.

17. Michael Dempsey, "American Graffiti by George Lucas, Francis Ford Coppola and Gary Kurtz," *Film Quarterly* 27, no. 1 (1973): 58.

18. Pauline Kael, "The Current Cinema: Un-People," *The New Yorker* (29 October 1973): 153.

19. Jameson, "Postmodernism or the Cultural Logic of Late Capitalism," 67.

20. Jameson, "Postmodernism and Consumer Society," 117.

21. Linda Hutcheon, *The Politics of Postmodernism* (London and New York: Routledge, 1989).

22. Hutcheon, *The Politics of Postmodernism*, 113.

23. Vivian Sobchack, "Introduction: History Happens," in *The Persistence of History. Cinema, Television and the Modern Event*, ed. Vivian Sobchack (London and New York: Routledge, 1996), 1-16.

24. Le Sueur, "Theory Number Five," 187-97.

25. Dwyer, *Back to the Fifties*, 17.

26. For many feminists, postfeminism is best understood as a regressive perspective on society where social equality would have been supposedly already attained. It is thus also characterized by a declined support for feminism because it would be considered outdated or disliked due to negative stigma. In other words, postfeminist logic first appropriates feminism's achievements in order to disregard them since they would not be needed anymore. See Elaine J. Hall and Marnie Salupo Rodriguez, "The Myth of Postfeminism," *Gender and Society* 17, no. 6 (2003): 878-902, and Pamela Abbott, Melissa Tyler and Claire Wallace, *An Introduction to Sociology: Feminist Perspectives* (London and New York: Routledge, 2006), 51-55.

27. Kathleen Loock, ""Whatever Happened to Predictability?": *Fuller House*, (Post)Feminism, and the Revival of Family-Friendly Viewing," *Television and New Media* 19, no. 4 (2018): 375.

28. Le Sueur, "Theory Number Five," 187.

29. Ibid., 188.

30. Boym, *The Future of Nostalgia*, 41-48.

31. Ibid., 49-56.

32. Le Sueur, "Theory Number Five," 189.

33. Ibid.

34. Svetlana Boym argues pretty much the same thing when she defines restorative nostalgia as a desire to re-create what has been lost in order to bring it into the present, see Boym, *The Future of Nostalgia*, 140.

35. Michel de Certeau, *The Writing of History*, trans. Tom Conley (New York: Columbia University Press, 1988), 69-70.

36. Pierre Sorlin, "Promenade dans Rome," *Iris—Revue de théorie de l'image et du son* 2, no. 2 (1984): 7.

37. de Certeau, *The Writing of History*, 90.

38. Le Sueur, "Theory Number Five," 192.

39. Ibid., 188.

40. Ibid., 192.

41. Oriana Schwindt, "'Stranger Things' Tests Limits of Netflix's Nostalgia Strategy," *Variety* (July 25, 2016), https://variety.com/2016/tv/news/stranger-things-netflix-fuller-house-nostalgia-strategy-1201822075.

42. Lizardi, *Nostalgic Generations and Media*, 113.

43. Bethonie Butler, "Is Netflix doing nostalgia better than anyone else right now?" *The Washington Post* (November 22, 2016), https://www.washingtonpost.com/news/arts-and-entertainment/wp/2016/11/22/is-netflix-doing-nostalgia-better-than-anyone-else-right-now/?noredirect=on&utm_term=.c819e5528238.

44. Jenna Scherer, "Get in the Ring: How 'GLOW' Recreates the Golden Age of Lady-Wrestling TV," *Rolling Stones* (June 23, 2017), https://www.rollingstone.com/tv/features/how-glow-recreates-the-golden-age-of-lady-wrestling-tv-w489354.

45. On this topic, see in particular Dwyer, *Back to the Fifties*.

46. For more information on feminist movements in the United States in the 1980s, see in particular Bradford Martin, *The Other Eighties. A Secret History of America in the Age of Reagan* (New York: Hill and Wang, 2011), 145-70; and Mary Fainsod Katzenstein, "Feminism Within American Institutions: Unobtrusive Mobilization in the 1980s," *Signs* 16, no. 1 (1990): 27-52.

47. Jenna Scherer, "Get in the Ring: How 'GLOW' Recreates the Golden Age of Lady-Wrestling TV," *Rolling Stones* (June 23, 2017), https://www.rollingstone.com/tv/features/how-glow-recreates-the-golden-age-of-lady-wrestling-tv-w489354.

48. See Dan Balz, "Trump and women: The big disconnect in American politics," *The Washington Post* (July 7, 2018), https://www.washingtonpost.com/politics/trump-and-women-the-big-disconnect-in-american-politics/2018/07/07/9469bdca-8145-11e8-b9a5-7e1c013f8c33_story.html?noredirect=on&utm_term=.4647e6fa7ec6; and Sabrina Siddiqui, "How has Donald Trump's first year affected women?" *The Guardian* (January 18, 2018), https://www.theguardian.com/us-news/2018/jan/18/how-has-donald-trumps-first-year-affected-women.

49. See Rosalind Gill, "Postfeminist Media Culture: Elements of a Sensibility," *European Journal of Cultural Studies* 10, no. 2 (2007): 147-66; Diane Negra, *What a Girl Wants? Fantasizing the Reclamation of Self in Postfeminism* (London: Routledge, 2009); and Loock, "'Whatever Happened to Predictability?': *Fuller House*, (Post)Feminism, and the Revival of Family-Friendly Viewing."

50. Abbott, Tyler and Wallace, *An Introduction to Sociology: Feminist Perspectives*, 211.

51. Hank Stuever, "Netflix's 'GLOW' fits right in with today's feminist TV, but mostly it's just ready to rumble," *The Washington Post* (June 17, 2017), https://www.washingtonpost.com/entertainment/tv/netflixs-glow-fits-right-in-with-todays-feminist-tv-but-mostly-its-just-ready-to-rumble/2017/06/15/f704fed8-4ad0-11e7-bc1b-fddbd8359dee_story.html?utm_term=.fd4ed395bc4a. My emphasis.

52. Tom Phillips, "Britain's real female wrestler activists are better and badder than GLOW's could ever be," *The Independent* (July 12, 2017), https://www.independent.co.uk/arts-entertainment/tv/features/britains-real-female-wrestler-activists-are-better-and-badder-than-glows-could-ever-be-a7836791.html. My emphasis.

53. Jenna Scherer, "Get in the Ring: How 'GLOW' Recreates the Golden Age of Lady-Wrestling TV," *Rolling Stones* (June 23, 2017), https://www.rollingstone.com/tv/features/how-glow-recreates-the-golden-age-of-lady-wrestling-tv-w489354. My emphasis.

54. Rachel Aroesti, "Stop! You're hurting me! Why GLOW's wrestling women aren't just an offence to fashion," *The Guardian* (June 29, 2017),https://www.theguardian.com/tv-and-radio/2017/jun/29/glow-netflix-wrestling-women-arent-just-an-offence-to-fashion.

55. On this topic, see in particular Rikke Schubart, *Super Bitches and Action Babes: The female Hero in Popular Cinema, 1970-2006* (Jefferson, NC: McFarland & Company, Inc., 2007) and Susan J. Douglas, *The Rise of Enlightened Sexism* (New York: St. Martin's Griffin, 2010). The concept "enlightened sexism" defined by Douglas makes it possible to better understand the complex relations between emancipation and exploitation. For Douglas, enlightened sexism refers to the fact that the media promote the sexualisation and exploitation of women as a form of emancipation when in reality these things maintain the same system which has always profited from women's bodies. Enlightened sexism makes women complicit in their own objectification through the language of a certain kind of feminism, in that women are seen as emancipated by their sexuality and exploitation, thereby making objectification and exploitation acceptable.

56. Caetlin Benson-Allott, "No Such Thing Not Yet: Questioning Television's Female Gaze," *Film Quarterly* 71, no. 2 (2017): 68.

57. Ibid.

BIBLIOGRAPHY

Abbott, Pamela, Melissa Tyler and Claire Wallace. *An Introduction to Sociology: Feminist Perspectives*. London and New York: Routledge, 2006.

Aroesti, Rachel. "Stop! You're hurting me! Why GLOW's Wrestling Women Aren't just an Offence to Fashion." *The Guardian* (June 29, 2017), https://www.theguardian.com/tv-and-radio/2017/jun/29/glow-netflix-wrestling-women-arent-just-an-offence-to-fashion.

Balz, Dan. "Trump and Women: The Big Disconnect in American Politics." *The Washington Post* (July 7, 2018), https://www.washingtonpost.com/politics/trump-and-women-the-big-disconnect-in-american-politics/2018/07/07/9469bdca-8145-11e8-b9a5-7e1c013f8c33_story.html?noredirect=on&utm_term=.4647e6fa7ec6.

Benson-Allott, Caetlin. "No Such Thing Not Yet: Questioning Television's Female Gaze." *Film Quarterly* 71, no. 2 (2017): 65-71.

Boym, Svetlana. *The Future of Nostalgia*. New York: Basic Books, 2001.

Butler, Bethonie. "Is Netflix Doing Nostalgia Better Than Anyone Else Right Now?" *The Washington Post* (November 22, 2016), https://www.washingtonpost.com/news/arts-and-entertainment/wp/2016/11/22/is-netflix-doing-nostalgia-better-than-anyone-else-right-now/?noredirect=on&utm_term=.c819e5528238.

Cross, Gary. *Consumed Nostalgia: Memory in the Age of Fast Capitalism*. New York: Columbia University Press, 2015.

de Certeau, Michel. *The Writing of History*, trans. Tom Conley. New York: Columbia University Press, 1988.

Dempsey, Michael. "*American Graffiti* by George Lucas, Francis Ford Coppola and Gary Kurtz." *Film Quarterly* 27, no. 1 (1973): 58-60.

Douglas, Susan J. *The Rise of Enlightened Sexism*. New York: St. Martin's Griffin, 2010.

Dwyer, Michael D. *Back to the Fifties: Nostalgia, Hollywood Film, and Popular Music of the Seventies and Eighties*. Oxford: Oxford University Press, 2015.

Gill, Rosalind. "Postfeminist Media Culture: Elements of a Sensibility." *European Journal of Cultural Studies* 10, no. 2 (2007): 147-66.

Grossberg, Lawrence. *We Gotta Get Out of This Place: Popular Conservatism and Postmodern Culture*. New York: Routledge, 1992.

Hall, Elaine J., and Marnie Salupo Rodriguez. "The Myth of Postfeminism." *Gender and Society* 17, no. 6 (2003): 878-902.

Hutcheon, Linda. *The Politics of Postmodernism*. London and New York: Routledge, 1989.

Jameson, Fredric. "Postmodernism or the Cultural Logic of Late Capitalism." *New Left Review* no. 146 (1984): 53-92.

Jameson, Fredric. "Postmodernism and Consumer Society." In *The Anti-Aesthetic. Essays on Postmodernist Culture*, edited by Hal Foster, 111-25. Port Townsend: Bay Press, 1985.

Jameson, Fredric. *Postmodernism, or, the Cultural Logic of Late Capitalism*. London: Verso, 1991.

Kael, Pauline. "The Current Cinema: Un-People." *The New Yorker* (October 29, 1973): 153-59.

Katzenstein, Mary Fainsod, "Feminism within American Institutions: Unobtrusive Mobilization in the 1980s." *Signs* 16, no. 1 (1990): 27-52.

Le Sueur, Marc. "Theory Number Five: Anatomy of Nostalgia Films: Heritage and Methods." *Journal of Popular Film* 6, no. 2 (1977): 187-97.

Lizardi, Ryan. *Mediated Nostalgia: Individual Memory and Contemporary Mass Media*. Lanham, MD: Lexington Books, 2014.

Lizardi, Ryan. *Nostalgic Generations and Media: Perception of Time and Available Meaning*. Lanham, MD: Lexington Books, 2017.

Loock, Kathleen. "'Whatever Happened to Predictability?': *Fuller House*, (Post)Feminism, and the Revival of Family-Friendly Viewing." *Television and New Media* 19, no. 4 (2018): 361-78.

Martin, Bradford. *The Other Eighties: A Secret History of America in the Age of Reagan*. New York: Hill and Wang, 2011.

Negra, Diane. *What a Girl Wants? Fantasizing the Reclamation of Self in Postfeminism*. London: Routledge, 2009.

Phillips, Tom. "Britain's Real Female Wrestler Activists Are Better and Badder Than GLOW's Could Ever Be." *The Independent* (July 12, 2017), https://www.independent.co.uk/arts-entertainment/tv/features/britains-real-female-wrestler-activists-are-better-and-badder-than-glows-could-ever-be-a7836791.html.

Scherer, Jenna. "Get in the Ring: How 'GLOW' Recreates the Golden Age of Lady-Wrestling TV." *Rolling Stones* (June 23, 2017), https://www.rollingstone.com/tv/features/how-glow-recreates-the-golden-age-of-lady-wrestling-tv-w489354.

Schubart, Rikke. *Super Bitches and Action Babes: The Female Hero in Popular Cinema, 1970-2006*. Jefferson, NC: McFarland & Company, Inc., 2007.

Schwindt, Oriana. "'Stranger Things' Tests Limits of Netflix's Nostalgia Strategy." *Variety* (July 25, 2016), https://variety.com/2016/tv/news/stranger-things-netflix-fuller-house-nostalgia-strategy-1201822075.

Siddiqui, Sabrina. "How Has Donald Trump's First Year Affected Women?" *The Guardian* (January 18, 2018), https://www.theguardian.com/us-news/2018/jan/18/how-has-donald-trumps-first-year-affected-women.

Simard, Denis. "De la nouveauté du cinéma des premiers temps." In *Le cinéma en histoire. Institutions cinématographiques, réception filmique et reconstitution historique*, edited by André Gaudreault, Germain Lacasse and Isabelle Raynauld, 29-56. Quebec/Paris: Nota Bene/Méridiens Klincsieck, 1995.

Sobchack, Vivian. "Introduction: History Happens." In *The Persistence of History: Cinema, Television and the Modern Event*, edited by Vivian Sobchack, 1-16. London and New York: Routledge, 1996.

Sorlin, Pierre. "Promenade dans Rome." *Iris—Revue de théorie de l'image et du son* 2, no. 2 (1984): 5-16.

Sprengler, Christine. *Screening Nostalgia: Populuxe Props and Technicolor Aesthetics in Contemporary American Film*. New York, NY: Berghahn Books, 2009.

Sprengler, Christine. "Complicating Camelot: Surface Realism and Deliberate Archa-
    ism." In *Analyzing Mad Men: Critical Essays on the Television Series*, edited by Scott F.
    Stoddart, 234-52. Jefferson, North Carolina and London: McFarland & Company,
    2011.
Stuever, Hank. "Netflix's 'GLOW' Fits Right in with Today's Feminist TV, But Mostly
    It's Just Ready to Rumble." *The Washington Post* (June 17, 2017), https://www.
    washingtonpost.com/entertainment/tv/netflixs-glow-fits-right-in-with-todays-
    feminist-tv-but-mostly-its-just-ready-to-rumble/2017/06/15/f704fed8-4ad0-11e7-
    bc1b-fddbd8359dee_story.html?utm_term=.fd4ed395bc4a.

SIX

Shifting Nostalgic Boundaries

Archetypes and Queer Representation in Stranger Things, GLOW, *and* One Day at a Time

Heather Freeman

In the last few years, Netflix has found success with nostalgia-centered original content, from the wildly popular science-fiction series *Stranger Things* to 1980's women's-wrestling-centered *GLOW*, rebooted 1970s and 1980s sitcom *One Day at a Time*, and the 1990's-centric *Everything Sucks!* The success of *Stranger Things* in particular has been accompanied by a glut of critical think-pieces about collective American nostalgia for the 1980s. In this essay, I will look more closely at the ways nostalgia has been and is currently being theorized, focusing on regressive and progressive modes of nostalgic representation. I argue that the nostalgic model employed by *Stranger Things* and *GLOW* manifests in a troubling adherence to heteropatriarchal narrative paradigms. In both of these series, almost any hint of queer relationality is quickly overwritten with a heterosexual/romantic plotline. The internet has not failed to notice this lack; *The Advocate* even added both series to a "Shows we can't believe don't have queer characters" listicle.[1] (A brief note about terminology: for the purposes of this essay, "queer" encapsulates LGBTQIA+ as well as nonheteronormative modes of identity construction and relationality, following Annamarie Jagose's expansive insistence on "'the definitional indeterminacy' of queer.")[2] At the same time, many critics have pointed out the ways in which these nostalgia-driven series *do* play with 1980s stereotypes—namely, by rehabilitating their narcissistic "bad boy" characters into sympathizing, and therefore sympathetic, figures. These ex-

ceptions essentially prove the rule for this strain of boundary-driven contemporary nostalgia. Acceptable variation involves reinterpreting a paradigm by humanizing the arch-patriarchal "bad boys," rather than up-
ending that paradigm altogether by allowing nonheterosexual pairings to
drive plotlines.

The popularity of these series suggests that this limited, and limiting,
nostalgic model appeals to the widest audience. Series like *One Day at a
Time* and *Everything Sucks!*, though less successful, insist that more capacious alternatives do exist, though. Both of these shows incorporate queer
central characters and relationships into their nostalgia-driven narratives,
relying on a more galvanizing model of nostalgia that is fundamentally
inclusive, rather than excluding. The next section of this essay provides a
theoretical framework for my analysis of regressive and progressive nostalgia, after which I turn to an extended close analysis of queer representations (or the lack thereof) in the first two seasons of *Stranger Things,
GLOW, One Day at a Time,* and finally the single season of *Everything
Sucks!*

FORMS OF NOSTALGIA

Historically, nostalgia emerged as a pathologized concept,[3] but it has
been reformulated in the last few decades under a more explicitly ethical
framework. Fredric Jameson famously decried certain strains of nostalgic
media as present-ist and antihistorical,[4] while Svetlana Boym posited
two vastly different types of nostalgia, one progressive and one harmful.[5]
Much of this history informs my own exploration of Netflix programming's contemporary nostalgic turn, since these theories still inform the
way contemporary creators, critics, and audiences continue to deploy
and understand "nostalgia." At its core, nostalgia has perhaps been best
defined by Susan Stewart, in her book *On Longing,* "Nostalgia, like any
form of narrative, is always ideological: the past it seeks has never existed
except as narrative, and hence, always absent, that past continually
threatens to reproduce itself as felt lack."[6] Stewart's reminder that nostalgia is a "narrative" illustrates how and indeed why the concept has been
made into, by turns, the champion and whipping boy of so many theoretical models. "It" is actually plural, a compendium of possible stories.

This essay will focus on two major strands of nostalgia: a regressive,
solipsistic type in *Stranger Things* and *GLOW,* and a more capacious,
outwardly oriented type in *One Day at a Time* and *Everything Sucks!* The
former narrative insists on constraint and a past-oriented viewpoint,
what Emily Keightley and Michael Pickering call "retrotyping," in which,
"the past is rendered in such a way that the mnemonic imagination is
denied active presence, and connections to present and future are sty-
mied."[7] Media critics have long theorized this particular nostalgic im-

pulse, coding it by turns as necessary self-care, inevitable coping mechanism, or retrograde willful ignorance. In *Mediated Nostalgia*, Ryan Lizardi suggests that this form of nostalgia has become particularly problematic, arguing, "contemporary media nostalgia engenders a perpetual melancholic form of narcissistic nostalgia as opposed to a comparative, collective, or adaptive view of history."[8] In the last few years, the television industry itself has taken up this rhetoric, often with a positive spin: Hulu's vice president of content acquisition Lisa Holme likened "nostalgic programming" to "comfort food,"[9] comedian Kyle Mooney called it "a security blanket,"[10] and critic Myke Bartlett described it as a "panic room."[11] This consumer-soothing focus finds a parallel in the way creators of this nostalgia-driven content are often described. In "The Nostalgia Pendulum," Patrick Metzger argues of such creators, "[t]he art and culture of their childhood . . . helped them achieve comfort and clarity in their world, and so they make art that references that culture and may even exist wholly within that universe," resulting in a "feedback loop."[12] Once again, ideas of "comfort" and potential infantilization are at the forefront of how nostalgia gets discussed, and Metzger's notion of the "feedback loop" emphasizes the solipsistic potential of nostalgia-as-comfort. This particular narrative of nostalgia risks being fully *self*-reflexive, rather than *other*-oriented, complacent rather than galvanizing. Television critic Willa Paskin pinpoints this issue in *Stranger Things* in particular, calling its nostalgia "deeply solipsistic."[13] This creator-driven solipsism, which emerges postproduction as audience-centric comfort, is, I would argue, fundamentally at fault for the failure of imagination when it comes to queer or nonheteropatriarchal characters or pairings in regressive-nostalgia driven shows like *GLOW* and *Stranger Things*.

Capacious nostalgia focuses instead on the present and future. As Keightley and Pickering theorize, "Nostalgia is then not so much a search for ontological security in the past, but rather a means of taking one's bearings for the road ahead among the manifold uncertainties of the present."[14] Instead of the "ontological security" sought through regressive nostalgia, capacious nostalgia posits a radical "uncertaint[y]." Keightly and Pickering's argument begins to break down slightly, though, in its adherence to teleological narratives, as they conclude that, "Nostalgia informs the imaginative effort to connect who we were with who we are now, and reflect on the ways we have changed."[15] Not only does this formulation posit a progressive continuity of self from past through present, but it begs the question of who "we" is—and is not.

Unacknowledged assumptions about inclusion and exclusion form the bedrock of solipsistic nostalgia and result in the reproduction of heteropatriarchal boundaries in *Stranger Things* and *GLOW*. The queer-centric nostalgia of *One Day at a Time* and *Everything Sucks!*, perhaps unsurprisingly, questions these assumptions, resulting in an expansive narrative structure both within and around the series. Queer theories of nostalgia and time provide a crucial explanation for this difference, bringing into focus the difference between "traditional," heteronormative nostalgic narratives and "alternative" nostalgias created by/for/around those formerly excluded from such traditions. Whitney Monaghan summarizes the common ground of queer temporal theorists, stating that they "explore ways that dominant heterosexual ideology comes to shape our understandings of the temporality of social life. Such scholarship draws attention to the ways that heteronormative temporal logics valorise linear and progressive life narrative."[16] Drawing from Jack Halberstam's iconic *In a Queer Time and Place*, Nishant Shahani articulates one model of queer nostalgia, which is "not a restorative return to a fixed past. Instead, the ability to forge a space of belonging in the present is predicated on the affective force of the past. In moving backward, queer history becomes a valuable resource for the reparative process of assembling collective memory as the base materials for imagining a different future."[17] This argument echoes José Esteban Muñoz's insistence in *Cruising Utopia* that "[w]e must strive, in the face of the here and now's totalizing rendering of reality, to think and feel a *then and there* . . . we must dream and enact new and better pleasures, other ways of being in the world, and ultimately new worlds."[18] I would argue that both the rebooted *One Day at a Time* and *Everything Sucks!* employ this future-oriented nostalgic narrative, while more traditionally nostalgic and popular series like *Stranger Things* generally do not.

HETERONORMATIVE BOUNDARIES IN *STRANGER THINGS*

Stranger Things became a viral phenomenon within weeks of its Netflix debut in the summer of 2016, and online critical discourse immediately linked its popularity with its nostalgic content. Set in small-town Indiana in 1983, the series' first season focuses on four Dungeons & Dragons playing pre-teen friends, Will Byers, Mike Wheeler, Lucas Sinclair, and Dustin Henderson, and mysterious telekinetic child/government science experiment Eleven. From its opening title sequence on, the series is fully committed to reengaging the 1980s narrative archetypes popularized in the United States by Steven Spielberg and Stephen King: a small band of suburban children (including one exceptional girl) battle the supernatural and the government, which are somehow linked. In the first episode, Will gets transported into the supernatural "Upside Down" realm and must evade the monstrous Demogorgon within, and the rest of the season plays out predominantly in the "real" world, where his mother, brother, friends, and the local sheriff track him down while protecting Eleven, whose connections to the Upside Down are gradually revealed. Season 2 deals with the traumatic aftereffects Will and Eleven experience, and the gang must once again unite, albeit in more unexpected pairings, to save the town from the growing menace of the Upside Down.

Strikingly, though, the series' fantasy-tinged nostalgic play doesn't extend equally to all fields, or even to all characters. Notably, almost every suffering, abjected character is, at least initially, potentially queer, only to be killed off or forced into a heterosexual plotline by the second season. Cocreators Matt and Ross Duffer (notably white, cisgender, heterosexual men) can skillfully sketch a world where monsters kidnap and are thwarted by children, but they cannot seem to imagine a scenario in which those same children would want anything more, in the end, than a heterosexually appropriate dance partner for their middle school dance. Multiple characters and pairings bear out this aggressively hetero-patriarchal focus, though perhaps none more explicitly than the central lost child, Will Byers.

Will is introduced as the shyest of his four friends, an artistic and relatively quiet kid. He's not overtly coded as gay, but plenty of other characters speculate. When he disappears, local sheriff Hopper asks his mother if he could have temporarily run away, implying that this would be normal pre-teen behavior. Joyce Byers's whispered response to Hopper is that Lonny, her ex-husband, "used to say he was queer, called him a *fag*." Hopper quickly responds, "Is he?" to which Joyce understandably erupts, "*He's missing!*" [19] Obviously, as Joyce is insisting, Will's sexuality is not pertinent, and Hopper's curiosity is inappropriate, unprofessional, and borderline homophobic. And yet, it is Joyce herself who brings her ex-husband's slurs into the conversation, as if her son's lack of masculinity were proof of his vulnerability.

In a later episode, during a school assembly memorializing the presumed-dead Will, a horrific 1980s-style bully taunts, "What's there to be sad about anyway? Will's in fairyland now, right? Flying around with all the other little fairies, all happy and gay," at which point telekinetic Eleven causes him to urinate himself.[20] While this scene caused Daniel Reynolds in *The Advocate* to label Eleven a "queer avenging angel," and to applaud the series' handling of queerness and homophobia more generally,[21] I read these exchanges very differently. Obviously, the series adamantly punishes and/or villainizes overtly homophobic characters like this bully and Will's father Lonny, but it never acknowledges the idea that being gay could be acceptable, much less commendable. It's spoken about in accusatory whispers, or as the ultimate, inexcusable put-down, but never as a potentially neutral identifier. Throughout seasons 1 and 2 of the series, homophobia is unacceptable because homosexuality isn't really presented as an option, despite initial evidence to the contrary.

Since *Stranger Things* debuted, a vocal minority of fans and critics have speculated about Will's sexuality and the proto-queer nature of his friendship with Mike Wheeler, which emerges as a core force in the first season; and some fans have tried to claim Will's queerness as "canon."

Critic Beth Elderkin makes a case against this adoption, positing, "There's no reason to conform characters into expected roles, especially based on stereotypes. He's sensitive and people call him homophobic slurs, so the show should make him gay?"[22] Elderkin's argument does provide a useful potential corrective to my reading, emphasizing as it does the ways in which this series stretches the gender binary to support "sensitive" boys (and, through Eleven, fierce girls). Even if Will is not gay, or even queer, his effete qualities disrupt the association of masculinity with male heterosexuality, thereby challenging patriarchal norms even as heterosexual norms are preserved. The form of this challenge is telling: the Duffer brothers are willing to play with tropes of masculinity while maintaining the status quo in almost all other areas. And while stereotypes should not necessarily become narratively self-fulfilling prophecies, representation matters, and even Elderkin herself acknowledges that the series seems to want to have its cake and eat it too: "If the show wants to include so many negative slurs about the LGBT community, it seems rather cruel to not give them a voice or representation."[23] *Stranger Things* expends quite a lot of energy on this "cruelty," diminishing Will's potentially queer relationship with Mike Wheeler via the introduction, development, and simultaneous de-queering of Eleven.

Eleven first appears in *Stranger Things* via a slow-pan up, as a seemingly gender-neutral child with a shaved head, barefoot in the woods and wearing a torn hospital gown. The numeric name initially preserves this gender-neutral quality, though Eleven quickly encounters the trio of boys searching for their missing friend, and they soon shorten Eleven to "Elle." Newly synonymous with the French subjective feminine pronoun, "She" undergoes a quick schooling in gender norms and shame as the boys are embarrassed by her attempt to change clothing in front of them. Soon thereafter, she gets to experience that arch-patriarchal feminizing ritual, a makeover. Elle emerges literally reenvisioned by the three boys as a "pretty" girl in a blond wig and pink dress.[24] Eleven herself murmurs "pretty" at the transformation, and a few episodes later, upon losing her wig, she asks Mike, "Still pretty?" to which he eagerly responds, "Yeah!"[25] With this transition, the series has accomplished a series of heteropatriarchal deflections, eclipsing Mike's relationship to Will with his relationship to Eleven. Mike's relationship with Eleven is doubly stereotypical, as it also emerges *through* her heteronormative makeover from bald, gender-neutral child into idealized incarnation of white femininity. Throughout the first season, Eleven can be understood as "queer" in a number of overlapping ways: as gender neutral, as asexual, as a child, as a monstrously powerful creature, and/or as a fierce gender-nonconforming girl. Post-makeover, some of Elle's potentially queer identities remain accessible, but a viewer must read against type. Just as Will's potential gayness is overwritten or pushed aside in shameful, corrected whispers, Eleven's potential queerness is disguised and then effaced. Season 2 pursues this erasure even more aggressively through the introduction and failed development of new "tomboy" character Max, whose presence triggers a trite jealousy narrative that culminates, in the season's final scene, in the aggressively heterosexual Snow Ball.

Skater Maxine Mayfield, or Mad Max, was presumably introduced into the second season to act as a corrective to the perceived gender imbalance of season 1, particularly since Eleven was separated from the core quartet for much of the narrative. However, Max's character remains tellingly underdeveloped, and her budding relationship with the quartet of boys results in a love triangle with Dustin and Lucas, a friendship with Mike, and the jealous hatred of Eleven. Max's character, ostensibly a disruption of rigidly patriarchal gender binaries, actually serves as an engine that *over*-corrects any nonheteropatriarchal tendencies. By the final scene, Max pairs off with Lucas, Dustin becomes a baby-pickup-artist dancing with his friend's much-older sister Nancy, Eleven triumphantly reunites with Mike, and even newly exorcised Will gets a nameless female dance partner. Writing for *Buzzfeed*, Alison Willmore panned this scene as, "a blithely heteronormative happy ending that also came depressingly close to presenting romance as recompense for its characters' heroism."[26] Willmore's argument aptly focuses on the ways this "male-nerd-gets-the-girl-as-trophy" trope reflects "present-day cultural toxicity," but it also speaks to the near-erasure of nonheteronormative narrative options. The Snow Ball-as-season-finale emerges as a stark archetype of what queer theorist Jack Halberstam might call the "middle-class logic of reproductive temporality."[27] Viewers are left with, as Matt and Ross Duffer said in an interview, "these lovely boys," who are "dealing with a *girl*."[28]

This heteronormative erasure played out on a less intense narrative level, but a more intense fan-response level, in the first season with Mike Wheeler's older sister Nancy and her best friend Barb. Barb emerged as a huge fan favorite despite very little screen time, and her death sparked a Twitter hashtag #JusticeforBarb that resulted in a very in-depth season 2 plotline (which nonetheless managed to not include the character herself). For fans, Barb's reactions to best friend Nancy's new boyfriend Steve Harrington were coded as everything from "slut-shaming" and prudish to "every awkward queer girl in high school."[29] She jokingly asks Nancy, regarding her party-attire, "Is that a new bra?"[30] suggesting she's hardly prudish, though certainly judgmental of what critic Kat Rosenfield deemed Nancy's "douchebag boyfriend."[31] Many fans have coded Barb's relationship with Nancy as potentially lesbian or as an engagingly homosocial, arguably queer, alternative to a stereotypical high school romance plot. However, their relationship immediately takes a backseat to Nancy's relationship with Steve; and any potential queerness about the character, relationship, or narrative arc, is literally killed off with Barb's death at the beginning of episode three. Things get tied up neatly, and 1980's stereotypes prevail.

A notable exception to this paradigm, as briefly mentioned above, is the character of Steve Harrington. An 1980s-inflected "bad boy" arche-type, Steve is introduced as an aggressive bully and borderline-coercive boyfriend, a seeming center of arch-masculine heteropatriarchy, who undergoes a rapid narrative rehabilitation. By the second season, he transforms into a lovable, responsible babysitter-adventurer, who gets broken up with by Nancy and subsequently spends his time watching out for the younger children, later mentoring Dustin into a problematical-ly endearing young pick-up-artist. Many critics have pointed out the way his character arc plays with established 1980s types. Writing for *Vulture*, Kat Rosenfield states, "But where the Douchebag Boyfriend of yore was a one-note villain who mostly existed to make the hero look good by com-parison, *Stranger Things* makes something more of Steve, its teenage bad boy." She concludes, "And no matter how much you love the originals, it is kind of refreshing, at least this once, to see the popular bro with the power mullet turn out to be a decent guy after all."[32] Leaving aside whether or not Steve's behavior is, ultimately, "decent," the idea that this redemptive villain's arc is "refreshing" is troubling. *Buzzfeed*'s Alison Willmore aptly diagnoses the crux of Steve's problematic arc:

> The fact that [the actor who plays Steve] was promoted to series regu-lar in the second season after winning over fans in the first would seem to suggest that the Duffers have a better grasp on Steve's appeal than they ever did on Barb's. . . . And it's noticeable that he shifts in more significant ways than any of the other characters. . . . That Steve is the only figure who defies his preordained type speaks to how central types are to *Stranger Things*.[33]

In the end, Steve's character arc allows him to play first as a type, then against that type, and, in the end, to forge his own type altogether. His role hardly dismantles the idea of heteropatriarchal types, but it plays with and stretches those boundaries in a particularly aggressive, energiz-ing way, considering the bounded, overpoliced nature of so much of the series.

Ross Duffer links this back to the actor's skill, stating, "Joe was so good we started to fall in love with the idea that he has an arc himself,"[34] thus putting him in tandem with the quartet of "lovely boys" at the core of this series. Ironically, this response echoes his brother Matt's deflection in another interview, when asked to comment on fan outcry over the death of Barb, arguably a bigger favorite than Steve: "Shannon Purser who played Barb, we fell in love with her. . . . It was sad to lose her, but some people have to go."[35] In this instance, the Duffers' affective re-sponses of "love" failed to translate into imaginative potential or effort, and Purser's Barb, a character established in direct antagonism *to* Steve, remained limited to two-and-a-half episodes. The vastly diverging arcs of these two characters illustrates the link between nostalgic narratives, comfort, and solipsism; the Duffer brothers admit to finding the arch-heteronormative bad boy, and the man chosen to portray him, empathetic and intriguing enough to play with those norms, but "poor Barb," a potentially queer, antipatriarchal, antiheteronormative character, gets flattened by quick victimhood.

REGRESSIVE NOSTALGIA, TAKE TWO: *GLOW*

One could argue that *Stranger Things'* adherence to heteropatriarchal norms has more to do with its creators' worldview and blind spots and little, if anything, to do with any broader trends in nostalgic narrative convention, but an analysis of Netflix's other recent 1980s-set series *GLOW* would suggest otherwise. Aside from a peripheral lesbian pairing at the end of its second season, *GLOW*'s lack of queer representation, reliance on heteronormative paradigms, and advocacy of "bad boy" character complexity mimic those of its precursor series. *GLOW*, created by Liz Flahive and Carly Mensch, premiered in the summer of 2017 and provides a fictionalized spin on the behind-the-scenes development and production of the real 1980s women's wrestling series, the *Gorgeous Ladies of Wrestling*. The series centers around the large group of women cast in the show-within-a-show, who must learn to live and train together in a motel in Van Nuys. Each woman's character is tied to her newly developed wrestling persona, and many of these personas are racist, xenophobic, or otherwise problematic, as they were in the typically 1980s source material. The series' treatment of race and nationality merits an essay in itself, but it is worth noting that though the central characters are white, the secondary characters of color do get multiple plotlines in which they navigate their resistance to their stereotyped performative roles. The show's first season centers around struggling actress and protofeminist Ruth "Zoya the Destroya" Wilder, her best friend and successful soap opera star Debbie "Liberty Belle" Eagan (whose husband Ruth has slept with), and an even more interesting array of secondary characters, including the sweet but shy wrestling legacy Carmen "Macchu Pichu" Wade, the beyond-method Sheila the "She Wolf," and the British, sexually open Rhonda "Britannica" Richardson. The only central male characters are the washed-up middle-aged director Sam Silvia and young, rich trust-fund-financed producer Sebastian "Bash" Howard, whose fondness for white blazers with pushed up sleeves over T-shirts immediately telegraphs his 1980s playboy qualities. Reviewer Ben Yakas captures the predominant critical and fan response to the series, applauding its "complex female friendship[s]" as a "protofeminist text" that "deftly (and often hilariously) embraces, critiques, and challenges female stereotypes again and again through the personas of the wrestlers—all without fetishizing its actresses."[36] This characterization is generally apt, but it inadvertently draws attention to one of the most-commented-upon blind spots of the show's first season: its lack of "out" queer characters.[37] In response to fan outcry, the second season introduced out-and-proud lesbian Yolanda "Yoyo" Rivas, but her character is narratively sidelined for the majority of the season, and even her season-finale kiss with fellow wrestler Arthie "Beirut" Premkumar is overshadowed by the staged wedding of producer "Bash" Howard and "Britannica," a wedding that aggressively overwrites other potentially queer plotlines.

In the fourth episode of season 1, shortly after the women move into a seedy motel to begin more rigorous training, new roommates Carmen and Rhonda attempt to navigate their nighttime rituals, and *GLOW* seems to want to tease a queer romance while simultaneously undercutting it. The characters exchange the following dialogue, as Rhonda changes her shirt:

Rhonda: "Staring at my tits?"

Carmen: "I am, I'm sorry."

Rhonda: "It's OK, I don't care."

Carmen: "I just don't understand how they, um . . . stand up like that."

Rhonda: "Well, they like attention."

Carmen: "I've never lived with girls before so, I'll probably stare sometimes because you're basically just like an alien from another planet."[38]

This scene begins with a frankly stereotypical pornographic setup, albeit one framed less from a male gaze than from Carmen's female, shy, yet arguably lustful point of view. This female-centered reframing undermines the heteropatriarchal modes of viewership that usually dominate cinematic depictions of lesbian desire. However, this queer potential gets partially rerouted quickly via the dialogue; its matter-of-fact tone normalizes women living in intimate proximity to one another, and any remaining sexual tension is presumably undercut with Carmen's "alien" reference. After this exchange, though, the two women put lotion on together, and once again many of Carmen's facial expressions, framed in close-up, along with Rhonda's deeply embodied self-confidence, remind us of the sexual potential inherent in the scene. Arguably, even the choice to desexualize such a typically sexual scene is a departure from stereotypes, and thus it would seem to offer an intriguing alternative in terms of developing a homosocial paradigm of female friendship on-screen. However, even this nonsexual queer alternative is soon denied.

The scene quickly cuts, and the narrative never returns to this pair's budding relationship, sexual, or otherwise. By the end of this episode, both of these women are explicitly coded as heterosexual. Rhonda enters into a fraught sexual relationship with director Sam Sylvia, while Carmen enters into a charming, shy flirtation with producer "Bash" Howard, thereby preserving the heteronormative status quo. Carmen's plotline kills two birds with one stone, rehabilitating this show's "bad boy" Bash through his kindness, and overwriting her potential queerness with a schoolgirl-style crush on a sweeter model of 1980s archetypal masculinity.

Bash's arc partially mimics that of *Stranger Things*' Steve Harrington. He is, as critic LaToya Ferguson describes, "a giant, possibly coked up manchild. And a rich one at that," who suffers from "arrested development."[39] At the same time, the series invests a great deal of effort in rehabilitating his figure long before he can even achieve "douchebag" status, fashioning a hybrid figure who, as reviewer Eric Diaz diagnoses, "could fall easily into shitty, sexist cliches, and frankly . . . kind of [is] those stereotypes" but also "bring[s] a real humanity to [the] character."[40] Bash's relationship with Carmen serves as the core of his character's play against type in the first season, though the second season complicates things by hinting at his repressed "true" sexuality with the death of his butler Florian from what is clearly AIDS, followed by his grief-crazed, on-camera, green-card wedding to Rhonda, while Carmen looks heartbrokenly on. Bash's queerness keeps being teased even as its pushed to the side, in a way that perversely replicates the representational problems of season 1. He may be gay, but he must be closeted *and* repressed, denied even the hope of a nonheterosexual partner through the death of Florian. Once again, nostalgic norms can only be modified so far.

BREAKING BOUNDARIES: *ONE DAY AT A TIME* AND *EVERYTHING SUCKS!*

From 2016 to 2018, Netflix's programming also offered up more capacious models of "nostalgic" television. A temporal throwback of a different sort, *One Day at a Time* resurrects an older genre, the single-camera sitcom, while still hewing closely to contemporary progressive ideals of representation. The original sitcom, helmed by arch-progressive showrunner Norman Lear, ran from 1975 to 1984 and focused on a divorced mother raising two daughters, a premise that already belies contemporary rose-colored fantasies of the 1980s. The reboot retains Lear as executive producer and centers around a Latinx family consisting of a divorced veteran-turned-nurse mother, live-in grandmother, teen daughter, and preteen son. Notably, the original sitcom's creepy, overly flirtatious building superintendent Dwayne Schneider gets a contemporary make-over; the new "Schneider" is a trust-fund financed hipster whose initial flirtations quickly pivot into platonic empathy, at which point he becomes a fundamental part of the central family. This shift mimics the archetypal rich-bad-boy-made-good turn, but this series moves far beyond this basic twist, explicitly discussing and then dismantling notions of a heteropatriarchal paradigm.

The seemingly more traditional laugh-track-driven sitcom celebrates central teen character Elena Alvarez's lesbian identity from her coming out, to her acceptance by her mother and grandmother, through choosing a suit for her quinceañera, to getting a significant other—the genderqueer Syd—in the second season. Series writer Michelle Badillo speaks about how this centering of queerness was both internally and externally driven: "We did what we always do—pull from personal experience, and reach out to other people to educate ourselves on what we don't know. . . . I am a genderqueer person, and myself and other writers in the room have other nonbinary/GNC [gender-nonconforming] people in our circles we reached out to over the course of the season to keep us on track."[41] This practice explicitly breaks the solipsistic model of nostalgic creation, reaching outward while reaching back.[42]

The series continues to play with narrative paradigms of heterosexuality-as-default, with younger brother Alex "coming out" as heterosexual[43] and making meta jokes about how central his sister's identity is to the show: "Are you gay? I forgot, because you haven't mentioned it in the last five minutes."[44] Of course, the reboot is set contemporaneously, so one could argue that the writers and showrunners are not dealing with the same nostalgia-driven constraints as series set in the past. Critical reception would suggest otherwise, though, as many critics discuss the nostalgic factor of not only the series' source material but its format as well. Hank Stuever captures the duality of the series, writing, "It doesn't try to subvert or improve on the sitcom format; it simply exhibits faith that the sitcom genre can still work in a refreshing and relevant way . . . [i]t's much more than another nostalgia trip, yet it's worth noting how much of the original story has traveled the decades intact."[45] In other words, not only does this series belie the notion that nostalgia must be representationally limited in order to be effective, it makes the case that such limitations are hardly "true to period" themselves. After all, queerness and resistance to heteronormativity were obviously not invented in the last decade.

The buildup to the release of Netflix's mid-1990s-set *Everything Sucks!* was centered around nostalgia-for-nostalgia's sake, with a *Pop-Up-Video*-style teaser trailer full of jokes about how much technology has changed. The show itself quickly moved beyond this citational pleasure, though, creating a sweet alternative history in which protagonist boys discover that "nice guy" models of behavior are essentially toxic masculinity (and that they might not get the girl, and that that's OK), shy girls realize that they might be lesbians, and mean-girl bullies discover that they might be bisexual. The series centers on Black, heterosexual A/V geek Luke and white, lesbian A/V geek Kate, as they date, break-up, and reestablish their friendship while attempting to create a film with an assortment of their high school friends and enemies. The series is charming, and its brand of capacious, queer-centered, antipatriarchal nostalgia stands in marked contrast to the constrained variety employed by *Stranger Things* and *GLOW*. This expansive nostalgia, I would argue, begins to enact a version of queer theorist José Esteban Muñoz's idea of utopia, whereby "the past, or at least narratives of the past, enable utopian imaginings of another time and place that is not yet here but nonetheless functions as a doing for futurity, a conjuring of both future and past to critique presentness."[46] It is disappointing that such a synthetic, galvanizing mode of nostalgic television failed to gain popularity.

CONCLUSION: THE POPULARITY OF THE PANIC ROOM, OR, A UTOPIA DEFERRED

It speaks volumes that the two most popular 1980s-centered Netflix series, which content-wise have so little in common, share an affinity for heteronormative paradigms that can be bent only by archetypal representatives of such norms, but never fully broken. I have argued that these creator-inflicted constraints invoke a particular kind of regressive, bounded nostalgia that has long resonated with audiences, and the extreme popularity of *Stranger Things* shows that this resonance may only be getting stronger. This popularity, contrasted with the cancellation of *Everything Sucks!* and near-cancellation of *One Day at a Time,* arguably speaks to a contemporary complacency with reductive fantasies of the past, at least in the United States, or a perverse hesitation to, as Muñoz put it, "critique presentness." It also, of course, speaks to the demographics of those in power as creators and/or consumers: the majority is white and heterosexual and (with regard to creators) male. In the regressive, echo-chamber version of nostalgic representation, variation is only allowed within the double boundaries of what the "past" gets imagined as and what contemporary creators can relate to. In the process, collective nostalgias become defined by individual fantasies of the past, often regardless of marginalized or otherwise nondominant audience desires.

In essence, an adherence to some 1980s Reaganite fantasy of heteronormative patriarchy may result in a comfortingly secure "panic room" for some, to return to critic Myke Bartlett's striking metaphor, but that begs the question of who gets to access said panic room and what, or indeed, *who* the panic room keeps out. The answer, it seems, is most "others," defined broadly—and historically—by those already in the room. The stakes of this metaphorical isolationism remain high; as nostalgia theorist Svetlana Boym wrote in *The Future of Nostalgia* in 2001, "Fantasies of the past determined by needs of the present have a direct impact on realities of the future."[47] In other words, nostalgia is powerful. Popular nostalgic narratives not only rewrite our pasts, but they also dictate our futures. And as Netflix has become a narrative and cultural juggernaut, the relative popularity of its nostalgic series suggest that while there is room to hope, there may be more room to panic.

NOTES

1. Tracy E. Gilchrist, "13 Shows We Can't Believe Don't Have LGBT Characters," *The Advocate*, July 21, 2017, http://www.advocate.com/arts-entertainment/2017/7/21/13-shows-we-cant-believe-dont-have-queer-characters.

2. Annamarie Jagose, *Queer Theory: An Introduction* (New York: NYU Press, 1996), 1.

3. Svetlana Boym, *The Future of Nostalgia* (New York: Basic Books, 2001), xiv.

4. Frederic Jameson, *Postmodernism, or, The Cultural Logic of Late Capitalism* (London: Verso, 1991).

5. Boym, *Nostalgia*.

6. Susan Stewart, *On Longing: Narratives of the Miniature, the Gigantic, the Souvenir, the Collection* (Durham, NC: Duke UP, 1993), 23.

7. Emily Keightley and Michael Pickering, *The Mnemonic Imagination: Remembering as Creative Practice* (New York: Palgrave Macmillan, 2012), 11.

8. Ryan Lizardi, *Mediated Nostalgia: Individual Memory and Contemporary Mass Media* (Lanham, MD: Lexington Books, 2015), 7.

9. Qtd. in Meg James and Yvonne Villarreal, "Nostalgia TV makes a comeback. How Hulu and Netflix are breathing new life into old TV shows," *The Los Angeles Times*, August 20, 2017, http://www.latimes.com/business/hollywood/la-fi-ct-timeless-tv-streaming-20170820-story.html.

10. Qtd. in Alan Siegel, "The Year Nostalgia Took Over," *The Ringer*, December 20, 2017, http://www.theringer.com/pop-culture/2017/12/20/16797242/nostalgia-brigsby-bear-lady-bird-stranger-things-disaster-artist-the-room.

11. Myke Bartlett, "Rose-Coloured Rear View: *Stranger Things* and the Lure of a False Past," *Screen Education* 85 (June 2017): 22.

12. Patrick Metzger, "The Nostalgia Pendulum: A Rolling 30-Year Cycle of Pop Culture Trends," *The Patterning*, February 13, 2017, http://thepatterning.com/2017/02/13/the-nostalgia-pendulum-a-rolling-30-year-cycle-of-pop-culture-trends/.

13. Willa Paskin, "*Stranger Things*," *Slate*, July 12, 2016, http://www.slate.com/articles/arts/television/2016/07/stranger_things_a_spielberg_homage_by_the_duffer_brothers_on_netflix_reviewed.html.

14. Keightley and Pickering, *Mnemonic*, 137.

15. Keightley and Pickering, *Mnemonic*, 137.

16. Whitney Monaghan, *Queer Girls, Temporality, and Screen Media: Not "Just a Phase"* (New York: Palgrave Macmillan, 2016), 14.

17. Nishant Shahani, "'Between Light and Nowhere': The Queer Politics of Nostalgia," *The Journal of Popular Culture* 46, no. 6 (December 2013): 1227. [full article 1217-1230]

18. José Esteban Muñoz, *Cruising Utopia: The Then and There of Queer Futurity* (New York: NYU Press, 2009), 1.

19. Matt and Ross Duffer, *Stranger Things*, "The Vanishing of Will Byers," (season 1, episode 1), directed by Matt and Ross Duffer, July 15, 2016, Netflix.

20. Justin Dobie, *Stranger Things*, "The Body," (episode 4), directed by Shawn Levy, July 15, 2016, Netflix.

21. Daniel Reynolds, "Homophobia Is the Real Monster in *Stranger Things*," *The Advocate*, July 26, 2016, http://www.advocate.com/television/2016/7/26/homophobia-real-monster-stranger-things.

22. Beth Elderkin, "*Stranger Things* Actor Addresses Will's Sexual Orientation," *Gizmodo*, October 16, 2016, http://io9.gizmodo.com/stranger-things-actor-addresses-wills-sexual-orientatio-1787859710.

23. Elderkin, "*Stranger Things*."

24. Dobie, "The Body."

25. Justin Dobie, *Stranger Things*, "The Bathtub," (episode 7), directed by Matt and Ross Duffer, July 15, 2016, Netflix.

26. Alison Willmore, "*Stranger Things* Is Nostalgic for a Time Before Nerds Were Toxic," *Buzzfeed Reader*, November 9, 2017, http://www.buzzfeed.com/alisonwillmore/how-stranger-things-redeemed-and-then-ruined-the-nerd?utm_term=.yt8jJodgW#.itOGaKQ7o.

27. Jack Halberstam, *In a Queer Time and Place* (New York: NYU Press, 2005), 4.

28. Matt and Ross Duffer, interviewed by Alan Sepinwall, "*Stranger Things*' Creators Explain It All about Season 1," *Uproxx*, July 26, 2016, http://uproxx.com/sepinwall/stranger-things-creators-explain-it-all-about-season-1/.

29. Courtney Enlow, "What's the Appeal of Barb from *Stranger Things*?" *Pajiba*, September 1, 2016, http://www.pajiba.com/netflix_movies_and_tv/whats-the-appeal-of-barb-from-stranger-things-shes-every-awkward-queer-girl-in-high-school.php.

30. Matt and Ross Duffer, *Stranger Things*, "The Weirdo on Maple Street," (episode 2), directed by Matt and Ross Duffer, July 15, 2016, Netflix.

31. Kat Rosenfield, "How *Stranger Things* Subverts the 'Douchebag Boyfriend' '80s-Movie Trope," *Vulture*, July 21, 2016, http://www.vulture.com/2016/07/stranger-things-douchebag-boyfriend-trope.html.

32. Rosenfield, "Douchebag Boyfriend."

33. Willmore, "*Stranger Things*."

34. Matt and Ross Duffer, interviewed by Geoff Berkshire, "Stranger Things Finale: Duffer Brothers Talk Cliffhangers, Death and Season 2," *Variety*, July 18, 2016, http://variety.com/2016/tv/news/stranger-things-finale-duffer-brothers-interview-season-2-1201816664/.

35. Duffer, interviewed by Geoff Berkshire.

36. Ben Yakas, "Netflix's *GLOW* Explores Female Identity & '80s Nostalgia," *Laist.com*, June 23, 2017, http://laist.com/2017/06/23/glow_review.php.

37. Faith Choyce, "*GLOW* Does A Lot of Things Right, Just Not Queer Representation," *Autostraddle*, July 10, 2017, http://www.autostraddle.com/glow-does-a-lot-of-things-right-just-not-queer-representation-386252/.

38. Sascha Rothchild, *GLOW*, "The Dusty Spur," (episode 4), directed by Melanie Mayron, June 23, 2107, Netflix.

39. LaToya Ferguson, "The Less Glamorous Men of *GLOW* Take Things outside the Ring," *The AVClub*, June 25, 2017, http://tv.avclub.com/the-less-glamorous-men-of-glow-take-things-outside-the-1798191656.

40. Eric Diaz, "*GLOW* Celebrates Everything Wonderfully Tacky about the '80s," *Nerdist*, June 21, 2017, http://nerdist.com/glow-review-netflix-80s-alison-brie/.

41. Pilot Viruet, "*One Day at a Time* Has a Nuanced Nonbinary Character," *Into*, February 2, 2018, http://intomore.com/into/One-Day-At-A-Time-Has-a-Nuanced-Nonbinary-Character/ef5bab901f184a12.

42. It is also worth noting that the series' writing staff and showrunners include queer and heterosexual Latinx people, which further separates it from the vast majority of television series.

43. Debby Wolfe, *One Day at a Time*, "Exclusive," (episode 7), directed by Pamela Fryman, January 26, 2018, Netflix.

44. Becky Mann and Audra Sielaff, *One Day at a Time*, "Schooled," (episode 2) directed by Pamela Fryman, January 26, 2018, Netflix.
45. Hank Stuever, "In Netflix's Perfect Revival of *One Day at a Time*, There's Hope for the Future of Sitcoms," *The Chicago Tribune*, January 4, 2017, http://www.chicagotribune.com/entertainment/tv/ct-one-day-at-a-time-review-netflix-20170104-story.html.
46. Munoz, *Cruising Utopia*, 106.
47. Boym, *Nostalgia*, xvi.

BIBLIOGRAPHY

Bartlett, Myke. "Rose-Coloured Rear View: *Stranger Things* and the Lure of a False Past." *Screen Education* 85 (June 2017): 16–25.

Boym, Svetlana. *The Future of Nostalgia*. New York: Basic Books, 2001.

Calderon Kellet, Gloria, Mike Royce, and Norman Lear, creators. *One Day at a Time*. Netflix, 2017–2018. Digital.

Choyce, Faith. "*GLOW* Does a Lot of Things Right, Just Not Queer Representation." *Autostraddle*, July 10, 2017. http://www.autostraddle.com/glow-does-a-lot-of-things-right-just-not-queer-representation.

Diaz, Eric. "*GLOW* Celebrates Everything Wonderfully Tacky about the '80s." *Nerdist*, June 21, 2017. http://nerdist.com/glow-review-netflix-80s-alison-brie/.

Duffer, Matt and Ross, creators. *Stranger Things*. Netflix, 2016-2017. Digital.

Duffer, Matt and Ross. "*Stranger Things* Finale: Duffer Brothers Talk Cliffhangers, Death and Season 2." Interview by Geoff Berkshire. *Variety*, July 18, 2016. http://variety.com/2016/tv/news/stranger-things-finale-duffer-brothers-interview-season-2-1201816664/.

Duffer, Matt and Ross. "*Stranger Things*' Creators Explain It All about Season 1." Interview by Alan Sepinwall. *Uproxx*, July 26, 2016. http://uproxx.com/sepinwall/stranger-things-creators-explain-it-all-about-season-1/.

Elderkin, Beth. "*Stranger Things* Actor Addresses Will's Sexual Orientation." *Gizmodo*, October 16, 2016. http://io9.gizmodo.com/stranger-things-actor-addresses-wills-sexual-orientatio-1787859710.

Enlow, Courtney. "What's the appeal of Barb from *Stranger Things*?" *Pajiba*, September 1, 2016. http://www.pajiba.com/netflix_movies_and_tv/whats-the-appeal-of-barb-from-stranger-things-shes-every-awkward-queer-girl-in-high-school.php.

Ferguson, LaToya. "The Less Glamorous Men of *GLOW* Take Things Outside the Ring." *The AVClub*, June 25, 2017. http://tv.avclub.com/the-less-glamorous-men-of-glow-take-things-outside-the-1798191656.

Flahive, Liz, and Carly Mensch, creators. *GLOW*. Netflix, 2017. Digital.

Gilchrist, Tracy E. "13 Shows We Can't Believe Don't Have LGBT Characters." *The Advocate*, July 21, 2017. http://www.advocate.com/arts-entertainment/2017/7/21/13-shows-we-cant-believe-dont-have-queer-characters.

Halberstam, Jack. *In a Queer Time and Place*. New York: New York University Press, 2005.

Jagose, Annamarie. *Queer Theory: An Introduction*. New York: New York University Press, 1996.

James, Meg, and Yvonne Villarreal. "Nostalgia TV Makes a Comeback: How Hulu and Netflix Are Breathing New Life into Old TV Shows." *The Los Angeles Times*, August 20, 2017. http://www.latimes.com/business/hollywood/la-fi-ct-timeless-tv-streaming-20170820-story.html.

Jameson, Frederic. *Postmodernism, or, The Cultural Logic of Late Capitalism*. London: Verso, 1991.

Jones, Ben York, and Michal Mohan. *Everything Sucks!* Netflix, 2018. Digital.

Keightley, Emily, and Michael Pickering. *The Mnemonic Imagination: Remembering as Creative Practice*. New York: Palgrave Macmillan, 2012.

Lizardi, Ryan. *Mediated Nostalgia: Individual Memory and Contemporary Mass Media.* Lanham, MD: Lexington Books, 2015.

Metzger, Patrick. "The Nostalgia Pendulum: A Rolling 30-Year Cycle of Pop Culture Trends." *The Patterning*, February 13, 2017. http://thepatterning.com/2017/02/13/the-nostalgia-pendulum-a-rolling-30-year-cycle-of-pop-culture-trends/.

Monaghan, Whitney. *Queer Girls, Temporality, and Screen Media: Not "Just a Phase."* New York: Palgrave Macmillan, 2016.

Muñoz, José Esteban. *Cruising Utopia: The Then and There of Queer Futurity.* New York: New York University Press, 2009.

Paskin, Willa. "*Stranger Things.*" *Slate*, July 12, 2016. http://www.slate.com/articles/arts/television/2016/07/stranger_things_a_spielberg_homage_by_the_duffer_brothers_on_netflix_reviewed.html.

Reynolds, Daniel. "Homophobia Is the Real Monster in *Stranger Things.*" *The Advocate*, July 26, 2016. http://www.advocate.com/television/2016/7/26/homophobia-real-monster-stranger-things.

Rosenfield, Kat. "How *Stranger Things* Subverts the 'Douchebag Boyfriend' '80s-Movie Trope." *Vulture*, July 21, 2016. http://www.vulture.com/2016/07/stranger-things-douchebag-boyfriend-trope.html.

Shahani, Nishant. "'Between Light and Nowhere': The Queer Politics of Nostalgia." *The Journal of Popular Culture* 46, no. 6 (December 2013): 1217–1230.

Siegel, Alan. "The Year Nostalgia Took Over." *The Ringer*, December 20, 2017. http://www.theringer.com/pop-culture/2017/12/20/16797242/nostalgia-brigsby-bear-lady-bird-stranger-things-disaster-artist-the-room.

Stewart, Susan. *On Longing: Narratives of the Miniature, the Gigantic, the Souvenir, the Collection.* Durham, NC: Duke UP, 1993.

Stuever, Hank. "In Netflix's Perfect Revival of *One Day at a Time,* There's Hope for the Future of Sitcoms." *The Chicago Tribune*, January 4, 2017, http://www.chicagotribune.com/entertainment/tv/ct-one-day-at-a-time-review-netflix-20170104-story.html.

Viruet, Pilot. "*One Day at a Time* Has a Nuanced Nonbinary Character." *Into*, February 2, 2018. http://intomore.com/into/One-Day-At-A-Time-Has-a-Nuanced-Nonbinary-Character/ef5bab901f184a12.

Willmore, Alison "*Stranger Things* Is Nostalgic for a Time before Nerds Were Toxic." *Buzzfeed Reader*, November 9, 2017. http://www.buzzfeed.com/alisonwillmore/how-stranger-things-redeemed-and-then-ruined-the-nerd.

Yakas, Ben. "Netflix's *GLOW* Explores Female Identity & '80s Nostalgia." *Laist.com*, June 23, 2017. http://laist.com/2017/06/23/glow_review.php.

SEVEN

"Heaven Is a Place on Earth"

Digital Nostalgia, Queerness, and Collectivity in Black Mirror's *"San Junipero"*

Keshia Mcclantoc

In the unrelenting demands of digitally driven lives, nostalgia is a key player in cultivating a well of collective memories. Consumers embrace these memories, whether through the "Timehop" feature on Facebook or use of the popular #throwbackthursday or #flashbackfriday hashtags. Nostalgia through a digital lens is a collaboration of past and present, reminding consumers to both embrace and be wary of rapidly growing technology. As Simon Massey says, "digital nostalgia doesn't simply provide an escape from the demands of technology but actively augments and complements it."[1] Consumers embrace nostalgia because companies have the tools that allow them to consistently replicate and brand it. Nostalgia branding within the digital realm has become the norm, with Netflix taking full advantage of this strategy. With popular shows like *Stranger Things, GLOW,* and *Everything Sucks!* feeding the yearning of an unrelenting audience, Netflix has positioned itself as one of the digital giants actively marketing and branding nostalgia. Netflix's embrace of nostalgia is particularly potent when it becomes a reflective commentary, delivering a world where digital nostalgia becomes a literal heaven on earth. Such is the case in *Black Mirror* series 3, episode 4, "San Junipero," where those who embrace digital nostalgia are those who find the happy ending.

Black Mirror a British science fiction television series created by Charlie Brooker, is an anthology where each forty-five- to ninety-minute epi-

sode delivers a different story revolving around the unexpected consequences of technology. Though the show is not considered a "Netflix
original," Netflix's acquisition of the series brought it international interest and acclaim by making it available to a larger, nostalgia hungry audience.[2] *Black Mirror* is known for its dark and satirical undertones, warning the audience about the costs of losing themselves in technology rather
than embracing a technologically mediated world. Like the name of the
series suggests, the episodes attempt to very literally hold a mirror to the
audience and show the grave consequences possible when confronting
technology. The characters' encounters with technology usually leads
them to unhappy circumstances by the episode's end. "San Junipero,"
was the first to break that pattern, embracing technology, nostalgia, and a
happy ending. Brooker wanted the episode to be "a palate cleanser, a
reinvention that offered a different vision of what the show could do."[3]
The episode succeeds not just in creating a compelling emotional narrative but also in leveraging nostalgia in a way that breeds hope, rather
than fear, for the possibilities of future technology. It is the leveraging of
this nostalgia that makes the experience of watching "San Junipero" so
reflective, where both the characters and audience participate in nostalgia
therapy.

"San Junipero" is unique because it allows the audience to fulfill their
desire to consume nostalgia in a way that moves beyond the recreational
nostalgia of period narratives. Rather than being set in a certain era that
would nostalgically trigger the audience, the episode, like many *Black
Mirror* episodes, takes place in a near future. In the "San Junipero" universe, characters can participate in a simulation that places them in the
era of their choice. As the characters consume nostalgia, so does the audience, creating a reflective narrative where the layering of nostalgia is
saturated with both metacommentary and irony. By watching this episode, the audience enables a mirroring of one's self unlike the other *Black
Mirror* episodes. The mirror effect of the other episodes is usually
charged with technological warnings via aggrandized satires of current
technology. In "San Junipero," the technological warning comes from this
simulated nostalgia, as the characters actively participate in and consume
this technology. As the audience watches the characters consume nostalgia by simulation, they too are taking part of the simulation, consuming
nostalgia by watching the episode. In viewing "San Junipero," the audience holds up the mirror themselves, cultivating a reflective metacommentary that forces them to acknowledge their consumption of nostalgically driven media, as both the characters and audience can benefit from
nostalgia therapy. However, for most viewers, this mirroring experience
is thrilling, creating an emotionally charged episode that invites them to
take part in the narrative by embracing the nostalgia presented. Paired
alongside the dual consumption of nostalgia, the episode also uses the
irony of queer nostalgia. In a simulated 1987, the two female leads are

married, something which was not yet legal in real-life 1987. The digital nostalgia present in the characters' lives allows them to reinvent a version of the 1980s where queer love was approved of and celebrated. Both its use of nostalgia and use of queerness is what earned "San Junipero" its rapid popularity, proving itself worthy to a fast-paced audience waiting for its next nostalgic treat. By looking at the overlapping ideas of digital nostalgia, queerness, and collectivity in "San Junipero," this episode cultivates a cultural commentary that is simultaneously reflective and ironic. This commentary is potent, demonstrating consumer wants and needs, with consumption of this narrative literally creating a brief heaven on earth for the audience.

"San Junipero" opens to the neon lit streets of a small seaside town, aptly called San Junipero. With brightly colored clothes, arcade games, and lights, it is a visceral, nostalgic 1980s dream. The episode soon introduces shy Yorkie and sociable Kelly. The pair are instantly attracted to each other, but Yorkie turns down Kelly's advances, citing a fiancé. A week later, Yorkie seeks out Kelly and the two have sex. Afterward, Kelly reveals that she was previously married to a man but has always known that she was bisexual. When Yorkie cannot find Kelly the following week, she seemingly bounces between eras, going from the 1980s to the 1990s to the early 2000s. In each era, touches of music, lighting, costumes, and product placement indicate the time. When Yorkie finally finds Kelly in 2002, the episode shifts, revealing the technological underbelly of a seemingly nostalgic paradise.

Kelly and Yorkie are not young, and San Junipero is not a real place. Instead, it is a simulation where the minds of the elderly or ailing are uploaded on a weekly basis in five-hour slots, allowing them to consume nostalgia in the era of their choice as a form of immersive therapy. In this near-future reality, Kelly is a seventy-year-old cancer patient while Yorkie has been quadriplegic for forty years, after coming out to her parents and getting in a bad accident. Yorkie's fiancé is her nurse, Greg, who she plans on marrying so he can sign off on her to being euthanized and permanently uploaded into the simulation. Outside of San Junipero, Kelly visits and marries Yorkie instead. Later, the two celebrate in San Junipero, Yorkie now a permanent resident and Kelly still visiting on a five-hour weekly basis. They soon argue about this status, Kelly saying she would never pass over to San Junipero, because her husband and daughter, who both died years before, were not uploaded into the simulation. Kelly leaves Yorkie alone, but struggles as her cancer continues to spread. She changes her mind, joining Yorkie in San Junipero in the final moments of the episode. Belinda Carlisle's iconic "Heaven on Earth" plays while the pair drive happily into the sunset. In reality, their minds are uploaded into a server, surrounded by thousands of others.[4] The happy ending they are allowed is the ability to use technologies to sideline the actuality of death and stay within this nostalgic paradise forever.

Unlike traditional nostalgia, digital nostalgia is a form of nostalgia mediated by technology. This mediation of nostalgia via technology is a central theme of "San Junipero," as technology-driven nostalgia is a daily occurrence in the lives of these characters. In today's consumer-driven world, digital nostalgia is what leads to the most effective branding and marketing. As the audience's relationship to "San Junipero" is that of a consumer and Netflix's *Black Mirror* is the marketer and brander of nostalgia, consumption of this episode becomes the technological mediation that affords digital nostalgia. At its core, nostalgia can be defined as "sentimental imagining or evocation of a period of the past."[5] Nostalgia can be both individually lived and collectively unlived, as those who are sentimental for the past can either be yearning for a past specific to their experiences or imagining a past they had not lived through. Both politically and socially, the latter form of nostalgia is the one that holds more potential to be marketed and branded. Though nostalgia of a lived past can certainly be manipulated in the same way, the imagined nostalgia is a more influential tool in forging sentimental narratives like "San Junipero."

In Michael Cabon's "The True Meaning of Nostalgia," he says that "nostalgia is a valid, honorable, ancient human emotion."[6] Nostalgia seems to be an ache that all humans share, one that Cabon says is forged in "the consciousness of lost connection."[7] This loss of connection is what allows consumers to cultivate nostalgia as means of collectivity. Nostalgia of an unlived past does just this, by imagining a world of what-ifs and missed opportunities, of moments that feel lost because of what could have been. In short, nostalgia creates a sense of connection between the known and unknown, pulling either from lived or unlived memories, or both, to create a sense of collective sentimentality. The collective nature of nostalgia is one that says, "you are connected; you have placed a phone call directly into the past and heard the answering voice."[8] When technology becomes the answering voice at the end of this line, it becomes digital nostalgia, using technological mediation to enhance this sense of collectivity. In many ways, the irony of digital nostalgia comes from the use of technology itself. The digital world has become an ever-increasing well of information, meaning, and collectivity, yet it also cultivates a virtual void. When nostalgia is mediated through technology, it simultaneously creates the void as well as fills it, bringing imagined connection to the past and answering a sentimental call. To continue digitally driven lives, consumers not only want digital nostalgia but also need it to fill the void the technology invokes. Svetlana Byom's says that "A cinematic image of nostalgia is a double exposure, or a superimposition of two images—of home and abroad, of past and present, of dream and everyday life."[9] The irony of digital nostalgia is exactly its ability to be both the home and not home, lived and unlived, individual and collective, or pleasurable and painful. The digital nostalgia therapy of "San Junipero" is complex in this same way, but it is also a reality that does not seem so far-fetched. Technology is already mediating many of the ways in which people consume nostalgia. Embrace of digital nostalgia, and the juxtaposed positions it brings, seems not only preferable but also inevitable.

When companies like Netflix market and brand this nostalgia, digital nostalgia becomes a consumer-friendly product. Instead of consumers cultivating nostalgia, media now packages and delivers nostalgia via technology. In "How the Digital Age Turbo-Charged Nostalgia," Holly Baxter says that nostalgia "is no longer an internal emotion or a quiet yearning for what has passed. Instead, it is a deafening roar of collective online voices about how far we've come." [10] In particular, Netflix uses nostalgia branding to reach out to specific sets of audiences that they believe will bring higher subscriber numbers. Oriana Schwindt's *"Stranger Things* Tests Limits of Netflix's Nostalgia Strategy," discusses the way that company is now using popular shows to give audiences "a reanimated chunk of their childhood." [11] The demographic that Netflix aims for is the near-tokenized millennial generation, audience members between the ages of eighteen and thirty-four, who were born primarily throughout the 1980s and 1990s. Nearly all of Netflix's nostalgic canon takes place in the 1980s or 1990s, or are remakes of series originally released during that time period. [12] By marketing nostalgia to the generation defined by an influx of technology, Netflix posits itself as a prime practitioner of digital nostalgia. In "San Junipero," the audience is positioned, like Yorkie and Kelly, as consumers of nostalgia, creating a reflective metanarrative that makes the *Black Mirror* series live up to its name. "San Junipero" loads its episode with nostalgic triggers, most of which are present in the costumes, lighting, music, and product placement. These triggers are what pull the audience in, creating a sense of the imagined sentimental world, one of happy, consumable memories. When this world is revealed to be a simulated one, the veil over that world lifts. Here, the audience can be either disappointed that they were so easily manipulated into believing the world as is or thrilled by the potential of this technology, following suit with contradictory nature of nostalgia itself.

The most visceral part of the "San Junipero" lies in the way costumes and lighting are manipulated to create an ephemeral dream-like quality in the simulation, starkly contrasting the pale scenes of reality. At the start of the episode, Yorkie enters in a striped sweater, khaki shorts, and round glasses. The outfit is seemingly neutral, one that could fit into nearly any era. As soon as she walks into the club, however, the crowd is full of an over-the-top extravaganza of 1980s costumes. Big hair, shoulder pads, acid-wash denim, and polyester track suits all make the cut as the camera, acting as Yorkie's eyes, scans the crowd. Everything is bathed in smoke and neon lights, creating the illusion of a dream, one where seemingly happier times could be projected. Moments before entering the club, Yorkie spots Kelly, wearing a brightly bedazzled jacket and a corset.

When the two first speak moments later, Kelly compliments Yorkie's glasses and says of the crowd "People try so hard to look how they think they should look, they probably saw it in some movie."[13] Ironic, considering how Kelly seems deeply endowed in the stereotypical 1980s fashion herself. This comment is an important moment, serving as the audience's first subtle hint that this world is not natural, but constructed, just like the crowd constructed its fashion choices by mimicking movies. In Suzanne Lai's "Nostalgia, Sexuality, and Existere in *Black Mirror*'s 'San Junipero,'" she posits that "visual pleasure or seduction is the first step or prerequisite of nostalgia . . . the yearning and desire for the past rooted in our affection towards the way an era looks—the way it fulfils our aesthetic needs."[14] For the first half of "San Junipero," the episode does just this, pulling in the audience by aesthetically feeding into their version of an imagined 1987.

In the next scene, Yorkie preps for her next rendezvous with Kelly. She switches between different cassettes, trying on new and exciting outfits with each song. The first song to play is The Smiths, "Girlfriend in a Coma," an irony not lost when the audience later learns that Yorkie is quadriplegic. She then plays "Don't You (Forget about Me)," wearing a floral Molly Ringwald-esque frock. "Heart and Soul" by T'Pau plays next, then "Addicted to Love," by Robert Palmer, both memorable songs accompanying a highly stylized costume. Finally, Yorkie settles on a style similar to what she had worn the previous week, and "Wishing Well," by Terrance D'Arby plays as the scene switches to Kelly.[15] The scene lasts just over a minute, but it embodies the aesthetic needs of the audience, indulging them in a visually appealing 1980s montage by working with costumes. However, what is most significant about the scene is music, each costume accompanied by a significant song from the 1980s. Music, more than costume, becomes the nostalgic trigger in this scene, pulling not just on the visual aesthetics of audience need but also on their need to immerse as many senses as possible into this nostalgic vision.

Though psychology has long held smell as the sense most triggering of memories, hearing is significant too. In "Neural Nostalgia: Why Do We Love the Music We Heard as Teenagers," by Mark Stern, he says that "psychologists and neuroscientists have confirmed that . . . songs hold disproportionate power over our emotions."[16] The emotional connection to songs is prevalent in cultivating nostalgia because music stimulates a neurological trigger. As Stern explains, music connected to memory triggers your prefrontal cortex and releases dopamine and serotonin, the "neurochemicals that make us feel good."[17] In turn, musical nostalgia is neurologically triggering, literally feeding the listener happy thoughts and emotions in connection with the music. Though not all audience members were present during the release of the songs played during Yorkie's changing scene, many of the songs are frequently referenced in popular culture, thus contributing to the individual and collective nature of lived and unlived nostalgia. Stern says that "the nostalgia that accompanies our favorite songs isn't just a fleeting recollection of earlier times; it's a neurological wormhole that gives us a glimpse into the years when our brains leapt with joy." [18] By including musical triggers within the episode, in both this scene and more, "San Junipero," fills the audience with a nostalgic bliss. Again, this pulls the audience in as consumers of media, using the episode and its nostalgic triggers as its own form of simulation. This becomes even more prominent when the episode confronts the audience as consumers by placing reminiscent games, movie posters, and products throughout the episode.

Before entering the club, Yorkie passes a row of television sets, which advertise, "new for '87." This visual marker makes the audience aware of the era, using consumer products to nostalgically set the time frame. In the club, she goes to the arcade and plays Bubble Bobble. Someone approaches her and asks her if she wants to play Top Speed, which she kindly rejects. [19] Every moment in San Junipero is filled with these markers, ones that reinforce the era to the audience via consumer products. The games are particularly compelling because for just a few quarters, consumers can spend a few happy moments immersed in a nostalgically digital world, like Bubble Bobble or Top Speed. In the simulation, the characters do the same. When Yorkie jumps through eras, this nostalgic product placement continues. In 1980, the scene opens to an advertisement for a Chrysler Toyota and people in the arcade now play PAC-MAN. In 1996, more television sets are displayed, Yorkie walks under a poster for "Scream," and Alanis Morrisette plays in the background. In 2002, flat-screen televisions are advertised, and Yorkie finds Kelly playing Dance Dance Revolution. [20] Regardless of era, these markers function as nostalgic triggers, informing the audience of the era and reminding them nostalgia is that which they commercially consume. Though costumes and music work as markers of each era, these product placements become the most significant markers of the time because they are the nostalgic triggers that work as artifacts of consumer culture. Though Yorkie's time hopping is what first breaks the illusion of the San Junipero simulation for the viewers, it is the inclusion of all these eras that makes "San Junipero" such a visceral, nostalgic, and consumable episode.

This viewer consumption of "San Junipero" is only reinforced when the episode brings the audience back to the reality, the near future where both older and ailing versions of Kelly and Yorkie exist. This world pales in comparison to the bright, exciting world of the San Junipero simulation. It is bathed in dull light and pastel colors. Most of these scenes take place in Yorkie's hospital, where everything is sterile, and people move slowly and quietly. Only ominous, soft music plays in the background. When Kelly convinces Greg to secretly upload both her and Yorkie to the simulation for a few moments, the difference between the two settings in staggering. San Junipero is bright and warm, with slapping ocean waves and each of the women bathed in vibrant colors.[21] This scene only lasts a moment, returning the audience to reality quickly. For the consumers, this scene only works to ground them in the intoxicating nostalgia of San Junipero. The near future depicted here is one that seems desolate, while technology provides a nostalgic heaven. Rather than make them fear the implications of technology, "San Junipero," entices the audience with technology, showing the real world as the place to avoid and the simulation as the place to be.

Along with being saturated in color, music, costumes, and products that the audience is likely familiar with, "San Junipero" also leverages queer nostalgia. When Kelly visits Yorkie in the hospital, they are married in lieu of a marriage between Yorkie and Greg. Soon after, Kelly signs the paperwork that allows Yorkie to be uploaded to the simulator permanently. In her weekly San Junipero visit, Kelly appears in a wedding dress and the two celebrate their union.[22] The irony here is that in the real-world 1987, gay marriage was not yet legal. However, in the simulation of 1987, Yorkie and Kelly can be their queer, feminine, fully realized selves. Originally, Charlie Brooker conceptualized the episode around a heterosexual couple. However, realizing the potential within the simulation, he soon wrote a queer couple, saying "you can gift them that in this world. And it felt like a nice thing to do for the characters apart from anything else and it chimed with the theme of going back and exploring facets of things that you hadn't gotten to do at the time, really. Which is kind of what both of them were trying to do."[23] Their queerness is celebrated in San Junipero, because like so many other things that the simulation promises, it allows you to experience nostalgia therapy by doing what you had not done before. Just like the concept of imagined nostalgia allows the audience to sentimentally immerse themselves in what could have been, what can be for Yorkie and Kelly is a queer marriage in a simulated 1987. The queering of this simulated past serves the purpose of nostalgia by using both media and technology to idealize what would have otherwise been an unhappy ending for Yorkie and Kelly. There is a dissonance between the real 1987 that viewers have experienced through either lived of unlived nostalgia and this simulated, sentimental 1987. As such, despite celebrating the fictional union, the viewers know this happiness only comes from a reinvented past.

Gilad Padva's *Queer Nostalgia in Cinema and Pop Culture* explores the potential for queer nostalgia in reinventing the tragic past of LGBT+ individuals. Queer nostalgia is a branch of a nostalgia that "is not about appropriation of a given heteronormative nostalgia, but rather, it highlights the need for a joyful recall and therapeutic recollection of queer personal and communal experiences."[24] Queer nostalgia means to reconcile with the past that not only reinvents past narratives as queer, but also allows those narratives to subvert the norm, painting history as a place where queer individuals existed. For Yorkie, this use of queer nostalgia was particularly useful in her mental recovery. Outside of the simulation, Kelly and Greg talk candidly about how Yorkie became quadriplegic, with Greg saying, "One night, she's 21, comes out to her folks. They're a little uptight about it, you might say, tell her they don't want a gay daughter, it's not natural, and so forth. They fight, she gets in her car, runs it off the road, boom."[25] Greg also informs Kelly that Yorkie wishes to be euthanized, but her "big-time religious," parents are keeping her from this wish, hence, why he agreed to marry her. This is the moment that Kelly volunteers instead.[26] When Kelly insists that she marry Yorkie, no protest is made by Greg nor the surrounding characters. It seems the near future that they occupy is one where their marriage is legal, but the world is not yet free of homophobia. The fight that Yorkie has with her parents literally rips her youth and ability to move away from her; it is these same parents that refuse her access to a permanent solution. For Yorkie, the San Junipero simulation is a form of queer nostalgia because it allows her a world where she can walk, dance, speak, and love freely — affectively reinventing what was taken from her due to homophobia.

Yorkie's recovery via queer nostalgia allows the audience to use the San Junipero simulation as means to consume a queer narrative. In Tamara De Szegheo Lang's "The Demand to Progress: Critical Nostalgia in the LGBTQ Cultural Memory," he says, "For LGBTQ people who must find their own community, mass media becomes an important space of self-discovery and identity negotiation, even when these 'official memories' are not necessarily created by or for the marginalized communities whose histories they represent."[27] To Lang, official memories represent what is typically recorded in history, which usually pushes marginalized people into the background. In turn, they lack in a shared sense of history and rely on queer nostalgia and reinvention narratives provided by the media to find that history. Additionally, Lang adds that "while tragic memories of the past are repeated through channels like media and history projects, happy aspects of the past must be forgotten in order to maintain the image of the present as both satisfactory for and accepting of LGBTQ people."[28] As such, narratives about queer pasts tend to be painted only as moments of trauma, ignoring any potential for a happy queer past. Queer nostalgia subverts that because it allows queer people to recover from possible traumatic pasts but also invites opportunities for a shared history that was happy. In this way, the queer past can become part of official memories, bringing in the simultaneous narratives of trauma and happiness. For viewers, Yorkie's traumatic past being reinvented by the San Junipero simulation allowed this. This representation becomes another nostalgic trigger for an audience, especially for queer consumers, who can immerse themselves in Kelly and Yorkie's happy ending.

This form of queer nostalgia is important because it also tackles the wildly popular "bury your gays," trope, by simultaneously killing off the queer characters and allowing them to have a happy ending. According to J. E. Reich, "'burying your gays' refers to casually killing off LGBT characters, often as a sacrificial lamb to keep the plot rolling for their straight counterparts."[29] This trope has been around since the early 1990s and remains one of the biggest complaints about queer representation; media will deliver queer characters and then kill them off. Soon after Kelly marries Yorkie, she signs paperwork for her to be euthanized, killing off her physical quadriplegic self. After an argument about whether Kelly herself would permanently join Yorkie in San Junipero, the audience sees the elderly Kelly struggling with her cancer and finally saying "I guess I'm ready . . . for the rest of it."[30] As Reich says, "'San Junipero' undeniably kills its queer characters, but it also gives them a new lease on life where they can flirt, kiss, and have 'fucking awesome' sex."[31] "San Junipero" subverts the "bury your gays," trope because while it does bury its gays, it also allows them a happy ending. This happy ending is important, because it is only through queer nostalgia and the available means of technology that Kelly and Yorkie can live on and love each other. Technology affords them the ability to sideline the typical death that usually comes with "bury your gays," and live in a queer nostalgic heaven. The audience also takes this in, immersing themselves in a love story from the start, and celebrating the ending in which the two queer characters both die and have a happy ending. By doing so, it reinvents the official memories for the audience, allowing them to embrace a nostalgic 1980s where queer love would have been celebrated.

However, not all parts of this nostalgic heaven seem dreamy and idealistic. Despite the episode working as the "palette cleanser," that Brooker intended it to be, it does contain some of the thematic darker *Black Mirror* undertones. While their minds live on in a simulated afterlife, in reality, Kelly and Yorkie are dead by episode's end. They are not the only ones. At one point, in reference to the other townspeople in San Junipero, Yorkie asks Kelly "how many of them are dead, like what percentage" to which Kelly responds, "eighty, eighty-five."[32] As visitors, Kelly and Yorkie are the minority in San Junipero, with many of the other citizens being people who have already died. This scene is important in breaking the illusion of San Junipero, because while it seems populated with seemingly happy, alive people, it is primarily populated by the dead. The weight of this statement is made heavier when the pair fight later in the episode, with Kelly refusing "to spend eternity in this fucking graveyard you're so in love with."[33] Kelly is not necessarily saying something untrue, as San Junipero is a graveyard, one that only seems alive because it simulates an afterlife. When Kelly finally chooses to stay within the simulation, it does not feel like she is choosing death. Instead, she is choosing to take on the assured afterlife rather than an unsure one.

The more details the audience learns about San Junipero, the darker the undertones of the simulation become. By introducing the idea of the pain slider, a tool that allows the citizens in San Junipero to control how much pain they can or cannot feel, the simulation plays with the notion as nostalgia as simultaneous pain and pleasure. This heaven is a place where pain, like death, can be sidelined. In the same way, pleasure seems to be encouraged and embraced without any consequences. In one scene, Kelly smokes, an amusement that she can enjoy without the fear of a cancer; ironic since she herself is dying of cancer. At one point, on her search for Kelly, Yorkie goes to the Quagmire, a dark BDSM-like club whose only purpose seems to provide drugs, alcohol, and sex. Outside of these darker spaces of pleasure, San Junipero is portrayed as a place where there are no limits on fun. The background characters are always dancing, playing games, and laughing in an endless stream of life. Even beyond all the nostalgic triggers, San Junipero is an ideal world, one where pain and death can be sidelined, and the pleasure becomes endless.

As such, the reality within "San Junipero" is a pale comparison to the simulation, where pain seems to run in surplus. Those who use the system are only allowed to use it once a week on a five-hour time limit. Until they die, their taste of heaven is limited. This means that the near-future world of "San Junipero" is one where reality has the potential to become meaningless. Although Yorkie's euthanized death seems justified, due to her quadriplegic status, the episode implies many people within this universe seek the same without the same justifications. The darker implications in this episode holds up a mirror to the human desire for nostalgia, showing the audience a reality where technology allows a painless heaven, making the real world all but obsolete. In Matt Leggatt's *Cultural and Political Nostalgia in the Age of Terror*, he addresses this topic, saying "we have been for some time heading toward a future in which perfection is possible through the building of a new digital world."[34] In "San Junipero," the afterlife simulation is that perfected digital world. By promising what seems like an assured eternity through the uploading of the subconscious post-death, the technology in the episode of *Black Mirror* effectively eliminates the meaning of living a real life. Though most members of the audience perceived "San Junipero" as the first *Black Mirror* episode to have a happy ending, the technological implications of that ending work in the same way the rest of the series does, by holding a mirror to the audience and showing them the darker implications of their technological desires.

Overall, *Black Mirror's* "San Junipero," leverages nostalgia to show the audience a reflection of themselves. While Kelly and Yorkie consume nostalgia through the San Junipero simulation, the audience consumes nostalgic triggers throughout the episode. The episode shows the hope possible with technology, "the utopian potential of a nostaligized existence made possible through virtual reality technology."[35] At its core, San Junipero is a utopia where technology can reinvent narratives, death and pain can be sidelined, and consumers can happily immerse themselves in nostalgia. This nostalgic utopia holds the power to be both terrifying and subversive. However, the nostalgia in this episode also cultivates a sense of a collectively shared past, one that provides a hopeful message. With technologies like the San Junipero simulation, that shared past can become the heaven waiting for those who choose to be there. Although this has the potential to make reality meaningless, the human need to take part in a collective existence outweighs these darker implications. Despite these undertones, it is ultimately the audience's job to determine the way that they consume this form of digital nostalgia. Companies like Netflix will continue to leverage nostalgia in attempts to draw in an audience, but consumers are the ones who have the power to use and interpret that nostalgia. If the happy ending and rampant popularity of "San Junipero" proves anything, it is that consumers are choosing to look at digital nostalgia as a source of hope and means to find their own heaven on earth.

NOTES

1. Simon Massey, "Opinion: Embracing the Power of Digital Nostalgia," *Transform Magazine,* September 9, 2016, http://www.transformmagazine.net/articles/2016/opinion-embracing-the-power-of-digital-nostalgia/.

2. Emily Whitney, "'Black Mirror' Is the One Show You Need to Watch On Netflix over the Holidays," *Huffington Post,* December 14, 2014, https://www.huffingtonpost.com/2014/12/24/black-mirror-netflix_n_6348764.html.

3. Helen O'Hara, "The Story of San Junipero: Why Charlie Booker's Emmy-Winning Vision of Heaven Will Live Forever," *The Telegraph,* September 18, 2017, https://www.telegraph.co.uk/on-demand/2017/09/16/san-junipero-revisited-black-mirrors-heartbreaking-vision-heaven/.

4. "San Junipero." *Black Mirror,* series 3, episode 4, Netflix, 21 Oct. 2016. *Netflix.* https://www.netflix.com/watch/80104625?trackId=200257859.

5. "nostalgia, n." OED Online. Feb. 2018. *Oxford University Press.* http://www.oed.com/view/Entry/128472?redirectedFrom=nostalgia (accessed January 26, 2018).

6. Michael Cabon, "The True Meaning of Nostalgia," *New Yorker,* March 25, 2017, https://www.newyorker.com/books/page-turner/the-true-meaning-of-nostalgia.

7. Cabon, "True Meaning."

8. Cabon, "True Meaning."

9. Svetlana Boym, "Nostalgia," *Atlas of Transformation,* 2011, http://monumentto-transformation.org/atlas-of-transformation/html/n/nostalgia/nostalgia-svetlana-boym.html.

10. Holly Baxter, "How the Digital Age Turbocharged Nostalgia," *The Guardian,* October 30, 2013, https://www.theguardian.com/commentisfree/2013/oct/30/digital-age-nostalgia-online-generation.

11. Oriana Schwindt, *"Stranger Things* Tests Limits of Netflix Nostalgia Strategy," *Variety,* 25 July 2016, https://variety.com/2016/tv/news/stranger-things-netflix-fuller-house-nostalgia-strategy-1201822075/.

12. Schwindt, *"Stranger Things."*

13. "San Junipero."

14. Suzanne Lai, "Nostalgia, Sexuality, and Existere in *Black Mirror*'s 'San Junipero,'" *Buhk.me* (blog), *Wordpress,* November 2, 2016, https://buhk.me/2016/11/02/san-junipero/.

15. "San Junipero."
16. Mark Stern, "Neural Nostalgia: Why Do We Love the Music We Heard as Teenagers," *Slate,* August 12, 2014, http://www.slate.com/articles/health_and_science/science/2014/08/musical_nostalgia_the_psychology_and_neuroscience_for_song_preference_and.html.
17. Stern, "Neural Nostalgia."
18. Stern, "Neural Nostalgia."
19. "San Junipero."
20. "San Junipero."
21. "San Junipero."
22. "San Junipero."
23. Formo, "Black Mirror."
24. Gilad Padva, *Queer Nostalgia in Cinema and Pop Culture* (New York: Palgrave Macmillan, 2014), 230.
25. "San Junipero."
26. "San Junipero."
27. Lang, "The Demand to Progress: Critical Nostalgia in the LGBTQ Cultural Memory," *Journal of Lesbian Studies* 19, no. 2 (2015): 232.
28. Lang, "The Demand," 231.
29. J.E. Reich, "How *Black Mirror* Decided to Bury Its Gays," *Slate,* October 27, 2016, http://www.slate.com/blogs/outward/2016/10/27/black_mirror_upends_tv_s_bury_your_gays_trope.html.
30. "San Junipero."
31. Reich, "How *Black Mirror.*"
32. "San Junipero."
33. "San Junipero."
34. Matt Leggatt, *Cultural and Political Nostalgia in the Age of Terror: The Melancholic Sublime* (New York: Routledge, 2018), 82.
35. Leggatt, *Cultural and Political,* 104.

BIBLIOGRAPHY

Baxter, Holly. "How the Digital Age Turbocharged Nostalgia." *The Guardian,* October 30, 2013. https://www.theguardian.com/commentisfree/2013/oct/30/digital-age-nostalgia-online-generation.
Black Mirror. "San Junipero." Directed by Owen Harris. Written by Charlie Brooker. Netflix Streaming Services. October 21, 2016.
Boym, Svetlana. "Nostalgia," *Atlas of Transformation,* 2011, http://monumenttotransformation.org/atlas-of-transformation/html/n/nostalgia/nostalgia-svetlana-boym.html.
Cabon, Michael. "The True Meaning of Nostalgia." *New Yorker,* March 25, 2017. https://www.newyorker.com/books/page-turner/the-true-meaning-of-nostalgia.
Formo, Brian. "'Black Mirror': Charlie Brooker and Gugu Mbatha-Raw Talk 'San Junipero' in Our Spoiler Interview." *Collider,* October 27, 2016. http://collider.com/black-mirror-san-junipero-explained-netflix-interview/.
Lai, Suzanne. "Nostalgia, Sexuality, and Existere in *Black Mirror*'s 'San Junipero.'" *Buhk.me* (blog), *Wordpress,* November 2, 2016. https://buhk.me/2016/11/02/san-junipero/.
Lang, Tamara De Szeghee. "The Demand to Progress: Critical Nostalgia in LGBTQ Cultural Memory." *Journal of Lesbian Studies* 19, no. 2 (2015): 230-48. doi:10.1080/10894160.2015.970976.
Leggatt, Matthew. *Cultural and Political Nostalgia in the Age of Terror: The Melancholic Sublime.* New York; London: Routledge, 2018.
Massey, Simon. "Opinion: Embracing the Power of Digital Nostalgia." *Transform Magazine,* September 9, 2016. http://www.transformmagazine.net/articles/2016/opinion-embracing-the-power-of-digital-nostalgia/.

"nostalgia, n." OED Online. Feb 2018. *Oxford University Press.* http://www.oed.com/view/Entry/128472?redirectedFrom=nostalgia (accessed January 26, 2018).

O'Hara, Helen. "The Story of San Junipero: Why Charlie Booker's Emmy-Winning Vision of Heaven Will Live Forever." *The Telegraph,* September 18, 2017. https://www.telegraph.co.uk/on-demand/2017/09/16/san-junipero-revisited-black-mirrors-heartbreaking-vision-heaven/.

Padva, Gilad. *Queer Nostalgia in Cinema and Pop Culture.* Basingstoke (GB): Palgrave Macmillan., 2014.

Reich, J. E. "How *Black Mirror* Decided to Bury Its Gays." *Slate,* October 27, 2016. http://www.slate.com/blogs/outward/2016/10/27/black_mirror_upends_tv_s_bury_your_gays_trope.html.

Schwindt, Oriana. "*Stranger Things* Tests Limits of Netflix Nostalgia Strategy," *Variety,* 25 July 2016, https://variety.com/2016/tv/news/stranger-things-netflix-fuller-house-nostalgia-strategy-1201822075/.

Stern, Mark. "Neural Nostalgia: Why Do We Love the Music We Heard as Teenagers." *Slate,* August 12, 2014. http://www.slate.com/articles/health_and_science/science/2014/08/musical_nostalgia_the_psychology_and_neuroscience_for_song_preference_and.html.

Whitney, Emily. "'Black Mirror' Is the One Show You Need to Watch on Netflix over the Holidays." *Huffington Post,* December 14, 2014, https://www.huffingtonpost.com/2014/12/24/black-mirror-netflix_n_6348764.html.

EIGHT

After Jim Kelly

Hybrids of Hip Hop and Kung Fu as Nostalgia

Ande Davis

In the late 1960s and early 1970s, the kung fu film genre ascended in the US zeitgeist, developing a devoted following in theater audiences across the country. These new films imported from Hong Kong attracted interest because of how they integrated into the existing film canon, particularly in how they came to influence such genres as action and blaxploitation after their arrival. In the context of this anthology, the popularity of both the kung fu and blaxploitation genres among audiences of color would seem to be rife for nostalgia, a fertile ground Netflix cultivates to capitalize on the potential of the past. However, perusing the selections available through Netflix's US streaming catalog of "classics" include *The African Queen* (1951), *Cheers* (1982-1993), *White Christmas* (1954), *The Andy Griffith Show* (1960-1968) and others in this vein, with a distinct lack of classic kung fu and related blaxploitation films,[1] giving some weight to the question of *whose* nostalgia the company intends to capitalize on. Making available old movies and shows, however, is but one of the strategies that Netflix uses to engage viewers' nostalgic desires. As not merely a distributor of content but also a creator of original content, another strategy is through incorporating elements of popular genres from the past into new productions, a method they enlist by incorporating tropes, plots, and motifs from kung fu films into shows centering around Black characters and storylines, as in *The Get Down* (2016-2017) and *Luke Cage* (2016-).

Contemporary criticism of kung fu movies from the early 1970s notes that "the viewer of a 'Chop Suey Eastern' always knows who's the 'good guy' and who's the 'bad guy,'"[2] though the difference "is a matter of some contention."[3] Kung fu's presence in a space of interstitial morality was complicated by the amount violence of the films, since—as the name of the genre suggests—a significant portion of a film's running time was devoted to fighting, though as B. P. Flanigan argues, "this is not at all inconsistent when we admit that we are members of a society that uses force, often violent force, as the ultimate conflict resolver."[4] Among the stars in this popularity surge is the Chinese-American actor Bruce Lee, whose presence managed to subvert and shift representations of Asians on US movie screens, as he "reinvents the Asian masculine body and reinscribes it with political and cultural significance, making his films relevant as an expression of Asian American politics and culture."[5] Following Lee's rise, Black martial artist Jim Kelly appeared in his first major role as Williams in *Enter the Dragon*, Lee's final film before his premature death. Kelly would go on to star in several more kung fu movies, but his role as the politically conscious fighter in *Enter the Dragon* set the stage for Black entry into martial arts for years to come.

Even before Kelly's appearance on-screen, kung fu films had been popular among Black audiences. As part of a trend in the media industry of the seventies toward targeting low-budget, violent films—such as kung fu films and the related blaxploitation genre—toward "ethnic" audiences, it would be an altogether simplistic assumption to credit this popularity to the films' violence. Rather, as Fred Ho points out, "[o]bvious political 'readings' can be made of the 'nonwhite' Third World beating, defeating the 'white' First World as a statement of anti-imperialist and nationalist pride,"[6] and that these movies "offered for the first time a heroic world not populated by whites but by a Third World people,"[7] adding to the cross-cultural appeal that has persisted for decades.

As Amy Abugo Ongiri notes, this relationship "provides a telling moment of slippage and indeterminacy in which notions of the totalitarian nature of power and western notions of aesthetics, culture, and dominance are undone."[8] This slippage in the links between African Americans and kung fu films is one way in which the Black–White binary in US discussions can be subverted and destabilized by allowing us to "grapple with both how racial identity is constructed and how it can be reconstructed."[9] The long-standing and widely noted connections between African Americans and kung fu films has persisted despite "images of the 'Black-Korean conflict,' debates around affirmative action, and 'model minority' mythmaking" that situate "African Americans and Asian Americans as polar opposites ever doomed to conflict in America's racial ideological landscape."[10] The Black presence in kung fu films—and inversely, the presence of kung fu in African American media and communities—remains a distinct terrain upon which the US racialized constructs and hierarchies can be problematized and reexamined, presenting nostalgia as a potential progressive site for thinking about alternative futures.

As hip hop began developing in the mid-to-late 1970s shortly after the arrival of kung fu movies on US shores at the beginning of the decade, its DNA became infused with the aesthetic and political implications of Bruce Lee's movies. The cultural cachet accumulated by hip hop in its formative years made it an intriguing site for political messaging. However, as S. Craig Watkins notes, "Whatever social or political impact hop hop has had on young people has come primarily in the world of popular culture," and because of this, "they have not been able to directly engage or affect the institutions that impact young people's lives."[11] It is precisely this apparent political impotency that helps the link between kung fu and hip hop thrive. As a genre in which characters embody a search for justice and retribution outside of the institutions, norms, and hierarchies of a dominant subjugating society—often through violent means—kung fu provides a template within which hip hop might model its counter-hegemonic thrust. This appeal for political resonance is reinforced by numerous crossings of liminal cultural spaces between the worlds of hip hop and kung fu, stretching in all directions, acting as an embodiment of the hybridity present in Homi K. Bhabha's Third Space of enunciation.[12] Such a space allows for racialized subjectivities to escape the binary of the Black/White paradigm and displace sites of meaning outside of imperialist hierarchies, becoming a way for groups to "move away from always speaking to the dominant and rarely speaking to each other."[13] These crossings are important to an ethnofuturist mission that aims for a new means of understanding manufactured ideas of race and culture in an attempt at looking toward future society that resists the constructs of ubiquitous Whiteness.

The Netflix original series *The Get Down* and *Luke Cage* each provide some form of this cultural overlap that sees kung fu, hip hop, and blaxploitation influences coalesce into new products that provide alternate ways of approaching familiar ideas about race. Far from engaging in a process of appropriation, however, these shows participate in the effort of forging, as Anthony Sze-Fai Shiu asserts, "a pathway toward a future removed from racialist property rights but firmly grounded in a negotiation of racialized identity."[14] In doing so, the shows work within Netflix's tendency toward nostalgia in creating and marketing their content. These nostalgic directions proceed to draw in viewers because of how they prompt "behaviors that directly promote social connections,"[15] leading to a sense of community belonging with those who participate in viewing, while also playing to viewers' narcissism that prompts a greater sense of agency through validating their views of the past.[16]

In the case of *The Get Down* and *Luke Cage*, both shows find their roots in issues contemporary to their setting, such as in the emergence of hip hop among increasing poverty and ghettoization, or in the reclaiming of agency through Black Lives Matter and related movements, while they also use hip hop's focus on "learning, adaptation, innovation, and radical reinvention."[17] In this sense, hip hop provides the perfect framework, as the art form of DJing is innately nostalgic, relying on sampling from past tracks to remix and re-present memory. While being necessarily backward-looking, this act of remixing also acts to construct a new future by using these radical reinventions to shape meaning in an elastic present. The choice in each of these shows to overlap cultural influences, to engage in the long-standing relationship between African Americans and the kung fu genre, is more than an aesthetic choice. Both *The Get Down* and *Luke Cage* integrate kung fu and hip hop, though in vastly divergent ways, to suggest the "possibility of resistance even in the zero-sum moment of material resources,"[18] doing more than hint toward an Orientalized fascination. Instead, they engage in a dialogue on racialized identification in the United States by incorporating a nostalgic connection to kung fu films that taps into key historical periods of community and political agency, while also temporally displacing these concepts to make them useful ways of perceiving future communities.

Set in the Bronx in 1977 at the emergence of hip hop, the first half[19] of *The Get Down* draws liberally from the tropes of kung fu movies to rewrite the story of hip hop and its early practitioners. The premise of the show functions through two layers of historical nostalgia—the show's "present" is a concert in 1996 New York where rapper Mr. Books (the stage name of the show's main character Ezekiel Figuero) talks about growing up during hip hop's emergence in the late seventies. This construct enables viewers at different ages to engage with the show's content through nostalgia: both millennials who were in their formative years during the show's "present" as well as older generations who remember the seventies, in which most of *The Get Down*'s action takes place. Viewing the themes of the show through multiple historical prisms allows the political spaces and historical imperatives of the different periods to travel into the actual present of the viewer, giving the show its political thrust.

The act of viewing the narrative through the performance of rapping also helps connect with a sense of authenticity that is inherently necessary in hip hop. In the opening scenes of the show, for instance, Books raps, "got my name from the city / Where, the most dangerous city,"[20] calling on the performative authenticity noted by Lester K. Spence, who writes, "MCs take contemporary representations of poor urban neighborhoods in part devised and articulated by experts, politicians, and other artists and use them in their lyrics as marketing tools, becoming experts through the aesthetic choice of adopting first-person point of view and choosing the same type of urban subject matter."[21] In this rap, Books is not simply relaying representations of urban blight and entrenched poverty, but also presenting a knowledge of political situations in 1977 when he raps, "The president neglected us, him and six masterminds / Six powerful men put New York through some drastic times,"[22] in a manner that transcends mere authenticity signaling and—along with a montage of historical footage interspersed with scenes shot for the show—helps connect the viewer to the narrative via a nostalgia for the time. This opening also sets up the tone for the series, in which the stories of Black and Latinx characters are foregrounded, and in which White characters are placed in antagonistic roles of power—"The rich and selfish ones / Feed on the welfare ones,"[23] indicating the record executives, producers, politicians, bureaucrats appearing throughout the series—who act as gatekeepers to the loci of power the protagonists attempt to access. This situation replicates the societal imperative in which the interpolation of the kung fu film and its anticolonialist implications becomes a useful tool in relating the narrative.

The aesthetic of *The Get Down* plays on well-established themes and motifs of kung fu movies to reposition ideas surrounding the genre of hip hop, as well as the political and narrative situations of the show. Throughout the season, the show draws on these tropes to draw together the nostalgia of hip hop's early days and the nostalgia of kung fu films to redraft the founding of the musical genre as the discovery of an ancient, mystical tradition. From the start, the series uses historical figures such as Grandmaster Flash—who they reconfigure in the role akin to martial arts master—along with a fictional central cast, such as Flash's protégé Shaolin Fantastic. When we first see Shaolin, he runs and jumps through a detritus-filled alleyway before acrobatically scaling a fire escape to land at the feet of his master, Flash, all while a funky guitar-riff backed by Asian-inspired flutes reminiscent of kung fu and blaxploitation films plays in the background. In the intervening conversation, Flash refers to Shaolin as "grasshopper,"[24] while giving him a quest to prepare not in martial arts, but in the art of DJing. Shaolin himself is cast as the noble and mysterious warrior, emphasized at the end of the scene with him silhouetted by the rising sun, staring off into the distance before running off, the audience never once seeing the entirety of his face.[25] These motifs, presented early on in the series, give overt cues pointing toward the mutual influences of hip hop and kung fu.

Brushing up against an Orientalist impulse to create a magical and mystifying other, *The Get Down* stops just short of such indulgences. These motifs exist as a recognition of the long-standing relationships between the genres of kung fu and hip hop, particularly the impact of the former upon the latter—the "grandmaster" in Grandmaster Flash, after all, embodies the influence of kung fu on early practitioners, with the creation of "Shaolin" Fantastic as a continuation of that kung fu-inspired stage nomenclature. The training that Flash provides to Shaolin is tied heavily to the archetypes of kung fu films, with the experienced DJ providing the novice with only a crayon to figure out how to master his mixing technique.[26] The practice that Shaolin goes through to unlock the secret is as rigorous as any martial arts training depicted in kung fu movies. Young Books ties into the kung fu tropes, as well—as the biracial Black and Puerto Rican emcee chosen by Shaolin in his assigned quest for a "wordsmith," we see him as reluctant in taking up his craft when his teacher asks him to take credit for a poem he wrote. It is only when he sees the power of MCs at a hip hop show that he decides to seek the tutelage of Grandmaster Flash alongside Shaolin, running parallel to the reluctant fighter trope strung throughout kung fu films. These interpolations of the historical and the fictional in the series also call up the political lineage between Maoism and the Black Power movement.[27] Vijay Prashad argues that "links between Asia and Africa in the middle of the previous century came on the terrain of a sort of anticolonial solidarity,"[28] that affinities for cultural exchange between Black and Asian American communities stem from a shared oppression in the shadow of Western hegemony.

For there to be real, political ramifications to this linkage, there must be something beyond cursory winks at a shared oppression. There must be something larger at stake. For *The Get Down*, the nascent musical form must be wielded to undermine and speak around the (White) political powers. Ho points out that Bruce Lee made the conscious choice to show Whites being defeated by Asians in his movies,[29] a theme transposed in a scene from *The Get Down* where Books uses his linguistic skills as a weapon against the political establishment. Books, interning for a Bronx community leader, is asked to speak as a token minority youth at a rally for mayoral candidate Ed Koch, whose platform is heavily antigraffiti, an artform central to hip hop and Books's circle of friends. Throughout the scene, Koch refers to "vile, lawless graffiti animals," "graffiti thugs," "graffiti bums," and vowing that "graffiti will die under Ed Koch."[30] Whereas other martial arts characters such as the Samurai are "essentially middle-class and motivated by the common good, the kung fu hero's motives are always personal and familial,"[31] which is a motif that carries over to Books during his moment in the spotlight. Struggling internally, torn between his job and staying true to his MCing crew and the younger citizens of the Bronx, Books abandons his prepared statement and instead delivers a speech featuring graffiti messages from trains that routinely pass through the neighborhood. His message slips past the confused adults in the crowd but is easily recognized by the younger members of the audience sitting at the fringes. The action lives in the same space as hip hop itself, an art form dedicated to reaching young audiences. As Murray Forman contends, "the street has been a consistent site for emergent hip-hop practices" and "has had important implications for hip-hop throughout its evolution, providing a thread between contemporary practices and the formative practices upon which they are founded."[32]

Black politics have likewise consistently emerged in the streets in US history through uprisings, sit-ins, demonstrations, and marches, giving the "street authority" provided by hip hop a ready political connection. As a result, hip hop's and kung fu's shared ties to poorer, oppressed populations coalesce into a uniquely shared goal.

To this end, Books concludes his speech by saying, "The young people aren't the problem, we're the solution,"[33] hailing the intended audience for his speech among those youth on the margins of the crowd, in turn signaling to those in the home viewing audience. Those who were "the young people" in the seventies are now part of the establishment, forced to reckon with the solutions in which they may or may not have taken part. Younger viewers who are now "the youth" are encouraged through the bestowing of a disobedient, activist lineage—participation in Black Lives Matter or grassroots movements for stricter gun laws in response to school shootings are a continuation of the struggles implicated in the show. It becomes irrelevant that history shows Koch winning the mayoral race, as in *The Get Down*, Books's intended audience was receptive to the message; he points toward the future instead of remaining in the present, a strong indication of nostalgia's progressive potential in remaking the future. The series brushes aside Koch's temporary political hold to emphasize the importance of the minority youth communicating with each other and doing so past White powerholders. The defeat of the colonialist power is made public through *The Get Down* in a true-to-form kung fu film fashion. Before leaving the stage, Books admonishes that "the battle for the South Bronx has just begun,"[34] which in the moment contains a double meaning, referring to the hip hop battle that he is heading for as well as the political moment in which he has inserted his voice. In this way, kung fu merges with hip hop in *The Get Down* as a unifying counterhegemonic force that subverts and speaks past the dominance of a ubiquitous Whiteness to harness ethnofuturist potentials.

In *The Get Down*, the temporal setting is an inroad for nostalgia to do the work of bringing the past into a contemporary dialogical space. By not simply telling a story from the dawn of hip hop, but instead recasting that story as a kung fu narrative, the show manages to connect the political imperatives and racial dynamics of multiple time periods. For *Luke Cage*, the use of nostalgia functions quite differently. As a superhero show that fits into Marvel's Cinematic Universe, Cage works within parameters set by the various commercial and production interests that determine the boundaries for the show's existence. Still, showrunner Cheo Hodari Coker was given considerable freedom to create a show that draws upon the comic book character's past while connecting that past to a present political moment. In doing so, the nostalgia inherent in the series must do the heavy lifting of connecting viewers to a constructed past, while using a narrative rooted in the present. To accomplish this, it enlists ties to kung fu films.

For the character of Luke Cage, his existence in comics has long been tied to kung fu influences, as he began life in the seventies as a hero influenced by blaxploitation (a genre that is itself deeply rooted in kung fu movies) and was frequently partnered with Iron Fist, a hero inspired by the kung fu craze of the seventies. In creating the series for Netflix, these influences manifested through how the show creators built hip hop into the DNA of *Luke Cage*. Coker and other writers drew on the lyrics and imagery of rap and hip hop to develop both the look and tone of the show, which is set in Harlem, to complement the themes and motifs of a bulletproof Black man wearing a hoodie that incorporates a number of issues in the contemporary sphere. The result is creating a character "so culturally Black that [his] existence is more deeply embedded in Black culture than the pop culture canon."[35] The show stands out from other Marvel Netflix shows by promoting a vision of Black political consciousness, from confronting the use of racial slurs[36] to the inclusion of Black-authored texts in the hands of its characters.[37] Carried by these details in which "Cage's struggles don't feel like the struggles of superhero, but more specifically the struggles of a *Black* superhero,"[38] one where the "focus on Cage's indestructible skin, of course, evokes issues of race and the sociohistorical troubles African-Americans face in the U.S.,"[39] the setting of *Luke Cage* is more than simply another superhero show; it is steeped in the historical imperatives of US racial hierarchies, tied to history as much as the present.

In addition to infusions of Black literature, philosophy, and history—as well as a thorough hip hop influence—Coker and the show's writers also decided to embed *Luke Cage* with elements relating to the character's blaxploitation past from his comic book origins, with the cultural crossings between hip hop and kung fu acting as the space where nostalgia does the work of connecting contemporary and historical political immediacies. The first season's most obvious reference to kung fu comes during a flashback sequence showing Cage's previous life in prison:

Cage: You used to box?

Squabbles: I used to live on 42nd Street back in the day. *Five Deadly Venoms, Clan of the White Lotus, Five Fingers of Death.*

Cage: You think you can fight because you used to watch kung fu flicks?

Squabbles: I *know* I can fight because I owned that corner back when I sold dope. And any asshole who tried to take anything from me learned up close how I became Golden Gloves champ for seven years. Watched kung fu flicks when I wasn't on the corner.

Cage: What was your favorite movie?

Squabbles: Jet Li, the remake of *Chinese Connection*[40]—*Fist of Legend*, better than the original.

Cage: You choose Jet over Bruce?

Squabbles: [*Nods.*]

Cage: Nah, you can't oversee my training. [*Begins doing pushups.*]

Squabbles: I can have an opinion.

Cage: Just like assholes—everyone's got one.[41]

This scene, while not central to the overall development of plot or character is important as a tool for authentication and gatekeeping, validating the show's position in the kung fu-blaxploitation lineage by having Cage (cheekily) question his friend's qualifications based on his apparent poor choice in kung fu movies. The authenticating that happens here is essential to drawing connections between hip hop and kung fu, as "the desire to affirm authenticity and skill is a ubiquitous artistic quality in the 'rap game.' The criteria for authenticity, however, are dynamic."[42] The criteria being used in this scene are both personal fighting experience and kung fu knowledge and appreciation, with Cage testing Squabbles to see if he can be trusted. The history surrounding kung fu films and television shows are replete with the types of Orientalist mischaracterizations that "declare an independence from the real" while it also "co-opts or colonizes the real,"[43]—examples ranging from the classic *Kung Fu* television series to Marvel's recent *Iron Fist* series on Netflix help illustrate this trend—leading to a great deal of mistrust around inauthenticity. This dual reliance on authenticity is critical in ensuring that the nostalgia inherent in *Luke Cage* is able to perform its necessary functions.

More subtle, yet more prevalent throughout the series, is the way in which *Luke Cage* adapts various tropes from the kung fu genre by recontextualizing them. Notable is the show's use of the calm older figure of Pop to help encourage and guide the young combatant:

Pop: You should be out there helping people, that's all, like them other fellas downtown. [Referring here to the Avengers from their eponymous movies.]

Cage: Reva [Cage's deceased wife] used to say the same thing.

Pop: Yeah, well, she was right. You don't ever think about all the people you could help? You should be more ambitious.

Cage: What if my ambition is to sweep hair, wash dishes, and be left the hell alone?

Pop: Well that would be a waste.

Cage: You think I asked for any of this? I was framed, beaten, and put in some tank like an exotic fish. Came out with . . . abilities.

Pop: Saved your life.

Cage: More like ruined it. Reva's dead. I'm a fugitive.

Pop: So, take my advice, brother. The past is the past. The only direction that matters in life is forward, never backwards.[44]

Not only is Pop trying here to lead Cage down a path of social justice— mirroring the master archetype fulfilled by Grandmaster Flash in *The Get Down*, much as Cage mirrors Books's reluctant warrior—but also the folk sayings Pop brings in toward the end of the scene act as a reconfiguration of the spiritual guidance provided by such masters in typical kung fu movie tropes. *Luke Cage* links its hip hop aesthetic to kung fu much more subtly than does *The Get Down*, but the connections it does provide between cultural influences engages viewers' nostalgia by linking a present community crisis to a remembered past of solidarity and (fictionalized, stylized) action against wrongdoing.

The differences between *The Get Down* and *Luke Cage* extend to how each of these shows subvert racial hierarchies by relocating the dialog on race and political agency out from under a Eurocentric context. While *The Get Down* does this by having its characters talk past White seats of power and those complicit with them, *Luke Cage* contains almost no White characters among its cast. Instead, the antagonists in power are Black villains, who play a dual role in the creation of the show's Black aesthetic. On the one hand, the antagonists of the early part of the season, Cottonmouth Stokes and Mariah Dillard, project a belief "that even dirty money should be used to rebuild Harlem for the people,"[45] while on the other hand these characters "function as sites of infection, as they each act in the manner of antigens, vying to take over the 'body politic' of Harlem,"[46] standing in contrast to the bulletproof skin of Cage, an embodiment of "the innate immune system, of which our skin serves as one of its integral defense mechanisms, flushing, trapping, and shedding away infections agents."[47] The threats in *Luke Cage* come from within Harlem, as do the solutions.

In both shows, through the different ways they recontextualize kung fu tropes, remix them in a hip hop context, and resituate them in an unflinchingly Black worldview, we are provided with useful examples for the potential redefinition of racial structures and given a way of envisioning a future outside of a homogenous, assimilationist society where the concept of "postrace" assumes default Whiteness. These crossings rely on nostalgia to do the heavy lifting of drawing on an idealized past in which community solidarity led to political action toward social justice, a time that aligns with the rise of both hip hop and kung fu cinema.

The nostalgia strengthens its urgency in the aftermath of the 2016 election, where a rise in White supremacist activity and reported hate crimes leaves many searching for a community response. Psychological studies suggest evidence that "when people feel alone, they may desire to mentally time travel to a point in which they had relationship success[48];" in the case of these shows, that relationship is a sense of community action toward justice and growth. The distinct time period these two shows are referencing, shortly after the end of the Civil Rights era and the death of Martin Luther King, Jr., offers a distinct rallying call toward political action through hip hop.

It is no coincidence, after all, that *The Get Down* uses the figure of Grandmaster Flash as its hip hop sifu—he and the Furious Five would go on to release "The Message," a song which "indicated that a place for socially conscious rap music also existed in the marketplace"[49] and propelled hip hop from parties to the political arena for the first time. The famous hook from that song contains the lines "It's like a jungle sometimes / It makes me wonder how I keep from going under." It's this spirit that the nostalgia of *The Get Down* and *Luke Cage* are attempting to tap into by combining the use of hip hop and kung fu, reaching into the past to quite literally interact with "The Message." In doing so, they shift their view from the past to the future for the purpose of providing moments of slippage in racial binary hierarchies, making a dialogical space to configure alternatives for thinking about the world in terms of possibilities of cultural identification rather than its burdens.

NOTES

1. As of the time of writing, the only classic kung fu movie available to stream on Netflix is the early Jackie Chan film *Young Tiger* (1973), though a broad selection of more modern kung fu films are available; these differ considerably in aesthetic, tone, and budget from those that originally arrived in the United States in the seventies.

2. B. P. Flanigan, "Kung Fu Krazy: or The Invasion of the 'Chop Suey Easterns,'" *Cinéaste* 6, no. 3 (1974): 10. The phrase "Chop Suey Eastern" is an obvious (dated, Orientalized) play on "Spaghetti Western," emphasizing the role kung fu films played in relation to Westerns, a nostalgic link, as both a point of convergence and divergence in US film genre studies.

3. Flanigan, "Kung Fu Krazy," 10.

4. Flanigan, "Kung Fu Krazy," 10. The use of violence as conflict resolution is yet another point of similarity between kung fu movies and Westerns.

5. Yuan Shu, "Reading the Kung Fu Film in an American Context: From Bruce Lee to Jackie Chan," *Journal of Popular Film and Television* 31, no. 2 (2003): 53.

6. Fred Ho, "Kickin' the White Man's Ass: Black Power, Aesthetics, and the Asian Martial Arts," in *AfroAsian Encounters: Culture, History, Politics*, edited by Heike Raphael-Hernandez and Shannon Steen (New York: New York University Press, 2006), 297.

7. Ho, "Kickin' the White Man's Ass," 298. The labels of "first world" and "third world" are Ho's and will not be used by the author of this chapter outside of quotation.

8. Amy Abugo Ongiri, "'He Wanted to Be Just Like Bruce Lee': African Americans, Kung Fu Theater and Cultural Exchange at the Margins," *Journal of Asian American Studies* 5, no. 1 (2002): 39.

9. Janine Young Kim, "Are Asians Black?: The Asian American Civil Rights Agenda and the Contemporary Significance of the Black/White Paradigm," in *Blacks and Asians: Crossings, Conflict, and Commonality*, edited by Hazel M. McFerson (Durham: Carolina Academic Press, 2006), 190.

10. Ongiri, "He Wanted to Be Just Like Bruce Lee," 31.

11. S. Craig Watkins, *Hip Hop Matters: Politics, Pop Culture, and the Struggle for the Soul of a Movement* (Boston: Beacon Press, 2005), 149.

12. Homi K. Bhabha, *The Location of Culture* (London: Routledge, 1994), 36-39.

13. Elaine H. Kim, "At Least You're Not Black: Asian Americans in U.S. Race Relations," in *Blacks and Asians: Crossings, Conflict, and Commonality*, edited by Hazel M. McFerson (Durham: Carolina Academic Press, 2006), 206.

14. Anthony Sze-Fai Shiu, "Styl(us): Asian North America, Turntablism, Relation," *CR: The New Centennial Review* 7, no. 1 (2007): 88.

15. Clay Routledge, *Nostalgia: A Psychological Resource* (New York: Routledge, 2016) 68.

16. Routledge, *Nostalgia*, 106.

17. Murray Forman, "No Sleep 'Til Brooklyn," *American Quarterly* 54, no. 1 (2002): 126.

18. Ongiri, "He Wanted to Be Just Like Bruce Lee," 39.

19. This chapter will mainly focus on part I of the first (and only) season, the first six episodes, as these contain the strongest connection to a kung fu narrative, while the second half more draws more on drug dealing and gangs.

20. *The Get Down*, "Where There Is Ruin, There Is Hope for Treasure," Netflix, August 12, 2016, written by Baz Luhrmann, Stephen Adly Guirgis, and Seth Zvi Rosenfeld, directed by Baz Luhrmann.

21. Lester K. Spence, *Stare in the Darkness: The Limits of Hip-Hop and Black Politics* (Minneapolis: University of Minnesota Press, 2011), 28.

22. *The Get Down*, "Where There Is Ruin."

23. *The Get Down*, "Where There Is Ruin."

24. This term is borrowed from the seventies US television series *Kung Fu* starring David Carradine. The series is problematic as "a hegemonic moment in which the American popular imaginary once again re-created its Asian spiritual 'other'" and "allowed an unmitigated Orientalist portrayal of Eastern philosophy, as well as of the behavior of its Eastern characters." Jane Naomi Iwamura, *Virtual Orientalism: Asian Religions and American Popular Culture* (Oxford: Oxford University Press, 2011), 115.

25. *The Get Down*, "Where There Is Ruin."

26. *The Get Down*, "Seek Those Who Fan Your Flames," Netflix, August 12, 2016, written by Sam Bromell, Sinead Daly, and Jacqui Rivera, directed by Ed Bianchi.

27. Vijay Prashad, *Everybody Was Kung Fu Fighting: Afro-Asian Connections and the Myth of Cultural Purity* (Boston: Beacon Press, 2001), 140-42.

28. Prashad, *Everybody Was Kung Fu Fighting*, 144.

29. Ho, "Kickin' the White Man's Ass," 297.

30. *The Get Down*, "Raise Your Words, Not Your Voice," Netflix, August 12, 2016, written by Seth Zvi Rosenfeld and Sam Bromell, directed by Ed Bianchi.

31. Rex Krueger, "Aaron McGruder's *The Boondocks* and Its Transition from Comic Strip to Animated Series," *Animation: An Interdisciplinary Journal* 5, no. 3 (2010): 325.

32. Murray Forman, *The 'Hood Comes First: Race, Space, and Place in Rap and Hip-Hop* (Middletown: Wesleyan University Press, 2002), 83.

33. *The Get Down*, "Raise Your Words."

34. *The Get Down*, "Raise Your Words."

35. Samantha Blackmon, "'Be Real Black for Me': Lincoln Clay and Luke Cage as the Heroes We Need," *The CEA Critic* 79, no. 1 (2017): 97-98.

36. Most prominently seen in *Luke Cage*, "Code of the Streets," Netflix, September 30, 2016, written by Cheo Hodari Coker, directed by Paul McGuigan. The episode is bookended by a confrontation in which a black teenaged mugger calls Cage "nigga" while holding a gun to his head, leading to a lecture from Cage on the use of the word. The respectability politics inherent here become complicated when Cage shouts the term back at the mugger later in the exchange.

37. A detail noted by a number of websites who have collected the references into various iterations of the "*Luke Cage* Syllabus." Viz. Tara Betts, "The Luke Cage Syllabus: A Breakdown of All the Black Literature Featured in Netflix's *Luke Cage*," *Black Nerd Problems*, http://blacknerdproblems.com/the-luke-cage-syllabus-a-breakdown-of-all-the-black-literature-featured-in-netflixs-luke-cage/.

38. Blackmon, "Be Real Black For Me," 98.

39. Larrie Dudenhoeffer, *Anatomy of the Superhero Film* (New York: Palgrave Macmillan, 2017), 280.

40. Squabbles is referencing the 1972 film *Fist of Fury* which, due to a marketing and translation error, was released in the United States under a title meant for a different movie (originally called *The Big Boss* in China), a mistake not rectified until 2005. In calling the film by the mistaken (original) name, Squabbles provides another coded authentication, showing that (despite preferring Jet Li to Bruce Lee) he is no neophyte to the genre, tracing his bona fides back for decades.

41. *Luke Cage*, "Step in the Arena," Netflix, September 30, 2016, written by Charles Murray, directed by Vincenzo Natali.

42. Jeffrey O. G. Ogbar, *Hip-Hop Revolution: The Culture and Politics of Rap* (Lawrence: University Press of Kansas, 2007), 42.

43. Iwamura, *Virtual Orientalism*, 112.

44. *Luke Cage*, "Moment of Truth," Netflix, September 30, 2016, written by Cheo Hodari Coker, directed by Paul McGuigan.

45. Blackmon, "Be Real Black For Me," 101.

46. Dudenhoeffer, *The Anatomy of the Superhero Film*, 280.

47. Dudenhoeffer, *The Anatomy of the Superhero Film*, 280.

48. Routledge, *Nostalgia*, 31.

49. Watkins, *Hip Hop Matters*, 21.

BIBLIOGRAPHY

Bhabha, Homi K. *The Location of Culture*. London: Routledge, 1994.

Blackmon, Samantha. "'Be Real Black for Me': Lincoln Clay and Luke Cage as the Heroes We Need." *The CEA Critic* 79, no. 1 (2017): 97-109.

Coker, Cheo Hodari. *Marvel's Luke Cage*. Netflix. 2016.

Dudenhoeffer, Larrie. *Anatomy of the Superhero Film*. New York: Palgrave Macmillan, 2017.

Flanigan, B. P. "Kung Fu Krazy: or The Invasion of the 'Chop Suey Easterns.'" *Cinéaste* 6, no. 3 (1974): 8-11.

Forman, Murray. *The 'Hood Comes First: Race, Space, and Place in Rap and Hip-Hop*. Middletown: Wesleyan University Press, 2002.

———. "No Sleep 'Til Brooklyn," *American Quarterly* 54, no. 1 (2002): 101-127.

Ho, Fred. "Kickin' the White Man's Ass: Black Power, Aesthetics, and the Asian Martial Arts." In *AfroAsian Encounters: Culture, History, Politics*, edited by Heike Raphael-Hernandez and Shannon Steen, 295-312. New York: New York University Press, 2006.

Iwamura, Jane Naomi. *Virtual Orientalism: Asian Religions and American Popular Culture*. Oxford: Oxford University Press, 2011.

Kim, Elaine H. "At Least You're Not Black: Asian Americans in U.S. Race Relations." In *Blacks and Asians: Crossings, Conflict, and Commonality*, edited by Hazel M. McFerson, 203-213. Durham: Carolina Academic Press, 2006.

Kim, Janine Young. "Are Asians Black?: The Asian American Civil Rights Agenda and the Contemporary Significance of the Black/White Paradigm." In *Blacks and Asians: Crossings, Conflict, and Commonality*, edited by Hazel M. McFerson, 171-201. Durham: Carolina Academic Press, 2006.

Krueger, Rex. "Aaron McGruder's *The Boondocks* and Its Transition from Comic Strip to Animated Series." *Animation: An Interdisciplinary Journal* 5, no. 3 (2010): 313-329.

Luhrmann, Baz, and Stephen Adly Guirgis. *The Get Down*. Netflix. 2016.

Ogbar, Jeffrey O. G. *Hip-Hop Revolution: The Culture and Politics of Rap*. Lawrence: University Press of Kansas, 2007.

Ongiri, Amy Abugo. "'He Wanted to Be Just Like Bruce Lee': African Americans, Kung Fu Theater and Cultural Exchange at the Margins." *Journal of Asian American Studies* 5, no. 1 (2002): 31-40.

Prashad, Vijay. *Everybody Was Kung Fu Fighting: Afro-Asian Connections and the Myth of Cultural Purity*. Boston: Beacon Press, 2001.

Routledge, Clay. *Nostalgia: A Psychological Resource*. New York: Routledge, 2016.

Shiu, Anthony Sze-Fai. "Styl(us): Asian North America, Turntablism, Relation." *CR: The New Centennial Review* 7, no. 1 (2007): 81-106.

Shu, Yuan. "Reading the Kung Fu Film in an American Context: From Bruce Lee to Jackie Chan." *Journal of Popular Film and Television* 31, no. 2 (2003): 50-59.

Spence, Lester K. *Stare in the Darkness: The Limits of Hip-Hop and Black Politics*. Minneapolis: University of Minnesota Press, 2011.

Watkins, S. Craig. *Hip Hop Matters: Politics, Pop Culture, and the Struggle for the Soul of a Movement*. Boston: Beacon Press, 2005.

NINE

"We Can't Have Two White Boys Trying to Tell a Latina Story"

Nostalgia, Identity, and Cultural Specificity

Jacinta Yanders

Television remains an influential medium in American society despite an abundance of alternative options. Though television and how it's disseminated has changed significantly, the most popular television shows still reach millions of viewers. Thus, television still "plays a central role in the articulation, construction, and contestation of racialized identities in the United States."[1] Rather than simply reflecting society, "The way television represents the world always shapes our perception."[2] Television fosters aspirations, stokes fears, and cultivates desires. Currently, it's deeply invested in generating and capitalizing upon nostalgia, particularly via "reimaginings" (reboots, remakes, and so on), and one significant driving force behind the production of television reimaginings is Netflix.

Netflix might prefer to be known for its original programming rather than as a haven for works of the past. This seems evident given the company's continued shift away from being a repository for products it didn't produce and its habit of attaching the "Netflix Original" moniker to shows it imports from other countries and/or continues from other networks. However, it's worth noting that this orientation is also precipitated by the fact that Netflix has lost, and continues to lose, the rights to various programs it didn't produce. Nevertheless, in 2016, Netflix began promoting three reimaginings—*Fuller House*, *Gilmore Girls: A Year in the Life*, and *One Day at a Time*—together, suggesting that watching the three shows would allow viewers to return to the good ol' days of family and fun. *Fuller House* and *Gilmore Girls: AYITL*, capitalize on nostalgia with returning characters, familiar sets, etc. *One Day at a Time*, however, departs quite significantly from its predecessor. Rather than utilizing familiar characters or locations, *One Day at a Time* turns its attention to a different sort of specificity. The series is constructed to provide an authentic representation of a Cuban American family in the United States as opposed to the White American family portrayed in the original iteration. Both series address the complexities of life for single mothers trying to support their families, but the newer version expands upon its predecessor's gender-based focus to explore an array of issues, particularly in relation to race, mental health, and immigration. While the reimagining does hit many familiar multicamera family sitcom beats, it also intentionally attends to the political and cultural environment it exists in. Netflix has produced various critically acclaimed award-winning series, such as *Orange Is the New Black* and *House of Cards*. However, much of Netflix's most well-known original content has targeted adult viewers. Though Netflix does create programming for kids, it only recently made family viewing one of its primary interests.

At the outset of *Media and Nostalgia: Yearning for the Past, Present, and Future*, Katherine Niemeyer queries, "Who would have thought, given the 1990s' imagining of a future filled with technology, that the beginning of the new century would in fact be marked by an increase in expressions of nostalgia?"[3] Indeed, the intensity of this shift from futuristic postulations about what the new millennium might bring to an apparent desire to retreat into the past occurred somewhat unexpectedly. Changing cultural demographics and the demand for more—and better—representations of marginalized groups in media have resulted in a sort of tension. Despite public requests and praise for inclusive programming, such programming also often elicits backlash and desires to return to a more homogenous past. This sort of backlash was identifiably enmeshed in the campaign and presidential election of Donald Trump, which then quite directly impacted the contours of American television.

Particularly, broadcast networks seem to have taken the call to "Make America Great Again" as an imperative. This includes conventional networks such as CBS, whose Fall 2016 slate skewed intently toward White male protagonists, as well as ABC, which had previously garnered praise for being the most inclusive broadcast network. Between a bevy of shows from Shonda Rhimes and a collection of racially diverse comedies, such as *Blackish* and *Fresh off the Boat*, it had seemed as though ABC was a welcoming space for marginalized narratives.

Yet, following the 2016 election, newly installed ABC Network president Channing Dungey suggested the network had focused too much on representations of "well-to-do, well-educated people" while neglecting representations of "everyday Americans."[4] In discussing why ABC decided to reboot both *American Idol* and the increasingly controversial

Roseanne, Dungey asserted that while the network had done well with certain types of inclusivity, such as race and religion, it had neglected "economic diversity." Dungey also described *American Idol* as being about "a girl with a cowboy hat and a boy with a banjo and people from small towns where music has saved their lives in different ways."[5] Implicit in Dungey's critique of ABC's preexisting programming is the notion that those shows were *not* about "everyday Americans." If the Huangs and the Johnsons and Olivia Pope are not "everyday Americans," then who is? Furthermore, the rebooted *Roseanne* was constantly hampered by Roseanne Barr's off-screen prejudicial comments such that the series—after initially being renewed—was canceled. However, ABC ultimately decided to air a spin-off, *The Conners*, sans Barr. While being negatively received by many viewers whose marginalized identities were subject to Barr's vitriolic attacks, the rebooted *Roseanne* did well in the ratings overall. ABC had, indeed, recaptured the audience it desired.

Jason Mittell notes that "Whiteness has persisted as a norm throughout television history, with a presence so ubiquitous that most viewers do not even perceive most white characters as having any racial designation."[6] If Whiteness is assumed as the norm, then any attempts to divert from that norm would strike some viewers as an aberration in need of remedy. In the face of increased inclusivity, revisiting the past via an assortment of television reimaginings may serve as a means of pumping the brakes. Interestingly, many of these reimaginings include race swaps, gender flips, inclusion of more sexual orientations, etc. These changes could signal progression, but it tends to be the case that they have little noticeable impact on the narratives. As Ryan Lizardi explains, "The remake nostalgic ethos . . . serves to re-create, pacify, and distract, thereby reaffirming dominant ideologies and a hegemony of the past."[7] Furthermore, it's significant that the shows being reimagined are always shows that originally adhered to norms of Whiteness. Popular Black sitcoms of the past are not among the shows being reimagined. Thus, it's difficult to not see much of the recent reimagining initiative as indicative of a desire to return to the years of more comfortable—White—television. As Inkoo Kang recently queried, "Is there something problematic in the industry's embrace of *Roseanne*, *Will & Grace* and *The X-Files*, but not the iconic black sitcoms that also made the Clinton years an exhilarating time of experimentation and representation?"[8]

Original recipe *One Day at a Time* debuted in 1975, courtesy of prolific creator, Norman Lear. Known for popular television shows that challenged status quos about race and gender, such as *All in the Family* and *Maude*, Lear continued to push the envelope with *One Day at a Time*, which centered on a divorced White American woman, Ann Romano, figuring out the single life while raising her daughters, Julie and Barb. Capitalizing on contemporary feminist movements, the series focused on the lives of girls and women who could now — theoretically — do, say, and become whatever they wanted. Though the show was presumed to foreground the female characters' lives and perspectives, commentary and actions from the series' male characters — such as, Schneider, the intrusive building superintendent — often served to impose boundaries on Ann, Julie, and Barb.

Netflix's relatively new interest in remaking family-oriented television series could be read as a simple desire to capture the attention of all possible viewers. This makes sense given what Michael Samuel describes as a sort of "choice fatigue," a side effect of Peak TV in which viewers simply become overwhelmed by having too many options to choose from.[9] Television reimaginings are capable of standing out due to name recognition and/or familiar faces. Netflix in particular, with its algorithmic assessments, can push such content to the home pages of viewers it believes will be swayed by these reimaginings. In this way, Netflix's reimaginings function a bit differently than those on broadcast and cable television, which require viewers to seek them out. Given that each of the aforementioned Netflix reimaginings had original series that ran for at least seven seasons, Netflix could comfortably assume that these shows would, at least temporarily, capture attention.

Netflix, as a streaming service not beholden to advertisers, is invested in maintaining subscriptions. It might not seem like retreading the past would be an innovative way to accomplish such a goal. After all, part of what has made Netflix's original programming stand out has been its bent toward storytelling that isn't given space on linear television. Bearing that in mind, does it make sense for Netflix to reboot a series like *Full House*? Does doing so productively increase/maintain subscriptions? As it stands, Netflix does not share much in the way of viewership data. However, at the time of writing, *Fuller House* has been renewed for a fourth season while *One Day at a Time* has been renewed for a third. This suggests that these shows have effectively achieved Netflix's goals, which makes sense given that "In aggregate, in fact, reruns of comedies and cop shows draw far more viewers across all airings than high-rated serialized dramas like *The Walking Dead* or *Game of Thrones*, when you factor in reruns of the latter two."[10] *Full House* and *Gilmore Girls*, for example, have stayed in syndication since they ended. Netflix's goal with these reimaginings is cultivating rewatchability. This doesn't mean Netflix is abandoning its other original programming choices, but the service also wants to provide the sort of comfort that subscribers will want to regularly revisit. As Kathleen Loock explains while discussing Netflix's promotional materials that clustered the three reimaginings together, "This commercial strikes an emotional chord by recalling sentimental attachments to beloved characters (who have come to seem like the viewers' own family and friends) and well-known settings (which almost feel like the viewers' own homes), and stimulates a longing to reconnect."[11]

In January 2017, Netflix launched the *One Day at a Time* remake. Here, single mother, Penelope Alvarez, is raising her kids following a separation from her husband, Victor. As mentioned previously, the Alvarez family is described as Cuban rather than White, but it's worth noting here that there are both White Cubans and non-White Cubans (a distinction that becomes part of the series' narrative in its second season). Nevertheless, the clear intention is that the Alvarezes are a representation of a Latinx family, which is still relatively uncommon to see on American television.

Penelope's mother, Lydia, fills the co-parent gap left by Victor's absence. Lydia, a Cuban immigrant, often clashes with her daughter and granddaughter. As an elderly devout Catholic woman with heteronormative ideals, Lydia sees the world differently than her possibly agnostic veteran daughter and her granddaughter Elena, a student activist who often voices progressive ideals and displays a lack of conventional femininity. Meanwhile, the slightly younger Alex is primarily interested in popularity, sports, and looking good. As the baby of the family, Alex rarely clashes with his family members and mostly serves as comic relief. The Schneider character is still present, though with considerably less leeriness. He's also the most regularly appearing White character in the series, which often puts him in a position of learning from the Alvarez family about struggles he's never encountered. However, unlike many other series, which align the audience with the learning character and focus the narrative on how new knowledge has changed that character, *One Day at a Time* consistently maintains its focus on the Alvarezes.

The remake features a broad network for the family to interact with. Penelope is a nurse, and viewers are introduced to her boss, Dr. Berkowitz, as well as her coworkers, Scott and Lori. The dynamics of being the only non-White person—and particularly a woman of color—in the workplace play a role in multiple interactions that Penelope has with her coworkers. Such experiences allow Penelope to elucidate perspectives that are often disregarded in dominant narratives. She becomes friends with Jill, a Black female veteran, who introduces Penelope to a women veterans' support group via which Penelope also befriends Ramona, a gay Latina veteran. While Penelope's professional life requires her to navigate mostly White spaces, it's clear that her personal life is much more diverse. The remake itself is set in Echo Park, California, an area with a lengthy history of Cuban residency.

The first season is structured by a progression toward Elena's quinceañera celebration, which the young feminist does not wish to have given the practice's patriarchal roots. She eventually acquiesces, and making the arrangements for the celebration is woven throughout subsequent episodes. Meanwhile, the season also addresses sexism in the workplace, immigration issues, PTSD, queer identities, and gendered expectations. Most of these serious subjects are, in some way, coupled with a laugh. However, the series does evoke decidedly noncomedic tones at times, such as when Lydia emotionally recounts escaping Cuba via the Pedro Pan program and having to leave behind her older sister, who died before Lydia could see her again.

Very quickly, *One Day at a Time* makes viewers aware of how it will turn dominant narratives on their heads. In the first episode, when Penelope discusses a repair that needs to be done in the apartment, she says to Schneider, "You know you're the only non-Latino I trust to fix stuff. Is that racist? Who cares? It's just us."[12] The show asserts Penelope's affinity for her community while also playfully jabbing at phrases one might more readily expect to be uttered by White characters. In drawing attention to this exchange, *One Day at a Time* makes an implicit process explicit, but flips the expected power dynamic simultaneously. The show also acknowledges that, outside of the relatively safe space of her own home, Penelope has to regularly contend with more contentious societal narratives. When a patient continually calls her the wrong name—an experience recognizable to many people of color—Penelope remarks, "If that vieja calls me Maria one more time . . . " to which Dr. Berkowitz responds "She has Alzheimer's. . . . Just kidding. She's just racist."[13] This injection of humor coupled with serious matters enables the series to tackle complex topics without losing viewers who might otherwise find such storytelling unpalatable. It also provides viewers with moments of relief.

The family's Cuban ancestry is integrated into both the narrative and the mise-en-scène. Key components of this depiction include the décor in the apartment, the food the family typically eats, and the language used. Simultaneously, the show does not explain many of the cultural nuances it presents, nor does it typically translate the Spanish being used. As showrunner Gloria Calderón Kellett explains, "It was a creative choice not to have subtitles. I mean when I was growing up I didn't know what a Bar Mitzvah was until I saw it on TV."[14] Calderón Kellett draws attention to the fact that marginalized communities are expected to learn and abide by the norms of dominant society and/or more widely popular traditions. That which is lesser known is expected to be explained, which places an undue burden on marginalized communities. This series opposes that trend. It's up to the viewer to either make meaning through context or to do further research. The choice to integrate—and not explain—so many specific cultural nuances is risky, even bearing in mind that most questions viewers have could likely be answered in a few quick clicks. It's even more risky if one considers that remakes are always-already balancing the desires of multiple audiences. Yet, this is a risk that *One Day at a Time* believes is worth taking.

In addition to cultural references, several episodes throughout the first season address Elena's feminism and lack of conventional femininity as well as the various ways in which every member of the family is affected by sexism. In the second episode, viewers see this in a conversation about microaggressions and mansplaining spearheaded by Elena and also in Penelope's workplace, as her coworker Scott gets credit for her ideas and is revealed to make more money than Penelope. Most of the plot points in this episode are resolved by the end, but along the way, explicit conversations about sexism are brought to the forefront. Such conversations recur throughout the season, and though Lydia is portrayed as more conservative than both her daughter and grandchildren, the show often reveals her to be more liberal than one might expect. For example, when challenging the notion that God could be a woman, Lydia quips, "If God was a woman, there'd be less problems."[15]

Kristin J. Warner argues that if a previously White character is going to be cast with a non-White actor, it's not enough to simply throw in a non-White actor, make minimal changes, and call it a day. Warner says, "It is not enough that a Black character be named LaQuisha, for example. Rather, LaQuisha's characterization and storyline should resonate at multiple levels. . . . Details make characters real and their realness is what makes them relatable, not their 'similarity to me.' Specificity adds those details and enables characters to become than types."[16] It's the sense of specificity that's most often lacking when actors of color are cast in roles that weren't written for them, and it's the specificity that notions of color-blindness and postracialism attempt to avoid by way of flattening identities into idealized notions of equality. This diminishes the representational significance of such characters and also increases the likelihood of perpetuating undesirable tropes.

One Day at a Time gravitates toward the specific in a variety of ways, such as when Penelope brings home pastries from Porto's, a bakery known for its Cuban goods. According to Mexican-Salvadoran writer Vanessa Erazo, "It's those small moments that offer a peek into the showrunners' commitment to authentic details."[17] Discussions of "authenticity" are always fraught, but as I've argued elsewhere, being able to ultimately prove something is authentic is less important than it *feeling* authentic.[18] The decision to include these small details suggests care, and that feeling can make viewers—especially those used to being ignored—feel seen more than simply casting an actor of color.

Both Calderón Kellett and Norman Lear have emphasized the necessity of specificity. Calderón Kellett draws attention to the flattening of cultural identity that typically occurs in television shows featuring Latinx characters as a means of trying to represent the entire community. Along a vein similar to Warner, Calderón Kellett says, "The specificity goes away, and when that goes away, you lose something" and Lear adds, "The interesting thing about that specificity is, it's recognized as our common humanity. It's real. They're not pretending they're more American or something. They're Cuban-American, and they're real. People relate to that reality."[19] That realness makes viewers connect with characters. This isn't because the show's viewers necessarily come from the same background, but because the fully fleshed out characters are not stock types. As Cuban writer Alex Alvarez noted about the series, "It did a good job of being culturally specific to Cubans and to a distinctly Latinx experience while also being universally relatable in so many ways. It's inviting anyone into this story."[20]

The series did not get to this place by accident. Previously, Lear had been out of direct involvement with productions for quite some time. However, Brent Miller, an executive at Lear's Act III production company, wanted to get Lear involved again. Miller partnered with Sony Pictures Television, who brought in Mike Royce to head up the show. Though Royce had a history of television success, Miller told Lear, "We can't have two white boys trying to tell a Latina story."[21] Miller recognized and wished to remedy what he perceived to be a gap in their knowledge base, which is choice that is still fairly uncommon across the industry. They would not have been the first or the last to create a show—ostensibly *about* people of color—with no people of color behind the scenes. But instead, they brought in Calderón Kellett, who is Cuban American, to co-run the show.

According to Calderón Kellett, the *One Day at a Time*'s writers' room is markedly diverse, with a wide range of ages, races, genders, and sexual orientations present.[22] These identities have contributed a variety of perspectives, which have shaped many of the series' storylines and characterizations. Calderón Kellett also tweeted, "Proud to say that aside from our inclusivity in front of & behind the camera, @onedayatatime passes the Bechdel test, Mako Mori test, Sphinx test, Vito Russo test, Sexy lamp test & DuVernay test. All take into account inclusivity in storytelling. Look 'em up! Be inspired!"[23] Recent critiques of the overabundance of Whiteness and maleness in the industry have sometimes elicited rebuttals that the "best" person for the job was hired and/or that it was too difficult to find someone else. But what Calderón Kellett suggests is that being intentional and inclusive is not actually that difficult and that, as a show already doing these things, *One Day at a Time* is deserving of attention and recognition.

Writer Alex Alvarez expressed skepticism going into watching the show, and as many viewers from marginalized communities can attest, this is not uncommon. Viewers often clamor for more inclusive representation, but what's provided often disappoints. Erazo was surprised to find the show enjoyable and said, "We are so used to being disappointed with a show about Latinos. We come in apprehensive. It's hard to get a show like that right, to get the cultural references, generational differences, and then on top of that to land the jokes and have it be actually funny."[24] Calderón Kellett had been approached by executives to make the family Mexican, presumably to be more legible to American viewers. She said she could do so, but she wouldn't be able to do it as well.[25] In other words, part of the reason that she is able to tell this story is *because* she's able to imbue it with details from her own background. This is not to say that people who don't have similar backgrounds aren't capable of doing similar work, but it would require more effort to get it right, and this sort of additional labor is not yet commonplace.

In addition to sustained cultural specificity, *One Day at Time*'s refashioning of representation also includes telling stories that often go untold. Viewers see Penelope, as a veteran, dealing with her own postwar anxiety, a lingering shoulder injury that she struggles to get adequately attended to by the VA, and a veteran ex who prefers to treat his PTSD with alcohol rather than therapy. According to Calderón Kellett, Penelope was not initially going to be a veteran, but "We thought, Gosh, if we make it her, we're going to spend more time with her and speak about the female military experience, which is not something that's often talked about."[26] The series also focuses extensively on the human side of immigration. Again, these heavy storylines regularly inject humor, such as in the episode about Elena's best friend Carmen, whose parents have been deported. In the episode, Schneider reveals that he immigrated illegally from Canada. Scott remarks, "So, you're an illegal alien?" to which Schneider responds "Well, we prefer undocumented."[27] On one hand, the show is clearly poking fun at Schneider's attempt to claim allegiance with Latinx immigrants who are obviously at more risk. On the other hand, *One Day at a Time* clarifies the language that should be used. Later, in a decidedly less humorous moment, Carmen comments, "My parents didn't do anything wrong. . . . We're a normal American family."[28] Given that *One Day at a Time*'s release was nearly simultaneous with Donald Trump's Inauguration and an uptick in legislative aggression against immigrants, Carmen's statement was particularly timely.

In the second season, the series intentionally reflected anxieties about Trump's election without ever mentioning his name. In the first episode, Alex shares the increased racist language that's directed toward him, which shocks Schneider who'd thought of Los Angeles as a progressive place and results in Elena commenting "Ever since somebody decided to call an entire group of Latinos, rapists and criminals, everyone thinks they can say whatever racist thought occurs to them."[29] The backbone of the series' second season addresses the precarious immigration statuses of Lydia and Schneider, driving Elena to eventually query, "What if one day, they decide to send all non-citizens back to where they came from?"[30] Very real concerns of the Latinx diaspora are foregrounded in a way that's far removed from the "Very Special Episode" of years past. Viewers don't get the sense that the Alvarez family will necessarily overcome every roadblock. Instead, these problems are ongoing struggles, sometimes navigated successfully and sometimes not. And lest viewers begin to feel emotionally overwhelmed, the series' laughs often tap into its most incisive cultural critiques, such as the following discussion about the US Citizenship test:

Schneider: You only have to get 60% right to pass.

Elena: So basically, to become an American, you have to prove you're a D-minus student.

Schneider: Yep, it's the same requirement as it is to become president.[31]

One of the most underrepresented narratives that the remake chooses to highlight focuses on Elena's sexual identity. In Elena, viewers come to know a queer Latina who is ultimately much more comfortable attending her quinceañera in a suit rather than a dress. The series does not relegate this story to a one-off episode and then forget it happened. Instead, Elena's self-discovery is ongoing with only Lydia suspecting initially that her granddaughter might not be heterosexual. Elena questions her attractions, attempts to date a boy, watches porn in an attempt to figure out what she likes, and has heartfelt conversations with her family. The series utilizes the people closest to Elena to demonstrate a range of possible reactions to her sexuality. Lydia is momentarily bothered but comes around quickly, Penelope says she isn't bothered but actually takes more time to adjust, Alex is completely unbothered, and Schneider is only bothered to the extent that he's one of the first to find out and feels burdened by keeping the secret. Elena's friends are immediately accepting. That most people in Elena's life are accepting offers a productively nontragic outcome. However, much like real life, that does not mean there won't be challenges. For Elena, the most direct challenge comes from her father.

Victor's arrival for Elena's quinceañera sends ripple effects through the lives of several characters. Elena feels like she has to hide her sexuality, Penelope halts a burgeoning romantic relationship, and Schneider feels uncomfortable about fulfilling the fatherly role he had come to play with Alex and Elena. The only people that are easygoing in Victor's return are Lydia, who still wants Victor and Penelope to reunite, and Alex, who is just happy to see his father. However, Lydia's perspective changes when it's revealed that Victor hasn't been in treatment and is still drinking to cope with PTSD. Though Victor is still invited to the quinceañera, he's no longer welcome as a potential romantic partner for Penelope. Furthermore, when Elena comes out to him, Victor responds poorly. He lashes out at both Elena and Penelope, saying, "She's not. . . . She's not that way."[32] Victor and Elena's relationship was already strained. Unlike his easy bond with Alex, Victor doesn't know how to connect to his daughter. After some cajoling from Penelope, Victor attends the quinceañera. But upon seeing Elena in a suit, he leaves early—before the father-daughter dance—hurting his daughter in the process.

However, the series is unwilling to let the story rest on this familiar sad note. In Victor's absence, Penelope joins Elena for the father-daughter dance, and eventually, the whole family is on the dance floor. They embrace Elena, reminding her of the support that she does have. For many viewers, particularly young queer viewers of color, such a storyline is not typically offered. That this story was told, and told in a way that doesn't come across as defeating, is a credit to the thoughtfulness evident in the construction of *One Day at a Time*.

Thus far, this particular remake has received critical and commercial acclaim. Noting that its first season dropped in January of 2017, it was often discussed in the popular press—despite the content it addresses—as a bit of respite from contemporary American life. Following its second season, the series' showrunners, critics, Latinx cultural organizations, and viewers campaigned for another season, which Netflix ultimately gave the green light. It remains to be seen whether the remake will eclipse the prominence of the original, but perhaps it doesn't need to. As veteran character Pam—played by Mackenzie Phillips who starred as Julie on the original series—quipped about a movie she saw "Another remake. Well, it was nothing like the original. But I like 'em both."[33]

When writing about another Netflix original series, the very nostalgic *Stranger Things*, television critic Todd VanDerWerff commented, "When we say we want something 'original,' what we really mean is that we want something familiar, but just different enough to feel novel."[34] Ryan Lizardi has also said, "It is not so much that these texts are classic, instead it is the time period itself that is classic for those constructed nostalgics."[35] If we hold these ideas together simultaneously, then there is space for a series like *One Day at a Time* to both fulfill its role of providing familiar comforts while also working to challenge the status quo. This makes the series distinguishable from many of its televisual compatriots, which is something that is quite important given the abundance of viewing options contemporarily. In a way, the series functions as a sort of Trojan Horse. Its familiar conceits and overall feel-good aesthetic get viewers in the door, but the actual content inside is different enough to give the series measures of importance and uniqueness that further stoke viewer interest.

However, it's worth noting that being "different" doesn't always pan out as expected, especially when a given reimagining's construction runs completely counter to its nostalgic referent. The creators of the *Heathers* television adaptation discovered this recently after making the choice, unlike the filmic predecessor that punched up at the normative upper echelons of society, to write students from groups that are marginalized in real life as the series' bullies. The students who are "normal" are the targets of these bullies. As Samantha Allen comments, having seen the first episode, "The sole idea in the new *Heathers* seems to be that it's now uncool to be straight, white, and cisgender. . . . The new *Heathers* is for people who want to see a heteronormative status quo restored before it has even been meaningfully disrupted."[36] One might argue that this purportedly inclusive representation is yet another attempt to "correct" the path and return to a world of sameness. However, the series was publicly derided from the moment its first trailer was released. After releasing the pilot in February 2018, the series was meant to premiere officially in March 2018, but was delayed, according to Paramount Network, because of the Parkland School Shooting. The intense critical and cultural backlash, made widely present via social media, probably also had an impact. The Paramount Network canceled the series officially in the summer of 2018, but subsequently decided to air a heavily edited version in October of the same year. Notably, the series was not able to garner much of an audience.

So what comes next? About television, John Fiske once wrote, "It is wrong to see it as an originator of social change, or even to claim that it ought to be so, for social change must have its roots in material social existence; but television can be, must be, part of that change, and its effectivity will either hasten or delay it."[37] And so, television broadly, and Netflix more specifically, plays a critical role in developing society. Part of how Netflix contributes to this development is reliant on how it functions in this remaking project. Will it continue to provide spaces to shows like *One Day at a Time* that both provide the comfort Netflix seeks to capitalize upon while also challenging dominant ideologies and providing space for underrepresented narratives? Furthermore, it's undeniable that Netflix is an influential company whose impact can be identified in various facets of the entertainment industry. One such place where that influence, particularly with respect to *One Day at a Time*, seems to be bearing out is in a slate of new reimaginings (The CW's *Roswell*, Freeform's *Party of Five*, and The CW's *Charmed*). As Inkoo Kang notes, these three reimaginings will be comprised of Latinx casts, and the first two shows' plot descriptions indicate that immigration issues will be central to the stories they're telling.[38] The influences here are likely far more extensive than Netflix and *One Day at a Time*, but given the critical and audience acclaim the series has received, it makes sense that other televisual outlets would want a piece of the pie. What remains to be seen is whether these reimaginings will be allowed to imbibe their production processes and narratives with the degree of cultural specificity that *One Day at a Time* has modeled or if the current conventions of broadcast and cable network expectations will foreclose such possibilities.

NOTES

1. Sarah Nilsen and Sarah E. Turner, *The Colorblind Screen: Television in Post-Racial America* (New York: New York University Press, 2014), 4.

2. Jason Mittell, *Television and American Culture* (New York: Oxford University Press, 2009), 270.

3. Katherine Niemeyer, *Media and Nostalgia: Yearning for the Past, Present and Future* (London: Palgrave Macmillan UK, 2014), 1.

4. Josef Adalian, "ABC Wants to Focus More of Its Programming on the Working Class in the Age of Trump," *Vulture*, December 1, 2016, http://www.vulture.com/2016/12/abc-changing-programming-philosophy-due-to-trump.html.

5. Jackson McHenry, "ABC Held a Meeting after Trump's Election That Lead to Reviving Roseanne," *Vulture*, March 30, 2018, http://www.vulture.com/2018/03/trumps-election-lead-to-abc-reviving-roseanne-idol.html.

6. Mittell, *Television and American Culture*, 315.

7. Ryan Lizardi, "The Nostalgic Revolution Will Be Televised," in *Remake Television: Reboot, Re-Use, Recycle*, ed. Carlen Lavigne (Lanham, MD: Lexington Books, 2014), 42.

8. Inkoo Kang, "Critic's Notebook: The Blinding Whiteness of Nostalgia TV," *The Hollywood Reporter*, March 28, 2018, https://www.hollywoodreporter.com/news/blinding-whiteness-nostalgia-tv-1097193.

9. Michael Samuel, "Time Wasting and the Contemporary Television-Viewing Experience," *University of Toronto Quarterly* 86, no. 4 (December 1, 2017): 84,https://doi.org/10.3138/utq.86.4.78.

10. Sam Thielman, "Netflix's Algorithms of Nostalgia: Why Sitcoms from Your Childhood Are Back," *The Guardian*, April 22, 2015, http://www.theguardian.com/media/2015/apr/22/netflix-sitcom-full-house-data-algorithms.

11. Kathleen Loock, "'Whatever Happened to Predictability?': Fuller House, (Post)Feminism, and the Revival of Family-Friendly Viewing," *Television & New Media* 19, no. 4 (November 30, 2017): 367, https://doi.org/10.1177/1527476417742972.

12. Pamela Fryman, "This Is It," *One Day at a Time* (Netflix, January 6, 2017).

13. Fryman, "This Is It."

14. Ana Sofía Peláez, "Meet the Woman Who Gave 'One Day at a Time' Its Bicultural, Latino Flavor," *NBC News*, January 26, 2017, https://www.nbcnews.com/news/latino/meet-woman-who-gave-one-day-time-its-bicultural-latino-n711476.

15. Phill Lewis, "No Mass," *One Day at a Time* (Netflix, January 6, 2017).

16. Kristen J Warner, *The Cultural Politics of Colorblind TV Casting* (New York: Routledge, 2015), 7.

17. Vanessa Erazo, "This Is What Happened When 5 Cubanas Sat Down to Watch Netflix's 'One Day at a Time,'" *Remezcla*, January 10, 2017, http://remezcla.com/features/film/5-cubanas-watch-netflix-one-day-at-a-time/.

18. Jacinta Yanders, "Interactions, Emotions, and Earpers: 'Wynonna Earp,' the Best Fandom Ever," *Transformative Works and Cultures* 26 (March 15, 2018), https://doi.org/10.3983/twc.2018.1129.

19. Maria Elena Fernandez, "After Two Decades Away, Norman Lear Has a New TV Show," *Vulture*, January 2, 2017,http://www.vulture.com/2016/12/norman-lear-one-day-at-a-time-c-v-r.html.

20. Erazo, "This Is What Happened."

21. Fernandez, "After Two Decades Away."

22. Fernandez, "After Two Decades Away."

23. Gloria Calderón Kellett, "Proud to Say That aside from Our Inclusivity in Front of & behind the Camera, @onedayatatime Passes the Bechdel Test, Mako Mori Test, Sphinx Test, Vito Russo Test, Sexy Lamp Test & DuVernay Test. All Take into Account Inclusivity in Storytelling. Look 'em up! Be Inspired!," *Twitter* (blog), March 7, 2018, https://twitter.com/everythinggloria/status/971415550638227456.

24. Erazo, "This Is What Happened."

25. Fernandez, "After Two Decades Away."

26. Fernandez, "After Two Decades Away."

27. Phill Lewis, "Strays," *One Day at a Time* (Netflix, January 6, 2017).

28. Lewis, "Strays."

29. Pamela Fryman, "The Turn," *One Day at a Time* (Netflix, January 26, 2018).
30. Phill Lewis, "Roots," *One Day at a Time* (Netflix, January 26, 2018).
31. Gloria Calderón Kellett, "Citizen Lydia," *One Day at a Time* (Netflix, January 26, 2018).
32. Pamela Fryman, "Quinces," *One Day at a Time* (Netflix, January 6, 2017).
33. Phill Lewis, "One Lie at a Time," *One Day at a Time* (Netflix, January 6, 2017).
34. Todd VanDerWerff, "*Stranger Things* Proves We Don't Want Totally Original Stories. We Want Familiar Ones," *Vox*, August 10, 2016, https://www.vox.com/2016/8/10/12416672/stranger-things-netflix-review-original-story.
35. Ryan Lizardi, *Mediated Nostalgia: Individual Memory and Contemporary Mass Media* (Lanham: Lexington Books, 2014), 136.
36. Samantha Allen, "The New 'Heathers' Is a Trumpian, LGBT-Bashing Nightmare," *The Daily Beast*, February 23, 2018,https://www.thedailybeast.com/the-new-heathers-is-a-trumpian-lgbt-bashing-nightmare.
37. John Fiske, *Television Culture* (New York: Routledge, 2011), 45.
38. Inkoo Kang, "Critic's Notebook: The Blinding Whiteness of Nostalgia TV," *The Hollywood Reporter*, March 28, 2018, https://www.hollywoodreporter.com/news/blinding-whiteness-nostalgia-tv-1097193.

BIBLIOGRAPHY

Adalian, Josef. "ABC Wants to Focus More of Its Programming on the Working Class in the Age of Trump." *Vulture*, December 1, 2016. http://www.vulture.com/2016/12/abc-changing-programming-philosophy-due-to-trump.html.
Allen, Samantha. "The New 'Heathers' Is a Trumpian, LGBT-Bashing Nightmare." *The Daily Beast*, February 23, 2018. https://www.thedailybeast.com/the-new-heathers-is-a-trumpian-lgbt-bashing-nightmare.
Calderón Kellett, Gloria. "Citizen Lydia." *One Day at a Time*. Netflix, January 26, 2018.
———. "Proud to Say That aside from Our Inclusivity in Front of & behind the Camera, @onedayatatime Passes the Bechdel Test, Mako Mori Test, Sphinx Test, Vito Russo Test, Sexy Lamp Test & DuVernay Test. All Take into Account Inclusivity in Storytelling. Look 'em up! Be Inspired!" *Twitter* (blog), March 7, 2018. https://twitter.com/everythinggloria/status/971415550638227456.
Erazo, Vanessa. "This Is What Happened When 5 Cubanas Sat Down to Watch Netflix's 'One Day at a Time.'" *Remezcla*, January 10, 2017. http://remezcla.com/features/film/5-cubanas-watch-netflix-one-day-at-a-time/.
Fernandez, Maria Elena. "After Two Decades Away, Norman Lear Has a New TV Show." *Vulture*, January 2, 2017. http://www.vulture.com/2016/12/norman-lear-one-day-at-a-time-c-v-r.html.
Fiske, John. *Television Culture*. New York: Routledge, 2011.
Fryman, Pamela. "Quinces." *One Day at a Time*. Netflix, January 6, 2017.
———. "The Turn." *One Day at a Time*. Netflix, January 26, 2018.
———. "This Is It." *One Day at a Time*. Netflix, January 6, 2017.
Kang, Inkoo. "Critic's Notebook: The Blinding Whiteness of Nostalgia TV." *The Hollywood Reporter*, March 28, 2018. https://www.hollywoodreporter.com/news/blinding-whiteness-nostalgia-tv-1097193.
Lewis, Phill. "No Mass." *One Day at a Time*. Netflix, January 6, 2017.
———. "One Lie at a Time." *One Day at a Time*. Netflix, January 6, 2017.
———. "Roots." *One Day at a Time*. Netflix, January 26, 2018.
———. "Strays." *One Day at a Time*. Netflix, January 6, 2017.
Lizardi, Ryan. *Mediated Nostalgia: Individual Memory and Contemporary Mass Media*. Lanham, MD: Lexington Books, 2014.
———. "The Nostalgic Revolution Will Be Televised." In *Remake Television: Reboot, Re-Use, Recycle*, edited by Carlen Lavigne. Lanham, MD: Lexington Books, 2014. http://site.ebrary.com/lib/alltitles/docDetail.action?docID=10852558.

Loock, Kathleen. "'Whatever Happened to Predictability?': Fuller House, (Post)Feminism, and the Revival of Family-Friendly Viewing." *Television & New Media* 19, no. 4 (November 30, 2017): 361–78. https://doi.org/10.1177/1527476417742972.

McHenry, Jackson. "ABC Held a Meeting after Trump's Election That Lead to Reviving Roseanne." *Vulture*, March 30, 2018. http://www.vulture.com/2018/03/trumps-election-lead-to-abc-reviving-roseanne-idol.html.

Mittell, Jason. *Television and American Culture*. New York: Oxford University Press, 2009.

Niemeyer, Katherine. *Media and Nostalgia: Yearning for the Past, Present and Future.* London: Palgrave Macmillan UK, 2014. http://ebookcentral.proquest.com/lib/ohiostate-ebooks/detail.action?docID=1699403.

Nilsen, Sarah, and Sarah E. Turner. *The Colorblind Screen: Television in Post-Racial America*. New York: New York University Press, 2014.

Peláez, Ana Sofía. "Meet the Woman Who Gave 'One Day At A Time' Its Bicultural, Latino Flavor." *NBC News*, January 26, 2017. https://www.nbcnews.com/news/latino/meet-woman-who-gave-one-day-time-its-bicultural-latino-n711476.

Samuel, Michael. "Time Wasting and the Contemporary Television-Viewing Experience." *University of Toronto Quarterly* 86, no. 4 (December 1, 2017): 78–89. https://doi.org/10.3138/utq.86.4.78.

Thielman, Sam. "Netflix's Algorithms of Nostalgia: Why Sitcoms from Your Childhood Are Back." *The Guardian*, April 22, 2015. http://www.theguardian.com/media/2015/apr/22/netflix-sitcom-full-house-data-algorithms.

VanDerWerff, Todd. "*Stranger Things* Proves We Don't Want Totally Original Stories. We Want Familiar Ones." *Vox*, August 10, 2016. https://www.vox.com/2016/8/10/12416672/stranger-things-netflix-review-original-story.

Warner, Kristen J. *The Cultural Politics of Colorblind TV Casting*. New York: Routledge, 2015.

Yanders, Jacinta. "Interactions, Emotions, and Earpers: 'Wynonna Earp,' the Best Fandom Ever." *Transformative Works and Cultures* 26 (March 15, 2018). https://doi.org/10.3983/twc.2018.1129.

TEN

Netflix's *Cable Girls* as Reinvention of a Nostalgic Past

Paola Maganzani

For its first original Spanish series, Netflix chose a female-oriented melodrama focusing on four very different women working as switchboard operators in 1928 Madrid, Spain, struggling with universal themes such as love, sacrifice, pain, betrayal, and the fight for freedom in a patriarchal society. *Cable Girls'* first season premiered on Netflix in over 190 countries on 28 April 2017; the second season aired on 25 December 2017, the third season came out on September 2018 and a fourth season is scheduled. As with their other original TV series, Netflix released the entire season all at once every time to allow fans to binge-watch the period-drama series in every country that has video on demand (VOD) platforms.

The series' title carries an implicit reference to a past in which information flowed through the cables of a central switchboard through people which at the time allowed telephone communication; the title is also reminiscent of films made between the 1920s and early 1930s when the cable technique was almost outdated. However, these films were among the first to show female workers, their work environment, fashion and feminine complicity, and they captured social changes.

In the posttelevision era, the production of retro imagery has moved into the field of television seriality, a contemporary storytelling form which allows for the development of more extensive stories about the many experiences of characters, as well as complex plots due to the huge amount of time available and also because of its discontinuous and basically unfinished structure. According to Katharina Niemeyer, series evoke a feeling of nostalgia because "they are based on the imperative to always leave a void, [. . .] the void a long-watched series leaves when it finally ends, or the never-arriving closure of an unfinished narrative."[1] On a theoretical level, all TV series are structurally nostalgic, but the nostalgic feeling can have different widths. The nostalgic approach seems to have completely replaced the historical one at all levels, becoming indistinguishable from the latter. Nostalgia has become a consumer product; it works as a commercial operation, given the increasing trend in the number of nostalgic products on the streaming platforms, and it is spreading almost everywhere today: successful series like *Boardwalk Empire* (HBO, 2010–2014) and *Mad Men* (AMC, 2007–2015), bring back to the fashions of the early 1920s and 1960s, raising interest for a time and place otherwise unknown among those who had only heard of them but had never experienced them. Like other successful serial experiences, *Cable Girls* reworks the story of a past that seems to be far away, recovering the aesthetic appeal of the 1930s. Behind a commercial operation, there is something more complex and interesting which calls into question the way we put ourselves in relation to the past and to "consume" memories.

This chapter analyzes Netflix's success strategy in producing a series aimed at new European markets which blends the old and new media in a captivating period drama mixing elements of the past, such as costumes, decor and historical details with modern pop music in a form of entertainment that encompasses storytelling and nostalgic representations.

FROM THE PAST TO NOSTALGIC RE-EVOCATION

Netflix's Spanish series goes back to the late 1920s and tells the story of four women who are hired as operators for Compañía Telefónica, Spain's first major national telephone company. *Cable Girls* takes place in a historical context scarcely covered by the world of cinema; it is set in Spain, but it could be the 1920s in any other city. In 1928, the telephone company opens its headquarters in the center of the city, and hundreds of young women stand in line to find work as "switchboard girls"; for each of them, the act of wearing headphones and plugging in the cables of the switchboard becomes the first true step toward emancipation. Most women did not have a voice in a society that was still based on a patriarchal model with traditional expectations of marriage, children and home. These four women, differing in character, provenance, social class and habits, unexpectedly end up forming tight friendships. Each of them must face the difficulties linked to family issues and to their own past lives. They must assert their own independence and emancipate themselves in a country where women's rights are far from being recognized by the legal system or by society.

The first episode introduces us into the spirit of the time and to the lives of the main characters: the protagonist Lidia/Alba, whose real name is Alba but who is hiding behind a false identity in an attempt to escape from her past; Carlota, the rebellious daughter of a strict colonel; Marga, a naive twenty-one-year-old from a remote country village; and Ángeles, one of the best operators of the company and the perfect wife of a husband whom nobody would wish to have. Very important roles are also played by some male characters: Francisco, Carlos, Pablo, Mario, Miguel and the inspector Beltrán, six totally different men who will influence the stories of the protagonists. The jealousies, envy and betrayals that play out inside the company are mixed with the ambition, friendship and love that involve the four protagonists.

Ever since the epoch of silent movies, cinema has shown this phase of renewal many times, bringing to the screen a new category of female workers who were neither manual workers nor office clerks but new professional figures, not specialized, not working in a factory or in a traditional office. Telephone operators appeared very often in films of the early 1930s as characters phoned each other through the operators. Hotel switchboard operators were, for example, the heroines of *Orchids and Ermine* (1927) and *I've Got Your Number* (1934). Switchboard operators working in the telephone companies were present in *The Telephone Girl* (1927), the sound adaptation of *The Secret Call* (1931) and a few years later, the dramatic *Looking for Trouble* (1934).

The operators' task was to connect the lines at the manual telephone switchboard; and since there were still few women in the workplace, their recruitment was symbolic of the modernity of a telephone company. Even after the advent of sound cinema, telephone operators were protagonists of musical comedies generally associated with German cinema and inspired by the tradition of Viennese operettas. Set in telephone switchboard offices with working spaces arranged in long lines, showing the young operators struggling with misunderstandings, mistaken identities and twists that inevitably led to happy endings, these romantic comedies entertained the audiences throughout Europe.

Among the typical examples, we may mention the German comedy *Fräulein — Falsch Verbunden,*[2] (*Wrong Number, Miss!*) by Emmerich W. Emo that led to some successful remakes such as the Italian *La telefonista* (*The Telephone Operator,* 1932) and the English *Give Her a Ring* (1935). In these comedies the cinematographic space is organized on the basis of scenic and architectonic models inspired by Art Déco, in which secretaries, telephone operators and typewriters all appear on the screen; young girls, enterprising and considered quite liberated for their time, though never crossing the limits of what is moral, have humble jobs but are modern, and they become icons of important social changes.[3] However, male supremacy is everywhere, from professional responsibilities to personal decisions, while women are bound to male perspectives and interests. In other words, the female identity constructed on the screen is a subordinate gender identity; the ambition of the female protagonist is not to make a career as a telephone operator but rather to find a good prospect for marriage and to improve her social status. Later, the figure of the telephone operator slowly disappeared, both from reality and the screens, and only cinematographic sequences, company photos, documents and personal memories are left as testimonies to the epoch of the switchboard girls who had become part of the collective imagination.

The image of the working woman as shown through cinema is redefined by Netflix, which uses Telefónica as a literal and figurative icon of communication to show the changing world and women's conditions in the 1920s. Through the contemporary storytelling, the series makes one think about the connections of the past to the present, showing that "nostalgia is not just the preserve of the past, but can be directed just as well toward the future or even the present."[4] A wider scenario opens up in which the series' perspective focuses mainly on female characters who dream of equality with men as the spirit of independence was so remarkable when they were just entering into that vast, promising future and desired freedom. Nostalgia in its regressive and progressive moods opens up issues of historical persistence and ambiguity between the return to an earlier idealized past and the desire not to return "but recognize aspects of the past as the basis for renewal and satisfaction in the future."[5]

NETFLIX IN EUROPE: A NEW PRODUCTIVE AND COMMERCIAL GEOGRAPHY

Cable Girls is one of the first original European productions with which Netflix, the giant of streaming, set out to conquer new markets. In the last three years, Netflix has gravitated toward original productions considered to be more effective in capturing new users outside of the USA. It was not by chance that much of the seven billion dollars spent on its contents were invested in such projects, considering that the local tastes are the predilection that certain countries or certain geographical areas have for content that can also please elsewhere. Local productions such as the period series *Cable Girls*, the German thriller *Dark* and the Italian mafia drama *Suburra* were, from the outset, symptomatic of the international strategy of the company, and they continue to be part of the global launch. According to Reed Hastings, Netflix has invested over 1.75 billion dollars in European productions, including licensed programs, original content and coproductions because the American streaming giant is increasingly looking toward the international side of its business to drive growth.[6]

Netflix's business model does not include advertising revenues but is based exclusively on subscriptions, while broadcast networks and cable channels make money by selling audiences to advertisers. Netflix has developed original series for subscribers in non-US markets that are also available to US subscribers. The increase in the number of viewers who want to see Netflix content, and who therefore take out or renew subscriptions, has clearly led to a growth in profits. Moreover, the strategy adopted by Netflix to expand throughout the continent of Europe, with the intention of increasing its share of the market and searching for new subscribers from the other side of the ocean, is also aimed at contrasting with the progressive saturation of the USA market.[7]

Netflix has its strong point in network expansion that makes even more tangible its versatility in adapting and evolving in the direction of what the public really wants. For this reason, it has focused on local productions and more realistic stories in which the public can recognize themselves in the settings and characters. Each story has different characteristics but, above all in Europe, there is the value of perceiving that national/continental identity is invaluable. Through internet distribution, Netflix can serve several audiences simultaneously and separately, providing users with the desired content and then creating an addiction to it, thus increasing its permanence on the platform. Attention to users is the strength of Netflix that has completely changed the paradigm of consumption of products on demand and that has been able to capture a certain type of behavior—binge-watching—and to transform it from the typical activity of the fandom into the normal behavior of the consumer. Netflix's success comes from the amount of content and distribution everywhere, both as a producer as well as a distributor of other content, such as classic films; however, to keep up with other competitive and quality platforms, Netflix has recently increased its investments into more original series that are the requirement for quality TV on demand at competitive prices because it is through the quality of the contents that other platforms, such as HBO, compete and exert more pressure to be superior. Of course, HBO has also long relied on subscribers, which explains the distinctiveness of many HBO programs despite its distribution by cable.

By making this Spanish series, Netflix gave local producers the chance to gain access to a global audience, thanks to international production for an international platform. In addition, *Cable Girls* follows a model of production already consolidated for Bambú Producciones, the Spanish television producer founded in 2007 that has several years of experience behind them in the form of costume dramas such as *Velvet* (2014–2016) and *Gran Hotel* (2011–2013), which were broadcast by Antena 3, one of the main television channels in Spain.

The production and distribution geography of the on-demand platform has changed in recent years. Netflix has concluded new agreements with important producers outside of the United States, thus inaugurating new commercial outlets on a worldwide level and coproductions which have given new vigor to the on-demand platform, merging creativity and tradition: being loved by its own nation and at the same time ensuring global success with a "Spanish" period drama and an American budget.

It is hard not to think of the Spanish tradition of "telenovelas," especially with regard to the revelations and the intrigues that link all the characters together. In fact, the series presents certain elements typical of the genre: it is conceived for a female audience, it is a romantic period drama, and it is a historical series in terms of costumes, but it differs especially in the way it is narrated. The narrative scheme evolves through flashbacks, and a comment on the events narrated by an off-screen voice brings the viewer a message, a key to interpretation, something to remember and to make one's own, so that the off-screen voice becomes an element of the representation aimed at interacting in a different way with the image that is shown on the screen.

The sequences closely adhere to the subjective view of the protagonist who, as André Bazin reminds us, may even be absent or implicit; it is sufficient to hear her voice off-screen.[8] The off-screen voice is in this case also a ploy to draw the viewer's attention to the historical period; it has the purpose of illustrating a time, it alludes to some significant object that can offer information about an epoch which the viewer must know about in order to appreciate the next development in the story.[9] The political background and tensions are accompanied by new details about the pasts of the four main characters, while the subplots of their friends and colleagues explore various different themes such as abuse, sexism, sexual freedom and the vindications of the female figures; viewers cannot help empathizing with them, regardless of whether they had lived in the 1930s or live in the present. Struggling for freedom and independence, Lidia, Marga, Ángeles and Carlota are somehow no less real than we are.

NOSTALGIA AND POP CULTURE ON DEMAND

According to Fred Davis, nostalgia implies a positive preference for the past and negative sentiments toward the present or the future. The audio-visual products created in a nostalgic vein include the Hollywood remakes that take their inspiration from old films or from famous people of the past. More generally, "nostalgia uses the past [. . .] but is not a product thereof."[10] In this sense, *Cable Girls* represents an ideal media subject because it acts on the fascination for components of a nostalgic past in order to attract an audience that is seeking content that will take them back in time to a lost dimension. The cultural repercussions and the responses of the audience depend on the personal, individual or collective associations existing in the past. In the first place, nostalgia can be felt only if one has experienced the original event, classified as real nostalgia according to the types of nostalgia proposed by Stacey M. Baker and Patricia F. Kennedy,[11] a form of simple nostalgia that produces a longing for the past (according to Davis). Collective nostalgia, on the other hand, represents a sentimental desire felt by entire cultures, generations or nations. Russell W. Belk suggested that collective nostalgia is specific to a generation, so a younger cohort prefers music, films and other cultural expressions different from those of their parents.[12]

Emiliano Morreale reminds us that "such collective emotion is created by the mass media more than by the large-scale propagators. Nostalgia comes from the media, it exists thanks to the media and for the media."[13] The term "nostalgia" implies the inclination to look to the past from an emotional perspective, so as to turn it into the object of a particular (re)consideration in the light of the present.[14] For an audience of the millennial generation, the perception of the past does not come in a direct form but is a mediated knowledge of a period and of a previous culture that the young "millennial" has not experienced and tries to understand in terms of reimagined content. This kind of nostalgia evokes an interpreted form of nostalgia, as Davis suggests. The feeling of nostalgia helps to highlight important memories and in practice translates into the appreciation of vintage objects with the aura of legitimacy. According to Marta Blazquez Cano,[15] the way in which people find their route to the past through vintage items in the form of nostalgia is commonly linked to specific objects. Vintage is not only a style but is also a form that organizes nostalgia and valorizes segments of the past according to a logic linked to fashion and styles. The study by Morris B. Holbrook on the tendency toward nostalgia suggests that age and the predisposition to nostalgia seem to act independently as separate aspects of models of nostalgic preferences.[16] In his study carried out on a sample heterogeneous in age, Holbrook concluded that age does not appear to influence feelings of nostalgia, whereas gender plays an important role, with women apparently being more inclined toward nostalgia than men.

Holbrook and Robert M. Schindler define nostalgia as "the preference toward objects (persons, places, or things) that were more common (popular, fashionable, or widely circulated) when one was younger (in early adulthood, in adolescence, in childhood, or even before birth)."[17] In a later study, they confirmed that pleasurable sensory experiences are attributed to objects appreciated in an individual's past, and nostalgic associations arise in areas in which the individual has lived—moments in time, friendships and loved ones, gifts and leisure activities. Through the consumption of nostalgic products or brands, consumers can reconcile themselves with the past, and through online communities, it is possible to consume, so to speak, the past collectively, thus amplifying its importance.[18]

The costumes and the accessories used for this series are in part original and thus belong to the realm of vintage; they recall periods of the past

Figure 10.1.   Sara (Ana Polvorosa), Miguel (Borja Luna); still photography, *Cable Girls* **/ Netflix—Season 2.** *Source: Netflix/Bambú Producciones.*

or show the style of a certain era (see Figure 10.1). Alongside commodity vintage we find experiential vintage, which is the form that most notably permeates the contents of the media. The past reemerges in a modern key and attracts the public/consumer through an approach that is increasingly emotional and purposeful. In this perspective, one of the most innovative ideas of the series is, in fact, the correlation between the two forms of vintage. The White Lady, for example, is able to trigger this notion through the persuasive power of a vintage cocktail. The years of Prohibition in the USA have clear echoes in this series because they were already exploited in films like *C'era una volta in America* (*Once Upon a Time in America*, 1984) and in TV series such as *Boardwalk Empire* (2010–2014), as well as in the film *The Great Gatsby* where another "vintage" beverage, the Gin Rickey (the cocktail mentioned in Francis Scott Fitzgerald's novel), reappears in Baz Luhrmann's remake of the same name. And like Luhrmann's film, the new Netflix series has a soundtrack made up of modern songs, featuring a selection of pop songs in English and just one in Spanish, *Hablarán de ti y de mí,* sung by Vanesa Martín and used only during the closing credits of the last episode of the first season. Even though we are in the 1920s, the music selected does not include jazz and swing, but on the contrary each episode contains twenty-first-century pop music, catchy and in particular sung by well-known voices of today's music scene, ranging from Jacob Miller to Lemaitre and Lana Del

Rey. These musical choices bring about a short circuit in the sense that the music of the series is perhaps the only element that detracts from nostalgia. Behind the use of modern music in a period drama is the intention of meeting the tastes of a younger audience, as Luhrmann did, by placing it in the foreground and using it to heighten the tones of the drama, murder and heartache, as in the song *Young and Beautiful* by Lana Del Rey. Lyrically, the song is written from the perspective of Daisy Buchanan, Gatsby's lover, and speaks to being young forever, to going to parties, to nostalgia and vulnerability as demonstrated in the lyrics "You'll love me again when I'm no longer young and beautiful."[19]

ALCHEMY OF A SERIES BETWEEN VINTAGE AND RETRO TASTE

With a look to the past, *Cable Girls* takes us inside the national telephone company, the only place that could represent a form of modernity for the women of the time. It takes us into the headquarters of the company that is not authentic but that has been reconstructed, along with the streets and buildings of Madrid during the 1920s, by imitating the real building design, a tall skyscraper of over ninety meters in height, built between 1926 and 1929, which was based on a plan by the architect Luis Ignacio de Cárdenas.[20] On the thirteen floors of the most representative building in the city, thousands of employees, telephone operators and executives worked in one of the sectors most indicative of the desire and impetus of the time toward the new era of communication. The building went on to host as many as 1,800 workers, most of whom were telephone operators who covered the busiest periods in shifts including up to 150 young women, as well as supervisors and other services associated with telephonic connection.

The two main locations of the series—the telephone exchange and the bar opposite—make up a very large set, with clear references to the architecture of the time. The set of the telephone exchange is the place most frequented by the protagonists of the series, and they had to learn how to use the cables and the systems of the switchboard with coaches and experts.[21] Almost the entire world of the protagonists is enclosed within the spaces of the telephone company, which becomes the center of jealousies, envy and betrayals but also of friendships and loves, following a narrative scheme that creates a synergy between the veracity of the events and fantasy, where behind every event that really happened, improbable deceits and conspiracies are hidden. The fashion and style of the period are brought back to life, thanks to the period costumes and accessories which define the context and reveal the characters, but the series focuses on nonmaterial aspects of the story instead of a world of appealing surfaces. However, the clothes of the series are the result of extensive research conducted personally by costume designer Helena Sanchis, who for almost two months selected original pieces of the 1920s and 1930s in the markets and shops, while patterns and fashion magazines became the main sources of research to give characters greater realism.[22]

The authors avoided a too-faithful reconstruction of the clothing of the past, as these original series should be seen as products destined for an international market as well. This explains why the clothes don't reflect exactly those of Spain in that period, but take their starting point from modernist culture, in particular with references to Paris of the time, as well, the sets and the design of the costumes were more European in *Midnight in Paris*, a 2011 American fantasy comedy set in Paris in the 1920s.[23]

In other words, Netflix's *Cable Girls* adopts an approach close to this model recurrent in Hollywood cinema, without forgetting the fact that they also included an element of "Spanish" expertise in terms of the historic adaptation. While remaining faithful to the aesthetics of the 1920s, the producers allowed themselves a certain amount of "poetic license," removing elements they considered "incoherent" or disturbing because the past would have irremediably become the past. For example, the uniforms have been made more sinuous and feminine in the series than in the reality of the time, as they were similar to "sacks"[24] (see Figure 10.2). In a sense, the series evokes the feeling of a past, does not represent the "real" past, but rather focuses on the "imaginary style of real past" as for "nostalgia film." The generalized sense of the past is rendered through objects and characteristic details described as "surface realism" produced "through the use of period markers such as dress, cars and settings," as well as *Cable Girls'* accessories, such as hats and scarves, which become fetishes for the construction of nostalgia.[25]

In the same way, cinematographic transpositions from the early 1930s showed the operators bundled up in high-necked overalls and long, loose sleeves (as they actually were in many telephone companies), but this was immediately neutralized by the photogenic beauty of the faces of the protagonist-divas who appeared in close-ups on the screen, in line with the prevailing model for divas of the time. In *Cable Girls*, Netflix's series proposes an aesthetic model that does not resemble the codified beauty of cinema actresses of the past but rather a modern-day kind of beauty. We do not see, for example, the famous thin-arched eyebrows typical of the most popular stars of the twenties. The choice to not reproduce exactly the image of the diva of the past (through the costumes and make-up) is in reality a strategy that we can recognize in the concept of realism offered by Nelson Goodman with reference to the image and performance of an actor: "Realism is relative, determined by the system of representation standard for a given culture or person at a given time."[26] In the end, rather than trying to resemble the past as much as possible, the performance becomes much more realistic when it succeeds in making us forget the presence of a code of representation of an artifice. The

Figure 10.2.   Carlota (Ana Fernández), Lidia (Blanca Suárez), Marga (Nadia de Santiago) and the female staff of the telephone company. Promotional image— *Cable Girls* **/ Netflix—Season 2.** *Source: Netflix/Bambú Producciones.*

performances of the actresses in the series who assume the roles of figures belonging to the past are convincing precisely because we do not notice how much their characters are infused with our past and how much they are realistic also in a modern context.[27]

A FEMALE VISION BETWEEN REALITY AND FICTION

Cable Girls expresses the wish to give greater space to series about women, against the retrograde views of the world of work in which women could aspire at most to become switchboard operators or secretaries, without falling into the stereotypes of the traditional Spanish soap operas. In line with the tradition of *Velvet* and *Gran Hotel*'s creators and producers, *Cable Girls* is targeted to a female audience and explores the place of women in the society of the 1920s, a period of great contrasts, caught between mentalities that are reactionary and linked to a past of rules and conventions and modern ideologies, ready to dislodge antiquated attitudes and behavior. In some particularly intense moments, *Cable Girls* tackles various delicate themes, which are also commonplace in today's news: femicide, sexual violence and domestic abuse are placed side by side, on a narrative level, with the desire for redemption, change and that particular need for social and sexual freedom that leads female viewers to identify themselves with the protagonists. Although specifically set in Spain, stories transcend borders and culture, drawing attention to a past that never seems to go away and that reveals how the difficulties of a time are still relevant today. According to the authors, the setting of the story in the past instead of the present makes it possible to highlight the social changes that took place in the 1920s and 1930s in favor of the independence of the whole female gender, and this allowed the representation of the sexes to be even more credible in the 1930s, since the social gap was more marked. In a sense, the series returns to an earlier time marked by progress, yet nostalgic viewing is often seen as regressive: what appears unacceptable is the raw reality. Despite the gap in time, the women in the series have much in common with contemporary women; even after the important advances in women's rights achieved during the twentieth century, women in Spain continue to experience "inequality, maltreatment and discrimination at work,"[28] and the series aims to honor "the struggle that these women have had to undertake in order to find a place in society." Through the interpretive lens of nostalgia, the attempt to tackle the legacy of the past tends to operate on a collective level and works as the active "use of the past in a progressive manner within the present."[29]

CONCLUSION

Netflix's business perspective is to focus mostly on the original productions through efforts and investments, and it expects to reach 8 billion in 2018 by doing agreements with other operators, such as those with Fox-Disney and Sky, as well as numerous agreements with overseas producers. Series with content that contains nostalgia seem to gain positive feedback, especially those addressing characters and universes that people around the world have over time learned to know and love. *Cable Girls* is in tune with Netflix's seriality tendencies and provides a series of distinctive signs in the contemporary panorama that are also the elements of its success. It shows gender policies in the Spanish environment of the early 1930s in line with the aesthetic of a period drama while paying great attention to the daily challenges facing women today, as the characters still speak for the struggle for independence outside of traditional and domestic expectations. Despite the broader definition offered by some scholars of contemporary seriality according to which all TV series are in themselves nostalgic, *Cable Girls'* strength is in the context of setting since it appropriates a particular aesthetic and narrative universe that is not reworked from preexisting series models; it focuses on its original themes in an original way. The design team worked hard to make everything feel and look real, a realness that resonates with the audience not just in fetishistic detail but also drawing attention to the many undesirable aspects of that history. In this way, the Netflix platform relaunches all the expressive potential of film language in the logic of contemporary storytelling, in which viewers connect with the interiority of the characters through the exteriority of the spaces. In this sense, nostalgia helps to relate to "a way of living, imagining and sometimes exploiting or (re)inventing the past, present and future."[30] As nostalgia is the hallmark of many contemporary narrative works, especially in the field of television series, *Cable Girls* is nostalgic not in terms of an ontological realism but in its evocative style.

NOTES

1. Katharina Niemeyer and Daniela Wentz, "Nostalgia Is Not What It Used to Be: Serial Nostalgia and Nostalgic Television Series," in *Media and Nostalgia* , ed. K. Niemeyer (London: Palgrave Macmillan, 2014), 134.

2. *Fräulein—Falsch Verbunden*, dir. Emmerich Wojtek Emo, 1932, Berlin, Germany: Filmjuwelen, 2015, DVD.

3. On the gender models conveyed by cinema in fascist Italy, see Maria Casalini, ed., *Donne e cinema. Immagini del femminile dal fascismo agli anni Settanta* (Roma: Viella, 2016); Victoria De Grazia, *Le donne nel regime fascista,* trans. Stefano Musso (Venezia: Marsilio, 1993).

4. Niemeyer and Wentz, "Nostalgia Is Not What It Used to Be," 134.

5. Michael Pickering and Emily Keightley, "The Modalities of Nostalgia," *Current Sociology* 54, no. 6, (2006): 921.

6. Ed Meza, "Netflix Invests Nearly $2 Billion in European Productions, Promises More," *Variety*, 1 March 2017, http://variety.com/2017/biz/global/reed-hastings-netflix-berlin-100-million-subscribers-1201999745/.

7. Francesca Sironi, "Gli Stati Uniti non bastano più: ecco come Netflix va alla conquista del mondo," *L'Espresso*, July 2, 2017: 82–85.

8. André Bazin, *Che Cosa è il Cinema* (Milano: Garzanti, 1986), 198.

9. Andrea Fioravanti, *La "storia" senza storia: racconti del passato tra letteratura, cinema e televisione* (Perugia: Morlacchi , 2006), 131.

10. Fred Davis, *Yearning for Yesterday: A Sociology of Nostalgia* (New York: Free Press, 1979), 10–18.

11. Stacey Menzel Baker and Patricia F. Kennedy, "Death by Nostalgia: A Diagnosis of Context-Specific Cases," in *NA—Advances in Consumer Research Volume 21*, eds. Chris T. Allen and Deborah Roedder John (Provo, UT: Association for Consumer Research, 1994), 169–74, http://acrwebsite.org/volumes/7580/volumes/v21/NA-21.

12. Russell W. Belk, "Possessions and the Sense of Past," in *SV—Highways and Buyways: Naturalistic Research from the Consumer Behavior Odyssey*, ed. Russell Belk (Provo, UT: Association for Consumer Research, 1990), 114–30.

13. Emiliano Morreale, *L'invenzione della nostalgia. Il vintage nel cinema italiano e dintorni* (Roma: Donzelli, 2009), 12.

14. Emiliano Morreale, "Dalla Nostalgia al Vintage," in *L'ombra del Passato: la nostalgia tra cinema e televisione*, ed. Leonardo Gandini (Trento: Fondazione Museo Storico Trentino, 2011), 35–42.

15. Marta Blazquez Cano, "Do Fashion Blogs Influence Vintage Fashion Consumption? An Analysis from the Perspective of the Chinese Market," in *Vintage Luxury Fashion—Exploring the Rise of the Secondhand Clothing Trade,* eds. Daniella Ryding, Claudia E. Henninger and Marta Blazquez Cano (Manchester: Palgrave, 2018), 167–183.

16. Morris B. Holbrook, "Nostalgia and Consumption Preferences: Some Emerging Patterns of Consumer Tastes," *Journal of Consumer Research* 20, no. 1 (February 1993): 245–256.

17. Morris B. Holbrook and Robert M. Schindler, "Echoes of the Dear Departed Past: Some Work in Progress on Nostalgia," in *NA—Advances in Consumer Research Volume 18*, eds. Rebecca H. Holman and Michael R. Solomon (Provo, UT: Association for Consumer Research, 1991), 330–33.

18. Morris B. Holbrook and Robert M. Schindler, "Nostalgia for Early Experience as a Determinant of Consumer Preferences," *Psychology & Marketing*, 20, no. 4 (2003): 275–302.

19. Lana Del Rey, *Young And Beautiful*, The Great Gatsby: Music from Baz Luhrmann's Film, Interscope Records, 2013.

20. Espacio Fundación Telefónica, "History of the Building," accessed 8 July 2018, https://espacio.fundaciontelefonica.com/en/visit-us/history-of-the-building/.

21. Alice Zampa, "Las chicas del cable. Interviste alle attrici del cast," *Pianetadonna*, 8 May 2017, https://www.pianetadonna.it/notizie/tempo-libero/las-chicas-del-cable-netflix-cast-attrici.html.

22. Manuel Campagna, "Las Chicas del Cable: la prima serie spagnola di Netflix, L'intervista alla costumista Helena Sanchis," Amica, 1 May 2017, https://www.amica.it/2017/05/01/las-chicas-del-cable-la-prima-serie-spagnola-di-netflix/.

23. Alice Zampa, "Las chicas del cable: anteprima esclusiva sulla nuova serie Netflix tutta al femminile," 28 April 2017, https://www.pianetadonna.it/notizie/tempo-libero/las-chicas-del-cable-netflix.html.

24. Zampa, "Interviste."

25. Marc Le Sueur, "Theory Number Five Anatomy of Nostalgia Films: Heritages and Methods," *Journal of Popular Film* 6, no. 2 (London: Routledge, 1977): 193.

26. Nelson Goodman, *Languages of Art: An Approach to a Theory of Symbols* (Indianapolis/Cambridge: Hackett Publishing, 1968), 37.

27. Antonella Giannone and Patrizia Calefato, "Il costume cinematografico," in *Manuale di comunicazione, sociologia e cultura della moda*, 5, *Performance* (Roma: Meltemi, 2007): 17-39.

28. Efe-epa, "'Las Chicas del Cable' Stars Are Pioneers in Fiction and Reality," *Agencia EFE*, 7 April 2017, https://www.efe.com/efe/english/entertainment/las-chicas-del-cable-stars-are-pioneers-in-fiction-and-reality/50000264-3232435.

29. Michael Pickering and Emily Keightley, "Retrotyping and the Marketing of Nostalgia," in *Media and Nostalgia* , 84.

30. Katharina Niemeyer, "Introduction: Media and Nostalgia," in *Media and Nostalgia*, 2.

BIBLIOGRAPHY

Baker, Stacey Menzel, and Patricia F. Kennedy. "Death by Nostalgia: A Diagnosis of Context-Specific Cases." In *NA—Advances in Consumer Research*. Vol. 21. Edited by Chris T. Allen and Deborah Roedder John. Provo, UT: Association for Consumer Research, 1994. http://acrwebsite.org/volumes/7580/volumes/v21/NA-21.

Bazin, André. *Che cosa è il cinema*. Milano: Garzanti, 1986.

Belk, Russell W. "Possessions and the Sense of Past." In *SV—Highways and Buyways: Naturalistic Research from the Consumer Behavior Odyssey*. Edited by Russell Belk. Provo, UT: Association for Consumer Research, 1991.

Cable Girls. Netflix Official Site. https://www.netflix.com/it-en/title/80100929.

Campagna, Manuel. "Las Chicas del Cable: la prima serie spagnola di Netflix, L'intervista alla costumista Helena Sanchis." *Amica*, 1 May 2017. http://www.amica.it/2017/05/01/las-chicas-del-cable-la-prima-serie-spagnola-di-netflix/

Casalini, Maria, eds. *Donne e cinema. Immagini del femminile dal fascismo agli anni Settanta*. Roma: Viella, 2016.

Davis, Fred. *Yearning for Yesterday: A Sociology of Nostalgia*. New York: Free Press, 1979.

De Grazia, Victoria. *Le donne nel regime fascista*. Translated by Stefano Musso. Venezia: Marsilio, 1993.

Del Rey, Lana. "Break My Fall." Recorded 2010. Album unreleased.

Efe-epa. "'Las Chicas del Cable' Stars are Pioneers in Fiction and Reality." *Agencia EFE*, 7 April 2017. https://www.efe.com/efe/english/entertainment/las-chicas-del-cable-stars-are-pioneers-in-fiction-and-reality/50000264-3232435.

Espacio Fundación Telefónica. "History of the Building." https://espacio.fundaciontelefonica.com/en/visit-us/history-of-the-building/.

———. Photographic Archive. https://en.fundaciontelefonica.com/art-digital-culture/artistic-and-technological-collections/photographic-archive/.

Fioravanti, Andrea. *La "storia" senza storia: racconti del passato tra letteratura, cinema e television.* Perugia: Morlacchi, 2006.

Fräulein—Falsch Verbunden, 1932. Directed by Emmerich Wojtek Emo. Filmjuwelen, Alive—Vertrieb und Marketing, 2015. DVD.

Gandini, Leonardo, Daniela Cecchin and Matteo Gentilini, eds. *L'ombra del passato: La nostalgia tra cinema e televisione.* Trento: Fondazione Museo Storico Trentino, 2011.

Giannone, Antonella, and Patrizia Calefato. *Manuale di comunicazione, sociologia e cultura della moda. 5. Performance.* Roma: Meltemi, 2007.

Goodman, Nelson. *Languages of Art: An Approach to a Theory of Symbols.* Indianapolis/Cambridge: Hackett Publishing, 1968.

Holbrook, Morris B. "Nostalgia and Consumption Preferences: Some Emerging Patterns of Consumer Tastes." *Journal of Consumer Research* 20, no. 1 (February 1993): 245–56. https://doi.org/10.1086/209346.

Holbrook, Morris B., and Robert M. Schindler "Echoes of the Dear Departed Past: Some Work in Progress on Nostalgia." In *NA—Advances in Consumer Research.* Vol. 18. Edited by Rebecca H. Holman and Michael R. Solomon. Provo, UT: Association for Consumer Research, 1991.

———. "Nostalgia for Early Experience as a Determinant of Consumer Preferences." *Psychology & Marketing* 20, no. 4 (2003): 275–302.

Le Sueur, Marc. "Theory Number Five Anatomy of Nostalgia Films: Heritages and Methods." *Journal of Popular Film* 6, no. 2. London: Routledge, 1977: 187–97.

Meza, Ed. "Netflix Invests Nearly $2 Billion in European Productions, Promises More." *Variety*, 1 March 2017. http://variety.com/2017/biz/global/reed-hastings-netflix-berlin-100-million-subscribers-1201999745/.

Morreale, Emiliano. *L'invenzione della nostalgia. Il vintage nel cinema italiano e dintorni.* Roma: Donzelli, 2009.

Niemeyer, Katharina, and Daniela Wentz. "Nostalgia Is Not What It Used to Be: Serial Nostalgia and Nostalgic Television Series." In *Media and Nostalgia.* Edited by Katharina Niemeyer. London: Palgrave Macmillan, 2014.

Pickering, Michael, and Emily Keightley. "The Modalities of Nostalgia." *Current Sociology* 54, no. 6 (2006): 919–41.

Ryding, Daniella, Claudia E. Henninger, and Marta Blazquez Cano, eds. *Vintage Luxury Fashion—Exploring the Rise of the Secondhand Clothing Trade.* Manchester: Palgrave, 2018.

Sironi, Francesca. "Gli Stati Uniti non bastano più: ecco come Netflix va alla conquista del mondo." *L'Espresso*, July 2, 2017: 82–85.

The Great Gatsby. 2013. Directed by Baz Luhrmann. Warner Home Video, 2013. DVD.

Zampa, Alice. "Las chicas del cable: anteprima esclusiva sulla nuova serie Netflix tutta al femminile." *Pianetadonna*, 28 April 2017. https://www.pianetadonna.it/notizie/tempo-libero/las-chicas-del-cable-netflix.html.

———. "Las chicas del cable Interviste alle attrici del cast." *Pianetadonna*, 8 May 2017. https://www.pianetadonna.it/notizie/tempo-libero/las-chicas-del-cable-netflix-cast-attrici.html.

ELEVEN

"Weaponizing Nostalgia"

Netflix, Revivals, and Brazilian Fans of Gilmore Girls

Mayka Castellano and Melina Meimaridis

Among mass culture, television has been repeatedly defined as an industry particularly accustomed to repetition as its *modus operandi*, relying on the repetition of successful products and formulas. Such a quality would even be one of its distinctive characteristics. In this sense, television programming has been filled with remakes, reboots, and revivals, which use familiarity and nostalgia to attract viewers. In this scenario, Netflix stands out for "resurrecting" several canceled/finished series, as well as for *weaponizing nostalgia*, that is, producing content aimed at nostalgic fans in a process we'll characterize as *Audience Recall*. This process began in 2013, when it brought back *Arrested Development* (Fox, 2003–2006/Netflix, 2013–). Since then, Netflix has produced *Fuller House* (2016), a reboot of the sitcom *Full House* (ABC, 1987–1995) and a revival of the original show *Gilmore Girls* (The WB, 2000–2006/CW, 2006–2007), *Gilmore Girls: A Year in the Life* (2016),[1] which this chapter will evaluate.

In Greek nostalgia is defined as the pain felt when longing for home and/or homeland. This sentiment was initially defined around the year 1688 and used to describe a type of melancholy that Swiss soldiers felt when they were fighting abroad.[2] The emergence of the word is linked to the construction of a pathology, associated with a particular sentiment (*Heinweh desiderium patriae*), which appears in medical vocabulary and is listed as a disease. Nostalgia, then, begins to describe a peculiar type of melancholy associated with the separation from the everyday environment.[3] However, the entry into the more expanded lexicon only occurred in the nineteenth century, Jean Starobinski points out the term only appeared in the *Dictionaire de l'Académie* in 1835.[4] This entry is significant in recognizing the concept's transition from a medical use to a cultural use, linked to literary practices and, therefore, more imprecise meanings.

According to Starobinski this particular affliction became a universal entity. Moving away from a pathological condition, nostalgia is increasingly associated with a kind of intimate disorder strongly related to memory. Recently, references of a "Culture of Nostalgia"[5] or a "Nostalgia Boom"[6] describe a change in our own perception concerning the term, which no longer refers to a "negative" sentiment, closely tied to war times, but connotes something potentially good linked to the remembrance or recovery of a more or less distant past.

Considering Netflix's relevance in the last decade throughout the world, this chapter seeks to argue that nostalgia, despite being a resource historically used by several TV series, has been weaponized by Netflix: used as one of the company's main strategies, boosting its reach based on subscriber consumption preferences. Our main hypothesis is that through weaponizing nostalgia Netflix can reawaken fandoms, while also providing the company with a "safer investment." In order to present our argument, we'll analyze *Gilmore Girls'* revival and its curious impact on Brazilian fans, who just days after the revival's release decided to gather and "re-create" the town of Stars Hollow in Rio de Janeiro at the event "Stars Hollow in Four Seasons,"[7] which was intended to revive the series' experience, which had been off the air, in Brazil's free-to-air channels, since 2011.

MEMORY AND REPETITION IN AMERICAN FICTIONAL TV SERIES

Nostalgia was initially characterized as a social malaise, associated with a pathology that mainly affected the military, and was approached by physicians and psychologists who sought to find a cure for such a condition.[8] Over the years, the term became more popular, moving away from a pathology and being described as an incurable condition of modernity.[9] More recently, we find a wide and present discussion concerning nostalgia in several fields of knowledge, such as sociology,[10] history,[11] literature,[12] and communication.[13]

In this chapter, Svetlana Boym's definition of nostalgia will be of great use. The author defines the term as "a longing for a home that no longer exists or has never existed. Nostalgia is a feeling of loss and displacement, but it is also a romance with one's own fantasy."[14] For the author, nostalgia goes beyond an individual psychological question, being related to a yearning for a distinct temporal moment and expresses a particular relation with time: "Nostalgia is rebellion against the modern idea of time, the time of history and progress. The nostalgic desires to obliterate history and turn it into private or collective mythology, to revisit time like space, refusing to surrender to the irreversibility of time that plagues the human condition."[15]

By transforming time into a returnable space, nostalgia allows individuals to relive moments from the past. It is a time management strategy in a context in which time seems increasingly elusive. In view of recent technological advances, this return has become apparently "viable" and thus what began as an illness has developed into a profitable marketing resource, since "selling a sweet image of the past brings big bucks."[16]

We consider socially significant the strategical use of nostalgia by several industry segments; therefore, we opted to focus our analysis on the specific relationship between nostalgia and American television. For decades, television shows from the United States have had a nostalgic quality. According to Grainge and Niemeyer there are several reasons behind the current nostalgia boom; therefore, the phenomenon could hardly be reduced to a response derived from only one theoretical framework. The spatial limitations here, however, led us to approach nostalgia from only two distinct perspectives: a structural one—which involves a demand from the American television industry; and a contextual one—that considers the current sociocultural and industrial landscapes as one of the factors for the popularization of nostalgic narratives.

Structural Perspective

The television medium has a long-standing relationship with nostalgia. During its first decades, American channels, although organized with a programming schedule, did not have enough content to fill all the available timeslots, largely because the productions were still recorded live.[17] Years later with the emergence of new technologies that allowed the recording and storing of content, the television schedule began to be filled by both live and prerecorded programs. Serial fiction's high production cost has led to the popularization of reruns (airing the same episode more than once) as a way of profitably filling the "gaps" in each channel's daily schedule.[18] All the while, Buonanno points out that the increase of pay channels in the 1980s and in the subsequent decades created a scenario where the industry was not able to produce and air only brand-new content.[19] The author argues that the scarcity of money and ideas led the medium to incorporate its own memory in its programming.[20]

The frequent use of reruns describes an industrial practice based on a repetition aesthetic in which successful programs are licensed to other channels in the syndication model and stay on air for several years. According to Kompare, "Reruns represent not so much a dormant past as a dynamic television heritage: an ever-changing body of series, genres, stars, sights, and sounds, which culturally anchor the past few decades in the contemporary public memory."[21] The author further contends that repetition is one of television's fundamental strategies, which enables a profitable return from established programs by attracting viewers to a programming that is already familiar. In this sense, the author points out that one of American television's main qualities is its "regime of repetition."[22] Television's interest in the past provides a fertile environment for the emergence of nostalgic narratives.

Contextual Perspective

The contextual perspective can be divided into two angles: commercial and social. In the first case, the American television industry is currently living one of its most abundant periods, with almost five hundred scripted series produced yearly.[23] For the sake of comparison in 2010 this number was limited to 216 productions.[24] Despite this abundance of content, television executives believe that "viewers are more likely to spend time with something they know rather than something new,"[25] therefore, reinforcing the strategy of bringing back previously successful shows.

Although it is plausible to argue the existence of an apparent "media obsession" with nostalgia, this popularization is not only a marketing trend, but can also reveal deeper issues present in our contemporary society, which reflect positive or negative views on the relationship between time and space.[26] Fred Davis argues that nostalgic works and other forms of remembrance of the past tend to become popular in contexts of discontinuity and anxiety.[27] Thus, nostalgia can be understood as "a socio-cultural response to forms of discontinuity, claiming a vision of stability and authenticity in some conceptual 'golden age.'"[28] Davis, analyzing the "nostalgia boom" in the seventies, proposes that nostalgia, although a social emotion, can also be considered an aesthetic modality that arises in response to the yearning for continuity in moments of transition.[29]

The current sociocultural context of the so-called postmodernity may be influencing the return of past works, since there would be a desire to relive a "better time," a period conceived in a romanticized way as prior to the decline of principles and customs.[30] The cyclical political and economic crises in the capitalist system and the migratory movements potentialized by globalization are also pointed out as inductors of this desire, by providing a sense of stability and belonging, made possible, on the one hand, by familiarity with certain fictional universes and, on the other, by the affective memory brought by fruition. In this way, nostalgic narratives create a distorted picture that things were better in past decades, an image with which the present cannot compete with because "it is always the adoration of the past that triumphs over the lamentations for the present."[31]

Such narratives, in addition to appropriating this romanticized celebration of the past, can also function as escapist works by distracting viewers and helping them to distance themselves from their social realities, which may involve personal, work, or wider problems relating to society, politics, dilemmas, and issues, especially in adult life, that were not present in the same way in the past.

NETFLIX AND THE NOSTALGIA ALGORITHM

American television has changed a lot since its early days, both in technological and commercial terms, as well as in aspects related to consumption and spectatorship. During the 1980s and 1990s, the emergence of the videocassette recorder (VCR) made time-shifting possible, as well as, allowed viewers to build their own video "libraries" of television content.[32]

The notion of a library of content is consolidated with Netflix. The company is currently one of linear television's main competitors[33] and has a contradictory discourse about its insertion in the market: although it claims to produce TV, the company makes a point of constantly marketing its productions as a "new" kind of television.[34] This strategy has already been discussed by Castellano and Meimaridis; the authors indicate that the service has relied on discourses of distinction as a marketing strategy to distance itself from linear television.[35]

In Brazil, Netflix has become wildly popular. To understand this, one must first observe that Brazil has one of the most overpriced pay television services in the world. Still, those who have access to American television shows on pay cable channels complain of time gaps between the official broadcast in the United States and the broadcast in Brazil, that can vary from days, weeks, or even months. This scenario encourages fans to search the web for streaming services, online pirated links, or downloads to watch their favorite shows in a timely manner. In this sense, Netflix's one-drop release model and its relatively cheap cost have made the company increasingly popular in Brazil. In 2016, the company doubled the number of Brazilian subscribers from three to six million. The rapid growth has attracted attention from Netflix's CEO, Reed Hastings, who in an interview said, "Brazil is a rocket, the growth here is impressive and we want to increase our investments in local content."[36]

Among all of the possible analytical avenues, we'll seek to explore a marketing strategy that has attracted our attention and that we characterize here as weaponizing nostalgia. The expression began to circulate in 2014, referring to the hashtag #ThrowbackThursday, or #TBT, on social networks,[37] which consisted of (re)posting old images or personal photos on a specific day of the week. Here, we understand the expression weaponizing nostalgia as a phenomenon that describes the use certain media producers have made of the recent "nostalgia boom."[38]

We propose in this sense the concept of Audience Recall, that is, the awakening of an audience that already exists and that, therefore, needs little effort to be engaged. Similar strategies have been developed within the framework of the so-called convergence culture, when the public's migratory behavior leads large media companies to explore, for example, the same narrative universe in as many platforms as possible.[39] Here, however, we refer to a specific process, in which a particular audience is not being stimulated, due to the absence of new elements relating to that product. It is important to emphasize that we are not referring to a fandom, the more articulate fan community of these productions, since fandoms in large part remain active and stimulated even during long periods of hiatus from new content, mainly by the existence of parallel productive logics, such as those represented by fanfics and other fan creations.

Audience Recall is used here to analyze Netflix's strategy of reviving canceled series, a phenomenon that began in 2013 when the company produced a new season of *Arrested Development,* a comedy that despite having an active fan community had been canceled by Fox in 2006 for not delivering high enough ratings. In the following years, Netflix produced *Fuller House.* The show's teaser is made up of iconic images from the original show and the sound of the country song "The House That Built Me" by Miranda Lambert.[40] The artist sings about her childhood memories and about her impossible desire to return to the house that is no longer her own. In 2016, Netflix also announced another successful revival, *Gilmore Girls: A Year in the Life.*

REVIVING *GILMORE GIRLS*

From a commercial and media point of view *Gilmore Girls: A Year in the Life* was a success. The season was made up of four ninety-minute episodes that brought the original cast back together. Created by Amy Sherman-Palladino, the original series follows the life of Lorelai Gilmore (Lauren Graham), who begins the show thirty-two years old, and her teenage daughter nicknamed Rory (Alexis Bledel), sixteen years old. In the first episodes, we are informed that Lorelai's unexpected pregnancy led to a strain in her relationship with her parents, Emily (Kelly Bishop) and Richard (Edward Herrmann), members of a traditional and affluent family from Hartford, Connecticut. Rory's birth coincides with Lorelai's move to the small town of Stars Hollow, where she resumes life as a maid at the local Independence Inn. The plot focuses on the professional, romantic and family dramas of the duo over the years and explores the mother and daughter relationship closely.

The idea for the revival was motivated by the uproar on social media after Netflix added all seven seasons of *Gilmore Girls* to its American catalog in 2014.[41] The tone of the posts revolved around the excitement of being able to watch again a show from the past. Most of the messages were posted by young adults who were teenagers, the target audience of the show, when *Gilmore Girls* aired. The mother-daughter theme also set the tone for the celebration, of teen girls who once identified with Rory, now adults having the opportunity to see the show through Lorelai's perspective. It should be noted that the show would only be added to the Brazilian catalog in 2016.

The series was well received by Netflix's subscribers and awakened the company's interest in taking advantage of this nostalgic wave with a new iteration of an existing series, that is also available on the platform. Added to this, we cannot ignore the algorithm, a rich mechanism for measuring the preferences of subscribers that the company has at its disposal and which certainly influences the decision to invest or not on certain products. This situation has been characterized by some authors as "Algorithm Culture."[42] Logically, *Gilmore Girls* fans' feedback associated with a cross-referencing of the public's access data revealed the potential for a new season.

After months of rumors and negotiations with the creators (Amy and her husband, coauthor Daniel Palladino), in January 2016, official news confirmed that Netflix would bring *Gilmore Girls* back. The seventh and (last) season of the original version was penned without the show's creators input, because they had left the production at the end of season 6 over financial disagreements. The main frustration fans have mentioned over the years is the fact that Amy was not able to finish the story she created. The showrunner, throughout the years, would often say that she knew the four last words she wanted to conclude the show with, yet she never was able to employ them in the original run. *Gilmore Girls* abrupt cancellation in the seventh season led to an ending that, while frustrating for the fans, left room for the story to be continued.

The confirmation that Amy could finally make a worthy finish to the *Gilmore Girls'* saga (and ultimately reveal the four final mythical words) prompted a new wave of celebration from fans around the world. The excitement was capitalized by Netflix, who frequently encouraged the buzz with posts and news on their social media profiles. The post on Netflix's Brazilian profile announced in Portuguese "From Stars Hollow to Netflix. #GilmoreGirls returns with a new Netflix original eighth season. And yes all of the classic seasons are coming to Netflix also. In 2016, only on Netflix" (Netflix, 2016). The post had over thirty-three thousand likes and over four thousand comments, with fans using popular phrases from the original show like "I don't like Mondays" and "Coffee, coffee, coffee."[43] The revival debuted on November 25, 2016, after ten months of intense speculation and debate by fans on how the show would return. The whole revival is punctuated by the return of elements from the original story, mainly because the new episodes were recorded in the same place of the original seasons. From the aesthetic point of view, most of the nostalgic elements of the revival can be perceived in the maintenance of the environments and objects of the original work, which is justified by the reluctance of several characters to abandon old habits, something that is in keeping with their personalities.

Every local spot remained virtually identical in the revival such as the main characters' homes, Emily's mansion, the inn, Luke's Diner, as well as the town itself. Another important element was the presence of all of the original cast members, with the notable exception of Edward Herrmann, Lorelai's father, who died in 2014. The actor's death was included in the plot with Richard's demise off-screen. This significant loss is the revival's starting point in which the three main characters (Lorelai, Emily, and Rory) try to move forward in life. In the first episode, we see, in a flashback, the patriarch's funeral. Richard's absence is an important element in the revival's attempt to both "continue" previous storylines and present new developments for the characters, especially Emily and Lorelai, who were more directly impacted by the loss.

The revival is full of moments that bare resemblance to storylines from the original show. In the first episode, it is revealed that Lorelai and Emily fought right after Richard's wake. This strain in their relationship, however, is not strange to fans of the original production, since the troubled relationship between the two characters is present throughout all of *Gilmore Girls*. So, starting the revival with this particular fight is a very familiar way to bring viewers to a place they've once been very accustomed to and remind them of all of the struggles these characters have faced along the years.

In the last episode of the seventh season Luke and Lorelai's relationship was left up in the air, a sore spot for many fans who were frustrated by this incomplete ending; however, the revival provided closure by having the couple get married. In one of the last scenes from the revival, Luke is strolling through town in his pickup truck, with Lorelai and Rory standing in the cargo area. The scene plays out to Sam Phillips's song "Reflecting Light." The song, which continues throughout the whole scene, is also familiar to viewers, as it had already been used in one of the couple's most intimate moments in the episode "Last Week Fights, This Week Tights" (season 4, episode 21). The song becomes the perfect soundtrack for the couple's impromptu wedding late in the night. The couple chooses to anticipate the experience of the following day by holding a private and more intimate ceremony at the town square.

During the revival, longtime viewers were able to watch Lorelai, now forty-eight years old, in crisis about not having any children with Luke; Emily's mourning and the need to find joy in her life since her affairs in Hartford's high society seemed frugal after her husband's death; and Rory, now a thirty-two-year-old adult struggling to find a steady job and searching for answers about life's meaning. Throughout the course of the four new episodes, the young woman has shallow relationships and maintains an affair with an ex-boyfriend. Near the end of the last episode of the revival we discover that the final four words, safely guarded by Amy Sherman-Palladino for so many years, revealed Rory's unplanned pregnancy. This revelation provided a sentiment that the narrative had come full circle. Rory, now pregnant, begins a new journey, the same age as Lorelai when the original show began.

RECALLING THE BRAZILIAN *GILMORE GIRLS'* FANDOM

Although American television series have aired in Brazilian TV since the sixties in free-to-air channels, more recently these productions have found a larger audience through cable channels, streaming services, and illegal downloads and torrents. In this way, certain specificities concerning access to these productions in Brazil should be considered. Although some shows are still shown in free-to-air channels, such as Globo and SBT, most of these channels air incomplete seasons. Meanwhile, pay television channels air these productions fully; however, viewers complain of the asynchronous distribution of content in which the official broadcast in the United States and the airing in Brazil can vary from days, weeks, or even months. All the while, pay-cable television is still limited to a rather small portion of the population, not reaching 10 percent of Brazil's two hundred million population.[44] This whole scenario encourages fans to search the web for streaming services, online pirated links, or downloads to watch their favorite shows in a cheap and timely manner.

In Brazil, *Gilmore Girls* aired on SBT inconsistently for many years and fully on a couple of cable channels, such as Warner Channel, Boomerang, and MTV, cultivating, in this way, a large fan base in the country. The complete series has also been available on Netflix since July 2016. Although Netflix tried to bring Stars Hollow to life by appropriating elements from the town and creating an efficient marketing campaign that preceded the debut of the revival, most of these efforts were limited to an American audience, for example the over two hundred American coffee shops that Netflix took over and transformed into mini Luke's Diners in October 2016.[45] However, Brazilian fans of the television show, decided to gather and "re-create" the town of Stars Hollow for themselves in Brazil. The organizers of the event "Stars Hollow in Four Seasons" dressed up a small park in Rio de Janeiro with many symbols and references from the show, and from the revival's new episodes. On December 3, 2016, just days after the new episodes debuted, a gathering of fans enjoyed their shared enthusiasm for the show by visiting the park and somehow having the "feeling" of being in Stars Hollow.

The celebratory event happened in a park in the district of Méier. The place was chosen because "the square has a beautiful gazebo, one of the few available in Brazilian cities," explained one of the organizers of the event. The event was called "Stars Hollow in Four Seasons" and was made viable through a crowdfunding campaign on the Brazilian website Catarse.me that was supported by ninety-seven people.

With the phrase, "Have you ever imagined spending a whole day in Stars Hollow, with music, books, food and a FREE ENTRANCE? Oy with the poodles already!" the organizers of the event presented their idea for the gathering through a Facebook event that had over seven hundred confirmed invites and over a thousand interested individuals.[46] The theme of the event was the town of Stars Hollow. Because each new episode in the revival referenced a specific season of the year, the square was divided and decorated accordingly. In summer, people could sit in beach chairs and participate in the debate "Feminism and Representation in *Gilmore Girls.*" At the same time, they could compete in a *Gilmore Girls* trivia game, or listen to the lectures "Characters and Fans: Shared Lives" with Professor Luísa Melo from Puc-Rio University and "The *Gilmore Girls* in a Feminist World: A Journey in Time" with journalist Mônica Chaves.

In fall, people found food trucks, and in spring, they were able to purchase or exchange books, clearly in reference to Rory's reading habit. Singers who sang some of the show's most popular songs, as well as their own original music also attended the event. These artists preformed in "troubadour style" a quirky Stars Hollow feature. The most crowded part of the party, however, was the gazebo completely decorated in winter theme. There were styrofoam snowflakes scattered all over the gazebo, which created a fun contrast with the scorching summer day in Rio de Janeiro. The 104-degree heat sensation did not stop fans from standing in line to take pictures with the gazebo, or with a very peculiar snowman (who imitated one made by Rory and Lorelai on the show's tenth episode of the second season). There was also a replica of the Stars Hollow welcome sign which was a must-have snapshot for most visitors.

During the event, it was interesting to note the number of adult women along with female friends of the same age, who probably shared the habit of watching the series as teenagers. In addition, many were accompanied by small children and shared with them the facts about the series as they walked through the park filled with references to that narrative universe. It was noticeable among the participants that they wanted to share with close friends and people who they just met the impressions about the revival, whether to point out what they had loved or to discuss what they thought was frustrating. It is important to remember that the event was created, organized, and financed by fans, with no participation of external donors involved with the series. Below, figure 11.1 shows the Gazebo dressed in winter elements and figure 11.2 shows plaques of several Stars Hollow signature places.

Figure 11.1. The gazebo decorated with winter elements and the snowman from the show's second season. *Source: Courtesy of Melina Meimaridis.*

Figure 11.2. Plaques of signature places from Stars Hollow. *Source: Courtesy of Melina Meimaridis.*

NOTES ON TIME AND MEMORY: FINAL CONSIDERATIONS

The return of canceled television shows is emblematic of the current television landscape, in which the cutthroat environment has enabled successful narratives from the past to come back and be reimagined. To assert that television is undergoing a transformational process is an oversimplified statement, since frequent change is one of the medium's hallmarks. Perhaps this explains the multiplicity of processes we perceive in ways of producing, distributing, and consuming television. New agents, such as streaming services, innovate practices that, as we have seen, are not entirely new. The appeal to the viewer's memory, both as a narrative resource and as a form of Audience Recall, is quite old. *Gilmore Girls'* return has reawakened a very enthusiastic audience around the world, but particularly in Brazil.

In this chapter, we analyzed Netflix's practices of reviving canceled series, specifically analyzing *Gilmore Girls'* revival. We found some indications that the revival, framed here as a case of weaponized nostalgia, worked several narrative elements in order to activate fans' memories. From the commercial point of view, the idea was a success. The series got Netflix's third biggest audience debut in 2016, according to Symphony Advanced Media over five million viewers, ages eighteen to forty-five, watched the show in its premiere weekend.[47] While we do not wish to propose further investigation into the reception of the revival by the public, it is interesting to note that our empirical research has brought some conflicting perceptions about the production.

Dealing with memory and nostalgia, both complex and current themes, even from the notion of weaponizing nostalgia, as we propose here, brings with it subjective questions that cannot be neglected. It was interesting to note that some fans were disappointed with the revival, and that the explanations for this usually revolved around an inability of the show to reproduce the "original work's spirit." A recurrent critique of revivals and other shows that seek the difficult task of remaking a past success. The question that we put forward is that if nostalgia can act as a lure to audiences, guaranteeing an initial public that does not demand much effort to be engaged, it also imposes difficulties in its execution.

When commenting on Kant's conception of nostalgia, Starobinski states that for the Prussian philosopher, the desire of the nostalgic is not the place of his youth, but youth itself, childhood itself, linked to an earlier world, a time of his unrecoverable life.[48] Revisiting known narrative universes can thus offer the reassuring pleasure of reunion and, at the same time, the nuisance about the perception that time has passed, that those people on the screen are no longer the same, that we are no longer the same and that time also acts inexorably in our experiences with cultural objects. Netflix's television consumption practices, because of its recent nature, still preclude peremptory statements about its effectiveness. The *Gilmore Girls'* revival, although promoted as a window into the past, has created a desire for continuation in its fan community, especially because of the cliffhanger at the end. If we'll continue to follow the *Gilmore Girls'* saga over time, only time (and Netflix) will tell.

NOTES

1. Todd VanDerWerff, "*Stranger Things* Doesn't Just Reference '80s Movies. It Captures How It Feels to Watch Them," *Vox*, August 2, 2016, https://www.vox.com/2016/8/2/12328900/stranger-things-netflix-review-emotions

2. Harvey A. Kaplan, "The Psychopathology of Nostalgia." *Psychoanalytic Review*, 74 (Winter 1987), 465-86.

3. Jean Starobinski, *L'encre de la Mélancolie* (Paris: Le Seuil, 2013).

4. Starobinski, *L'encre de la Mélancolie*.

5. Paul Grainge, "Nostalgia and Style in Retro America: Moods, Modes, and Media Recycling." *The Journal of American Culture* 23 (Spring 2000), 28.

6. Katharina Niemeyer, *Media and Nostalgia* (Basingstoke: Palgrave Macmillan, 2014), 1.

7. Cristine Gerk, "Fãs de 'Gilmore Girls' Vão Recriar a Cidade de Stars Hollow no Rio," O Globo, November 26, 2016. https://oglobo.globo.com/cultura/revista-da-tv/fas-de-gilmore-girls-vao-recriar-cidade-de-stars-hollow-no-rio-20540606

8. Fred Davis, "From Yearning for Yesterday: A Sociology of Nostalgia," in *The Collective Memory Reader*, ed. by Jeffrey K. Olick, Vered Vinitzky-Seroussi, and Daniel Levy (Oxford: Oxford University Press, 2011), 446-451.

9. Svetlana Boym, *The Future of Nostalgia* (New York: Basic Books, 2001).

10. Michael Pickering and Emily Keightley, "The Modalities of Nostalgia," *Current Sociology* 54 (November 2006), 919-941.

11. André Bolzinger, *Histoire de la Nostalgie* (Paris: Campagne Première, 2007).

12. Starobinski, *L'encre de la mélancolie*.

13. Amy Holdsworth. *Television, Memory and Nostalgia* (London: Palgrave Macmillan, 2011).

14. Boym, *The Future of Nostalgia*, xiii.

15. Boym, *The Future of Nostalgia*, xv.

16. Charles Panati, *Panati's Parade of Fads, Follies, and Manias* (New York, NY: Harper Perennial, 1991).

17. Michele Hilmes, *Only Connect: A Cultural History of Broadcasting in the United States* (Third Edition, California: Wadsworth Cengage Learning, 2011).

18. Derek Kompare, *Rerun Nation: How Repeats Invented American Television* (New York: Routledge, 2006).

19. Milly Buonanno, *The Age of Television: Experiences and Theories* (Bristol, UK: Intellect Books, 2008).

20. Buonanno, *The Age of Telvision*, 17.

21. Derek Kompare, "I've Seen This One Before: The Construction of 'Classic TV' on Cable Television," in *Small Screens, Big Ideas: Television in the 1950s*, ed. by Janet Thumin (London: I.B. Tauris, 2002), 20.

22. Kompare, *Rerun nation*, xvii.

23. Caroline Framke, "500 Scripted Shows in 2017 and 71 Netflix Originals: The Future of TV Is Crowded," *Vox*, August 10, 2016. http://www.vox.com/2016/8/10/12413968/peak-tv-500-shows-john-landgraf.

24. Maureen Ryan, "TV Peaks again in 2016: Could It Hit 500 Shows in 2017?" *Variety*, December 21, 2016. http://variety.com/2016/tv/news/peak-tv-2016-scripted-tv-programs-1201944237/.

25. Robert V. Bellamy, Daniel G. McDonald, and James R. Walker, "The Spin-Off as Television Program Form and Strategy." *Journal of Broadcasting & Electronic Media* 34, no. 3 (April 1990), 283-297.

26. Niemeyer, *Media and Nostalgia.*

27. Davis, "From Yearning for Yesterday."

28. Grainge, "Nostalgia and Style," 28.

29. Davis, "From Yearning for Yesterday."

30. Frederic Jameson, *Postmodernism, or, the Cultural Logic of Late Capitalism* (North Carolina: Duke University Press, 1991).

31. Davis, "From Yearning for Yesterday," 448.

32. Amanda D. Lotz, *The Television Will Be Revolutionized* (New York: New York University Press, 2007).

33. Amanda Lotz, *Portals: A Treatise on Internet-Distributed Television* (Michigan: Michigan Publishing, 2017).

34. Chuck Tryon, "TV Got Better: Netflix's Original Programming Strategies and the On-Demand Television Transition." *Media Industries Journal* 2 (2015).

35. Mayka Castellano and Melina Meimaridis, "Netflix, Discourse of Distinction and New Modes of Televison Production." *Contemporanea -Revista de Comunicação e Cultura* 14 (August 2016), 193-209.

36. Daniel Gallas, "Como a Netflix Driblou a Pirataria e Fez do Brasil seu 'Foguete'" November 23, 2015, https://www.bbc.com/portuguese/noticias/2015/11/151123_netflix_pirataria_brasil_dg_fn.

37. James Poniewozik, "Every Day Is Throwback Thursday: The Weaponized Nostalgia of the Internet," *Time*, October 2, 2014. http://time.com/3455924/internet-nostalgia-social-media/.

38. Niemeyer, "*Media and Nostalgia.*"

39. Henry Jenkins, *Convergence Culture: Where Old and New Media Collide* (New York: New York University Press, 2006).

40. Netflix, "*Fuller House* I Teaser [HD] I Netflix," December 15, 2015. https://www.youtube.com/watch?v=uhInIOKwGXU.

41. Kirsten Harris, "The Best Twitter Reactions to 'Gilmore Girls' Coming to Netflix," *Buzzfeed*, September 11, 2014. https://www.buzzfeed.com/kristinharris/the-best-twitter-reactions-to-gilmore-girls-coming-to-netfli?utm_term=.amVZDaZYQ#.hwxkQak9A.

42. Blake Hallinan and Ted Striphas, "Recommended for You: The Netflix Prize and the Production of Algorithmic Culture," *New Media & Society* 18 (January 2016), 117-137.

43. Netflix, "De Stars Hollow para a Netflix," Facebook, January 29, 2016, https://www.facebook.com/netflixbrasil/photos/a.218069644916503/1062547397135386/?type=3&theater.

44. Maria I. V. Lopes, Maria and Guilhermo O. Gómez, *(Re)Inventions of TV Fiction Genre and Formats* (Porto Alegre: Sulina, 2016).

45. Libby Hill, "Fans Get Their 'Gilmore Girls' on at Luke's Diner Pop-Up Coffee Shops," *LA Times*, October 5, 2016, http://www.latimes.com/entertainment/tv/la-et-st-gilmore-girls-anniversary-coffee-shop-20161005-snap-story.html.

46. Stars Hollow em Quatro Estações, Facebook, https://www.facebook.com/events/1797201633885579/.

47. Michael O'Connell, "'*Gilmore Girls*' Revival Appears to Be a Huge Ratings Hit for Netflix," December 1, 2016. https://www.hollywoodreporter.com/live-feed/gilmore-girls-netflix-ratings-third-biggest-2016-951967.

48. Starobinski, *L'encre de la mélancolie.*

BIBLIOGRAPHY

Bellamy, Robert V., Daniel G. McDonald, and James R. Walker. "The Spin-Off as Television Program Form and Strategy." *Journal of Broadcasting & Electronic Media* 34, no. 3 (1990): 283-297. Accessed September 4, 2018. https://doi:10.1080/08838159009386743.

Bolzinger, André. *Histoire de la Nostalgie.* Paris: Campagne Première, 2007.

Boym, Svetlana. *The Future of Nostalgia.* New York: Basic Books, 2001.

Buonanno, Milly. *The Age of Television: Experiences and Theories.* Bristol, UK: Intellect Books, 2008.

Castellano, Mayka, and Melina Meimaridis. "Netflix, Discursos de Distinção e os Novos Modelos de Produção Televisiva//Netflix, Discourse of Distinction and New Modes of Televison Production." *Contemporanea-Revista de Comunicação e Cultura* 14, no. 2 (2016): 193-209. Accessed September 4, 2018. http://dx.doi.org/10.9771/1809-9386contemporanea.v14i2.16398.

Davis, Fred. "From Yearning for Yesterday: A Sociology of Nostalgia." In *The Collective Memory Reader*, edited by Jeffrey K. Olick, Vered Vinitzky-Seroussi, and Daniel Levy, 446-451. Oxford: Oxford University Press, 2011.

Dean, Peter. "DVDs: Add-Ons or Bygones." *Convergence: The International Journal of Research into New Media Technologies* 13 (May 2007): 119-128. Accessed September 4, 2018. http://dx.doi:10.1177/1354856507075239.

Framke, Caroline. "500 Scripted Shows in 2017 and 71 Netflix Originals: The Future of TV Is Crowded," *Vox.* August 10, 2016. http://www.vox.com/2016/8/10/12413968/peak-tv-500-shows-john-landgraf.

Gallas, Daniel. "Como a Netflix Driblou a Pirataria e Fez do Brasil seu 'Foguete'" November 23, 2015, https://www.bbc.com/portuguese/noticias/2015/11/151123_netflix_pirataria_brasil_dg_fn

Gerk, Cristine. "Fãs de 'Gilmore Girls' Vão Recriar a Cidade de Stars Hollow no Rio," *O Globo.* November 26, 2016. https://oglobo.globo.com/cultura/revista-da-tv/fas-de-gilmore-girls-vao-recriar-cidade-de-stars-hollow-no-rio-20540606

Grainge, Paul. "Nostalgia and Style in Retro America: Moods, Modes, and Media Recycling." *The Journal of American Culture* 23 (Spring 2000): 27-34. Accessed September 4, 2018. http://dx.doi:10.1111/j.1537-4726.2000.2301_27.x.

Hallinan, Blake, and Ted Striphas. Recommended For You: The Netflix Prize and the Production of Algorithmic Culture. *New Media & Society*, 18 (January 2016): 117-137. Accessed September 4, 2018. http://dx.doi:10.1177/1461444814538646.

Harris, Kirsten. "The Best Twitter Reactions to 'Gilmore Girls' Coming to Netflix," *Buzzfeed.* September 11, 2014. https://www.buzzfeed.com/kristinharris/the-best-twitter-reactions-to-gilmore-girls-coming-to-netfli?utm_term=.amVZDaZYQ#.hwxkQak9A

Hill, Libby. "Fans Get Their 'Gilmore Girls' on at Luke's Diner Pop-Up Coffee Shops." *Los Angeles Time.* October 5, 2016. http://www.latimes.com/entertainment/tv/la-et-st-gilmore-girls-anniversary-coffee-shop-20161005-snap-story.html

Hills, Matt. 2007. "From the Box in the Corner to the Box Set on the Shelf." *New Review of Film and Television Studies* 5 (March 2007): 41-60. Accessed September 4, 2018. http://dx.doi:10.1080/17400300601140167.

Hilmes, Michele. *Only Connect*: A Cultural History of Broadcasting in the United States. Third Edition, California: Wadsworth Cengage Learning, 2011.

Holdsworth, Amy. *Television, Memory and Nostalgia.* London: Palgrave Macmillan, 2011.

Jameson, Frederic. *Postmodernism, or, the Cultural Logic of Late Capitalism.* North Carolina: Duke University Press, 1991.

Jenkins, Henry. *Convergence Culture: Where Old and New Media Collide.* New York: NYU Press, 2006.

Kaplan, Harvey A. "The Psychopathology of Nostalgia." *Psychoanalytic Review*, 74 (Winter 1987): 465-86.

Kompare, Derek. "I've Seen This One Before: The Construction of 'Classic TV' on Cable Television." In *Small Screens, Big Ideas*: Television in the 1950s, edited by Janet Thumin, 19-34. London: I.B. Tauris, 2002.

———. *Rerun nation: How Repeats Invented American Television*. New York: Routledge, 2006.

Lopes, Maria I.V. and Guilhermo O. Gómez. *(Re)Inventions of TV Fiction Genre and Formats*. Porto Alegre: Sulina, 2016.

Lotz, Amanda. D. *The Television Will Be Revolutionized*. New York: NYU Press, 2007.

———. *Portals: A Treatise on Internet-Distributed Television*. Michigan: Michigan Publishing, 2017.

Netflix's Facebook page. Accessed 08 December 2016. https://www.facebook.com/netflixbrasil/photos/a.218069644916503/1062547397135386/?type=3&theater.

Niemeyer, Katharina. *Media and Nostalgia*. Basingstoke: Palgrave Macmillan, 2014.

O'Connell, Michael. "'Gilmore Girls' Revival Appears to Be a Huge Ratings Hit for Netflix," *Hollywood Reporter*. December 1, 2016. https://www.hollywoodreporter.com/live-feed/gilmore-girls-netflix-ratings-third-biggest-2016-951967.

Panati, Charles. *Panati's Parade of Fads, Follies, and Manias*. New York, NY: Harper Perennial, 1991.

Pickering, Michael, and Emily Keightley. "The Modalities of Nostalgia." *Current Sociology* 54 (November 2006): 919-941. http://dx.doi:10.1177/0011392106068458.

Poniewozik, James. "Every Day Is Throwback Thursday: The Weaponized Nostalgia of the Internet." *Time*. October 2, 2014. http://time.com/3455924/internet-nostalgia-social-media/.

Ryan, Maureen. "TV Peaks again in 2016: Could It Hit 500 Shows in 2017?" *Variety*. December, 21, 2016. http://variety.com/2016/tv/news/peak-tv-2016-scripted-tv-programs-1201944237/.

Starobinski, Jean. *L'encre de la Mélancolie*. Paris: Le Seuil, 2013.

Tryon, Chuck. "TV Got Better: Netflix's Original Programming Strategies and the On-Demand Television Transition." *Media Industries Journal* 2 (2015). http://dx.doi:10.3998/mij.15031809.0002.206.

VanDerWerff, Todd. "*Stranger Things* Doesn't Just Reference '80s Movies. It Captures How It Feels to Watch Them," *Vox*, August 2, 2016, https://www.vox.com/2016/8/2/12328900/stranger-things-netflix-review-emotions.

TWELVE

Nostalgic Things

Stranger Things *and the Pervasiveness of* *Nostalgic Television*

Joseph M. Sirianni

HAWKINS, INDIANA; 1983—A group of adolescent boys—Mike, Dustin, Lucas, and Will—are tucked away in the basement of a Midwestern suburban home playing a feverish game of Dungeons & Dragons. The wood paneled walls surrounding them holds a poster of John Carpenter's *The Thing* and among their frantic gameplay, Mike's mom—complete with 1980s iconic, layered feathered hair—yells for them to wrap it up. Upstairs in the living room, dad fiddles with the rabbit ear antenna, and outside the boys take off on their BMX bikes. And with that scene, viewers are transported back to the 1980s and into Netflix's hugely popular series, *Stranger Things*.

But something even more transportive happens at the eight-minute mark of the pilot episode. In a hue of neon red, the title of the series slowly reveals itself in a typeface reminiscent of the covers of early Stephen King novels, and the theme music recalls the early synth film scores of John Carpenter. But the pop cultural references of the era don't stop there as the plot synopsis from Netflix reads: *When a young boy vanishes, a small town uncovers a mystery involving secret experiments, terrifying supernatural forces and one strange little girl.* From that description alone, films such as *Poltergeist*, *E.T.*, and *Firestarter* are noted and the homages persist throughout the series, calling upon other noteworthy films of the 1970s and 1980s including *Jaws*, *Close Encounters of the Third Kind*, *Alien*, *The*

Empire Strikes Back, A Nightmare on Elm Street, The Goonies, Stand by Me, and *Predator.*

For those who grew up in the 1980s, *Stranger Things* is a time machine disguised as a television series that is destined to remind viewers of the era's most memorable films. But it's not just the winks to the decade's entertainment that transports audiences. The fashion, the set design, the score, *the bikes,* all serve as memory pathways that has established the series' reputation for being an 1980s time capsule. For many viewers, the immersive appeal of *Stranger Things* lies within its ability to generate intimate memories of the era—it's an emotional portal to one's past, it's nostalgia. Since the show's premiere, nostalgia was immediately attributed to the appeal of the series with critics declaring: "*Stranger Things* is terrifyingly good '80s nostalgia,"[1] "Netflix's *Stranger Things* basks in '80s nostalgia but doesn't drown in it,"[2] and "With *Stranger Things,* Netflix delivers an eerie nostalgia fix."[3]

NOSTALGIC TELEVISION

Nostalgia can be defined as a yearning for the past, or a fondness for tangible or intangible possessions and activities linked with a previous era that is no longer attainable.[4] Peak research interest in nostalgia emerged in the 1970s under sociologist Fred Davis who viewed nostalgia as a fondness for the past marked by positive yet bittersweet feelings.[5] Nostalgic sources exist profusely with researchers designating anything from a visit to a childhood home to collecting sports memorabilia as potential stimuli.[6] Considering the massive success of *Stranger Things,* and other programs within its periphery, television is arguably being used as one of the prime sources for generating nostalgia today and Netflix appears to be leading the pack. Period television shows such as *The Get Down, Black Mirror's* "San Junipero," *GLOW, Everything Sucks,* and *Dark* have offered Netflix viewers a reimagined yet familiar escape back in time. On the other hand, reboots like *Queer Eye, Bill Nye Saves the World, One Day at a Time, Voltron, Wet Hot American Summer,* and *Lost in Space* are appeasing viewers with a modern take on old favorites. And finally, Netflix has revived shows such as *Arrested Development, Fuller House, Gilmore Girls,* and *Mystery Science 3000* inviting subscribers to sit back and catch up with their old favorites.

This of course isn't the first time the industry has tapped into audiences' sense of nostalgia. *Happy Days,* along with other television shows of the 1970s like *The Waltons* and *Little House on the Prairie,* were part of what Davis referred to as "the nostalgia wave of the seventies."[7] In describing these shows Davis states, "onto the market has also come that strange hybrid form, the new old show, shows that are "new" perhaps in the strict technical sense of not having been produced before but are so unabashedly permeated by qualities of genre revivalism as to make them appear authentic "leftovers" from an earlier era."[8] By today's standards, that hybrid form is no longer aberrant; it's commonplace on broadcast, cable, and streaming outlets with *Stranger Things* being the current archetype. At the moment, hybrid forms, more appropriately referred to as period television here, exist along reruns, reboots, revivals—not to mention an expansive streaming library of past shows—in a genre known as nostalgic television.

Nostalgic television can be defined as television programs that are intended to evoke a feeling of yearning within audiences for a previous time period that they may feel attached to, yet is currently irretrievable. Keep in mind nostalgia is a subjective experience; what is nostalgic for one person might not be nostalgic for another person. What's crucial, at least from this perspective, is that nostalgic television is specifically created and or marketed by networks to engender nostalgic feelings within audiences, and can be viewed as an advantageous opportunity for networks to increase their viewing audiences. *Stranger Things* is part of what *Variety* magazine calls Netflix's "nostalgia strategy"—an attempt to attract and keep subscribers who might be swayed by a reanimated chunk of their childhoods.[9] Current streaming technologies have no doubt perpetuated the nostalgia cycle. Viewers can catch up on more recent nostalgic shows like *The Goldbergs* and *Mad Men* via streaming services, and popular shows of the past can also easily be accessed using the same platforms.

AUDIENCE RECEPTION

In order to account for today's pervasiveness of nostalgic television and the ways in which nostalgia has contributed to the success of shows like *Stranger Things*, a closer look at examining nostalgic television as a product and audience receptions toward nostalgic television is crucial. Not only is the nostalgic mode important, but so is the nostalgic mood. In differentiating between the two, Grainge describes the nostalgia mood as a structure of feeling predicated on past experiences and the mode as a commodified style.[10]

In guiding consumer choices, nostalgia typically generates positive rather than negative responses about the past and can influence consumers both emotionally and cognitively.[11] Items that remind us of our past have the ability to signal and reinforce our self-identity based on our individual experiences and give way to favorable memories and emotions.[12] When consumers self-identify with specific products, higher value is attributed to those products, leading to purchases.[13] Television networks have been known to commodify nostalgia as a way for viewers to construct and maintain a sense of identity in an effort to slow down the present while evoking the past.[14] Nostalgic television shows can, there-fore, be viewed as media products able to generate memories about our past selves for a period for which we long. While watching a nostalgic television show, viewers might experience varying levels of nostalgia based on self-identification.[15]

The first level, real nostalgia, occurs at the individual level and can only be experienced if a person has lived through the event. *Stranger Things* viewers might recall vivid, intimate recollections of the era and become nostalgic due to the series' many film references, music, fashion, and other period markers. The second level of nostalgia, collective nostal-gia, occurs when an experience is widely shared by a culture, generation, or nation.[16] For these viewers, nostalgia might be triggered by the gener-ational symbols that were unique to the era such as playing Dungeons & Dragons, hanging out at the arcade, or the presence of Reagan/Bush '84 presidential election signs. The last level of nostalgia, simulated nostal-gia, is nostalgia that is experienced through external sources such as mo-vies, books, or stories from an era in which an individual has not directly experienced.[17] Younger viewers of *Stranger Things* may find themselves yearning for the show's setting and novelties, especially if they are watching with adults who share their real nostalgic memories with them. It's interesting to note that the Duffers were born in 1984—one year after season 1 takes place and the same year as season 2. When the Duffers presented *Stranger Things* to networks, they described the series as a love letter to the Golden Age of Steven Spielberg and Stephen King.[18] If the Duffers' idea for *Stranger Things* was generated by nostalgia for the works of the era, then it was certainly at the simulated level provoked by enter-tainment that they experienced later in life.

MEDIA MEMORIES AND AESTHETIC EMOTIONS

If the nostalgia mode and mood can work together in eliciting nostalgia, understanding why specific elements of nostalgic television can engen-der these responses is important. Writing in the 1970s, Davis noted a shift from private and intimate memories (e.g., childhood homes and streets) to memories generated by the mass media.[19] The media maintains the capability for lending itself to private associations with media images of the past and can be objects of our personal memory.[20] Moreover, Hoff-man and Kutscha state individuals may recall media content, such as television and film, better than personal family memories due to the in-tensive emotions that they elicit during the initial experience with that content.[21] Media memories can also become integrated within our per-sonal lives and may serve as points of biographical reference.[22] Adding to this, television series have the power to "transmit" memories of actions and events that have not been personally experienced.[23] The media, specifically film and television, therefore, can serve as emotional touchstones for real nostalgia and also for simulated nostalgia.

So if television has the capability to generate memories, thus eliciting nostalgic responses within audiences at varying levels, the question as to *how* to locate these responses remains vital. Following Armbruster's method for locating these responses within nostalgic television, a textual analysis that examines potential nostalgia triggers—including narration, cinematography, setting, music, art design, and characters—will be conducted.[24] Of importance will be analyzing the aesthetic emotions (a form of the nostalgia mood) elicited by the series and defined as the different ways that the audiovisual text can provoke emotional reactions within viewers[25] thus contributing to viewers' nostalgic responses. Since the intensity of aesthetic emotions most likely lies within many of the series' textual references, an intertextual analysis of both the series and references will be essential to this study. Specifically, the presence of artifact nostalgia—an emotional response to certain stylistic elements of a text that have lost their dominance resulting in a longing desire for the return of such artifacts or an experience that was related to it—will be useful.[26] In addition to the series' authentic re-creations of the era, it is suggested that artifact nostalgia will be stimulated by the intertextual references and filmic style of the era contained within *Stranger Things,* thus prompting emotional yearning within audiences for a return of these elements and for past experiences associated with the show.

TEXTUAL ANALYSIS

Contextual Notes

The early 1980s was a time of economic crisis in the United States with a deep recession that saw business bankruptcies, rising interest rates, agricultural turmoil, and high unemployment rates. Although the United States experienced an economic rebound in 1983—the year *Stranger Things* begins—a series of other events including the AIDS crisis, the Just Say No drug program that incarcerated mass amounts of minorities from the inner-city, and the Cold War between the United States and the Soviet Union loomed over the nation. Despite the presence of these social plights, *Stranger Things* chooses to forgo any direct mention of them. Instead, the show focuses on the cultural impact of film during that time. By 1983, films like *Jaws,* the *Star Wars* trilogy, *Close Encounters of the Third Kind, Raiders of the Lost Ark,* and *E.T.*—all films that are referenced in *Stranger Things*—were box office and commercial successes. By the end of 1983, all of these films were in the top twenty highest grossing domestic films of all time, further demonstrating their pervasiveness in American culture and their ability to become imbued in the memories of audiences.[27]

From its inception, *Stranger Things* was propelled by the allure of nostalgia for the era and the many films and pop cultural artifacts that defined it. To sell the show to networks, the Duffers created a pitch book that resembled a Stephen King paperback with the show's original title, *Montauk*, attached to the cover of a *Firestarter* paperback. Images and references to *Jaws*, *Close Encounters of the Third Kind*, *E.T.*, and *Stand by Me* were used to establish the show's narration, cinematography, setting, art direction, music, and characters; but more notably, to remind network execs of the unforgettable feelings that those films evoked within audiences.

Narration

For their network pitch, the Duffers explicitly indicated that the entire series would be structured like one, long film similar to the Hollywood three-act structure with a definitive beginning, middle, and end to allow for complete character arcs and satisfactory storytelling.[28] Because the Duffers had drawn inspiration from numerous 1970s and 1980s films that follow a three-act structure, it seemed natural that they would also break down the first season of *Stranger Things* using the same format, treating it like an eight-hour film. Most notably, season one of *Stranger Things* shares a similar three-act structure to one of its most inspirational sources, *E.T.* As indicated in their pitch book, act 1 of *Stranger Things* sees Mike encounter Eleven, just as Elliot encounters E.T. Act 2 of *Stranger Things* and *E.T.* share further similarities as Mike and his friends go to great lengths to hide Eleven from government forces, just as Elliot and his siblings do for E.T. In act 3, Mike and his friends band together to protect Eleven from the government forces which mimics the third act of *E.T* as well. Likewise, *Stranger Things* also follows the same three-act structure of its other source inspiration, *Poltergeist*, with act 1 dealing with children who have gone missing due to supernatural forces, act 2 depicting their mothers stopping at nothing to find them, and act 3 following the mothers into a supernatural realm to bring their children home.

Stranger Things also eschews complex storytelling devices that so many television shows encompass today. *LOST*, *Breaking Bad*, *Westworld*, and *The Handmaid's Tale* are part of a long list of television shows that have incorporated either an abundance of flashbacks, flash-forwards, and/or morally challenged characters into their narratives as part of a genre labeled complex television.[29] *Stranger Things'* narrative structure with its archetypal characters, enriching themes of friendship and family, escalating action, and coherent story is a reminder of simpler storytelling devices, one that brings back memories and a potential yearning for equally simpler times.

Not only does *Stranger Things* implicitly incorporate nostalgic film references within its narrative, it explicitly refers to them as well. Throughout the series, characters make specific references to films of the period that lend itself to the narration, characterization, and evocation of nostalgia. In "The Weirdo on Maple Street" (season 1, episode 2), Mike compares Eleven's telekinetic abilities to Yoda from *Star Wars*. In "The Bathtub" (season 1, episode 7), Dustin becomes suspicious of Hopper's walkie-talkie and mutters, "Lando" recalling Lando Calrissian's betrayal of Han Solo in *The Empire Strikes Back*. Later when considering facing the Demogorgon without Eleven, Mike comments that it would be like R2-D2 going to battle against Darth Vader. In "The Vanishing of Will Byers" (season 1, episode 1), Joyce experiences a flashback while searching for Will in his backyard hut. During this scene, Joyce reflects on a previous memory where she surprises Will with two tickets to *Poltergeist*. Joyce's own nostalgia for a happier time, potentially mirrors the audience's own nostalgia associated with the film. Season 2 of *Stranger Things* continues to explicitly incorporate film references into its narrative with references to *Mad Max*, *Ghostbusters*, and *Halloween*.

Finally, in an ode to Stephen King, the episodes of *Stranger Things* are all uniquely organized in book chapters. At the beginning of each episode, a chapter title appears on the screen in a typeface that recalls early King novels. The series, according to Matt Duffer, was intended to be a cinematic version of a long King book.[30] With the chapter titles, plus the many homages to Stephen King's novels and film adaptations, the narrative works to not only trigger nostalgic associations with the source material, but to engender the feeling that audiences are being guided through a King novel in the form of a television series—a feeling that potentially evokes memories of reading the author's novels from a period that has passed.

Cinematography

Stranger Things was shot in 2:1 aspect ratio on a RED dragon camera to achieve a cinematic look, in conjunction with a Leica lens which is similar to the softer, flatter lenses of the 1970s and 1980s. Cinematographer Tim Ives commented, "My dream and my job was to help make [*Stranger Things*] feel like it was shot back then. That was our goal, to make this thing feel like something that you'd lost and you hadn't seen in such a long time . . . the script and their packaging wreaked of this nostalgia that I fell instantly into."[31]

The cinematography isn't just used to invoke nostalgia within audiences through the series' authentic look; it also deliberately captures the cinematography of specific film scenes from various Spielberg films. In "The Vanishing of Will Byers" (season 1, episode 1), Will investigates a strange sound coming from his backyard shed in a scene that shares a likeness to one from *E.T.* Both scenes are set against a night-filled sky, with an eerie fog enveloping the yard, and a soft, yellow, light beaming from the shed. The scenes are also framed equivalently in a medium shot that places Will and Elliot at the opposite end of the shed. Season 2 ("MadMax," episode 1) hosts another scene with Will where he is lured to his front door by a sequence of bright lights flashing from outside, just like Barry is in *Close Encounters of the Third Kind*. The scenes are both framed in a wide shot from behind the characters as the door opens, allowing vibrant red and orange lights to fill their living rooms. A nod to *Jaws* is also evident in season 1 when the camera, in a close-up of Hopper's typewriter, focuses in as the word "Missing" is typed, just as the word "Shark Attack" is typed by Chief Brody.

Setting

The interior and exterior spaces in *Stranger Things* work to establish scenic realism which refers to the extent to which a film's setting evokes an accurate depiction of actual places.[32] The filmic image, as suggested by Corrigan and White,[33] has the potential to evoke nostalgia based on the viewers' belief that the film accurately portrays the details of our world realistically. For viewers, the interior of the Wheelers' suburban home may elicit memories of family dinners during the 1980s, or the arcade, with its rows of classic video games, might transport viewers back to their local arcade where they spent hours with friends. Scenic realism and nostalgia also works on an intertextual level when they convey realistic portrayals of fictional settings. The Wheelers' living room bears a resemblance to Elliot's in *E.T.*, and this is most evident when Eleven, like E.T., discovers the Wheelers' living room television set, becoming mesmerized by it ("Holly Jolly," season 1, episode 3). As Hopper and Joyce explore the nocturnal realm of the Upside Down ("The Upside Down," season 1, episode 8), viewers are reminded of the dark, desolate chambers of the alien spacecraft in *Alien*. Exterior settings also work on an intertextual level, conveying scenic realism. Scenes of the kids riding their bikes through the suburban streets and dense woods of Hawkins recalls similar settings and scenes from *E.T.*, *The Goonies*, and *The Explorers* whereas the forest train tracks that the kids navigate, bring to mind similar scenes from *Stand by Me* ("The Flea and the Acrobat," season 1, episode 5).

Decor, Props, and Costumes

Along with settings, these elements also operate within the mise-en-scène to elevate the scenic realism of the era. Textual elements such as decor, props, and costumes can serve as a nostalgic source of historical realism and historical escapism for the audience member.[34] Trapper keepers, cans of pudding, walkie talkies, radio boom boxes, Rubik's cube, *Star Wars* toys, white wicker bedroom furniture, movie and music posters, wood paneling, ruffled blouses, and corded telephones are all period markers of the 1980s visible in *Stranger Things*. Additionally, period colors of the era are ubiquitous with earth tones of reds, browns, yellows, and greens dominating the interiors. Lynda Reiss, the prop master of the series, commented, "I [didn't] want to do a nostalgia-tinged product. I want[ed] it to be the '80s. I [didn't] want it to be what everyone just thinks is the '80s. Our baseline was the reality of the Midwest in 1983."[35] Reiss used a series of props that predates 1983 (e.g., Will's late 1970s Panasonic boom box, Jonathan's 1981 Fisher MC-4550 stereo) in order to present a realistic depiction of the era and to avoid simplistic nostalgic triggers. Furthermore, the absence of props from previous eras within a text can negatively affect the nostalgic experience making the realism for period television "artificial and unsettling."[36]

The series' props are also conspicuously marked by intertextual references. Throughout season 1, Eleven develops an obsession with Eggo waffles, and they become an iconic image associated with her, just as Reese's Pieces did for E.T. In both texts, their respective foods are left in the forest, signifying the characters' presence. One of the most iconic props from *Stranger Things* are the bikes that carry our young characters on their adventures across Hawkins. The bikes not only act as intertextual period markers for 1980s films like *E.T.* and *The Goonies* but they also serve to evoke carefree memories within the viewers where the act of bike riding with friends symbolically represented independence and liberation from adult authority.

The costumes in *Stranger Things* are quintessential to the era and are greatly elevated by their scenic realism. Characters are dressed in plaid, flannel, denim, corduroy, and khaki with colors consisting primarily of muted earth tones. Season 1 costume designer Kimberly Adams drew inspiration from film characters of the period, catalogs, magazines, family photo albums and Midwestern states yearbooks from 1983.[37] The costumes also maintain a high degree of intertextuality. Eleven's pink dress and blonde wig that the boys disguise her in, is reminiscent of the clothes that Gertie dresses E.T. in. Hopper's brown and tan sheriff's uniform stands apart from the other police officers just as Chief Brody's did in *Jaws*, whereas his brown fedora evokes images of Indiana Jones. In a nod to *The Goonies*, Barb's hairstyle and glasses recall Stef, who is also the best-friend character. The Halloween setting of season 2 also calls attention to several films of the era with characters dressed in costumes from *Ghostbusters*, *Halloween*, and *Risky Business*.

Music

Both the score and popular music of the era play a significant role in creating mood and establishing the time period in *Stranger Things*. According to Sprengler music has the ability to elicit nostalgia by generating memories associated with hearing a song for the first time or with the time it was commonly listened to.[38] Collective horror film audiences who feel nostalgic toward its synth soundtrack by Survive will recognize the inspiration extracted from genre films like *Zombie, The Fog,* and *Day of the Dead.* In one of its most signature uses of music, The Clash's, *Should I Stay or Should I Go,* is uniquely used as a nostalgia trigger for both viewers and within the narrative. On one hand, viewers may be reminded of endearing times associated with the song. On the other hand, the song generates nostalgic feelings within Jonathan when he hears it following Will's disappearance ("The Weirdo on Maple Street," season 1, episode 2). In a flashback sequence, Jonathan is reminded of a happier time when the two brothers bonded by listening to the song together. Moreover, Jonathan uses the song to bring Will out from under the control of the Mind Flayer in season 2 ("The Gate," episode 9) and—to refer back to the etymology of nostalgia—to help him return home.

Characters

According to Cardwell, nostalgia may be provoked through the empathetic connection that viewers share with on-screen characters.[39] In this sense, adult viewers are likely to experience nostalgia during emotional moments between characters that are adolescent in nature, and thus nostalgic for any adult audience. When *Stranger Things* viewers see Mike and Eleven share their first kiss, or Jonathan and Will's brotherly bonding, or the middle school dance full of awkward and tender moments, they are encouraged to connect emotionally with the characters by drawing upon personal memories. Although these scenes are not uniquely akin to the time period, emotional empathy for the protagonists invites viewers to split off in their own nostalgic sentiments.[40]

Nostalgia is also experienced through the high level of intertextuality contained within the characters. As discussed, the relationship between Mike and Eleven is intended to evoke memories of the friendship between Elliot and E.T. The Duffers clearly established this relationship early on by writing in their pitch book, "If Mike is the Elliot of our show, Eleven is our E.T." As nostalgic sentiments are evoked, viewers might be reminded of the emotions that they felt during their initial viewings of the film. For Hopper, the Duffers pulled inspiration from Chief Brody of *Jaws.* While Hopper is much more hard-nosed than Brody, both have the same outfit, drive Chevrolet Blazers, have scars of the past (Hopper's daughter's death, Brody's undisclosed injury), and both hunt an unseen "monster" that lurks beneath the surface.[41] If Hopper fails to match Brody in terms of personality, then he definitely succeeds in evoking another iconic Spielberg character: Indiana Jones. Aside from the fact that they both wear fedoras, Hopper and Indiana are gruff, impatient men with similar demeanors and moral codes.[42] David Harbour who plays Hopper comments, "Indiana Jones was one of the iconic characters that me and the Duffers grew up watching and it's what they wanted to bring to [Hopper]."[43] In additional Spielberg fashion, Joyce Byers stands in for Diane Freeling of *Poltergeist* (a Spielberg production) and Jillian Guiller of *Close Encounters of the Third Kind* with all three being mothers whose children have been abducted by unseen supernatural forces. Likewise, Joyce shares a similarity with Roy Neary of the latter film as both characters become obsessed with deciphering cryptic supernatural messages and as a result, are perceived to be unstable by their friends and family. Moreover, the use of lights is used in both texts to communicate with the supernatural; Will contacts Joyce through Christmas lights, and the aliens communicate with Roy via the spaceship's lights.

The characters in *Stranger Things* also bear a resemblance to those of Stephen King's work. "The Body" (season 1, chapter 4) is an homage to King's short story of the same name which would later be adapted into the feature film, *Stand by Me*. According to the Duffers, "We love that story and that film with all of our boyish hearts, and its DNA is written all over the show." In both texts, the characters are young boys who must transition into adulthood when their carefree adolescence is abruptly interrupted by loss and tragedy. Likewise, the same theme is captured in King's novel, *It*, and in both *The Body/Stand by Me* and *It*, archetypal bullies play a role in thwarting the protagonists' mission, just as they do in *Stranger Things*. *Stranger Things* also shares character similarities with King's *Firestarter* as both Eleven and Charlie respectively possess telekinetic powers as a result of their mothers partaking in government experiments during college.

The current study has sought to account for the pervasiveness of nostalgic television by examining the role that nostalgia plays in guiding networks' programming decisions and the ways in which nostalgia can influence audience viewing preferences. As demonstrated, various textual referents of the past contained within television shows have the ability to elicit emotional responses within audiences. Such referents may operate to engender nostalgic feelings on the real, collective, or simulated level predicated on how audiences self-identify with the content. By analyzing nostalgia as both a mode (nostalgic television) and mood (aesthetic emotions) through textual analysis, this study has demonstrated how nostalgic associations within period television shows like *Stranger Things* appeals to audiences. Armbruster[44] also applied this method to reruns and remakes, and future studies should take these subgenres, in addition to revivals, into consideration.

It should be noted that this study's intent hasn't been to expose the corporate greed of television networks who seek to capitalize off of audiences' nostalgia. If *Stranger Things* and other nostalgic television programs can work to generate positive feelings within the present, provide a temporary safe haven from current troubles, and serve as a source of aspiration for the future[45] then audiences should embrace nostalgia. On the other hand, with the increasing ubiquity of nostalgic television, problems might exist when nostalgia hinders present-day progression for those who remain fixated on the past, unable to let go of it. A concern also exists if nostalgic television—like other nostalgic media—becomes the dominant television genre giving way to creative exhaustion, cultural homogeneity, and fixed representations of the past.[46] Additionally, nostalgia has been known to be a competitively advantageous tool for marketers when exploited effectively, especially in the television industry.[47] Perhaps this is why Netflix has rejected the claim of having a nostalgia strategy[48]; however, given their season 2 marketing campaign that featured reimagined film posters from the era, nostalgia-themed cross-promotional deals with Reebok, Target, and Eggo, plus their numerous shows that seem to beckon audiences with nostalgia (e.g., *Wet Hot American Summer: First Day of Camp, Fuller House, Gilmore Girls: A Year in the Life, One Day at a Time, Bill Nye Saves the World, The Magic School Bus Rides Again, GLOW, Mystery Science Theater 3000, Dark, Everything Sucks!*) makes it difficult to ignore the role that nostalgia has played in their decision making. The Duffers also appear to distance themselves from nostalgic associations commenting: "And so while there is nostalgia [in *Stranger Things*], we don't want people focused on, 'Oh, that was so cute, I remember that from the '80s.' We want people to fall in love with the characters in the story."[49] The Duffers seem to be confusing recollection with nostalgia, and they deny the powerful feelings that nostalgia can engender. Whether it was their own nostalgia which resulted in the creation of the series, or viewers' nostalgia which has been a significant factor for the popularity of the series, nostalgia has been a key proponent for the success of *Stranger Things*. For the nostalgic viewer, watching *Stranger Things* isn't just about remembering the 1980s; it's about *feeling* the 1980s. The strength of *Stranger Things* lies within its ability to capture not just the authentic look of the 1980s, but the sensation of watching the films it references again for the very first time. Whether real, collective, or simulated, *Stranger Things* allows the audience to experience nostalgia for an era that was marked by some of the industry's most unforgettable films, characters, and creators. But above all, the series instills within viewers the same feeling of awe and excitement that they felt when Elliot and E.T. rode into the night, or the feeling of friendship and camaraderie that the young adults in *Stand by Me* shared, or the sense of adventure, thrills, and childhood freedom that defined *The Goonies*. It takes us to a place that we long to visit again; albeit for a temporary time, a place of wonder, excitement, fantasy, and adoration; all by the way of nostalgia—and *that* is good nostalgic television.

NOTES

1. JW McCormack, "*Stranger Things* Is Terrifyingly Good '80s Nostalgia," *Vice*, July 25, 2016, https://www.vice.com/en_us/article/mvkayy/stranger-things-is-terrifyingly-good-80s-nostalgia.

2. Alan Sipenwall, "Netflix's *Stranger Things* Basks in 80s Nostalgia but Doesn't Drown in It," *Uproxx*, July 13, 2016, https://uproxx.com/sepinwall/review-netflixs-stranger-things-basks-in-80s-nostalgia-but-doesnt-drown-in-it/.

3. Neil Genzlinger, "With *Stranger Things*, Netflix Delivers an Eerie Nostalgia Fix," *New York Times*, July 14, 2016, https://www.nytimes.com/2016/07/15/arts/television/review-with-stranger-things-netflix-delivers-an-eerie-nostalgia-fix.html.

4. Fred Davis, *Yearning for Yesterday: A Sociology of Nostalgia* (New York: The Free Press, 1979); Morris B. Holbrook, "Nostalgia and Consumer Tastes," *Journal of Consumer Research* 20, no. 2 (1993): 245–256.

5. Fred Davis, "Nostalgia, Identity and the Current Nostalgia Wave," *Journal of Popular Culture* 11, no. 2 (1977): 418, https://doi.org/10.1111/j.0022-3840.1977.00414.x.

6. Russell W. Belk, "The Role of Possessions in Constructing and Maintaining a Sense of Past," *Advances in Consumer Research* 17 (1990): 670; Davis, *Yearning*, 133; Jeremy J. Sierra and Shaun McQuitty, "Attitudes and Emotions as Determinants of Nostalgia Purchases: An Application of Social Identity Theory," *Journal of Marketing Theory and Practice* 15, no. 2 (2007): 100.

7. Davis, "Nostalgia," 421.

8. Davis, *Yearning*, 134.

9. Oriana Schwindt, "*Stranger Things* Tests Limits of Netflix's Nostalgia Strategy," *Variety*, July 25, 2016, https://variety.com/2016/tv/news/stranger-things-netflix-fuller-house-nostalgia-strategy-1201822075/.

10. Paul Grainge, "Nostalgia and Style in Retro America: Moods, Modes, and Media Recycling," *American Culture* 23, no. 1 (2000): 28, https://doi.org/10.1111/j.1537-4726.2000.2301_27.x.

11. Sierra and McQuitty, "Attitudes and Emotions," 99.

12. Russell W. Belk, "Possessions and the Extended Self," *Journal of Consumer Research* 15, no. 2 (1988): 139; Marsha L. Richins, "Valuing Things: The Public and Private Meanings of Possessions," *Journal of Consumer Research* 21, no. 3 (1994): 504.

13. Americus Reed II, "Social Identity as a Useful Perspective for Self-Concept-Based Consumer Research," *Psychology and Marketing* 19, no. 3 (2003): 235–266; Richins, "Valuing," 507.

14. Kathleen Loock, "Whatever Happened to Predictability? Fuller House, (Post)Feminism, and the Revival of Family-Friendly Viewing," *Television & New Media* 19, no. 4 (2017): 6.

15. Stacey Menzel Baker and Patricia F. Kennedy, "Death by Nostalgia: A Diagnosis of Context-Specific Cases," *Advances in Consumer Research* 21, no. 1 (1994): 170.

16. Davis, "Yearning," 122; Baker and Kennedy, "Death."

17. Baker and Kennedy, "Death."

18. Ken Miyamoto, "How to Sell Your TV Series the *Stranger Things* Way," Screencraft, October 26, 2017, https://screencraft.org/2017/10/26/how-to-sell-your-tv-series-the-stranger-things-way/.

19. Davis, "Yearning," 125.

20. Andreas Böhn, "Nostalgia of the Media/in the Media," *Self-Reference in the Media* (Berlin, New York: Mouton de Gruyter, 2007): 146; Davis, "Yearning," 130.

21. Dagmar Hoffmann and Annika Kutscha, "Media Biographies: Consequences of Media Action, Aesthetic, Preference and Experience," in *Media Socialization Theories. New Models and Approaches in the Discussion,* eds. Dagmar Hoffmann and Lothar Mikos (Wiesbaden: VS Verlag, 2010), 226.

22. Tim O'Sullivan, "Television Cultures and Memories of Viewing," in *Popular Television in Britain: Studies in Cultural History,* ed. John Corner (London: BFI, 1991), 163.

23. Stefanie Armbruster, "Watching Nostalgia: An Analysis of Nostalgic Television Fiction and its Reception," in *Cultural Studies* 48, ed. Rainer Winter (Verlag: Transcript, 2016), 56.

24. Armbruster, "Watching Nostalgia," 96.

25. Armbruster, "Watching Nostalgia," 56.

26. Armbruster, "Watching Nostalgia," 66.

27. Box Office Mojo, "Domestic Grosses Viewing Chart as of Dec. 29, 1983," accessed September 10, 2018, https://www.boxofficemojo.com/alltime/domestic.htm?asof=1983-12-29&p=.htm.

28. Miyamoto, "How to Sell."

29. Jason Mittell, *Complex TV: The Poetics of Contemporary Storytelling* (New York: NYU Press, 2015), 17.

30. Eric Goldman, "How Steven Spielberg, John Carpenter and Stephen King Influenced *Stranger Things,*" *IGN,* July 7, 2016, http://www.ign.com/articles/2016/07/08/how-steven-spielberg-john-carpenter-and-stephen-king-influenced-stranger-things.

31. Matt Groba, "*Stranger Things* Cinematographer Tim Ives on Shooting the Upside Down," *Deadline,* August 26, 2017.

32. Timothy Corrigan and Patricia White, *The Film Experience: An Introduction* (London: Macmillan, 2012), 70.

33. Corrigan and White, *The Film Experience,* 121.

34. Andrew Higson, "Re-presenting the National Past: Nostalgia and Pastiche in the Heritage film." In *Fires Were Started: British Cinema and Thatcherism,* ed. Lester Friedman, (London: Wallflower Press, 2006), 97.

35. Tim Moynihan, "The Stories Behind *Stranger Things'* Retro '80s Props," *Wired,* July 27, 2016, https://www.wired.com/2016/07/stories-behind-stranger-things-retro-80s-props/.

36. Armbruster, *Watching Nostalgia,* 177.

37. Joe Kucharski, "*Stranger Things*—Costume Designing 1980s Nostalgia," *Tyranny of Style,* November 15, 2016, http://tyrannyofstyle.com/stranger-things-costume-design.

38. Christine Sprengler, "Screening Nostalgia: Populuxe Props and Technicolor Aesthetics," in *Contemporary American Film* (New York/Oxford: Berghahn, 2011), 76.

39. Sarah Cardwell, *Adaptation Revisited. Television and the Classic Novel* (Manchester/New York: Manchester University Press, 2002): 123.

40. Armbruster, *Watching Nostalgia,* 180.

41. Jacopo Della Quercia, "Spielberg Things: The Nostalgic Heart of *Stranger Things,*" in *Uncovering Stranger Things: Essays on Eighties Nostalgia, Cynicism, and Innocence in the Series,* ed. Kevin J. Wetmore, Jr. (Jefferson: McFarland, 2018), 114

42. Quercia, "Spielberg Things," 117.

43. Nardine Saad, "David Harbour Talks about How He almost Quit Hollywood before *Stranger Things,*" *LA Times,* June 7, 2017, http://www.latimes.com/entertainment/envelope/emmys/la-et-st-david-harbour-stranger-things-season-2-hellboy-20170607-htmlstory.html.

44. Armbruster, *Watching Nostalgia,* 93.

45. Davis, "Nostalgia," 418; Michael Pickering and Emily Keightly, "The Modalities of Nostalgia," *Current Sociology* 54, no. 6 (2006): 937.

46. Davis, *Yearning,* 128; Allison Graham, "History, Nostalgia and Criminality of Popular Culture," *Georgia Review* 38, no. 2 (1984): 364; Lyn Spigel, "From the Dark

Ages to the Golden Age: Women's Memories and Television Reruns," *Screen* 36 (Spring 1995): 17.

47. Sierra and McQuitty, "Attitudes and Emotions," 109; Rebecca Piirto Heath, "What Tickles Our Funny Bone?" *American Demographics* 18, no. 11 (1996): 51.

48. Bethonie Butler, "Is Netflix Doing Nostalgia Better Than Anyone Else Right Now?" *Washington Post*, November 22, 2016, https://www.washingtonpost.com/news/arts-and-entertainment/wp/2016/11/22/is-netflix-doing-nostalgia-better-than-anyone-else-right-now/?utm_term=.88ff217830a4.

49. Goldman, "How Steven Spielberg."

BIBLIOGRAPHY

Armbruster, Stefanie. "Watching Nostalgia: An Analysis of Nostalgic Television Fiction and Its Reception." In *Cultural Studies* 48, edited by Rainer Winter, 1–436. Verlag: Transcript, 2016.

Baker, Stacey Menzel and Patricia F. Kennedy. "Death by Nostalgia: A Diagnosis of Context-Specific Cases." *Advances in Consumer Research* 21, no. 1 (1994): 169–174.

Böhn, Andreas. "Nostalgia of the Media/in the Media." In *Self-Reference in the Media*, edited by Winfried Nöth and Nina Bishara. 143–164. Berlin, New York: Mouton de Gruyter, 2007.

Belk, Russell W. "Possessions and the Extended Self." *Journal of Consumer Research* 15, no. 2 (1988): 139–168. http://www.jstor.org/stable/2489522.

Belk, Russell W. "The Role of Possessions in Constructing and Maintaining a Sense of Past." *Advances in Consumer Research* 17, no. 1 (1990): 669–676.

Box Office Mojo. "Domestic Grosses Viewing Chart as of Dec. 29, 1983." Accessed September 10, 2018. https://www.boxofficemojo.com/alltime/domestic.htm?asof=1983-12-29&p=.htm.

Butler, Bethonie. "Is Netflix Doing Nostalgia Better Than Anyone Else Right Now?" *Washington Post*, November 22, 2016. https://www.washingtonpost.com/news/arts-and-entertainment/wp/2016/11/22/is-netflix-doing-nostalgia-better-than-anyone-else-right-now/?utm_term=.88ff217830a4.

Cardwell, Sarah. *Adaptation Revisited: Television and the Classic Novel*. Manchester/New York: Manchester University Press, 2002.

Corrigan, Timothy and Patricia White. *The Film Experience: An Introduction*. London: Macmillan, 2012.

Davis, Fred. "Nostalgia, Identity and the Current Nostalgia Wave." *Journal of Popular Culture* 11, no. 2 (1977): 418. https://doi.org/10.1111/j.0022-3840.1977.00414.x.

Davis, Fred. *Yearning for Yesterday: A Sociology of Nostalgia*. New York: The Free Press, 1979.

Genzlinger, Neil. "With *Stranger Things*, Netflix Delivers an Eerie Nostalgia Fix." *New York Times*, July 14, 2016. https://www.nytimes.com/2016/07/15/arts/television/review-with-stranger-things-netflix-delivers-an-eerie-nostalgia-fix.html.

Goldman, Eric. "How Steven Spielberg, John Carpenter and Stephen King Influenced *Stranger Things*." *IGN*, July 7, 2016. http://www.ign.com/articles/2016/07/08/how-steven-spielberg-john-carpenter-and-stephen-king-influenced-stranger-things.

Graham, Allison. "History, Nostalgia and Criminality of Popular Culture." *Georgia Review* 38, no. 2 (1984): 348–364. http://www.jstor.org/stable/41398680.

Grainge, Paul. "Nostalgia and Style in Retro America: Moods, Modes, and Media Recycling." *American Culture* 23, no. 1 (2000): 28–33. https://doi.org/10.1111/j.1537-4726.2000.2301_27.x.

Groba, Matt "*Stranger Things* Cinematographer Tim Ives on Shooting the Upside Down." *Deadline*, August 26, 2017.

Heath, Rebecca Piirto. "What Tickles Our Funny Bone?" *American Demographics* 18, no. 11 (1996): 48–52.

Higson, Andrew. "Re-presenting the National Past: Nostalgia and Pastiche in the Heritage film." In *Fires Were Started: British Cinema and Thatcherism*, edited by Lester Friedman, 110–124. London: Wallflower Press, 2006.

Hoffmann, Dagmar, and Annika Kutscha. "Media Biographies: Consequences of Media Action, Aesthetic Preference and Experience." In *Media Socialization Theories: New Models and Approaches in the Discussion*, edited by Dagmar Hoffmann and Lothar Mikos, 221–243. Wiesbaden: VS Verlag, 2010.

Holbrook, Morris B. "Nostalgia and Consumption Preferences: Some Emerging Patterns of Consumer Tastes." *Journal of Consumer Research* 20, no. 2 (1993): 245–256. https://doi.org/10.1086/209346.

Kucharski, Joe. "*Stranger Things*—Costume Designing 1980s Nostalgia." *Tyranny of Style*, November 15, 2016. http://tyrannyofstyle.com/stranger-things-costume-design.

Loock, Kathleen. "Whatever Happened to Predictability? *Fuller House*, (Post)Feminism, and the Revival of Family-Friendly Viewing." *Television & New Media* 19, no. 4 (2017): 1–18. https://doi.org/10.1177/1527476417742972.

McCormack, JW. "*Stranger Things* Is Terrifyingly Good '80s Nostalgia." *Vice*, July 25, 2016. https://www.vice.com/en_us/article/mvkayy/stranger-things-is-terrifyingly-good-80s-nostalgia.

Mittell, Jason. *Complex TV: The Poetics of Contemporary Storytelling*. New York: NYU Press, 2015.

Miyamoto, Ken. "How to Sell Your TV Series the *Stranger Things* Way." Screencraft, October 26, 2017. https://screencraft.org/2017/10/26/how-to-sell-your-tv-series-the-stranger-things-way/.

Moynihan, Tim. "The Stories Behind *Stranger Things*' Retro '80s Props." *Wired*, July 27, 2016. https://www.wired.com/2016/07/stories-behind-stranger-things-retro-80s-props/.

Meyers, Oren. "The Engine's in the Front, But Its Heart's in the Same Place: Advertising, Nostalgia, and the Construction of Commodities as Realms of Memory." *The Journal of Popular Culture* 42, no. 4 (2009): 733–755. https://doi.org/10.1111/j.1540-5931.2009.00705.x.

O'Sullivan, Tim. "Television Cultures and Memories of Viewing." In *Popular Television in Britain: Studies in Cultural History*, edited by John Corner, 159–189. London: BFI, 1991.

Pickering, Michael, and Emily Keightly. "The Modalities of Nostalgia." *Current Sociology* 54, no. 6 (2006): 919–941. https://doi.org/10.1177/0011392106068458.

Quercia, Jacopo Della. "Spielberg Things: The Nostalgic Heart of *Stranger Things*." In *Uncovering Stranger Things: Essays on Eighties Nostalgia, Cynicism, and Innocence in the Series*, edited by Kevin J. Wetmore, Jr., 112–127. Jefferson: McFarland, 2018.

Reed, Americus II. "Social Identity as a Useful Perspective for Self-Concept-Based Consumer Research," *Psychology and Marketing* 19, no. 3 (2003): 235–266. https://doi.org/10.1002/mar.10011.

Richins, Marsha L. "Valuing Things: The Public and Private Meanings of Possessions." *Journal of Consumer Research* 21, no. 3 (1994): 504–521. http://www.jstor.org/stable/2489689.

Saad, Nardine. "David Harbour Talks about How He almost Quit Hollywood before *Stranger Things*." *LA Times*, June 7, 2017. http://www.latimes.com/entertainment/envelope/emmys/la-et-st-david-harbour-stranger-things-season-2-hellboy-20170607-htmlstory.html.

Schwindt, Oriana. "*Stranger Things* Tests Limits of Netflix's Nostalgia Strategy," July 25, 2016. https://variety.com/2016/tv/news/stranger-things-netflix-fuller-house-nostalgia-strategy-1201822075/

Sierra, Jeremy J., and McQuitty, Shaun. "Attitudes and Emotions as Determinants of Nostalgia Purchases: An Application of Social Identity Theory." *Journal of Marketing Theory and Practice* 15, no. 2 (2007): 99–112. http://www.jstor.org/stable/40470284.

Sipenwall, Alan. "Netflix's *Stranger Things* Basks in '80s Nostalgia but Doesn't Drown in It." *Uproxx,* July 13, 2016, https://uproxx.com/sepinwall/review-netflixs-stranger-things-basks-in-80s-nostalgia-but-doesnt-drown-in-it/.

Spigel, Lyn. "From the Dark Ages to the Golden Age: Women's Memories and Television Reruns." *Screen* 36 (Spring 1995): 16–33. https://doi.org/10.1093/screen/36.1.16.

Sprengler, Christine. "The Nostalgia Film in Practice and Theory." In *Screening Nostalgia: Populuxe Props and Technicolor Aesthetics in Contemporary American Film.* 67–92. New York/Oxford: Berghahn, 2011.

THIRTEEN

"You Can't Rewrite the Past"

Analog and Digital Communications Technology in 13 Reasons Why

Patricia Campbell and Kathryn Pallister

Today's social media-obsessed teens would seem less likely to crave nostalgic content than their parents, yet the popularity of the Netflix Original series *13 Reasons Why* (based on Jay Asher's 2007 novel of the same name) demonstrates a hearty appetite for the past, a past that predates the birth of these "digital natives." While the series is perhaps best known for tackling social issues such as suicide, sexual assault, and white male privilege from an adolescent standpoint, the centrality of "old" communications technology (audio cassettes in season 1, Polaroid photographs in season 2) results in a persistent nostalgic impulse that filters out to other narrative elements. TV critic Inkoo Kang observes that "With its timely anxieties about phone-accelerated slut-shaming, Netflix's YA phenomenon *13 Reasons Why* may look like it bucks the nostalgia trend. But the secret to its success may very well lie in its adept channeling of the many ilks of teen wistfulness—those genuine and acutely felt, as well as those sentimental and patently faddish."[1] Indeed, the nostalgia that the teens ostensibly long for is not that of their own not-too-distant childhoods, but the past that lies somewhere in their mixtape-creating, Polariod-snapping predecessors' experiences that today's teens know about only indirectly, often through mediated knowledge. Kang refers to the "all-encompassing nostalgia" of the series, felt perhaps most acutely by lead character Hannah Baker, who yearns "for the innocence of childhood, for friendships that burst into life and fizzle just as fast, for the days of gallant

courtship, for a once-great America" as "the past can be the most comforting security blanket around."[2] The contradiction, of course, lies in the
fact that earlier generations of teens did not live in a perpetual loop of
John Hughes-infused high school fantasies, as they, too, felt the full
weight of mental illness, sexual assault, and toxic masculinity, albeit
without the "acceleration" of social media.

Though it presents an obvious technostalgia and explores narratives
of technological determinism, *13 Reasons Why* also underscores the ambivalences inherent in all technologies and the nostalgic impulse itself.
Through a discussion of the connections between technology, media, and
nostalgia, the series highlights the tensions between feelings of powerlessness and the potential for individual and collective agency in building
a more hopeful shared future.

NARRATIVES OF TECHNOLOGICAL DETERMINISM AND MEDIA NOSTALGIA

Most recent media studies scholarship challenges notions of technological determinism by stressing the role of social actors in shaping technology and the contingency surrounding technological development and use,
focusing on the differential relationships between users and technologies
in particular social contexts. However, narratives of technological determinism persist in popular conceptualizations of sociotechnical relations.
Wyatt suggests that in order to understand the relationship between humans and their technologies, it is important to examine the ongoing fascination with the technological determinist narrative.[3] Three aspects of this
narrative can be examined in relation to media nostalgia. First, media
forms have certain characteristics that lead to particular social effects;
second, technological progress is complete, transformational, and independent of human action; and third (a combination of the previous two),
there is a clear separation between "old" media and "new" media based
on their inherent characteristics, cultural implications, and historical positioning.

As Crowley points out, contemporary determinist narratives regarding the link between technological change and social change often explore the theme of "technology out of control, cut loose from the twin
anchors of politics and tradition,"[4] reflecting a technological world in
which humans are ultimately powerless, their actions driven by technology. This is certainly the case in some early studies of communications
technology where the dominant narrative endows technological forms
with certain characteristics that result in particular effects, both in terms
of sociopolitical transformation (as in the case of Harold Innis) and
psycho-cultural change (as in the case of Marshall McLuhan). Technological determinist narratives about social interaction with newer media

abound, from the early optimism of Negroponte's assertion that "like a force of nature, the digital age cannot be denied or stopped and that it has four very powerful qualities that will result in its ultimate triumph: decentralizing, globalizing, harmonizing, and empowering"[5] to alarmist claims that the internet is making us stupid[6] and more recently, stealing our attention.[7] From this determinist perspective, humans are subject to the effects of new technologies whose particular qualities have both personal and sociocultural impacts.

Another feature of these technological determinist narratives is the idea that the introduction of new media is absolute and transformational, that old media will necessarily disappear in the imperative of technological progress. Ballatore and Natale describe this phenomenon as the "myth of the disappearing medium,"[8] explaining how the introduction of a new medium creates a narrative linking the impending disappearance of the old to "fetishism, fears about the end of humanism and ideas of techno-fundamentalist progress."[9] They argue that understanding current technological cultural narratives requires a broader lens, one that acknowledges that this reactionary response to a new medium is not new. Though the long lens of history proves that communication media transformations are rarely total, Ballatore and Natale assert that the determinist narrative of technological change persists because it helps us to make sense of our individual experiences of new media and their impact on our everyday lives.[10]

The impulse to return to this narrative of technological determinism in which old media are in a sense "under threat" is clearly linked to the current nostalgia for analog media. Menke suggests that this individual and social media nostalgia is a coping mechanism for dealing with the stress of technological change and that the disappearing medium myth seems closely linked to nostalgic feelings and the desire to seek comfort in past media.[11] Menke differentiates between media nostalgia, a longing for past media forms (tape recorders, Polaroids) as cultural products themselves, and mediated nostalgia, a focus on texts, which characterizes much of the scholarship in the field. Ruppel agrees that this nostalgic response is a way of managing technological change; however, he problematizes this old/new media relationship further, exploring the "contradictory impulses of nostalgic longing and technological advancement"[12] that emerge in a new technology's introduction. The inherent paradox of this determinist narrative—unbridled technological progress that intermingles technology's past, present, and future—shapes users' relationship with technology, and in turn, users' identities, leading to both public nostalgia (shared imaginaries woven into broader cultural experience) and private nostalgia (individual experience with particular media forms). Furthermore, though the medium as object may not disappear, its meaning shifts in its juxtaposition to new media: "Yet, technology cannot recover the past. It can help to uncover the past, record the past, memorialize the past, duplicate the past, and, as in the previous examples, reflect and distort the past but it cannot return a subject to a previous era."[13] Even though new media may represent or revive the old media content through that nostalgic impulse, they cannot re-create the original context of their production and consumption.

A final technological determinist narrative underlies the two discussed above: the dichotomy between old and new media. As Natale notes, much discussion in communications studies focuses on definitions of old media in terms of artifacts, social uses, and technological progress that rely on a technological determinist approach based on the media's formal characteristics, their intended uses, and their position along the digital dividing line in media history.[14] In considering media nostalgia, Natale advocates for a more relational approach, "examining the possibility that the oldness of media might be sought not in the media themselves, but rather in our perception and imagination of technological change."[15] Natale suggests that the "perceived oldness" of media technologies shapes our emotional response to them and contributes to feelings of nostalgia, as "[n]ostalgia is often connected to aging, and because media employed in everyday life are constantly integrated within one's identity and experience, technostalgia can be regarded as a fascination with things that link to their, their parents', or previous generations' past."[16] Thus, a deeper understanding of media nostalgia or "technostalgia" requires going beyond the generalizing old/new (or analog/digital) media divide to examine the articulations between specific users and media in the context of technological change.

The discourse surrounding these technological determinist narratives connects clearly to broader discussions of mediated nostalgia. Niemeyer sees the sharp increase of nostalgic feelings in the twenty-first century as an ambivalent reaction to the fast pace of technological change, which exposes the desire to slow it down even while exploiting the opportunities offered by novel technologies.[17] Boym's work echoes Niemeyer's, positing that nostalgia "is actually a yearning for childhood, the slower rhythm of our dreams."[18] Moreover, Boym suggests that "technology and nostalgia have become co-dependent: new technology and advanced marketing stimulate *ersatz* nostalgia—for the things you thought you never had lost—and anticipatory nostalgia—for the present that flees with the speed of a click."[19] The shifts in perspective on time and space that accompany technological advancements also play into the nostalgic impulse, what Boym calls "the impossibility of mythical return," compounded by the mediated nostalgia that may idealize or otherwise re-present the past in other "impossible" ways.[20]

In a more rudimentary way, contemporary communications technology itself provides the means through which audiences consume nostalgic media, and Netflix provides a particularly popular platform for this consumption. The centrality of nostalgia in the Netflix brand centers on its built-in financial safety net, whether viewers binge-watch old network series like *Friends* or (re)experience 1980s popular culture in the Netflix Original *Stranger Things*. Hutcheon and Valdes remind that "nostalgia requires the availability of evidence of the past," though through the development of communications technology, "nostalgia no longer has to rely on individual memory or desire: it can be fed forever by quick access to an infinitely recyclable past."[21] Likewise, Davis, among others, emphasizes the role that mass media have in the collective aspect of nostalgia.[22] When an audience lacks an individual, firsthand experience with a particular time period, the nostalgic impulse mines a collective or mediated well of "memories." Thus, today's teenagers typically learn about cassette tapes through a series like *13 Reasons Why*, and they learn about 1980s alternative bands like Joy Division through YouTube.

Additionally, Wilson interrogates how nostalgia studies have addressed either a longing for a space/place (homesickness, essentially) or an earlier time (childhood, for many), arguing that both elements should comprise the construct of nostalgia. She also emphasizes the future orientation that nostalgia often brings, as "Nostalgia is not a mere passive longing for the past, but a potentially dynamic vehicle for (re)envisioning and (re)creating various pasts and futures."[23] This sort of progressive potential that Boym identifies contrasts with a perhaps more simplistic notion that nostalgia functions regressively, as an escape to an idealized, though flawed, past. Recognizing both the time and space dimension of nostalgic longing is particularly relevant in the context of media nostalgia since media themselves, as Innis noted, profoundly shape a culture's experiences of time and space.[24]

In relation to this "flawed past," Padva addresses the idealized versions of history that nostalgic texts seem to present, acknowledging that "reinventing or retelling the past is a major part of the creation of a gay, lesbian, bisexual and transgender heritage with its own role models, icons, symbols, emblems and glorified imageries" and that the "quest for a nostalgic haven in an alienated, unsafe, and homophobic world" becomes a central concern.[25] For many LGBTQ youth, neither the time of their childhood nor the space of their childhood home holds fond memories, so the nostalgic reimagining of the past that validates their identities becomes empowering. Likewise, nostalgic texts that erase or elide issues about race and ethnicity could function as a mediated reinvention of the past in a manner that embraces diversity, creating a new space in the present that demonstrates a sort of irreversible progress. In this space, *13 Reasons Why* questions technology alongside other narratives, highlighting tensions in "simpler times" of cassette tapes, homophobia, and miscegenation.

MEDIA TECHNOLOGY NARRATIVES IN *13 REASONS WHY*

Understanding various technological determinist narratives surrounding media use and their link to nostalgia helps us to understand the characters' relationship to media technologies in *13 Reasons Why*. Throughout the series, we see versions of these narratives arise repeatedly, both in the broader worldview of technology and in the individual relationships between characters and particular media forms: the pessimism surrounding new technologies; the longing for the old; the rejection of digital; the embrace of analog. However, much in the same way that more recent constructivist approaches to technology have challenged the determinism of early media studies, in order to understand fully the characters' appropriation of technology, we must also recognize the limitations of this narrative, the spaces in which ambivalences and tensions of the characters' media use break through. Examining the complexity of these sociotechnical relationships as they are embedded within the particular context of the series leads to a more nuanced understanding of the tensions inherent in the nostalgic impulse itself. Characters long for a technological past in which they never participated, simultaneously embrace and reject new technologies, and look to create new futures with old technologies.

Technological Determinism

In their attitudes toward technology, the teenage characters in *13 Reasons Why* evince the technological determinism narrative that ascribes certain characteristics to particular technological forms, which necessarily leads to broader psychic and sociocultural impacts. They seem to feel powerless in the face of rapid technological change and ubiquitous digital media. Their interpretation of this change also seems to reinforce the false old/new media dichotomy suggested by Natale, in which the older, analog technologies appear in nostalgic relief alongside newer, digital technologies.[26] From the very first words of the series, we are meant to understand the centrality of technology to the narrative, its power over human action, and the juxtapositon of old/new media. Hannah implores on the first cassette, "Don't adjust your . . . whatever device you're hearing this on. It's me, live and in stereo. No Google maps, no app, no chance for the interwebs to make everything worse, like it does."[27] Superficially, the show's portrayal of new media (as the characters seem to understand it) echoes many of the dire warnings found in contemporary technological determinist narratives: that new media challenge privacy protection, that they are making us stupid and driving us to distraction, that they are depersonalizing and dehumanizing. Old media, on the other hand, have a privileged position of authenticity and allow for more human participation and interaction.

Episode 1 ironically demonstrates how new media make users stupid and distracted.[28] When two girls take a selfie in front of Hannah's locker shrine, one girl inquires what hashtag to use, and the other reminds her: #neverforget. The theme of distraction reappears with alarming frequency throughout the series, with the teens' constantly chiming phones and computers in their bedrooms, distracting them twenty-four hours a day. Technological distraction in its extreme form occurs when Sheri, looking for her phone in her purse, hits a stop sign, which ultimately leads to Jeff's death. The teens' actions reinforce the popular dystopian discourse surrounding new media, including its deleterious effect on today's youth.

Other ubiquitious themes in the series that highlight the dangers of new media are privacy reduction and depersonalization, such as the sharing of the seemingly risqué photo of Hannah at the park with Justin and the photo of Courtney and Hannah kissing. Hannah herself reflects on this, narrating, "We're always watching someone. Following someone. And being followed."[29] Her comment underscores the narrative of powerlessness in the face of technological change, the inability to resist the pull of social media and its implied addictive gratification. Voyeurism, in fact, becomes linked to a certain passivity, such as when students film a schoolyard fight on their cell phones, making the watching itself an end, not a spur to future action. The teens also recognize the privacy implications of new media with their concern about possible cell phone monitoring in conjunction with the court case relating to Hannah's death. Clay feels the depersonalization of new media firsthand when he realizes by listening to the tapes that he masturbated to the image of Courtney and Hannah, a sharp juxtaposition to the warm and friendly face-to-face conversations he had shared with Hannah, and a particularly unsettling example of both depersonalization and privacy reduction.

As the teens live their daily lives saturated with new media, the use of "old" media often seems overt and obvious. The cassettes in season 1 and Polaroids in season 2 serve as the most frequent references to "old" media, though many others arise as well. For example, vintage posters line the characters' walls, and Hannah and Clay work at a movie theater. The series' most sympathetic characters—Hannah, Clay, Tony, and to some extent (particularly in season 2) Tyler—are all connected by their affinity for old media, a connection that reinforces and contributes to their positioning as outsiders. Consistent with the nostalgic impulse and media nostalgia in general, these teens view traditional mass media—from their cassette players to classic films—with fondness and longing.

In some cases, the longing for traditional media becomes directly linked to nostalgic views on the past. When Clay asks, "You're still on the old media, huh?" Tony responds, "Uh, it's so much better," to which Clay replies, "Everything was better before."[30] In other cases, such as Tyler's use of film cameras and a darkroom, old media are privileged through the notions of participation and control, a form of resistance to a world in which technology has taken over humanity (a paradoxic sentiment in the context of the participatory discourse surrounding new media). In that vein, after the circulation of "the list," Hannah yearns for "a button to fast-forward through all the shitty parts in life and go straight to the good parts."[31] Her affinity for cassettes shows again when Tony uses tapes as a DJ at the dance, which Hannah appreciates, prophetically observing that her parents' store sells blank ones.

Frequently, the conscious employment of analog technologies contrasts with the banality and ubiquity of the digital and becomes linked to a positive identity construction, an almost anachronistic positioning of characters like Hannah and Tony as outside of the present time and place. Hannah's overt vilification of new media, particularly social media, and affinity for old media are key to understanding her outsider status and personality. She calls herself "a paperback, write-in-the-margins kind of girl" when she meets a librarian who calls her "a kindred spirit," and he emphasizes the role of books in the community, calling libraries "a place where people can come together, find their tribe."[32] She references classic film when her mother gives her a box of chocolates, saying "You're not trying to turn me into Norman Bates or something, are you?" to which Olivia replies, "That movie theater job. . . . I don't think it's healthy for you."[33] Even in her own family, Hannah's preference for old media casts her as an outsider. Later in the series, Hannah tells Clay that "You got this rebel with a cause thing going on" as they are standing outside of the movie theater where they work.[34] The "traditional" medium of film overtly characterizes Hannah and Clay's relationship; their "unconsummated" relationship evidences a sort of innocence and simplicity, different from the other high schoolers' complex relationships.

Tony's characterization also consciously employs nostalgia, from the first shot of him in a leather jacket and pompadour hairstyle in front of his vintage Mustang. When he gives Clay a ride home, his Walkman and cassette collection are in plain sight, and Tony asks, "Can I play you a tape?," holding up a cassette with a homemade "Joy Division" label.[35] Tony makes the cassette tapes in the Bakers' pharmacy relevant to Hannah, telling her they are "For mixtapes of course. A lost and essential art," and he gives both Hannah and, later, Clay, a mixtape with the song they danced to, the minor key "Night We Met" with its nostalgic flavor.[36] By coding the mixtapes as anachronistic, Tony's technostalgia reaffirms his outsider status.

Closely related to imputing particular characteristics to old/analog and new/digital media is the determinist narrative of communications media transformation, in which one dominant medium replaces another in the technological imperative. The teens in the series don't seem to embrace the dominance of new technologies as progress, often mourning the loss of the old. A persistent iteration of the disappearing medium theme addresses how virtual, digital communication replaces face-to-face communication, leading to the inability to talk. Talking is seen as an unmediated (or at least less mediated) "pure" form of communication, and this loss of talk among teen characters appears frequently, such as in their interactions with their parents and in their communications class at school. Jessica, in particular, laments the overuse of technology, saying that social media is "the only communication you ever have any more,"[37] emphasizing that the high schoolers feel compelled to use digital media almost exclusively, underscoring the old media's obsolescence. At the end of season 1, we see the adolescents embracing perceived authentic conversation when Sky asks Clay, "Are you okay?" and he says "No, is that alright?"[38] The moment seems consistent with a nostalgic hopefulness, a desire to return to the "real" world of unmediated communication.

The loss of earlier media technologies also leads to the loss of related ways of life, such as poet and journalist, and in turn, a certain powerlessness over identity construction. Aspiration to these vocations exists only in Hannah's past; the digital present has disabused her of these childish dreams. When Hannah talks about the poetry group, she tells her mom, "No one has a career as a poet" and even says of journalists, "Do those still exist?"[39] Poetry becomes particularly problematic for Hannah when Ryan publishes her work without her consent; when her poetry gets used against her, she is ultimately outed by her handwriting (in contrast to digital anonymity). In response, she narrates that "Shit happens, and people suck. Maybe that's why I stopped writing and started eventually making tapes?"[40] These tapes ultimately come to represent paradoxically both Hannah's last attempt to control the legacy of her identity and a relinquishing of hope for any future identity construction.

TECHNOSTALGIC AMBIVALENCE

While there is ample evidence of the technological determinist narratives of attributing broad effects to media (in this case new media = bad, old media = good) and the disappearance of old media in the face of new, particularly from the perspective of the teenage characters, a fuller analysis of the series challenges these narratives to reveal the underlying ambivalence of technology and the nostalgic impulse itself. In the series, technology is often portrayed as having inherent characteristics with a clear separation between old and new media, yet a closer reading reveals a degree of contingency: it is not the technology itself that determines the effect, but the articulation between the user and the technology in particular contexts. At the same time, old media are clearly present; they have not disappeared, but have become reimagined in new practices. This ambivalence appears at multiple levels: in the media practices of individuals, among the teens, and between the generations, and in the sociocultural norms related to broader media representation.

Hannah herself embodies this ambivalence, as despite her repeated characterization of new media as negative, she happily embraces new technology when it suits her. She uses her sleek MacBook to video chat with her friend Kat, who has moved away, and texts with Justin to arrange their playground date. Even the juxtapositioning of Tony's mixtapes with Hannah's tapes illustrates an ambivalence that undermines the more overt technological determinance stance; in the hands of the same user, the technology's range of affordances and constraints results in both joy and pain. When Hannah meets Jessica to talk after their falling out, both conspicuously place their phones on the table, as if to represent the looming evils of new media, yet their conversation focuses on a paper list. Similarly, the reconstruction of Hannah's persecution focuses on the cyberbullying she has experienced, even though much of her pain has come from "the list" that resembles an old-school slam book and the bathroom graffiti that echoes prehistoric cave inscriptions.[41] Thus, the social ills of bullying and harassment become severed from technology, emphasizing the age-old nature of the issues, even in light of the accelerant that social media may provide. Neither "old" nor "new" communications media are inherently good or bad, but context dependent. The tapes themselves evidence the ambivalence about media fading from use, illustrating the mixing of old and new technology. Hannah's choice of cassette tapes (an interactive, participatory medium) to communicate after her death is at odds with the characterization of "traditional" media as one-way, as with radio or television broadcasts (all but absent from the series). Her old-media choice allows her to create her own message, similar to the interactive new media in which the other teens are immersed.

Through their relationship with technology, the other characters also illustrate this ambivalence. They perceive old media with a nostalgic longing, without overtly acknowledging that this same technology often has negative implications, depending on its use. When Hannah visits Tony to borrow his tape recorder, in order to tape her audio legacy, the scene can retrospectively be interpreted as a sort of cry for help with Tony's description: the tapes are "like a voice text on your iPhone, only with more style," providing an oxymoronic description of what will become her suicide note.[42] The two types of tapes (Hannah's and Tony's mixtapes) elide for Clay during his listening, evidencing the openness of technology in both use and interpretation. Similarly, the Polaroids that circulate in season 2 contrast with Justin's photo of Hannah that Bryce distributes via text message, yet it is precisely the nature of Polaroid technology (not easily duplicated, increasing the potential privacy of the images) that documents the systemic sexual predation of the Liberty High School baseball team. At the conclusion of season 1, Tony, Brad, Clay and Skye drive away from school, bookending the start of the season with Tony asking "Should I put a tape on?," and Clay responding "how about we just listen to the radio?"[43] indicating that they blame the technology (the tapes), not how it is used, as they shift to the more passive format of radio. The second season focuses on an extended narrative about testimony in the court cases, and even the medium of speech becomes questioned in its translation to conflicting versions of visual narration. This unreliablity of "unmediated" speech leads to broader questions about media and truth, suggesting the inherent ambivalence in all communication/mediation, which had been the focus of nostalgic longing in season 1. The old/new media distinction is also challenged in the characters' interactions. Clay's choice to use a vintage Walkman along with his modern Beats headphones to listen to the tapes indicates the comingling of media. Similarly, in the "Dollar Valentines" episode, old paper technology combines with computer algorithms to match up Hannah and Marcus, who both calls and texts Hannah to arrange the date. While this ambivalence seems lost on the students, it does challenge the disappearance of old media (like passing notes in class) and suggest that media characteristics are, at least to some extent, socially constructed.

The series also portrays an ambivalence in media nostalgia itself. The teenagers frame their use of "old" media, which stands out in the context of the digital, as novel, stylish, or a form of resistance to dominant media; however, they perceive the same media as outdated in the hands of the previous generation. When Clay borrows his dad's "boom box" to listen to the cassettes and can't open the tape door, this becomes a commentary on his dad's generation: the parents' adolescence, mirrored in the boom box, is obsolete, as are the parents themselves who are perceived by their childen as hopelessly out of touch. Later, when Clay's mom catches him listening to Hannah's tapes, Clay tells her they are for history class. Her response mimics that of his conversation with his father: "Cassettes are history now? Hm. Of course they are."[44] indicating that she, too, is antiquated. In its use of "old" print media, the school also serves as a site of ambivalence surrounding the technological generation gap. Seeing posters that are meant to help the students cope with the deaths of Hannah and Jeff, Alex rages, "Can't believe this fucking school. They're already putting up drunk driving posters,"[45] yet he, like many of the other teenage characters, adorns his bedroom walls with posters depicting nostalgic music and films. The teens' abilities to (re)produce and integrate old media in their daily practice further underscores the "myth of the disappearing medium." Tyler prefers film over digital photography and is skilled in darkroom practices. Similarly, Ryan is adept with a negative loupe, even though he is a high school student who would likely work exclusively with digital images rather than traditional film. Ambivalences surrounding old and new media arise in examining the social context of the technology's use within particular generations, in the reciprocal shaping of both the technological and the social.

Finally, the narrative reveals a broader ambivalence in the nostalgic impulse itself. The "reflective" nostalgia that Boym identifies "dwells on the ambivalence of human longing and belonging and does not shy away from the contradictions of modernity,"[46] and the series' focus on technology plays into this reflective nostalgia. While much of the narrative leans toward a more pessimistic view of new technology and a more idealized view of old technology, the negative aspects of earlier times become evident with a close reading. Tony's "retro" style and predilection for cassette tapes belie the fact that, as a gay Latinx teenager, he would have likely experienced systemic homophobia had he lived out his adolescence in the past that he seems to long for semiotically. Similarly, while new media enable cyberbullying and slut shaming to occur exponentially more significantly in the show, the #MeToo moment depicted in Jessica's time on the witness stand and the implicit critique of white male privilege and toxic masculinity exemplified in the characterization of Bryce stand in recognizable opposition. The Brock Turner-esque sentencing of Bryce following the trial that publicized his sexual assaults of Hannah and Jessica points to the typical "contradictions" of modernity, as his trial in the court of public opinion, both within the narrative and in "real" social media conversations elicited a more significant punishment. For example, several of the characters have Instagram accounts that went live after the second season, and comments on the feed of "brycemoney23" say things like "Like if u hate Bryce and monte" and "Yeah you drink to forget your a rapist but that's why I'm here to remind you," with some comments acknowledging that the account is for a fictitious character, not a real person.[47] Ultimately, technology becomes at once a symbol of regressive wistfulness for simpler times and progressive forward-thinking societal reform.

CONCLUSION

Narratives of technological determinism persist in popular conceptualizations of the relationship between society and technology, and the series *13 Reasons Why* is no exception. The teenage characters seem unable to escape the profound individual and socio-cultural effects of their technologized world as they seek solace in "old" media. However, the series also illustrates the ambivalence inherent in all media and the constructivist approach that individuals and society both shape and are shaped by technology. The tensions in these sociotechnical relationships problematize the nostalgic impulse itself, revealing the nuances between regression and progression, between looking back and moving forward. Despite the negative press that the series has received, perhaps there is a note of optimism embedded in the way that the series mobilizes nostalgia as evidence of the potential of human agency, the ability to eschew determinist narratives and to shape our engagements with technology and each other. This reading is particularly powerful in the context of the series' teenage viewers who often face pessimistic predictions for their future. As Clay says, "It has to get better. The way we treat each other and look out for each other. It has to get better somehow."[48]

NOTES

1. Inkoo Kang, *"13 Reasons Why* and the Most Powerful Teen Drug of All: Nostalgia," *MTV,* May 12, 2017, http://www.mtv.com/news/3012280/13-reasons-why-and-the-most-powerful-teen-drug-of-all-nostalgia/.

2. Kang, "Most Powerful Teen Drug.*"*

3. Sally Wyatt, "Technological Determinism Is Dead: Long Live Technological Determinism." In *Handbook of Science and Technology Studies,* ed. Edward J. Hackett, Olga Amsterdamska, Michael E. Lynch, and Judy Wajcman (Cambridge: MIT Press, 2008).

4. David Crowley, "Doing Things Electronically," *Canadian Journal of Communication* 19, no. 1 (Winter 1994): 5.

5. Nicolas Negroponte, *Being Digital.* (New York: Alfred K. Knopf, 1995), 231.

6. Nicholas Carr, "Is Google Making Us Stupid?" *Yearbook of the National Society for the Study of Education* 107 (2008): 89-94, https://doi.org/10.1111/j.1744-7984.2008.00172.x

7. Tim Wu, *The Attention Merchants: The Epic Scramble to Get Inside Our Heads* (New York: Knopf, 2016).

8. Andrea Ballatore and Simone Natale, "E-readers and the Death of the Book: Or, New Media and the Myth of the Disappearing Medium," *New Media & Society 18,* no. 10 (2015): 2379-2394, https://doi.org/10.1177/1461444815586984.

9. Ballatore and Natale, "E-readers,*"* 2379.

10. Ballatore and Natale, "E-readers."

11. Manuel Menke, "Seeking Comfort in Past Media: Modeling Media Nostalgia as a Way of Coping with Media Change," *International Journal of Communication* 11 (2017).

12. Marc Ruppel, "You Are Then, This Is Now: Nostalgia, Technology and Consumer Identity at CES 2007," *Social Identities* 15, no. 4 (2009): 537.

13. Ruppel, "You Are Then,*"* 553.

14. Simone Natale, "There Are No Old Media," *Journal of Communication* 66 (2016): 585-603, doi:10.1111/jcom.12235.

15. Natale, "There Are No Old Media," 586.

16. Natale, "There Are No Old Media," 596.

17. Katharina Niemeyer, "Digital Nostalgia," *Media Development* 4 (2016).

18. Svetlana Boym, "Nostalgia and Its Discontents," *The Hedgehog Review* 9, no. 2 (Summer 2007): 8, http://ezproxy.ardc.talonline.ca/login?url=https://search.ebscohost.com/login.aspx?direct=true&db=hlh&AN=26518932&site=eds-live.

19. Boym, "Nostalgia," 10.

20. Boym, "Nostalgia," 12.

21. Linda Hutcheon and Mario J. Valdes, "Irony, Nostalgia, and Postmodern: A Dialogue," online PDF, *Poligraphias* 3 (1998-2000): 20.

22. Fred Davis, "Nostalgia, Identity, and the Current Nostalgia Wave," *The Journal of Popular Culture* 11, no. 2 (1977): 414-424.

23. Janelle Wilson, "Here and Now, There and Then: Nostalgia as a Time and Space Phenomenon," *Symbolic Interaction* 38, no. 4 (2015): 490, doi.org/10.1002/symb.184Wilson.

24. Harold A. Innis. *The Bias of Communication* (Toronto: University of Toronto Press 1951).

25. Gilad Padva, *Queer Nostalgia in Cinema and Pop Culture* (New York: Palgrave Macmillan, 2014), 4.

26. Natale, "There Are No Old Media."

27. *13 Reasons Why*, "Tape 1, Side A," Netflix, March 31, 2017, written by Brian Yorkey, directed by Tom McCarthy, https://www.netflix.com/watch/80117471.

28. See Carr, "Is Google Making Us Stupid?"; and Wu, *The Attention Merchants*.

29. *13 Reasons Why*, "Tape 2, Side B," Netflix, March 31, 2017, written by Thomas Higgins, directed by Helen Shaver, https://www.netflix.com/watch/80117474.

30. *13 Reasons Why*, "Tape 1, Side A."

31. *13 Reasons Why*, "Tape 2, Side B."

32. *13 Reasons Why*, "Tape 4, Side B," Netflix, March 31, 2017, written by Kirk A. Moore, directed by Gregg Araki, https://www.netflix.com/watch/80117478.

33. *13 Reasons Why*, "Tape 3, Side B," Netflix, March 31, 2017, written by Nic Sheff, directed by Kyle Patrick Alvarez, https://www.netflix.com/watch/80117476.

34. *13 Reasons Why*, "Tape 3, Side A," Netflix, March 31, 2017, written by Julie Bicknell, directed by Kyle Patrick Alvarez, https://www.netflix.com/watch/80117475.

35. *13 Reasons Why*, "Tape 1, Side A."

36. *13 Reasons Why*, "Tape 3, Side A."

37. *13 Reasons Why*, "Tape 1, Side B," Netflix, March 31, 2017, written by Brian Yorkey, directed by Tom McCarthy, https://www.netflix.com/watch/80117472.

38. *13 Reasons Why*, "Tape 7, Side A," Netflix, March 31, 2017, written by Brian Yorkey, directed by Kyle Patrick Alvarez, https://www.netflix.com/watch/80117483.

39. *13 Reasons Why*, "Tape 4, Side B."

40. *13 Reasons Why*, "Tape 4, Side B."

41. *13 Reasons Why*, "Tape 2, Side A," Netflix, March 31, 2017, written by Dianna Son, directed by Helen Shaver, https://www.netflix.com/watch/80117474.

42. *13 Reasons Why*, "Tape 7, Side A."

43. *1 3 Reasons Why*, "Tape 7, Side A."

44. *13 Reasons Why*, "Tape 1, Side A."

45. *13 Reasons Why*, "Tape 5, Side B," Netflix, March 31, 2017, Nathan Louis Jackson, directed by Carl Franklin, https://www.netflix.com/watch/80117480; *13 Reasons Why*, "Tape 7, Side A."

46. Boym, *The Future of Nostalgia*, 13.

47. These comments appear on the May 14 "Cheers" post on the fictitious "bryce-money23" Instagram account.

48. *13 Reasons Why*, "Tape 7, Side A."

BIBLIOGRAPHY

Baral, Susmita. "How *13 Reasons Why* Upgraded Its Technology for Modern Users." *Refinery 29*. April 2, 2017. https://www.refinery29.com/2017/04/148191/13-reasons-why-technology-upgrade.

Ballatore, Andrea, and Simone Natale. "E-readers and the Death of the Book: Or, New Media and the Myth of the Disappearing Medium." *New Media & Society* 18, no. 10 (2015): 2379-2394. https://doi.org/10.1177/1461444815586984.

Boym, Svetlana. "Nostalgia and Its Discontents." *The Hedgehog Review* 9, no. 2 (Summer 2007): 7-18. http://ezproxy.ardc.talonline.ca/login?url=https://search.ebscohost.com/login.aspx?direct=true&db=hlh&AN=26518932&site=eds-live.

Carr, Nicholas. "Is Google Making Us Stupid?" *Yearbook of the National Society for the Study of Education* 107 (2008): 89-94. https://doi.org/10.1111/j.1744-7984.2008.00172.x.

Crowley, David. "Doing Things Electronically." *Canadian Journal of Communication* 19, no. 1 (Winter 1994): 5-22.

Davis, Fred. "Nostalgia, Identity, and the Current Nostalgia Wave." *The Journal of Popular Culture* 11, no. 2 (1977): 414-424.

Highfill, Samantha. "*13 Reasons Why*: Exclusive First Details on Season 2." *Entertainment Weekly*. May 9, 2017. http://ew.com/tv/2017/05/09/13-reasons-why-season-2-brian-yorkey/

Hutcheon, Linda, and Valdes, Mario J. "Irony, Nostalgia, and Postmodern: A Dialogue." Online PDF. *Poligraphias* 3 (1998-2000): 18-4.1

Innis, Harold A. *The Bias of Communication*. Toronto: University of Toronto Press, 1951.

Kang, Inkoo. "*13 Reasons Why* and the Most Powerful Teen Drug of All: Nostalgia." *MTV*. May 12, 2017. http://www.mtv.com/news/3012280/13-reasons-why-and-the-most-powerful-teen-drug-of-all-nostalgia/.

Menke, Manuel. "Seeking Comfort in Past Media: Modeling Media Nostalgia as a Way of Coping with Media Change." *International Journal of Communication* 11 (2017): 626-646.

Natale, Simone. "There Are No Old Media." *Journal of Communication* 6 (2016): 585-603. doi:10.1111/jcom.12235

Negroponte, Nicolas. *Being Digital*. New York: Alfred K. Knopf, 1995.

Niemeyer, Katharina. "Digital Nostalgia." *Media Development* 4 (2016): 27-30.

Padva, Gilad. *Queer Nostalgia in Cinema and Pop Culture*. Basingstoke (GB): Palgrave Macmillan, 2014.

Ruppel, Marc. "You Are Then, This Is Now: Nostalgia, Technology and Consumer Identity at CES 2007." *Social Identities* 15, no. 4 (2009): 537-555.

Seraro, Nivea. "*13 Reasons Why* Author on 'Bonus Content' the Netflix Show Adds to His Book." *Entertainment Weekly*. March 31, 2017. http://ew.com/books/2017/03/31/thirteen-reasons-why-jay-asher-netflix-tv-show/.

Wilson, Janelle. "Here and Now, There and Then: Nostalgia as a Time and Space Phenomenon." *Symbolic Interaction* 38, no. 4 (2015): 478-492. doi.org/10.1002/symb.184.

Wyatt, Sally. "Technological Determinism Is Dead: Long Live Technological Determinism." In *Handbook of Science and Technology Studies*, edited by Edward J. Hackett, Olga Amsterdamska, Michael E. Lynch, and Judy Wajcman, 165-180. Cambridge: MIT Press, 2008.

Wu, Tim. *The Attention Merchants: The Epic Scramble to Get Inside Our Heads*. New York: Knopf, 2016.

Yorkey, Brian. *13 Reasons Why*. March 31, 2017. Netflix. https://www.netflix.com/watch/80117471.

FOURTEEN

Carrying That Weight

Shinichiro Watanabe's Cowboy Bebop *and Nostalgia*

Kwasu D. Tembo

STREAMED NOSTALGIA: NETFLIX, CURATING, CREATING, AND
THE CONCEPT OF THE ARCHIVE

Developed by Sunrise Entertainment, Shinichiro Watanabe's Japanese
anime series *Cowboy Bebop* (1997–1998; hereon *Bebop*) is broadly considered to be one of the greatest anime series of all time. Since its release,
Bebop has garnered critical and commercial success in Japan and international markets, most notably the United States. In particular, critics have
noted the series' impressive score (by Yoko Kanno), narrative complexity,
nuanced voice performances, character design, and overall aesthetic and
narrative style. Tasha Robinson describes *Bebop*'s importance in terms of
the series being responsible for introducing Western viewers to anime
during the early post-millennium.[1] From *Ranker* to *Sbs*, the series typically places in the top twenty entrants of the vast majority of "best anime
series" lists. One of the latent implications of this universal praise is that
the series has accrued a reverential status over time. As a result, *Bebop* has
been imbued with both the aura of a rare or treasured object, as well as
the sense of timelessness that accompanies such objects. A concomitant
result of *Bebop*'s medial and cultural status is that the series is seen by
both ardent fans and cursory viewers as a text that is, at least, to be
admired, and at most, one that must be archived/preserved.

   Bebop is a prime example of aesthetic, narrative, and thematic nostalgic retrofuturism. The series' twenty-six episodes or "sessions" are set in

219

2071 approximately fifty years after a hyperspace gateway accident renders Earth near uninhabitable, and follow the misadventures of the bounty hunting crew of the spaceship *Bebop*. In response to said incident,
humanity colonizes most of the rocky planets and their respective satel-
lites in the Solar System. A consequence of this expansion is an increase
in interplanetary organized crime. To combat the epidemic, the Inter Solar System Police (ISSP) establish an official contract system whereby
"cowboys," that is registered bounty hunters, track down and apprehend
criminals in return for monetary rewards. The original crew of the *Bebop*
are two such bounty hunters: Spike Spiegel, an excommunicated former
hitman for the Red Dragon crime syndicate, and his partner Jet Black, a
former ISSP officer. Later in the series, Spike and Jet are joined by Faye
Valentine, an amnesiac con artist with a severe gambling addiction, Ed, a
highly idiosyncratic virtuoso hacker, and Ein, a genetically engineered
Corgi or data dog that expresses human level intelligence. The prepon-
derance of the series, which deals with the crew getting into a variety of
humorous, tragic, enlightening, surreal, and transformative situations in
the pursuit of their bounties, forms the backdrop for nuanced meditations on the pressures, inescapability, and confrontations with and of the
past. More thematically, the series' narrative premise, which concerns
outlaws and bounties, appeals to the Western/Noir archetypes of the
cowboy, the private-eye, and the golden-hearted shyster. All these and
other latently nostalgic themes, concepts, and ideas are reterritorialized
into a future setting which has the effect of exacerbating the sense of
nostalgia they carry.

This chapter will explore the relationship between the archive, archiving, and the archived object using Netflix as an example of a contemporary digital archive, and *Bebop* as a retrofuturistic archivable text. The
goal here is to explore and theorize the relationship between the archive
and the concept and praxes of "streamed nostalgia." It opens with an
examination of Netflix as a leading media platform and its relationship to
the concept of the archive. This is followed by a discussion of the relationship between Netflix and anime more broadly before concluding with a
close reading of these themes in relation to *Bebop* as a case study of a
"classic" in the medium, and its relationship to nostalgic genres.

Jana Radošinská provides the following succinct description of Netflix
in "New Trends in Production and Distribution of Episodic Television
Drama: Brand Marvel—Netflix in the Post-Television Era": "Netflix specializes in providing access to a significant amount of [existing and] original content; the service is advertisement-free, available in more than 190
countries all over the world, and it allows its users to choose from dozens
of episodic television dramas and feature films."[2] My use of the term
"streamed nostalgia" is based on Radošinská's identification of new
methods of consuming serialized television and film through digital media platforms, but more importantly, how these methods are predicated

on "basic market strategies of 'push' and 'pull,' representing new trends of television content [whereby] programme delivery is also shifting from 'over-the-air broadcast' where viewers have content 'pushed' to them, in favour of an expanding online environment where they 'pull' what they want to watch when they want to see it."[3] The implication here is that online digital media, provided through streaming services, online subscriptions, and video on demand (VOD) apparatuses including Netflix, Hulu, Amazon Prime, HBO NOW, and MUBI offer consumers vast databases of varied audio-visual media content culled from numerous networks and times. In this sense, the ever-updating Netflix catalog represents a digital space in which cultural texts are archived or dislodged from the sequential temporal imperatives of over-the-air broadcasting allowing consumers to *pull* content from any genre and any period.

In "Rethinking International TV Flows: Research in the Age of Netflix," Ramon Lobato theorizes this transition from the push of the broadcast to the pull *from* the archive as the transition from the schedule to the catalog. He notes that

> schedules are obviously different from catalogues in that the former are linear sequences of programmed content and the latter are interactive, curated databases. But the two objects are comparable in the sense that both index *the range of content available* through a particular distribution system, and thus delimit—without determining—the likely range of textual experiences available to audiences through that system.[4]

When considering the temporal limitations of traditional broadcast media and the archival nature of streamed media, platforms like Netflix have allowed nostalgia to become reified in contemporary media consumption praxes. Through the connectivity of Internet and communications technology, from fiber optic cable to the constantly evolving storage and playback capabilities of media devices and/or applications on them, what Radošinská terms "Internet-delivered television" allows consumers to exercise or, in a way, nourish their nostalgia in the inexhaustible tributaries of transtemporal media content.

Empirically, it is clear that Netflix has proven that streaming services, media content archives, and the praxes of online media production and consumption have changed the way human beings consume and produce what was once "televised programming."[5] The archival nature of Netflix allows media consumption to "partially or totally ignore once unavoidable 'side effects' of watching television (predefined, rigid programme schedule, often even the 'one episode a week' distribution strategy and other basic aspects of so-called seriality)" meaning that "one of the most significant consequences of watching episodic or serial narratives via online services and digital applications is the fact that the original concept of 'seriality' does not apply here."[6] As a direct result, "an ordinary viewer—free from institutionalized restrictions and ready to choose from vast amounts of entertainment—is unable to limit the range and timeframe of his/her own consumption of serial narratives, that is, to indulge in episodic stories in accordance with predetermined 'doses.'"[7] In this way, Netflix is retrofuturistic insofar as it uses current technology to unlock histories of media content without being impeded by the imminence of traditional broadcast programming: it is an apparatus of archive technology that idealizes, distills, or streamlines nostalgic praxes of consuming the mediated past.

If Netflix can be described as latently retrospective in a significant part of its operational model, then it is important to ask if and how Netflix engenders nostalgia in its consumers. According to Pierson and Bauwens's _Digital Broadcasting: An Introduction to New Media_ platforms like Netflix employ a repertoire of marketing, production, and programming strategies "to build an identity to differentiate themselves from others and establish a loyal relationship with audiences."[8] In this way, anime, like any other aesthetic and narrative technique of storytelling contained and disseminated through Netflix's archive, is done so through what Denis McQuail calls institutionalized fandom. Institutionalized fandom can be understood as a confluence of various types of nostalgically based methods of establishing a connection between media content and media audiences.[9] Essential to this strategy, Radošinská notes, is the creation and reproduction of "a hedonistic consumer category—a marketing and media projection of various cravings, dreams, expectations, experiences or pleasures desired by media audiences" which, of late, have all been marked in some way by nostalgia.[10] On the one hand, it may seem logical to conclude, as Martin Solik and Martin Klementis do, that "all products of popular culture must reflect on the everyday lives of their users. If the users do not 'find themselves' in the products of popular culture, such products will not be able to gain popularity."[11] On the other hand, the archival nature of Netflix specifically undoes this temporal imperative meaning that the platform allows the consumer to "look for themselves" in styles, genres, and periods not bound to the media being produced contemporaneously to them. In essence, Netflix allows consumers to time travel, that is, to find themselves both in the present unfolding of media history, but also in its past in a way that lends itself to speculation about the relationship between the archive and retrofuturism.

Although retrofuturism is typically understood to be a narrative and aesthetic tactic based on hindsight, that is, the use of tropes, styles and conventions considered futuristic reinserted into aesthetico-cultural frameworks of preceding eras, here the term also acknowledges the same effect can be achieved through the inverse action. In this sense, retrofuturism can also refer to reterritorializing or (re)projecting/(re)deploying style and aesthetic conventions from preceding epochs into the speculative imagining of future eras. In "Crafting Yesterday's Tomorrows:

Retrofuturism, Steampunk and the Problem of Making in the Twenty-First Century," Elizabeth Guffy states that retrofuturism

> builds on the "futurists" fevered visions of space colonies with flying cars, robotic servants, and interstellar travel but while futurists tool the promise of progress for granted, retro-futurism emerged as a more skeptical reaction. Indeed, retro-futurism makes no predications, nor can it be associated with claims for truth or honesty. Put simply, retro-futurism is a half-nostalgic, half-sentimental memorializing of popular futurism. It remains a sensibility, rather than a plan of action.[12]

Guffy's description of retrofuturism as a stylistic sensibility as opposed to a prescriptive aesthetico-narratological method applies directly to *Bebop* whose retrofuturism combines all the elements she names, while simultaneously infusing them with a sense of collage, drift, and/or bricolage. In *Bebop* Watanabe creates a *style* of visual and narrative storytelling that is at once nostalgic in its referential gestures to other genres and times, but also futuristic in terms of its setting and approach to the appearance and experience of the text's diegesis. In Rob Latham's "Our Jaded Tomorrows," retrofuturism is described as "an 'ambivalent fascination' with past utopia visions of the future"[13] while in "Nostalgia for the Future: Retrofuturism in Enterprise," Sharon Sharp goes further by making the important connection between retrofuturism and nostalgia by describing the former as using "iconic imagery of previous visions of the future, such as jet packs, homes of tomorrow, ray guns and other space age manifestations of technological progress, because our sense of the future is often inflected with a sense of nostalgia for imaginings of the future that never materialized."[14] For Scott Bukatman, the pervasiveness of nostalgia in contemporary approaches to media production and consumption is identical to the current epoch's retrofuturistic inclinations. According to Bukatman, we have entered an era of media that despite its unprecedented technological advances, is still defined as a "seemingly inexhaustible period of meganostalgia" with an "obsessive recycling of the past," a response to the sense that "the future is no longer distant and unattainable but has already arrived."[15] While the rhetoric here is latently critical of retrofuturism's ostensibly inextricable sense of derivation and unoriginality, Joanna Page notes in "Retrofuturism and Reflexivity in Argentine Science Fiction Film: The Construction of Cinematic Time" that Fredric Jameson, a theorist whose criticisms of nostalgia-based media production and consumption are, ironically, as incisive as they are recursive,

> does reserve a particular role for "collage" as a principle of organization in postmodern science fiction, defined as "the bringing into precarious coexistence of elements drawn from very different sources and contexts, elements which derive for the most part from older literary

models which amount to broken fragments of outworn older genres of
the newer productions of the media (for example, comic strips)."[16]

In *The Future of Nostalgia*, Svetlana Boym states that "a modern nostalgic
can be both homesick and sick of home" in that the audience wants "to go
back to a time that never existed, to relive times we never actually experienced [through] infinitely repeatable recordings [which] leave us with
nothing but 'the indexical trace' of themselves."[17] Here, Netflix can be
thought of as an apparatus of tertiary memory, an archive of saturated
indexical traces of various media which in themselves also stand as totemic of other times. Latent to the term "trace" here are also connotations
of incompletion, loss, and lack, specifically with regard to the ephemeral
albeit lauded phenomena of originality. Simon Reynolds cautions against
the dangers of nostalgia and its corrosive effects on originality and creativity in *Pop Culture's Addiction to Its Own Past*, stating that "retromania"
is akin to "a hipster stock market based around trading pasts, not futures," in which a crash is unavoidable: "the world economy was brought
down by derivatives and bad debt; [media] has been depleted of meaning
through derivatives and indebtedness."[18]

The tone and diction of the rhetoric here, again, seems negative, reflecting Eleanor Heartney's position in "Appropriation and the Loss of
Authenticity" in which she argues that "the empty nostalgia of our mediated memories holds no original and no original context."[19] While I agree
that this is theoretically sound, Heartney and others overlook the seemingly paradoxical albeit effective originality of bricolage. If one constructs
a bricolage of numerous media traditions, tropes, leitmotifs, and aesthetico-narratological praxes from the past and present and their respective
speculation of the future, then even nostalgically mediated conceptions
of the future can allow the emergence of a retrofuturistic authenticity.
Bebop stands as such an example in which Watanabe builds his own
retrofuturistic authenticity with both the severity and sincerity of genuine reverence, and a nuanced sense of humor that results from a critical
perspective and methodological self-awareness. In this sense, the ethos
behind *Bebop* is "far from reflecting any simple nostalgia for the bygone;
nor does it provide the basis for 'postmodern' pastiche," and furthermore, Bebop's "relation to the past is far from 'simple nostalgia' which
[. . .] seems equal to a cheap sentimentality that exploits the emotions of
loss and hope."[20] While for theorists including Jameson, Hobsbawm, and
Lowenthal nostalgia has (re)appeared as a "conservative," "sentimental,"
"invented," "falsifying," and "escapist" approach to the past," I am inclined toward Gronholm's primary position in "When Tomorrow Began
Yesterday: Kraftwerk's Nostalgia for the Past Futures" which suggests
that "nostalgia as a complex concept since it resonates with numerous
ways of relating to the past, ranging from personal melancholy and

home-sickness to a wide variety of forms of identity-making, retro-culture, entertainment, and the politics of memory."[21]

When considering anime specifically, the medium and its genres and subgenres have always been associated with nostalgia, whether period specific or retrofuturistic. Some notable examples include the following: Meditations on the extreme ancient praxes of Bushido in Hiroshi Hamasaki's *Shigurui: Death Frenzy* (2007); sci-fi Western explorations of the figure of the cowboy outlaw in Satoshi Nishimura's *Trigun* (1998); anime Gothico-horror interpolations of Shellian and Stokerian ideas combined with themes of Nazism and the occult in Umanosuke Iida's *Hellsing* (2001–2002); themes of gentilesse and chivalry in Shin Itagaki's *Bersek* (2016–2017); and perhaps the most famous anime meditation on the clash between past and future in techno-organic onto-existential terms in Mamoru Oshii's *Ghost in the Shell* (1995). When considering Netflix's approach to marketing for animated content, Roland Kelts notes that "Netflix's strategy is to amass personnel with proven track records who can generate properties in-house, as opposed to merely repackaging pre-existing material" going on to note "the company's budget for [anime] content spiked from $6 billion [in 2017] to over $8 billion in 2018."[22] Included in Netflix's push for new anime content is the first-ever animated version of the Toho franchise's *Godzilla* in Hiroyuki Seshita's *Godzilla: Planet of the Monsters* (2017), and Masaaki Yuasa's *Devilman Crybaby* (2018), an adaptation of Go Nagai's 1972 horror manga *Devilman*. The latter, which critics and consumers alike have labeled a masterpiece since its release in January, "could not exist without its explicit violence and eroticism" which "was only made possible by Netflix," Netflix here being regarded as "an ideal media outlet for anime adaptation" for a broad range of animated content.[23] With Netflix signing distribution and production contracts with noted anime production house Production I.G., and its subsidiary Wit Studio as well as Bones Inc., it is clear Netflix is committed to the expansion of the anime content of its archive, which will be increased this year with the creation and distribution of thirty exclusive anime series.[24]

Kayleigh Donaldson notes a similar trend in her article "Every Anime Available to Watch on Netflix" (2018), observing that Netflix has been building a substantial following in its anime content by acting as a repository for "a mix of classics and hot new favourites."[25] Such classics include Carl Macek's *Robotech* (1985), Kazuhiro Furuhashi's *Rurouni Kenshin* (1996–1998), both Watanabe's *Cowboy Bebop* (1997–1998) (hereon *Bebop*) and its now cult classic followup *Samuari Champloo* (2004–2005), and Hiroshi Nagahama's *Mushishi* (2005–2006). Netflix's strategy in certain cases is blatantly retrofuturistic, specifically, retrofuturism in the form of *manufactured* nostalgia through both adaptation and remake. Examples that have been circumscribed by the Netflix archive include Joaquim Dos Santos's *Voltron: Legendary Defender* (2016), and Noelle Stevenson's *She-Ra*

(2018), a remake of Gwen Wetzler's *She-Ra: Princess of Power She-Ra* (1985), itself a spin-off of the Lou Scheimer classic *He-Man and the Masters of the Universe* (1983), as well as Warren Ellis's *Castlevania* (2017), an adaptation of Hitoshi Akamatsu's 1989 video game *Castlevania III: Dracula's Curse.*

In view of Netflix's strategy toward the production and archiving of anime classics and adaptations, I contend that the relationship between Netflix and anime is *intrinsically* nostalgic. This relationship is one example of what Child and Faughnder have both independently described as a broader trend in contemporary media production and consumption centered on the past. This trend has led to what Rodrigo Gonzalez calls a nostalgia economy of media content in "The Nostalgia Economy: Netflix and New Audiences in the Digital Age":

> this situation marks a production tendency whose main strategies are the continuation and expansion of successful narrative franchises, the adaptation of past media products to contemporary contexts in terms of plot, and the reworking of an original material in a different medium. Hence, a nostalgia economy has appeared, being focused on creating mediatic iterations that mirror previous ones. The nostalgic component is found, narratively, in all the connections with the original material, and, economically, in the purpose of engaging past viewers, or fans, with the return of a "beloved" content and, at the same time, luring younger audiences to consume a product which appears to be new, but it is rooted in a sense of reminiscence.[26]

Here, Netflix's strategy to produce original anime content is based on developing "content that is anchored in a nostalgic sentiment," thereby taking "advantage of [the zeitgeist's] 'nostalgic desire' in distinct modes."[27] Therefore, Netflix is committed to producing and archiving original anime content, its ethos and success insofar as drawing out the patronage of fandoms, audiences, and subcultures such as anime otaku exists in an internet-delivered television nexus at whose center is a service-platform whose consumption practices rely on the past.[28]

TALES OF KILIMANJARO: INTERTEXTUAL NOSTALGIA-DRIVEN RETROFUTURISM IN *COWBOY BEBOP*

In many ways, *Bebop* is itself an archive of genre and themes. Watanabe makes this connection literally apparent in the series tagline "a new genre unto itself," one Brian Camp, Julie Davis, Jonathan Clements, and Helen McCarthy note is comprised of a bricolage of multiple genres, including comedy, noir, heist caper, action-adventure, Western, samurai, pulp fiction, and crime thriller.[29,30] This archival ethos is not limited to the series' aesthetic or narrative, but also its approach to use of music, as represented by the fact that most episode titles emphasize and collect various styles or genres of music from rhapsody, serenade, funk, to blues, or in some instances, specific song titles such as session 24 titled "Hard Luck Woman" (1999) and session 15 titled "My Funny Valentine" (1999). From a specifically sonic standpoint, *Bebop* is a retrofuturistic archive of genre and style. Series score composer Yoko Kanno went as far as to form a bricolage band called The Seatbelts which, though ostensibly a blues and jazz band, predicated their compositions for the series mainly on Western blues/blue grass, opera, and jazz. In an interview for *Red Bull Music Academy* in 2014 by Akahiro Tomita, Kanno gives the following account of the emergence of the collage and latently nostalgic ethos of the series score, perhaps the single most important element of *Bebop*:

> The seeds of the score were sown in middle school and high school when I was a member of the brass band. I'm not sure how it is nowadays, but back then all the songs kids were taught weren't at all cool, so I made and performed originals. But a part of me was always frustrated because I couldn't understand why everybody else was content playing the uncool music. I wanted to play brass music that shook your soul, made your blood boil, and made you lose it. This yearning became "Tank!" which was the opening theme. I wanted to make music which would light a fire in me when I played it. Also, when I was "convenient" during my university years, I transcribed a lot of black music. After I began to grasp and understand rhythm I thought, "How is it that they play the drums the same way, but the rhythm is so different between black people and white people?" So I took a trip to New Orleans to listen to jazz and funk.[31]

She goes on to state that during this trip, she "learned that even within a genre there are differences in the style" and cultural interpretations thereof.[32]

Fred Patten also notes how Watanabe makes explicit nostalgic references, both as homage and pastiche, to multiple films including *Midnight Run, 2001: A Space Odyssey, Alien,* and the works of specific auteurs including Bruce Lee and John Woo, and science fiction leitmotifs now inherent to the contemporary understanding of the genre developed in the fiction of William Gibson.[33] The design of the *Bebop*'s diegesis is also latently retrofuturistic. The cityscapes and metropolitan areas, including slums, suburbs, horse racing tracks, casinos, precincts, bars, ports, deserts and harbors shown on Mars, Ganymede, Titan, and Callisto all resemble the cityscapes of contemporary Tokyo or New York. Included in this retrofuturistic gesture to the architectural and cultural markers of the past, *Bebop*'s diegesis also contains Betamax video players, hyperspace gates, spaceships, explorations of eco-politics, channel-surfing, game shows, telemarketing, and mysticism in the form of the recurring prophesies of a First Nations shaman named Laughing Bull. Clements and McCarthy describe this retrofuturistic, nostalgic aesthetico-narratological bricolage or archive of genre and style as "one part Chinese diaspora and two parts wild west."[34] Similarly, Todd DuBois notes that the overall viewing experience of *Bebop* inextricably informed by the series' retrofuturistic bricolage is described by Watanabe as "80% serious story and 20% humorous touch."[35]

Watanabe's text relates back to Boym, Torlasco, and Reynold's suggestion of an inextricability between both the pleasure and pain of nostalgia in its very premise. All the main cast are characterized by a deep sense of loneliness or resignation to their fate and past whereby the past holds no nostalgic sentimentality, but rather a pervasive and inescapable sense of loss. For Spike, the past is a karmic cycle of loss and heartache, marked not only by the loss of the woman he loved, but also his friendship with his now rival Vicious. As a result, Spike is marked by an incisive sense of lethargic resignation nihilism. Spike's drifter persona is predicated on an acceptance of the fact that his past will eventually return to confront him and as such, there is no viable future available to him. His dry, and at times caustic, sense of humor and seeming carelessness stand as surety against his onto-existential and psycho-emotional limbo that cannot be assuaged by a utopian nostalgia for the past, nor a retrofuturistic optimism for the future.[36] This trauma of the past in the future also marks Jet in an ostensibly different, but latently undifferentiated way. In "Behind the *Bebop*—Murder, Mars and All That Jazz," Robert Bricken notes how Jet's cynicism is predicated on his loss of faith in his former life and the state of inter-Solar society, which includes the fact that his ex-girlfriend Alisa left him.[37] For Faye, large swathes of the past literally do not exist. A consequence of her cryogenic freezing is an almost total amnesiacal loss of memory. The verve, tenacity, addictiveness, sensuality, and acerbic character traits she expresses therefore seemingly emerge ex nihilo, out of reach of a utopian nostalgia for Earth-that-was, her youth, or family, as well as the possible restructuring thereof through a retrofuturistic sense of recombination and experimentation. As a result, for Faye, neither nostalgia nor retrofuturism solve or help her navigate her radical sense of onto-existential and psycho-emotional displacement. Even the seemingly carefree eccentricities of Ed can be read as an elaborate cover or manifestation of the traumatic loneliness generated by the fact that Ed's father abandoned her, again circumscribing the past as a temporal space whose foundation is trauma.

Retrofuturism and nostalgia exist beyond *Bebop's* "exchange" value and inhere in its "cult" status. Much in the same way Netflix has evolved from simply being a media archive to producing media for it own archiving, *Bebop* fandom has moved from simply consuming the series to co-producing, recirculating, and extending/expanding upon it. As Kyle Nicholas notes in his presentation "The Work Which Becomes a New Genre Itself: Textual Networks in the World of *Cowboy Bebop*," in recent years the advent of new media technologies has transformed our sense of adaptation and with it our sense of authorship and authenticity. Media consumers, or "readers," have always been active to some extent, selecting, combining and re-contextualizing portions of their favourite texts. But multimedia networks have both deepened and extended these activities in important ways. Employing digital duplication and production tools, global communities of network users now create and exchange media artifacts of ambiguous provenance. Members of these networks inhabit "the shifted mediascape produced by the Internet" that distributes production and desire.[38]

Nicholas's comments here seem somewhat oracular as in 2006, Netflix's business model was still predominantly archival; that is, limited to DVD rental by mail, before *Bebop* was a part of its archive and only distributed in the West via Cartoon Network, a year before the business began its media streaming service. As a direct result, platforms such as Netflix are blurring the boundaries between consumption and creation, between the archive and its expansion through production. For *Bebop*, this has taken the form of online communities, under the name *CowBe*, which Nicholas notes have been responsible for the distribution and influence of the series among Western consumers, but also responsible, I argue, for the manufacture of the nostalgia-based cult of the series since its release as well. As Nicholas notes, this cult was both archival *and* productive from the onset:

> Although the first episode shown was hardly a hit, the series developed a small but loyal following throughout its initial run. When it was not renewed for a full season, those fans got active in chatrooms and online gatherings and made their feelings known to producers at Sunrise Entertainment. Always attentive to fans in cyberspace and sensing a potential hit, Sunrise produced another 12 episodes and sold the entire 24 episode season to WOWOW cable television. Before airing the episodes, Sunrise also contracted with its parent company Bandai, a Japanese toy giant and one of the largest producers of Japanese entertainment in the United States, to combine some episodes to laser disk for direct sale. Sales of the disks (generally collector's items for dedicated fans) were brisk, and helped generate an online buzz for the cable episodes. As the episodes arrived (with a new Episode 1 helping to explain the series to new viewers) online anime communities in Japan and around the world used the series to explore their own creativity and interact with characters and each other.[39]

In this sense, internet-delivered media streaming services like Netflix only serve to accelerate the communal consumption and coproduction of cult media, the value and influence of its nostalgic characteristics, and promote further conglomeration between production and promotion of new and existing media content. The consumer becomes not only cocustodian of the archive, but coproducer in the expansion thereof. *Cowboy*

Bebop stands as an example of how platforms like Netflix can sharpen the already technically proficient and dialogic commercial-communal relationship between consumers and creators of nostalgia-based cultural artifacts. The result, Nicholas suggests, is that all media content, texts within the nebulous and ever-expanding remit of the streaming archive, means that "all texts are now networks of form and meaning," archives within archives, whose curation, in cases such as *Bebop* and other "cult" or "classic" media, regardless of genre or epoch, are curated with an express sense of nostalgia, which itself forms part of the ethos of archive itself.[40] *Bebop* stands as a microcosmic example of the relationship between nostalgia, cult media, and the acceleration of the archive. It is my contention that though the catalog of Netflix's archive will expand and morph based on its consumers, subscribers, and users' activities, tastes, and predilections, the content of the archive will always be influenced by the nostalgia surrounding the texts within its keep.

NOTES

1. Tasha Robinson, "Gateways to Geekery: Anime," *The AV Club*, Mar. 5, 2009, https://hearwww.avclub.com/gateways-to-geekery-anime-1798215994.

2. Jana Radošinská, "New Trends in Production and Distribution of Episodic Television Drama: Brand Marvel—Netflix in the Post-Television Era," *Communication Today*, Vol. 8, No. 1 (2017): 7.

3. Radošinská, "New Trends," 6.

4. Ramon Lobato, "Rethinking International TV Flows: Research in the Age of Netflix," *Television & New Media*, Vol. 19, No. 3 (2018): 243.

5. Todd Spangler, "Netflix Is Now More Valuable Than Disney," *Variety*, May 24, 2018, http://my.chicagotribune.com/#section/-1/article/p2p-99317850/

6. Radošinská, "New Trends," 7.

7. Ibid., 7.

8. Jo Pierson and Joke Bauwens, *Digital Broadcasting: An Introduction to New Media* (London: Bloomsbury New Media Series, 2015), 78.

9. Denis McQuail, *McQuail's Mass Communication Theory* (Thousand Oaks, CA: SAGE, 2010), 442.

10. Radošinská, "New Trends," 10.

11. Martin Solík and Martin Klementis, "Mimicry of Cultural Production for the Majority Development Tendencies of Mainstream Culture," *European Journal of Science and Theology* Vol. 11, No. 6 (2015): 103.

12. Elizabeth Guffy, "Crafting Yesterday's Tomorrows: Retrofuturism, Steampunk and the Problem of Making in the Twenty-First Century," *The Journal of Modern Craft*, Vol. 7, No. 3 (2014): 254.

13. Rob Latham, "Our Jaded Tomorrows." *Science Fiction Studies*, Vol. 36, No. 2 (2009): 340.

14. Sharon Sharp, "Nostalgia for the Future: Retrofuturism in Enterprise," *Science Fiction Film and Television*, Vol. 4, No. 1 (2011): 25.

15. Scott Bukatman, *Matters of Gravity: Special Effects and Supermen in the 20th Century* (Durham: Duke University Press, 2003), 14.

16. Joanna Page."Retrofuturism and Reflexivity in Argentine Science Fiction Film: The Construction of Cinematic Time," *Arizona Journal of Hispanic Cultural Studies*, Vol. 16 (2012): 227-244.

17. Svetlana Boym, *The Future of Nostalgia* (Michigan: Basic Books, 2001), 50; Domietta Torlasco, *The Heretical Archive: Digital Memory at the End of Film* (Minnesota: University of Minnesota Press, 2013), 92.

18. Simon Reynolds, *Retromania: Pop Culture's Addiction to Its Own Past* (London: Faber and Faber, 2011), 419-420.

19. Eleanor Heartney, *Critical Condition: American Culture at the Crossroads* (Cambridge: Cambridge University Press, 1997), 26-30.

20. Pertti Grönholm, "When Tomorrow Began Yesterday: Krafwerk's Nostalgia for the Past Futures," *Popular Music and Society*, Vol. 38, No. 3 (2015): 373.

21. Pertti Grönholm, "When Tomorrow Began Yesterday," 373.

22. Roland Kelts, "Netflix Is Animated about Anime," *The Japan Times*, February 25, 2018, https://www.japantimes.co.jp/culture/2018/02/25/general/netflix-animated-anime/#.W7TK_RxWWbw.

23. Roland Kelts, "Netflix Is Animated about Anime."

24. Lauren Orsini, "Why Netflix Making More Anime May Not Be a Good Thing for Fans." *Forbes*, February 1, 2018. good-thing-for-fans/.

25. Kayleigh Donaldson, "Every Anime Available to Watch on Netflix." *Screenrant*, 13 April 2018. https://screenrant.com/netflix-anime-best/.

26. Rodrigo Gonzalez, "The Nostalgia Economy: Netflix and New Audiences in the Digital Age" (PhD diss., The London School of Economics and Political Science, 2017), 3.

27. Rodrigo Gonzalez, "The Nostalgia Economy," 3.

28. Ibid., 4-5.

29. Brian Camp and Julie Davis, *Anime Classics Zettai!: 100 Must-See Japanese Animation Masterpieces* (Berkeley: Stone Bridge Press, 2007).

30. Jonathan Clements and Helen McCarthy, *The Anime Encyclopedia: A Guide to Japanese Animation Since 1917* (Berkeley: Stone Bridge Press, 2001).

31. Akahiro Tomita, "Interview: Anime Soundtracker Yoko Kanno," *Red Bull Music Academy Daily*, November 17, 2014, http://daily.redbullmusicacademy.com/2014/11/yoko-kanno-interview.

32. Tomita, "Interview: Anime Soundtracker."

33. Fred Patten, "'Cowboy Bebop: The Movie.' . . . At Last," *AWN*, March 31, 2003, https://www.awn.com/animationworld/cowboy-bebop-movie-last. Clements and McCarthy, *Anime*, 113.

34. Clements and McCarthy, *Anime*, 113.

35. Todd DuBois, "Otakon 2013: Press Conference and Public Q&A with Director Shinichiro Watanabe," *Toon Zone*, August 21, 2013, http://www.toonzone.net/2013/08/otakon-2013-with-shinichiro-watanabe/.

36. Robert Bricken, "Behind the Bebop—Murder, Mars and All That Jazz," *Jazzmess*, 2003, http://www.jazzmess.com/misc/animeinvasion.txt.

37. Robert Bricken, "Behind the Bebop."

38. Kyle Nicholas, "The Work Which Becomes a New Genre Itself: Textual Networks in the World of *Cowboy Bebop*," Paper presented at the annual meeting of the International Communication Association, Dresden International Congress Centre, Dresden, Germany, June 16, 2006: 1.

39. Kyle Nicholas, "The Work," 3.

40. Ibid., 2006.

BIBLIOGRAPHY

Boym, Svetlana. *The Future of Nostalgia*. Michigan: Basic Books, 2001.
———. "Estrangement as a Lifestyle: Shklovsky and Brodsky." *Poetics Today*, Vol. 17, No. 4 (1996): 511–530.
Bricken, Robert. "Behind the Bebop—Murder, Mars and All That Jazz." *Jazzmess*, 2003. http://www.jazzmess.com/misc/animeinvasion.txt.

Bukatman, Scott. *Matters of Gravity: Special Effects and Supermen in the 20th Century.* Durham: Duke University Press, 2003.

Camp, Brian, and Julie Davis. *Anime Classics Zettai!: 100 Must-See Japanese Animation Masterpieces.* Berkeley: Stone Bridge Press, 2007.

Child, Ben. "Don't Call It a Reboot: How 'Remake' Became a Dirty Word in Hollywood." *The Guardian*, August 24, 2016. https://www.theguardian.com/film/2016/aug/24/film-industry-remakes-hollywood-movies.

Clements, Jonathan, and Helen McCarthy. *The Anime Encyclopedia: A Guide to Japanese Animation since 1917.* Berkeley: Stone Bridge Press, 2001.

Donaldson, Kayleigh. "Every Anime Available to Watch on Netflix." *Screenrant*, April 13, 2018.https://screenrant.com/netflix-anime-best/.

DuBois, Todd. "Otakon 2013: Press Conference and Public Q&A with Director Shinichiro Watanabe." *Toon Zone*, August 21, 2013. http://www.toonzone.net/2013/08/otakon-2013-with-shinichiro-watanabe/.

Faughnder, Ryan. "Hollywood's Summer Problem? Reboots People Don't Want." *Los Angeles Times*, August 24, 2016. http://www.latimes.com/entertainment/envelope/cotown/la-et-ct-ben-hur-summer-box-office-20160817-snap-story.html.

Gonzalez, Rodrigo. "The Nostalgia Economy: Netflix and New Audiences in the Digital Age." PhD diss., The London School of Economics and Political Science, 2017.

Grönholm, Pertti. "When Tomorrow Began Yesterday: Kraftwerk's Nostalgia for the Past Futures." *Popular Music and Society*, Vol. 38, No. 3 (2015): 372–388.

Guffy, Elizabeth. "Crafting Yesterday's Tomorrows: Retrofuturism, Steampunk and the Problem of Making in the Twenty-First Century." *The Journal of Modern Craft* Vol. 7, No. 3 (2014): 249–266.

Heartney, Eleanor. *Critical Condition: American Culture at the Crossroads.* Cambridge: Cambridge University Press, 1997.

Hartley, John. *Television Truths: Forms of Knowledge in Popular Culture.* Michigan: Blackwell, 2008.

Kelts, Roland. "Netflix Is Animated about Anime." *The Japan Times*, February 25, 2018. https://www.japantimes.co.jp/culture/2018/02/25/general/netflix-animated-anime/#.WwsyLxxWWbx.

Latham, Rob. "Our Jaded Tomorrows." *Science Fiction Studies* Vol. 36, No. 2 (2009): 339–349.

Lobato, Ramon. "Rethinking International TV Flows: Research in the Age of Netflix." *Television and New Media*, Vol. 19, No. 3 (2018): 241–256.

McQuail, Denis. *McQuail's Mass Communication Theory.* Thousand Oaks, CA: SAGE, 2010.

Nicholas, Kyle. "The Work Which Becomes a New Genre Itself: Textual Networks in the World of *Cowboy Bebop.*" Paper presented at the annual meeting of the International Communication Association, Dresden International Congress Centre, Dresden, Germany, June 16, 2006.

Orsini, Lauren. "Why Netflix Making More Anime May Not Be a Good Thing for Fans." *Forbes*, February 1, 2018. https://www.forbes.com/sites/laurenorsini/2018/02/01/why-netflix-making-more-anime-may-not-be-a-good-thing-for-fans/.

Page, Joanna. "Retrofuturism and Reflexivity in Argentine Science Fiction Film: The Construction of Cinematic Time." *Arizona Journal of Hispanic Cultural Studies*, Vol. 16 (2012): 227–244.

Patten, Fred. "'Cowboy Bebop: The Movie.' . . . at Last." *AWN*, March 31, 2003. https://www.awn.com/animationworld/cowboy-bebop-movie-last.

Pierson, Jo, and Joke Bauwens. *Digital Broadcasting: An Introduction to New Media.* London: Bloomsbury, 2015.

Radošinská, Jana. "New Trends in Production and Distribution of Episodic Television Drama: Brand Marvel—Netflix in the Post-Television Era." *Communication Today*, Vol. 8, No. 1 (2017): 4–29.

Reynolds, Simon. *Retromania: Pop Culture's Addiction to Its Own Past.* London: Faber and Faber, 2011.

Robinson, Tasha. "Gateways to Geekery: Anime." *The AV Club*, March 5, 2009. https://www.avclub.com/gateways-to-geekery-anime-1798215994.

Sharp, Sharon. "Nostalgia for the Future: Retrofuturism in Enterprise." *Science Fiction Film and Television*, Vol. 4, No. 1 (2011): 25–40.

Spangler, Todd. "Netflix Is Now More Valuable Than Disney." *Variety*, May 24, 2018. http://variety.com/2018/biz/news/netflix-disney-more-valuable-market-cap-1202820952/.

Soliik, Martin, and Martin Klementis. "Mimicry of Cultural Production for the Majority Development Tendencies of Mainstream Culture." *European Journal of Science and Theology*, Vol. 11, No. 6 (2015): 93–105.

Tomita, Akahiro. "Interview: Anime Soundtracker Yoko Kanno." *Red Bull Music Academy Daily*, November 17, 2014. http://daily.redbullmusicacademy.com/2014/11/yoko-kanno-interview.

Torlasco, Domietta. *The Heretical Archive: Digital Memory at the End of Film*. Minnesota: University of Minnesota Press, 2013.

Afterword

In Love with the Past

Ann M. Ciasullo

As a child growing up in the 1970s, a good portion of my world centered on the large piece of furniture that occupied an entire wall of my family's living room: the console television. Every day after school, I sat myself in front of it to watch rerun after rerun of *Gilligan's Island*. A few times a year, my sister and I would forgo the antics of the castaways and tune into the more serious ABC *After School Special*. But the best television experience of my childhood occurred every Tuesday night from 8:00 to 9:00 p.m. That one glorious hour featured two of the most popular shows on television at the time: *Happy Days* and *Laverne and Shirley*, back-to-back ABC hits that were set in the United States in the 1950s. I loved these shows not only for their characters—because seriously, who doesn't love the Fonz?[1]—but also for their settings: the era of poodle skirts, leather biker jackets, and malt shops filled with juke box music. Watching these shows gave me a glimpse of what my parents' lives as teenagers must have been like (or so I thought): full of romance and making out and dancing and milkshakes and fun *all the time*. A loyal fan of both series, I watched them until well after they jumped the shark (literally, in the case of *Happy Days*, and figuratively in *Laverne and Shirley* when they moved from Milwaukee to Los Angeles). I reveled in the past that they presented, a past brought to me with formulaic regularity by my beloved, dependable best friend: the television.

Our televisions are still beloved, though in remarkably different and perhaps more complex ways than they were forty years ago. Then, we had three stations to choose from in the United States—ABC, CBS, and NBC—with an average of twenty to twenty-five primetime shows per channel at our disposal.[2] Now, as Sheri Chinen Biesen notes in chapter 3, viewers have seven hundred original series on Netflix to choose from *this year* alone.[3] With such an immense increase in viewing choices, it makes sense that many of the entries in our newest mode of television viewing—streaming—draw on one of the oldest strategies for capturing viewers' attention: presenting narratives about the "good old days," when things were seemingly better than they are in our ever-turbulent present.

While the eras identified now in television shows as the idealized past are less frequently the 1950s and 1960s and more frequently the 1980s and 1990s,[4] the sentiment remains the same: things were much simpler, and much better, back then. Using what Matthias Stephan calls in chapter 2 a "highly affective and emotional frame,"[5] Netflix has managed to position viewers just as ABC positioned me all those years ago: in a serious, committed relationship with the recent past. And with the relatively new phenomenon of binge watching,[6] the ante vis-à-vis that affective response is perhaps higher than ever. Thanks to Netflix, we can immerse ourselves in nostalgia for hours, days, and weeks at a time.

As a whole, the essays in this collection speak not only to the enormous influence of Netflix on viewing experiences and pleasures but also to the streaming platform's marketing savvy in creating a range of successful nostalgic iterations for a range of audiences. Indeed, the beauty — and brilliance — of Netflix is the *way* in which it packages and distributes nostalgia: through, as many of our authors have noted, reboots, revisions, and what Jacinta Yanders calls in chapter 9 "reimaginings,"[7] all multilayered texts that speak to multiple audiences. The sheer number of shows addressed in this collection — *Stranger Things, GLOW, Riverdale, Fuller House, Gilmore Girls, One Day at a Time, Black Mirror, The Get Down, Luke Cage, Cable Girls,* and *13 Reasons Why,* among others — bespeaks Netflix's reach across both time and genre. By tapping into what Giulia Taurino in chapter 1 describes as an "archive of historical and cultural memories,"[8] Netflix has created, in the words of John C. Murray in chapter 4, a "sophisticated model of distribution and consumption."[9] And with an annual profit of $558.9 million in 2017,[10] Netflix is not likely to change its approach anytime soon. If anything, the company will find ways to continue building upon its achievements, in particular what Biesen identifies as central to Netflix's branding strategy: its investment in a "nostalgia economy."[11]

Netflix's extraordinary success within this strategy lies in the company's understanding of the various qualities that make nostalgia work. These qualities include, first and foremost, content, that is, the plot and time period of the stories themselves. But they also include approach, for example, the aesthetics of the shows, the ways in which the shows narrate the past by using what Joseph M. Sirianni identifies in chapter 12 as "potential nostalgia triggers": "narration, cinematography, setting, music, art, design, and characters."[12] As Stephan similarly observes in chapter 2, setting and tone are often key, functioning as a wink to viewers that the creators of the project know what audiences want: tangible, even visceral reminders of the past (viz. the references to *E.T., The Goonies,* and the Reagan era in *Stranger Things*). And perhaps the most fascinating aspect of nostalgia that Netflix has seized upon is what Tom Vanderbilt calls "displaced nostalgia"[13] — that is, "nostalgia for times not even known to [viewers] firsthand."[14] This is the same version of nostalgia that characterized my relationship to *Happy Days* and *Laverne and Shirley*, but is amplified in our world of social media and online consumerism. As Janelle Wilson emphasizes in her book *Nostalgia: Sanctuary of Meaning*: "nostalgia for bygone times does not require having actually experienced those times. The dominant ideology, via the mass media, creates and sustains nostalgia . . . material culture embodies nostalgia."[15] The authors included in this collection all recognize, either explicitly or implicitly, how Netflix at once creates, sustains, and profits from the relationship between nostalgia and material culture. Even for the average American, it's easy to find proof of this relationship. Case in point: as of this writing, a search for *Stranger Things* on eBay yields over 47,000 items for sale. The past, as Netflix well knows, is highly profitable in the present.

A more cynical view might simply conclude that because Netflix's nostalgia strategy is purely profit-driven, its formula for success is boringly predictable: situate a show in the recent past, include beloved markers from that past, wrap it in a retro marketing poster, and wait for the money to roll in. What the authors included herein highlight, however, is that while the *marketing* of nostalgia may be simple, nostalgia itself is not. As a feeling, an entity, and a strategy, nostalgia takes a myriad of forms. One of the most compelling aspects of this collection is how carefully it identifies, reviews, and examines different kinds of nostalgia, from regressive to progressive (Freeman, chapter 6), from collective (Maganzani, chapter 10) to reflective (Stephan, chapter 2), from restorative to melancholic (Gauthier, chapter 5), from "technostalgia" (Campbell and Pallister, chapter 13) to digital nostalgia (Mcclantoc, chapter 7), from queer (Freeman, Mcclantoc) to hybrid (Davis, chapter 8). The essays furthermore describe how as an entity, nostalgia functions as a repository, an archive of memory, and a shared heritage (Stephan, chapter 2). Finally, they analyze *how* Netflix's nostalgia strategy is deployed: "weaponized," in the words of Mayka Castellano and Melina Meimaridis in chapter 11 and "serialized," in the words of Taurino in chapter 1. In his landmark book *Yearning for Yesterday*, sociologist Fred Davis draws attention the ineffable quality of nostalgia, observing that it is "a heavily fringed word and therefore susceptible to semantic vagueness, drift, and ambiguity."[16] Our contributors attempt to give it shape, specificity, and clarity, and doing so, they enhance our understanding of Netflix's nostalgia strategy as well as of the nature and complexity of nostalgia itself.

Many of these essays also underscore how the intricacies of nostalgia reside not only in its many forms but also in its internal contradictions. Svetlana Boym asserts that "[t]he first decade of the twenty-first century is not characterized by the search for newness, but by the proliferation of nostalgias that are often at odds with one another."[17] Taken as a whole and in conversation with each other, the essays contained here beautifully illustrate this point. On the one hand, Netflix's original nostalgia programming, exemplified in *Stranger Things*, taps into the more simplistic,

even regressive, aspects of nostalgia. On the other hand, through its reboots and reimaginings, Netflix gives us *One Day at a Time*, a series deeply engaged in the most pressing political and social issues of the day. The
reboots in particular complicate commonly-held ideas about nostalgia,
thereby interrogating its contours and tacit requirements. As Heather
Freeman observes in chapter 6, "[u]nacknowledged assumptions about
inclusion and exclusion form the bedrock of solipsistic nostalgia," often
resulting in a reinscription of the invisibility of historically marginalized
groups.[18] In their critique of the relative absence of queerness from traditionally nostalgic texts, Freeman (chapter 6) and Keshia Mcclantoc (chapter 7) emphasize the ways in which nostalgia can indeed be problematic
both representationally and emotionally. At the same time, they, along
with Ande Davis (chapter 8) and Jacinta Yanders (chapter 9), show us
how nostalgia can be familiar *and* can challenge the current status quo
around issues of race, gender, and sexuality. In offering their readings of
these Netflix creations, our authors stress the importance of questioning
the limits and boundaries of nostalgia—that is, whether nostalgia requires a certain kind of representation in order to be "authentic." Thus,
these essays underscore not only the complexity of shows themselves but
also the ideologically fraught relationship between past, present, and future.

Reading the essays in this collection, particularly those that focus on
Stranger Things and *GLOW*—both of which are set in the era when I came
of age—allowed me to occupy a position vis-à-vis the material that was at
once affective, analytical, and intellectual. This perhaps is why I feel compelled to share one more story, this time about present-day nostalgia. In
the course of writing this afterword, I went to a concert by Air Supply at
the local casino. For those of you unfamiliar with this group, a brief
overview: Air Supply was one of the most successful soft rock duos of the
early 1980s, amassing an impressive eight top-ten US hits within a three
year timespan. They are perhaps best known for the fact that "love"
appears in so many of their song titles ("All Out of Love," "Lost in Love,"
"Making Love Out of Nothing at All," etc.). The crowd of about twelve
hundred consisted primarily of people my age or older—somewhere in
the forty- to sixty-years-old range—and the most entertaining aspect of
the show was not the group themselves (who, incidentally, can still sing a
mean love song) but the clusters of tipsy, middle-aged women in the
crowd who hooted, hollered, and stood together swaying to the group's
most popular ballads. Behind them sat the more demure audience members, straining to look around them and see the band perform. Concert
etiquette be damned, the uninhibited dancing women declared; power
ballads must be sung along to actively and passionately, and in an up-
right position. Wilson asserts that "the past is kept alive via membership
in various social groups,"[19] and this concert reminded me that these
memberships are situational, enduring, and endearing. So, too, are view-

ers' relationships with the many series discussed herein. These shows are commodities, to be sure, and can be critiqued as such, but they are also doing important cultural work: connecting audiences both to the past *and* to each other.

In the conclusion of his 1979 study of nostalgia, Fred Davis reflects on the relationship between our "yearning for yesterday" and the media's role in both creating and sustaining that yearning: "the media in general and audio-visual media in particular," he observes, "can with such great facility nostalgically exploit their past cultural products for present pleasure and profit."[20] He continues:

> the mere revival of "old" hit shows [i.e., reruns] seems insufficient to appease the current American hunger for nostalgia, [so] onto the market has also come that strange hybrid form, the new-old show, shows that are "new" perhaps in the strict technical sense of not having been produced before but are so unabashedly permeated by qualities of genre revivalism as to make them appear authentic "leftovers" from an earlier era.[21]

The examples he proceeds to offer of these "new-old" shows include, of course, the very ones with which I opened this essay. Writing forty years ago, Davis at once identified a media trend and offered us a vision of our future. And at the same time, while "new-old" shows represent a part of Netflix's nostalgia programming, the streaming network has enlarged the scope of nostalgia in its commitment to reboots like *Gilmore Girls* and *Fuller House*. As such, as Biesen astutely declares in chapter 3, "Netflix has harkened back to reveal that what we previously thought and conceived of television itself is being reimagined entirely."[22] The essays in this collection lay the foundation for future work on viewers' experiences with both the past and the present through what is likely to remain, indefinitely, the primary mode of televisual experiences in the twenty-first century—a mode deeply invested in what Paola Maganzani in chapter 10 describes a "past that never seems to go away."[23] In the final chapter of this collection, Kwasu D. Tembo predicts that "the catalogue of Netflix's archive will expand and morph based on its consumers, subscribers, and users' activities, tastes, and predilections, [and] the content of the archive will always be influenced by the nostalgia surrounding the texts within its keep."[24] Like a loyal best friend or romantic partner, Netflix promises to stay in our lives, fulfilling our emotional needs and nostalgic impulses like no other media source in our current historical moment. And given Netflix's deep commitment to us—and ours to Netflix—it's clear that the past is here to stay in the present, and likely in the future, too.

NOTES

1. Seriously. I have never met a person who didn't like Fonzie, and if I ever do, that person will never be my friend.

2. Alex McNeil, *Total Television* (New York: Penguin, 1996), 1018-19.

3. Sheri Chinen Biesen, "Binge Watching the Past," 43.

4. Much has been written about the "cycles" of nostalgia, with writers claiming that it runs in twenty-, thirty-, and/or forty- year phases. For a brief synopsis of these theories, see Forest Wickman, "The 20-Year Nostalgia Cycle. Or Is It 40 Years? 15?" *Slate*, April 2012, https://slate.com/culture/2012/04/the-golden-forty-year-rule-and-other-nostalgia-cycles-could-trends-possibly-return-every-40-years-20-years-and-12-15-years.html.

5. Matthias Stephan, "Branding Netflix with Nostalgia," 26.

6. "Binge-watching" was named the "word of the year" in 2015 and was added to the Oxford English Dictionary in 2018. See Alison Flood, "Binge-Watching Declared the Word of the Year 2015," *The Guardian*, November 4, 2015, https://www.theguardian.com/books/2015/nov/05/binge-watch-2015-word-of-the-year-collins; and Haley Suh, "Words to Know by Now: Binge-Watching, Bechdel Test Added to Oxford English Dictionary," *Forbes*, June 15, 2018, https://www.forbes.com/sites/haleysuh/2018/06/15/words-to-know-by-now-binge-watching-bechdel-test-added-to-oxford-english-dictionary/#53e122de40c3.

7. Jacinta Yanders, "We Can't Have Two White Boys Trying to Tell a Latina Story," 137.

8. Giulia Taurino, "Crossing Eras," 18.

9. John C. Murray, "The Consumer Has Been Added to your Queue," 60.

10. Therese Poletti, "Netflix Is Growing at a Stunning Rate—and So Is Its Profit," *MarketWatch.com*, April 21, 2018, https://www.marketwatch.com/story/netflix-is-growing-even-faster-and-streaming-to-record-profit-totals-2018-04-16.

11. Biesen, 42.

12. Joseph M. Sirianni, "Nostalgic Things," 189.

13. Tom Vanderbilt, "The Nostalgia Gap," *The Baffler*, December 1993, https://thebaffler.com/salvos/the-nostalgia-gap.

14. Janelle L. Wilson, *Nostalgia: Sanctuary of Meaning* (Lewisburg: Bucknell University Press, 2005): 89.

15. Ibid., 99.

16. Fred Davis, *Yearning for Yesterday: A Sociology of Nostalgia* (New York: The Free Press, 1979), 7.

17. Svetlana Boym, "Nostalgia and Its Discontents," in *The Collective Memory Reader*, ed. Jeffrey K. Olick, Vered Vinitzky-Seroussi, and Daniel Levy (Oxford and New York: Oxford University Press, 2011), 456.

18. Heather Freeman, "Shifting Nostalgic Boundaries," 93.

19. Wilson, 41.

20. Davis, 132.

21. Ibid., 134.

22. Biesen, 48.

23. Paola Maganzani, "Netflix's *Cable Girls* as the Reinvention of a Nostalgic Past," 164.

24. Kwasu D. Tembo, "Streamed Nostalgia," 230.

BIBLIOGRAPHY

Boym, Svetlana. "Nostalgia and Its Discontents." In *The Collective Memory Reader*, ed. Jeffrey K. Olick, Vered Vinitzky-Seroussi, and Daniel Levy. 452–57. Oxford and New York: Oxford University Press, 2011.

Davis, Fred. *Yearning for Yesterday: A Sociology of Nostalgia.* New York: The Free Press, 1979.

Flood, Alison. "Binge Watch Declared the Word of the Year." *The Guardian*, November 4, 2015. https://www.theguardian.com/books/2015/nov/05/binge-watch-2015-word-of-the-year-collins.

McNeil, Alex. *Total Television.* New York: Penguin, 1996.

Poletti, Therese. "Netflix Is Growing at a Stunning Rate—and So Is Its Profit." *Market-Watch.com*, April 21, 2018. https://www.marketwatch.com/story/netflix-is-growing-even-faster-and-streaming-to-record-profit-totals-2018-04-16.

Suh, Haley. "Words to Know by Now: Binge-Watching, Bechdel Test Added to Oxford English Dictionary." *Forbes*, June 15, 2018. https://www.forbes.com/sites/haleysuh/2018/06/15/words-to-know-by-now-binge-watching-bechdel-test-added-to-oxford-english-dictionary/#53e122de40c3.

Vanderbilt, Tom. "The Nostalgia Gap." *The Baffler.* December 1993. https://thebaffler.com/salvos/the-nostalgia-gap.

Wickman, Forest. "The 20-Year Nostalgia Cycle. Or Is It 40 Years? 15?" *Slate*, April 2012. https://slate.com/culture/2012/04/the-golden-forty-year-rule-and-other-nostalgia-cycles-could-trends-possibly-return-every-40-years-20-years-and-12-15-years.html

Wilson, Janelle L. *Nostalgia: Sanctuary of Meaning.* Lewisburg: Bucknell University Press, 2005.

Index

ABC, 138–139, 235

accuracy/authenticity: in *Cable Girls*, 161–163, 164–165; in ethnic cultural representations, 143–144; in *GLOW* 1980s nostalgia mood, 32; historical, deformed in nostalgia, 29, 76–77, 79, 92, 224; *Mad Men* reinterpretation of, 86n13; synthetic culture relation to, 57, 61, 62, 63, 64; totemic nostalgia relation to historical, 28, 29

adaptations: *GLOW* case study of, 32–34, 36; *Riverdale* case study of, 26, 34–35, 36

advertisements, 45, 46, 52, 61–62, 64

affiliational thinking, 58, 60, 67, 68, 69

African Americans: *GLOW* stereotypes of, 33, 85; kung fu narratives appeal for, 123–125. *See also* Black culture and politics

Air Supply, 238

algorithmic-driven nostalgia, 11, 18–21, 173–174, 175

Alien, 185, 192, 227

Aliens, 31

Amazon, 43, 44, 49, 53n22

ambivalence, 204, 206, 211–214

AMC, 11–12, 43, 45

American Graffiti, 76, 80

American Idol, 138–139

anime, 225–226. *See also Cowboy Bebop*

anthology format, 16, 18

archaism, deliberate, 76, 78, 78–79, 86n13

Archie Comics TV and movie franchise, 26, 34, 35, 36. *See also Riverdale*

archives, 79; broadcast schedules shift to digital, 221; consumer as co-producer of, 228–229, 229–230, 239;

Cowboy Bebop role as, 219, 220, 226–227, 228, 230; memory, digital nostalgia as, 10, 14, 236, 237; Netflix library function as interactive, 10–11, 18–19, 58, 220, 221–222, 228–229, 229–230, 239; retrofuturism relation to, 222

Armbruster, Stefanie, 2, 3–4, 195–196

Aroesti, Rachel, 84

Arrested Development (revival), 60, 169, 174, 186

Arrow, 45, 46

artifact nostalgia, 115, 189

Asian Americans, 124, 128. *See also* kung fu narratives

Astin, Sean, 31

audience recall, 169, 174, 180

audience/viewership: generational/ intergenerational, 3, 13–14, 113, 138; Netflix percentage of global, 25. *See also* Brazilian audiences; consumers; generational perspectives

auto-play function, 66

Babylon Berlin, 42, 45–46, 50, 51

Baker, Stacey M., 159

Ballatore, Andrea, 205

Bartlett, Myke, 93, 103

Bauman, Zygmunt, 26–27, 29

Bauwens, Joke, 222

BBC, 17, 50, 51, 53n22

Benson-Allott, Caetlin, 84–85

Bentham, Jeremy, 63

Better Call Saul, 44–45, 46

Beyond Stranger Things, 31

Bhabha, Homi K., 125

bingewatching: anthology format and, 16; creation of, experience, 42; misconception of, 60; Netflix promotion of and influence on, 43,

About the Contributors

Mayka Castellano is a professor at the postgraduate program in communication and at the Department of Cultural and Media Studies at the Federal Fluminense University in Brazil. Currently she is developing research on television, new media, and representation politics, as well as the consumption of television serial fiction in new media platforms, mainly streaming services such as Netflix. She has several publications on topics such as cultural consumption, gender studies, fans, distinction, youth subcultures, trash culture, and self-help literature.

Sheri Chinen Biesen is professor of cinema-television and author of *Blackout: World War II and the Origins of Film Noir, Music in the Shadows: Noir Musical Films*, and *Film Censorship: Regulating America's Screen*. She received an M.A. and B.A. at University of Southern California, and PhD at University of Texas at Austin.

Patricia Campbell is a communications studies instructor at Red Deer College. She earned a PhD in communication and media studies (University of Calgary), as well as an MA in communications studies (McGill) and a BA in honors English (University of Alberta). Her research focuses on the social context of technology, and her areas of expertise include film art, communications history, and new media. Her work has been published in *Social Sciences and Medicine* and *Health Sociology Review.*

Ann M. Ciasullo is professor of English and women's and gender studies at Gonzaga University in Spokane, Washington. Her areas of expertise include literary theory and cultural studies, nineteenth- and twentieth-century American literature, women writers, and feminist theory. She has published on a wide range of topics, including the television series *Mad Men*, gender and humor in *MAD* magazine, women-in-prison narratives, and social justice in American literature.

Ande Davis is a PhD candidate at the University of Missouri-Kansas City in multiethnic American literature and humanities, where his research focuses on ethnofuturism, analyzing intersections in speculative and fantastic narratives that center an ethnic presence in their ideas about the future.

Heather Freeman is assistant professor of English at Florida Polytechnic University. Her research interests include nineteenth-century British literature, adaptations, television studies, fan studies, and the pathologized history of media consumption.

Philippe Gauthier lectures on media and popular culture at Queen's University (Canada). He recently completed a two-year SSHRC postdoctoral fellowship at Harvard University. In his research, Gauthier explores complex narratives in popular media franchises and revisits transmedia storytelling and social media through concepts such as interface, playfulness, and immersion. His work has appeared in a number of edited collections and in journals such as *New Review of Film and TV Studies, Animation, Film History, Cinemas: Journal of Film Studies, Cinéma & Cie* and *Studies in French Cinema*.

Paola Maganzani is a PhD candidate in music and performing arts in "La Sapienza" at The University of Rome. She received her training in cinema, television, and multimedia production at the University of Bologna, and she is working for the Department of Educational Sciences' medialab. She is currently researching the history of Italian cinema of the 1930s and 1940s with particular reference to Italian coproductions with European countries.

Keshia Mcclantoc is currently pursuing her MA degree in composition and rhetoric at the University of Nebraska–Lincoln, where she is writing her thesis on fan fiction and digital rhetorics. Her areas of interest include digital media, queer feminist rhetorics, and popular culture. She has published an article with a faculty mentor on "The New Frontier: Writing the First University Level Paper," in *Metamorphosis: Undergraduate Research, Scholarship and Creative Activity* as well as a paper on "Welcome to the Arena: Deconstructing the Female Character in Dystopian Literature" in the UNC–Asheville's undergraduate research conference proceedings.

Melina Meimaridis is a PhD candidate at the Federal Fluminense University. Her work analyses "comfort television series" in American TV. Currently she is researching the fictional representation of social institutions in television series. She has publications on topics such as fan studies, spoilers, Netflix, and gender politics in television series.

John C. Murray is professor of English at Curry College. He specializes in Victorian studies. He published *Technologies of Power in the Victorian Period* (Cambria, 2010), as well as articles and reviews in *Journal of Literature and Science, Journal of Contemporary Thought,* and the *British Society of Literature and Science*.

Kathryn Pallister teaches communications studies, sociology, and film at Red Deer College. Her research areas of interest include mass media, popular culture, gender, and parenting. She has contributed chapters to *Mediated Moms: Mothers in Popular Culture* (McGill-Queens University Press, 2012) and *Pops in Pop Cultures: Fatherhood, Masculinity, and the New Man* (Palgrave Macmillan, 2016).

Joseph M. Sirianni is assistant professor of communication studies at Niagara University. His research and teaching interests include the diffusion and utilization of new media by today's youth, film and cultural studies, media writing and reporting, and mass media theory. His research has been published in *Cyberpsychology: The Journal of Psychosocial Research in Cyberspace* and *The Journal of Sex Research*, and he has also presented his research at conferences such as the International Communication Association and the National Communication Association.

Matthias Stephan teaches at Aarhus University in Denmark. His main research topic is literary postmodernism, and his forthcoming book *Defining Literary Postmodernism for the Twenty-First Century*, suggests a definition of the term, using detective and science fictions as a frame, and explores the literary, film, and televisual implications of postmodernism. His current project looks toward grounded applications of postmodern theory, considering how literature has a role to play in ameliorating climate change, through considerations of cli-fi and the gothic. His work has appeared in *Scandinavian Studies, Coolabah, Otherness*: *Essays and Studies*, and *La Questione Romantica*: *Crime and the Sublime*. He serves as general editor for the interdisciplinary journal *Otherness: Essays and Studies*, and a coordinator of the Centre for Studies in Otherness.

Giulia Taurino is a PhD candidate in media studies at the University of Bologna and at the University of Montreal. Her research interests focus on narrative forms in contemporary television seriality. She took part in several international conferences and publications. She is currently collaborating with the research group Labo Télé (University of Montreal), where she works on a project for implementing data analysis and visualization in television studies.

Kwasu D. Tembo is a PhD graduate from the University of Edinburgh's language, literatures, and cultures department. His research interests include—but are not limited to—comics studies, literary theory and criticism, philosophy, particularly the so-called prophets of extremity—Nietzsche, Heidegger, Foucault, and Derrida. He has published on Christopher Nolan's *The Prestige*, in *The Cinema of Christopher Nolan: Imagining the Impossible*, ed. Jacqueline Furby and Stuart Joy (Columbia University

Press, 2015), and on Superman, in *Postscriptum: An Interdisciplinary Journal of Literary Studies* (2017).

Jacinta Yanders is a PhD candidate in the Department of English at The Ohio State University. She primarily researches mediated representations of identity as well as contemporary media trends. Her dissertation—*Remaking with a Twist: Television Reimaginings, Identity, and Representation in the 21st Century*—examines the productions, receptions, and narratives of television reimaginings in which characters' races, genders and/or sexualities are changed from what they were in the original texts. Additionally, her chapter, "Building and Breaking an Antihero: The Rise of Sonny Corinthos," was published in the book *Hero or Villain?: Essays on Dark Protagonists of Television,* and her essay "Interactions, Emotions, and Earpers: *Wynonna Earp*, the Best Fandom Ever" appears in the March 2018 issue of *Transformative Works and Cultures.*